THE SHADOWS-ON-THE-TECHE COOKBOOK

Cuisine of the Cajun Country

Hospitality—A Tradition along the Bayou

Published
by
THE SHADOWS SERVICE LEAGUE
of
New Iberia, Louisiana

THE SHADOWS SERVICE LEAGUE

The purpose of the Shadows Service League is to provide a wide range of volunteer services for the preservation, maintenance and improvement of The Shadows-on-the-Teche and, thereby, the community.

Copies may be obtained by addressing **The Shadows-on-the-Teche Cookbook,** P.O. Box 254, New Iberia, LA 70560.

ISBN 0-9609994-1-8

Library of Congress Catalog Card Number 82-62292

| First Printing | December 1982 | 10,000 copies |
| Second Printing | (revised) October 1983 | 20,000 copies |

· Printed in the United States of America
by
S.C. Toof and Company

CONTENTS

Cookbook Committee.   4

Introduction.   5

Hospitality—A Tradition At The Shadows.   6

Beverages, Wines and Appetizers. 17

Gumbos, Bisques and Soups. 47

Salads, Salad Dressings and Sauces. 69

Vegetables. 95

Eggs, Cheese, Grits, Pasta, Rice and
    Rice Dressings. 125

Meats. 149

Game and Poultry. 177

Seafood. 203

Breads, Bread Dressing, Jellies, Jams and Relishes. 249

Sweets. 277

How Men Cook. 323

COOKBOOK COMMITTEE

Chairmen: Susie Pharr and Virginia Kyle Hine

Co-Chairmen: Nancy Lewis, Beverly Shea and Yolanda Trahan

Office Managers: Cathi Gibbens, Connie Goodwin and Elenore Mestayer

Financial Manager: Joy Gerhart

Promotional Manager: Sherry Landry

Marketing Director: Keith Courrege

Individual Mail-Out Orders: Mac Beyt

Promotional Mail-Out: Barbara Kyle, Susie Smart and Donna Trappey

Wholesale Mail-Out: Jackie Gauthier and Shayne Wormser

Section Heads: Rose Mary Brooks, Dot Broussard, Sylvia Conrad, Celia Davis, Carol Ann Dumond, Trish Fletcher, Adele Forrest, Charlotte Guinn, Ellen Minvielle, Violeta Romero, Eva Schexnayder, Barbara Schwing, Mary Beth Woods

Proofreading: Tina Broussard, Jakie Forrest, Harriet Schwing, Pat Segura and Sonja Viator

Typing: Rachel Inzerella, Nancy Richard and Penny White

Inventory Coordinator: Julie Angers and Patricia Kahle

Business Consultants: Mark R. Pharr, Jr., McIlhenny Co., Paul McIlhenny and Dudley-Anderson-Yutzy

Legal Advisor: Jacob S. Landry

History: Manon Hunter and Shereen Minvielle

Transportation: Raymond Conner and Clement Knatte

Covers: Edward A. Minvielle

We would like to express our deep appreciation to the many members and friends of The Shadows Service League whose hard work, dedication, support and encouragement made this book possible.

INTRODUCTION

Acadiana can boast of being the section of southwest Louisiana where cooking and entertaining are integral parts of the joie de vivre. This unique area, called Cajun Country, lies along the Bayou Teche and extends south to the Gulf of Mexico, bounded on the east by the Atchafalaya Swamp. New Iberia lies in the heart of Cajun Country. The recipes included in this cookbook reflect the culinary art and gracious hospitality of this area.

The Acadian cuisine in New Iberia tastes pungent and spicy. It has been influenced by five main cultures. The Spaniards settled in 1779 and named their town Nova Iberia. The Indians already occupied the area using indigenous foods. Later, French settlers contributed their special herbs and spices. The Acadians were forced to leave Nova Scotia in 1753, and, after years of wandering, migrated to southwest Louisiana. They became known as Cajuns. From Africa came the blends and medleys that complete the unique cooking for which the Cajun Country has long been famous.

Recipes in this cookbook stem from the availability of foodstuffs abundant in the New Iberia area. The Gulf, lakes, bayous and marshes provide salt- and fresh-water fish, game of all varieties (alligators to birds), crawfish, crabs, shrimp and oysters. The soil yields rice, sugar cane, okra and yams. Sassafras (filé powder), bay leaf, parsley and shallots thrive and are used for seasoning. Hot red peppers grow wild and can be cultivated as a crop. Salt is mined or evaporated at nearby domes.

Many recipes in this cookbook proceed from one generation to the next. Some are guarded family "treasures," contributed only because of a strong willingness to help support The Shadows. In Acadiana when a Cajun says "Laissez les bons temps rouler," a visitor is guaranteed that the good times will roll and that the food will be superb!

Today The Shadows stands as a proud reminder of life in a bygone era. Its charm and elegance have graced numerous books, newspapers and magazines. Its reputation as an antebellum home spans both regional and national levels. Future generations will benefit only through current, continuous preservation.

In 1957, Helen Duprey Bullock wrote the following introduction for a Shadows-on-the-Teche cookbook. It appears exactly as it was written 28 years ago. She hoped to collaborate with William Weeks Hall on the book as a means to raise funds for the restoration of The Shadows. Now the members of The Shadows Service League offer this cookbook, from which all proceeds are dedicated to the restoration, preservation and continued operation of The Shadows-on-the-Teche as an historic house museum.

HOSPITALITY—A TRADITION AT THE SHADOWS

by

Helen Duprey Bullock
Director, Department of Information
National Trust for Historic Preservation

Bayou Teche has a long tradition of hospitality.

It flourished at **Shadows-on-the-Teche** through many generations. From the time the builder David Weeks first came to Attakapas or Nova Iberia in the 1830's to build his mansion, until his great-grandson Weeks Hall died on June 27, 1958, it extended a warm welcome to the great and near great of all the intervening generations.

As a final gesture of hospitality, Weeks Hall, known among his contemporaries as "the last of the Southern gentlemen," bequeathed his beloved **Shadows** and its contents to the National Trust for Historic Preservation. His purpose was to insure that the great mansion and gardens would welcome future generations to share their beauty and recall the way of life and tradition of the planter families of his native Louisiana.

In the rare and extensive library at **The Shadows,** which includes superb works on art, law, architecture, painting, botany, landscape architecture, history and literature, there is a much-used and extremely representative collection of several hundred cookbooks. The earliest ones are the best of the printed cookbooks which were available to southern housekeepers in the ante-bellum period. These were supplemented by hand-copied favorite family recipes interleaved in printed books or pinned to their pages, or by special copy book entries in the handwriting of the daughters and ladies of the family.

The voluminous correspondence, bills, accounts, legal papers and other records of this prominent planter family are now deposited in the Archives of Louisiana State University, under the direction of Dr. Vergil Bedsole. These are filled with reports on the fruits and vegetables growing in the gardens of the many scattered plantations owned by the children of the "home place." Letters call upon various members of the family to watch for the next packet boat on its trip up or down the Teche with a fresh mince pie, or perhaps a barrel of hams...and please to remember Ma's ice blankets.

This family lived well indeed, and generously shared its bounty with friends and strangers alike. **The Shadows** boasted a vegetable garden and numerous fruit trees; table necessities and luxuries not directly available at home were ordered from New Orleans or other cities. There is a receipted bill for sundries dated March 3, 1836 and directed to the Estate of David Weeks. (Ironically, after devoting several years to the building of his handsome mansion, David Weeks died in August 1834, at New Haven, Connecticut, where he had gone in a vain attempt to recover his health.) The receipt is from Peters & Millard of 34 Levee Street, New Orleans, for $180.24, and includes hams, brandy, tea, loaves of sugar, raisins, salt, mackerel, Madeira, barrels of flour, kegs of salmon, sardines, almonds, buckwheat, Irish potatoes and coffee.

Weeks' widow remained at **The Shadows** in seclusion until 1841, when she married a widower, Judge Moore, a prominent Virginia-born lawyer, destined to serve in both the Louisiana legislature and the United States Congress until the outbreak of the Civil War. On May 12, 1845, when the Henry Clay Club of Franklin met, it was Mrs. Mary Conrad Weeks Moore who paid $45 for the cask of Claret wine that livened the occasion. During these happy, ante-bellum years, **The Shadows** was the center of the town's social life. Children of both the Weeks and Moore marriages shared a happy life, amply testified by the visiting up and down the Teche and the exchange—via packet boat—of long, chatty letters. Mary Moore's letters to her husband, when he was absent in Washington on official business, reported the usual chronicle of Louisiana births, marriages, deaths, duels, balls, and gossip. But they invariably record the most important news of all, that concerning the happy family at **The Shadows,** the weather and the garden crops.

Writing on March 4, 1852, she was happy to tell him:

After a very severe winter, spring has to all appearances set in. The flowers that disappeared ever since the snow have again begun to bloom. The china and other trees to put out. The peach trees are full of bloom. I am very busy in the garden. Have planted many things in the new garden. I had green peas on the table every day when the freeze came in January.

Several years later, in hot mid-July, she told him that daughter Allie (Harriet Weeks Meade) was there on a visit with the children, and that they had the company of Bishop Polk all day, adding "Ice very much in demand."

The Bishop, and indeed any other visitors of distinction to New Iberia, inevitably were entertained at **The Shadows.** So much so that occasionally William Frederick Weeks, who managed his father's substantial estate, complained when the end-of-the-year bills arrived: "I see that we have been dancing too fast for the music."

The family had given generously to the funds for erecting the Church of the Epiphany. When it was consecrated in 1858, Mrs. Moore busily planned to entertain the Bishop, visiting clergy from New Orleans, and some ladies from St. Mary's. Probably in anticipation of all the festive cookery involved, she ordered from C. C.

Beirs & Co. of 95 Camp Street, New Orleans, a "No. 2 Cosmopolitan Range with Sett of Cooking utensils complete" at the extravagant price of $40. In March, 1861, it was superseded by a $125 cooking range from Alexander Todd's Foundry, but this was not destined for festive cookery.

In 1859 there was a great flurry of excitement in the Teche country when General Winfield Scott, hero of the War of 1812 and the Mexican War, paid a state visit to his loyal Whig supporters. "Old Fuss and Feathers'" visit was the occasion for all sorts of entertaining and hospitality, duly reported in the family letters. Allie Meade wrote her mother from Homa on July 19:

I have heard nothing new since I came home, except that Mrs. Dancy *the old lady* had just bought a velvet dress at Mrs. Biquerend's which will cost her when finished $150. She got it before General Scott came or before he was expected. A hundred and fifty dollars is a great deal to give for a dress. I wonder where she expects to wear it. Dr. Hawkins amused the Judge and myself on the boat telling us about twenty gentlemen going down with the new mail boat to call on the General, and all the refreshments that were handed were a big waiter of *oranges.*

But a happy era of hospitality was drawing to an ominous close. In January, 1861, William Frederick Weeks wrote to his stepfather, Judge Moore, "I still hope that nothing like coercion will be attempted. Should it be, we will be involved in a war that will destroy North and South. We will, however, have the satisfaction of fighting for our rights." The next month William wrote that he and his wife had visited his mother in New Iberia "to let the young folks see the circus."

Then came letters from the young boys in the family away at schools in Virginia and elsewhere seeking permission to join the Confederacy. Letters followed from camps, battlefields and hospitals...and death notices. **The Shadows** extended its unwilling hospitality to the Union forces which had captured New Iberia in 1863. Generals Stephen G. Burbridge and Nathaniel P. Banks took over the mansion and outbuildings, relegating the elderly Mrs. Moore to the attic chambers. A contemporary report on the conduct of Federal troops in Louisiana complained of the flaunting of a brigade flag over the entrance gate, and the privations suffered by Mrs. Moore that led to her death.

During Reconstruction, the scattered family attempted to regain some of its former possessions and bring them into some sort of order. **The Shadows** at only brief intervals in this era was able to extend its traditional hospitality. But, just as in the bleak years of the War, less fortunate members of the family and friends were welcome to share whatever it was, and with cordial good grace.

In 1922, young Weeks Hall returned from his art studies in Paris and found the once proud mansion drifting to ruin under its great oaks in the tangled remains of its beautiful gardens. He devoted the remaining years of his life to restoring the mansion and gardens, bringing back, in a vital way, the famous hospitality that had been its tradition.

Gone were the belles and beaux, bishops and generals of the ante-bellum era, and in their place came a throng of artists, writers, actors, bon vivants, famous stage and screen directors...and curious tourists. Weeks' mother, Lily Weeks Hall, had died in 1918. Her devoted sister Harriet, widow of Walter S. Torian, made it her special responsibility to see that "Tante's" favorite nephew, "Wee Willie," should entertain in proper style.

This was the beginning of another golden age of hospitality in the history of **The Shadows.** Although she retained a New Orleans residence, "Tante" was a frequent visitor and hostess at **The Shadows.** In her declining years she came there to live, and to be given the kindly attentions she had given to the hundreds of visitors who had been privileged to share her hospitality.

She greatly enhanced **The Shadows** collection of cookbooks, bringing to it not only her own, but adding numerous volumes from such distinguished visitors as Emily Post, Julian Street, Natalie Scott, Matilda Geddings Gray, Henry Miller, Edmund Wilson, Stark Young and Lyle Saxon. In 1924, David W. Griffith produced the film of Stark Young's "So Red the Rose," in which a studio reproduction of **The Shadows** was used. Griffith was a frequent visitor at the mansion on the Teche, and wrote to his host after one visit:

> ...Please give my kindest regards to Mrs. Torian, and, incidentally, you might tell her that neither East nor West, nor North or South, have I been able to find such a dinner as she provided for me that fatal winter night. Verily, she is the only hero or heroine, who has ever conquered that heavy weight vegetable, the sweet potato.

Mrs. Torian won a quiet recognition for her own culinary skill and that of Célèmine Burns who accompanied her on extended visits to **The Shadows.** Letters of appreciation for her famous sour orange preserves are to be found from such celebrities as Alfred Lunt, Lynn Fontanne, Julian Street, Emily Post and others. In December, 1940, her renown was reported in Walter Winchell's column. And steadily her collection of autographed and rare old cookbooks grew and grew, and her recipes constantly appeared in books on Creole cookery.

Of the several hundred volumes of cookbooks in **The Shadows** library, Mrs. Torian's are among the most interesting. It is easy to see which ones were most popular, and with what care she protected them with carefully pasted-on dust jackets of her own making. To select from them is difficult, but as a blackpot cook, a collector of cookbooks and author of one, I have made a choice from an embarrassment of riches of books, recipes and menus. As "Tante" wrote her nephew, thanking him for one of the many gift volumes in the collections, "the old fashioned ones are the best of all."

There is one set of six cookbooks, each containing from 4 to 8 recipes of the famous cooks of Mrs. Torian's friends in New Orleans. These are bound in bright-colored calicoes and ginghams, and adorned with watercolor portraits by L. Castellanos May. Among the cooks so recorded, and some of the choice recipes for which each was known are:

Zouzoute: Poisson Rouge au gratin—Praiines
Tante Calixte: Bisque aux Ecrevisses—La Bière Douce
Carmelites: Blanquettes de Veau—Canard aux Olives
Raphaela & Tante Melanie: Pain Perdu—Gombo Filé
Toinette: Daube Glacée—Nougate au Pacanes

"Tante's" nephew devoted his talent to appreciating good cookery and writing about it. Weeks Hall was a connoisseur of vast determination who could turn livid at the thought of a fruit salad, or write a two-page rhapsody on receiving a birthday gift of a mellowed Stilton in port. He was an accepted authority on Creole Cookery. A tribute to this talent was inscribed by Natalie Scott and Caroline Merrick Jones in their **Gourmet's Guide to New Orleans,** December, 1933, "For Weeks Hall, product and preserver of the wealth of old traditions, of which this small book represents just one— but not insignificant—element!" The book acknowledges 26 of Mrs. Torian's recipes, and 3 of Célèmine's, including the latter's "Oreilles de Cochon" (Pig's Ears).

This recipe was a great favorite of the host at **The Shadows.** When I first met him I was doubly welcomed as a friend: first because I came as a representative of the National Trust, which he hoped would accept and preserve **The Shadows**, and secondly because I had written a "proper" cookbook, a second edition of which was in that fabulous library before we ever met.

We often discussed by letter, or more frequently by tape recording, the possibility of a collaboration on a cookbook of **Shadows** recipes to augment a restoration fund. Oreilles was one of the recipes he recorded at great and amusing length to me. I use Célèmine's version rather than the longer but charming tape-recorded one:

ĆELÈMINE BURNS

OREILLES DE COCHON
(Pig's Ears)

2 cups flour
½ teaspoon salt
1 egg
1 teaspoon lard (heaping)

1 teaspoon butter
½ teaspoon vinegar
Ice water to make dough
Powdered sugar

(The secret of this famous unique recipe is released for the first time.)

Mix dry ingredients, add eggs and fats, stir vinegar and ice water in to make good dough. Roll very thin like paper, cut with saucer, drop in deep fat, twisting with fork as they fall to form oreilles (ears). Sprinkle with powdered sugar. Serve with coffee, tea or chocolate.

In his own article on "Louisiana Parish Cooking" published in **Harper's Bazaar** in January, 1941, Weeks gave a charming disquisition on the coffee that should accompany the Oreilles. He wrote of the role "the incomparable drip coffee plays in the lives of these people. It binds their daily lives together with a strong black thread of solace and cheer." He gave most explicit directions for its making and serving. His recipe for preparing Rufignac, as described by Raoul the butler, is:

RUFIGNAC

Use a big shell glass with a long silver spoon and put one zig of lemon syrup; then you put two zigs of Celestin Vichy. Then you go to the shelf and get that eight-dollar-a-gallon whisky and put one glug, and two good glugs; then you go to the Celestin Vichy and put one zing, two zings of Celestin; then stir with the long silver spoon; then serve it.

It is fitting that my first venture in writing of fabulous Creole cookery should appear in the Cajun-Creole Cane Festival issue of **The Daily Iberian.** Since our first meeting it was Weeks' thoughtful custom to mail me each issue annually. I hope somehow that my friend would have liked this small tribute of appreciation from one who had hoped to collaborate on a volume that would truly preserve the fabulous tradition of hospitality at **Shadows-on-the-Teche** which he exemplified.

DAUBE GLACÉE

2 lbs. beef round, larded and
   tied to keep compact
1 veal knuckle
1 pork shank and foot
3 large onions
1 bunch shallots
1 clove garlic
3 good-sized carrots
1 sprig thyme

2 French bay leaves
1 branch celery
3 sprigs parsley, a few
   leaves sweet marjoram
2 leaves sage
1 pod hot pepper
Salt and pepper to taste
A sprinkle of allspice
1 cup vinegar

To prepare meat: Season well with salt and pepper on both sides. Insert some garlic with the lardings.

Place chopped onions, shallots, garlic, carrots and the rest of the flavoring ingredients under and over the raw meat. Pour a cupful of strong vinegar in the crock, and let stand from one to three days, depending on size of daube.

Brown meat in a spoonful of hot lard, frying well on both sides without flour. Lower flame, and add to daube, all the ingredients contained in crock. Let cook slowly.

Add juices of knuckle, pork shank and foot, boiled with all the above mentioned ingredients until the bones are bare.

This soup, when thoroughly cooked, becomes the jelly. Add this soup to your daube, little by little, to moisten it. Then fill the pot nearly to the top with it, and let the meat simmer slowly for three or four hours until the daube is tender.

Scrape all vegetables and ingredients from cooked daube. Place it in a mold.

Then strain gravy through cheese-cloth, and pour over the meat. Chill and keep in icebox. When ready to serve, scrape fat on surface.

Unmold in a platter, and garnish to taste.

Editor's Note: This may be cut into squares and served on crackers.

POISSON ROUGE AU GRATIN
(Baked Red Fish)

(A red fish is known by the black dot near its tail.)

1 red fish, 2 or 3 pounds
1 large ripe tomato
1 large onion
1 large sweet pepper
1 pod garlic
2 green onions, tails and all
1 bunch shallots
1 pod hot pepper
Wineglassful sherry
1 sprig parsley

2 sprigs thyme
1 French bay leaf
2 dozen oysters
1 lemon
1 tablespoonful butter
1 can mushrooms
Salt and pepper to taste
Toasted bread crumbs, well
   pulverized

Clean fish thoroughly. Season with salt and pepper. Lay in fish baking-pan. Chop onion, garlic, hot pepper, shallots, parsley, and green onions with tails, very fine. Cover fish with all these ingredients. Sprinkle toasted bread crumbs on top. Lay sliced tomato, sweet pepper and sliced lemon, alternating, covering fish to the head. Dust with salt and pepper, and dot with butter. Add oysters and mushrooms. Place bay leaf and thyme in pan, with liquor of oysters, water from mushrooms and a teaspoonful of butter. Bake fish in moderate oven, basting it all the time. When done (in about thirty minutes) add a wineglassful of cooking sherry, and serve fish, piping hot, on fish dish, garnished to taste.

Editor's Note: The four previous recipes were not corrected. They appear exactly as Mrs. Bullock submitted them.

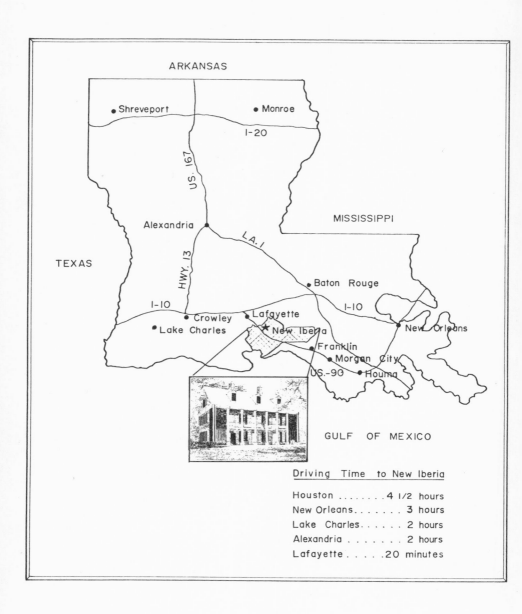

ARKANSAS

• Shreveport   • Monroe

I-20

US. 167

MISSISSIPPI

Alexandria •

LA. 1

TEXAS

HWY. 13

• Baton Rouge

I-10   • Crowley   • Lafayette   I-10   • New Orleans
     • Lake Charles   ★ New Iberia

Franklin •
• Morgan City
US.-90   • Houma

GULF OF MEXICO

Driving Time to New Iberia

Houston . . . . .4 1/2 hours
New Orleans. . . . . . . 3 hours
Lake Charles. . . . . . 2 hours
Alexandria . . . . 2 hours
Lafayette. . . . . .20 minutes

BEVERAGES, WINES AND APPETIZERS

Circa 1820-1940

For many years, the steamboat plied the Bayou Teche carrying mail, goods and passengers from New Orleans. As the excited crowd greeted the first arrival, the steamship "Louisianais" in 1819, they could not know that the steamboats would, in the future, carry the yellow fever mosquito into their midst.

The 1860's and 70's marked an era of luxurious steamboats plying the Teche. One of the most famous of these boats was the "Minnin Avery." It was owned by the firm of Price, Hine and Tupper, who maintained a Commission House in New Orleans. This firm had the mail contract from Morgan City to New Iberia by boat and thence by stagecoach from New Iberia as far west as San Antonio, Texas.

The steamboats used to come up the bayou into New Iberia as far as the depth of the water would allow. They would then unload at the warehouses on the bank. The steamboat's coming was always exciting—it brought the outside world to the Teche country. During the 1940's the steamboat began to be phased out by the railroad and the automobile.

Some of the materials used to build the Shadows came by steamboat up the bayou. The Weekses, like all families who lived on the bayou, depended greatly on the steamboats.

Beverages, Wines and Appetizers

BEVERAGES
Amaretto Stone Sour........... 17
Bloody Marys, Frozen.......... 17
Bourbon Slush................ 17
Cherry Bounce................ 18
Daiquiri, Frozen................ 18
Eggnog....................... 18
Egg Nog, Old Virginia Recipe..... 19
Gin Buck...................... 19
Margarita, Frozen.............. 19
Mint Julep.................... 20
Mint Julep, Southern........... 20
Old Fashioneds................ 20
Pink Squirrel.................. 21
Sazerac...................... 21
Whiskey Sour................. 21

PUNCH
Candy Cane Surprise........... 23
Champagne................... 22
Coffee....................... 22
Milk......................... 23
Planters..................... 23
Punch....................... 22
Red Rooster Christmas Drink..... 24
Sangria...................... 24
Sangria, White................ 25
Spiced Tea................... 25
Spirited Fruit................. 24
Wassail...................... 25

WINES
Suggestions for Serving......... 26

APPETIZERS
Almond Bacon Cheese Spread.... 28
Anchovy Wine Cheese Spread.... 28
Artichoke Balls............... 28
Bacon and Oysters............ 29
Braunschweiger Spread......... 29
Cheddar Cheese Puffs......... 29

Cheese Ball.......... 30
Cheese Straws................ 30
Chicken Glacé................ 31
Crab Ball..................... 30
Crabmeat Spread.............. 31
Crab Triangles................ 32
Crawfish, Scandinavian......... 32
Eggplant Antipasto............ 33
Ham Balls, Festive............ 33
Hidden Treasures............. 34
Jezebel Sauce................ 34
Maureen's Cheese............. 34
Mushroom Caps, Stuffed....... 36
Oyster Log, Smoked........... 38
Pastellitoes.................. 35
Pecans, Peppered............. 35
Ripe Olive Curry.............. 36
Shrimp Canapes.............. 37
Shrimp De Jonghe............ 37
Spinach Balls................ 38
Tiropites (Cheese Triangles)...... 39
Toast Cups.................. 36
Vegetables, Marinated......... 37

DIPS
Artichoke.................... 39
Chicken, Hot................. 39
Crabmeat.................... 40
Crawfish or Shrimp........... 40
Curry, Basic................. 41
Mushroom, Hot............... 41
Shrimp, Lemony.............. 42
Spinach..................... 42
Taco........................ 43

PÂTÉ
Chicken Liver I............... 43
Chicken Liver II.............. 43
Curry....................... 44
Pork........................ 44

Refer to additional recipes in "How Men Cook" section.

AMARETTO STONE SOUR

1 jigger of Amaretto
2 jiggers of orange juice

1 jigger of vodka
2 jiggers of Sweet and Sour
(Bar Mix)

Mix all ingredients and serve in a tall glass over ice. Garnish with fresh fruits.

Yield: 1 serving   *Charlotte Guinn*

FROZEN BLOODY MARYS

2 (46-ounce) cans V-8 juice
1 fifth vodka or gin
4 tablespoons lemon juice
2 tablespoons Worcestershire
sauce

⅛ to ¼ teaspoon Tabasco
pepper sauce or to taste
¼ teaspoon celery salt
⅛ teaspoon garlic powder
⅛ teaspoon onion powder

Mix all the above; freeze. When ready to serve, place in blender and process until slushy. Serve with a garnish.

Yield: 30 (4-ounce) servings   *Keith Courrege*

BOURBON SLUSH

2¼ cups pineapple juice
1½ cups ginger ale

¾ cup bourbon
Lemon-lime carbonated drink

Combine juice, ginger ale and bourbon. Stir well and freeze until firm. Break frozen mixture into chunks. Scoop into tall glasses, filling ⅓ to ½ full. Add carbonated drink, stir until slushy.

Yield: 4½ cups   *Virginia Minvielle*

CHERRY BOUNCE

2 quarts fresh wild cherries (stemmed and cleaned)
3 cups white sugar

1 quart ethyl alcohol (purchase at drug store, may substitute bourbon or vodka)

Put cherries in 1 gallon crock, add sugar, stir and cover with cloth. Stir every day for about 2 weeks. Add alcohol and let stand overnight. Strain through cheesecloth into bottles. Cork lightly.

Yield: 3 quarts

Ellen Minvielle

FROZEN DAIQUIRI

2 (6-ounce) cans frozen lemonade
2 (6-ounce) cans frozen limeade

6 ounces lemon juice, fresh
2 cups powdered sugar
48 ounces water
1 fifth rum

In large container, mix all ingredients and freeze.

Yield: 3 quarts

Charlotte Guinn

EGGNOG

1 quart milk
3 eggs, separated
1 cup sugar
4 scant tablespoons flour

1 (15½-ounce) can Carnation milk
2 tablespoons sugar
Nutmeg and whiskey to taste

Heat 1 quart milk to a skim. Do not boil. While heating milk, beat 3 egg yolks until creamy; then add sugar and flour gradually to eggs until blended. Next add this mixture to milk. Reheat all and allow to thicken for 5 minutes, continuously stirring. Remove from heat and let cool for 10 minutes, then add Carnation milk.

While mixture sets, add two tablespoons sugar to egg whites and beat until stiff. Put stiffened egg whites into mixture and beat in with an electric mixer until completely dissolved.

Nutmeg and whiskey may then be added to taste.

Yield: 6 servings

Miss Gladys Viator

OLD VIRGINIA RECIPE FOR EGG NOG

20 eggs, separated
3¾ cups granulated sugar
2 quarts milk

½ pint cream
1½ cups brandy
2 cups rum or whiskey
1 teaspoon vanilla

Beat yolks of eggs, add sugar and beat until creamy, then pour in milk and cream and when thoroughly mixed add stiffly beaten egg whites. Add liquor and vanilla, pouring gently and stirring continuously.

Yield: 6 quarts

An Old Weeks Family recipe

GIN BUCK

2 ounces gin (or vodka)
¾ ounce simple syrup

Juice of 1 Mexican lime or
½ Persian lime
Club soda to fill glass

Fill glass with crushed ice. Add gin and simple syrup. Fill glass with club soda; stir. Garnish with 1 orange slice.

Yield: 1 10-ounce glass

Putsy Beyt

FROZEN MARGARITA

2 ounces tequila
2 ounces Triple Sec

1 ounce fresh lime juice,
preferably Mexican
2 cups crushed ice

Blend and serve in glass with salted rim.

Yield: 2 drinks

10 ounces tequila
10 ounces Triple Sec

5 ounces fresh lime juice,
preferably Mexican

Add all ingredients to blender and fill with crushed ice. Serve in glasses with salted rim.

Yield: 1 quart

Putsy Beyt

MINT JULEP

7 sprigs of mint
1 teaspoon simple syrup

2½ ounces of bourbon
1 tablespoon light rum
Powdered sugar

Into a silver Julep cup or tall glass, muddle 4 sprigs of mint and 1 teaspoon simple syrup. Fill glass or Julep cup with crushed ice and 2½ ounces of bourbon whiskey. Stir until glass is frosted. Float 1 tablespoon of light rum on top and decorate with 2 or 3 sprigs of fresh mint lightly dusted with powdered sugar. Serve with short straws to capture the delicate aroma of the mint.

Yield: 1 serving   *Joe Regard*

SOUTHERN MINT JULEP

8 large mint leaves
2 ounces aged bourbon
   whiskey
1 ounce simple syrup

½ teaspoon rum
Crushed ice
Powdered sugar
1 (10-ounce) silver Julep cup

In a small bowl, crush the mint leaves in the bourbon; add the simple syrup and crush again. Pour through a bar strainer into a Julep cup filled with crushed ice. Stir vigorously to frost the cup. Float ½ teaspoon rum on top of drink and do not stir. Garnish with a sprig of mint dipped in powdered sugar.

Yield: 1 Julep cup   *Jim Mestayer*

OLD FASHIONEDS

1 gallon bourbon
1 cup simple syrup, recipe
   below

1 tablespoon bitters
Orange slices and cherries

Mix the above ingredients and serve over ice in old fashioned glasses, garnish with orange slices and cherries.

Simple syrup:
Place 1 cup of sugar in a 2 cup fireproof measuring cup. Add enough boiling water to sugar so that measuring cup is 1½ cups full. Stir until sugar is dissolved. Use 1 cup of this mixture in above recipe, refrigerate rest to use in something else.

Yield: 34 (4-ounce) servings   *A Friend of the Shadows*

PINK SQUIRREL

1 jigger Crème de Cacao
1 jigger Crème de Noya

2 jiggers half and half
1 small scoop vanilla ice cream

Blend. Serve in 4-ounce glasses.

Yield: 2 servings   *Charlotte Guinn*

SAZERAC

Cocktail shaker
1 teaspoon sugar
2 ounces water
3 dashes Angostura
   bitters

3 dashes Peychaud bitters
3 ounces whiskey, preferably
   rye whiskey (bourbon may
   be used)
⅛ ounce Absinthe
Slice of lemon

Add sugar to water and dissolve by stirring. Add the Angostura
and Peychaud bitters. Stir well and add whiskey. Add 4 to 6 ice
cubes and stir well. Into a dry glass, add Absinthe and twirl to coat
the inside of the glass. Pour the whiskey mixture into the glass
through a bar strainer. Run the rind of the lemon over the rim of
the glass, then drop into drink.

While sitting in front of an open fireplace on a cold winter night,
this is an unbeatable beverage, and it can be sipped in a leisurely
way because the finished drink has no ice in it.

Yield: 1 serving   *Jacob S. Landry*

WHISKEY SOUR

4 ounces water
1 heaping teaspoonful sugar
Juice of ½ lemon

3 ounces whiskey, bourbon,
   rye, sour mash, or blended
   whiskey
Slice of orange, lemon and
   cherry

Mix water and sugar stirring well until sugar is dissolved. Add
lemon juice and mix well. Adjust sugar and lemon juice to get
sweetness or tartness to suit personal preference of lemonade.
Add whiskey and fill tumbler with ice and garnish.

Yield: 1 serving   *Jacob S. Landry*

This is the safest drink to order when the bartender's talents are
not known as it's difficult to botch the job.

PUNCH

1 cup crushed pineapple
1 pint fresh strawberries (or 1 package frozen)
3 cups powdered sugar
¾ cup brandy
1 cup lemon juice

¾ cup orange juice
½ cup grenadine (or red food coloring)
1 fifth light rum or brandy
1 quart chilled soda

Mix first 4 ingredients and let stand 4 hours or overnight. Add next 4 ingredients. When ready to serve, add soda.

Yield: 3 quarts   *A Friend of the Shadows*

CHAMPAGNE PUNCH

1 quart ginger ale
1 quart soda

2 fifths champagne
2 ounces Crème de Cassis

Mix, chill and serve.

Yield: 4 quarts   *A Friend of the Shadows*

COFFEE PUNCH

6 quarts coffee (very black)
1 quart coffee ice cream
1 quart vanilla ice cream
⅔ cup sugar

2¼ tablespoons vanilla
¼ teaspoon nutmeg
1 quart heavy whipping cream

Chill black coffee. Pour over ice creams. Blend. Add sugar, vanilla, and nutmeg to cream and whip. Add to ice cream and coffee in punch bowl. Blend.

Yield: 9 quarts   *A Friend of the Shadows*

MILK PUNCH

1 fifth bourbon, chilled   ½ gallon vanilla ice cream
                            ½ gallon milk

Blend and serve. Sprinkle with nutmeg if desired.

Yield: 24 (4-ounce) cups   *Susie Pharr*

PLANTERS PUNCH

1 fifth dark rum   1 (6-ounce) can frozen pink
1 (6-ounce) can frozen orange   lemonade concentrate
    juice concentrate   3 tablespoons fresh lemon
Dash of grenadine   juice
                                 1 quart of water

Mix all ingredients. Best to drink after aging in refrigerator for at least 3 weeks. Will keep forever in refrigerator.

Yield: 16 (4-ounce) servings   *Mrs. Jacob S. Landry*

Note: Gallons have been served at the annual Jazz Brunch in the spring.

CANDY CANE SURPRISE PUNCH

2 (10-ounce) jars strawberry   4 pints soft peppermint stick
    jelly   ice cream
14 (1-liter) bottles 7-Up   Candy canes

Beat jelly until smooth, add 2 bottles boiling 7-Up, mixing until smooth. Chill. Before serving, spoon 3 pints ice cream into punch bowl. Add jelly mixture, stirring lightly. Slowly pour in remaining chilled 7-Up. Float scoops of remaining ice cream on top. Serve with candy cane in glass.

Yield: 45 servings   *Shara Viator*

RED ROOSTER CHRISTMAS DRINK

1 (12-ounce) can frozen
   orange juice concentrate,
   thawed

1 quart cranberry juice cocktail
3 cups vodka

Mix orange juice concentrate, cranberry juice and vodka. Freeze. Serve in punch cups.

Yield: 2 quarts   *Celia Davis*

SPIRITED FRUIT PUNCH

1 (8.5-ounce) can cream of
   coconut
1 (6-ounce) can frozen
   limeade concentrate
1½ cups rum

1 (46-ounce) can pineapple
   juice
1 (33-ounce) bottle gingerale,
   chilled
½ gallon vanilla ice cream

Combine first 4 ingredients and chill. To serve combine chilled mixture and gingerale in punch bowl with ice cream.

Yield: 3 quarts   *Virginia Minvielle*

SANGRIA

½ gallon burgundy or dry red
   wine
2 cups orange juice
½ cup lemon juice

¼ cup sugar
¼ cup brandy
⅛ cup Cointreau
2 cups soda (optional)

Mix all ingredients except soda and chill. Add soda immediately before serving.

Yield: 3½ quarts   *Carla Mouton*

WHITE SANGRIA

½ gallon white wine
40 ounces 7-Up
¼ cup simple syrup

½ cup orange juice
¼ cup brandy
Apples, oranges, bananas or
   other fruit

Mix all together. Add sliced apples, oranges, bananas or any other fruits; chill and serve.

Yield: 3½ quarts

Rose Mary Brooks

SPICED TEA

3 quarts boiling water
6 large tea bags
10 whole cloves
1 stick cinnamon
Fresh mint

1½ cups sugar
1 (6-ounce) can frozen orange
   juice
1 (6-ounce) can frozen
   lemonade concentrate

Pour boiling water over tea, cloves, cinnamon, and mint. Steep 15 minutes. Strain. Add sugar and stir to dissolve. Add orange juice and lemonade. Stir and add enough water to make 1 gallon. Serve over ice.

Yield: 4 quarts

Celia Davis

WASSAIL

1 cup sugar
½ cup water

3 lemon slices
2 cinnamon sticks

Boil 5 minutes and strain syrup.

2 cups cranberry juice cocktail
1 cup fresh lemon juice

1 quart red wine
1 cup brandy

Heat to the simmer stage. Add to syrup and serve hot.

Yield: 2 quarts

Sherry Landry

WINES

In selecting appropriate wines that will compliment these recipes, I have taken this occasion to recommend my personal selections. The wines suggested are usually stocked in most stores and are priced right for their excellent quality. This is opposed to rare vintages, aged, special or expensive wines, which are also excellent, but not so readily available. Accompanied by an appropriate wine, the delicate flavors of these recipes will be enhanced and overall enjoyment of the whole meal will result. A red and white wine should be present for every sumptuous repast.

David Foote

BEEF, ITALIAN DISHES, CHEESES

Mouton Cadet Rouge: Red French Bordeaux. Importer—Buckingham.

Médoc: Red French Bordeaux. Suggested labels—Sichel, Rothschild, any chateau listed in grand cru classification.

St. Emillion: Red French Bordeaux. Suggested labels—Nicolas, Rothschild, any chateau listed in grand cru classification.

Pommard: Red French Burgundy. Suggested labels—Moillard, Sichel, Joseph Drouhin.

Châteauneuf-du-Pape: Red French Côtés du Rhone. Suggested labels—Oreyfus Ashby, Nicolas.

Cabernet Sauvignon: Red California. Suggested labels—Robert Mondavi, Paul Masson, Simi, Arroyo, Mirassou, Sebastiani.

Pavillae: Red French Bordeaux. All chateau bottled wines.

St. Julien: Red French Bordeaux. All classified Bordeaux.

Margaux: Red French Bordeaux. Suggested labels—Sichel, chateaux as listed in grand cru classification.

Clos de Vougeot: Red Burgundy. Pinot Noir group. Suggested labels—Moillard, Joseph Drouhin.

LAMB, VEAL, PORK

Beaujolais: Red French, made from Gamay grape. Suggested labels—Nicolas, Sichel, Moillard, Joseph Drouhin, any of the grand cru beaujolais.

Zinfandel: Red California, grape variety. Suggested labels—Sebastiani, Paul Masson, Simi, Mirassou.

Côté du Rhone: Red French, blend of different grapes. Suggested labels—Delas Frères, Nicolas, Sichel.

POULTRY

Chablis: White French, made from Chardonnay grapes. Suggested lables—Moillard, Nicolas.

Zeller Schwärze Katz: Germany, white. Suggested label—Sichel.

Light Chablis: Less alcohol by volume, white California. Suggested labels—Paul Masson, Sebastiani.

SEAFOOD

Pouilly Fuissé: French white Burgundy. Suggested labels—Nicolas, Moillard.

Vouvray: French white Loire Valley wine. Suggested labels—Oreyfus Ashby, Pierre Chenier.

Mouton Cadet Blanc: French white Bordeaux. Importer—Buckingham.

Chardonnay: White California, made from Chardonnay group. Suggested labels—Paul Masson, Mirassou, Mondavi, Simi, Sebastiani.

Mendau: Vintage white wine. Suggested labels—Robert Mondavi's special blend, California.

Light Country Wine: White California, light in alcohol, fruity wine. Suggested labels—Sebastiani, Paul Masson.

Piesporter Goldtrop-Schen: Germany, white delicate. Suggested shipper—Sichel.

Mateus White: Portugal, special grape blend.

Blue Nun: White, Germany, Riesling blend.

Chenin Blanc: California, white, made from Chenin Blanc grapes. Suggested labels—Mirassou, Paul Masson, Robert Mondavi.

ALMOND BACON CHEESE SPREAD

¼ cup chopped toasted
  almonds
3 strips crisp bacon, crumbled
1 cup grated Cheddar cheese
¼ cup mayonnaise

1 tablespoon chopped green
  onions
⅛ teaspoon salt
Red pepper to taste

Mix all ingredients and serve at room temperature. Serve with crackers.

Yield: 1½ cups

Celia Davis

ANCHOVY WINE CHEESE SPREAD

1 (2-ounce) can anchovies,
  drained
2 (8-ounce) packages cream
  cheese

¼ cup sherry
2 tablespoons finely chopped
  stuffed green olives

Mash drained anchovies. Soften cream cheese and blend into fish. Beat in sherry until mixture is smooth. Add olives, cover and chill several hours to blend flavors. Serve with party rye bread or crackers.

Yield: 1½ cups

A Friend of the Shadows

ARTICHOKE BALLS

2 tablespoons olive oil
½ teaspoon chopped onion
3 cloves garlic, crushed
1 (14-ounce) can artichoke
  hearts, drained and mashed

1⅓ cups seasoned bread
  crumbs
3 eggs beaten until fluffy
1 cup grated Parmesan
  cheese

Heat oil in small skillet, sauté onion and garlic. Mix artichoke hearts and 1 cup bread crumbs. Add eggs, onions, garlic and ⅓ cup of cheese. Mix and refrigerate 1 hour. Form 1-inch balls and roll in mixture of ⅓ cup bread crumbs and ⅔ cup Parmesan cheese. Refrigerate until ready to serve.

Yield: 3 dozen

A Friend of the Shadows

BACON AND OYSTERS

12 selected Louisiana oysters   **12 thin slices of bacon**

Drain and wrap each oyster in bacon, using wooden toothpicks as skewers. Place in pan and bake in 350° oven until bacon is crisp.

Yield: 4 servings   *A Friend of the Shadows*

BRAUNSCHWEIGER SPREAD

12 ounces Braunschweiger, softened
1 (8-ounce) package cream cheese, softened
3 tablespoons minced green onion
1 tablespoon lemon juice

1½ teaspoons Worcestershire sauce
¼ teaspoon Tabasco pepper sauce
¼ teaspoon red pepper
¼ teaspoon garlic powder
Salt to taste

Mix. Pat into mound. Refrigerate and serve with crackers.

Yield: 80 cracker servings   *Adele Forrest*

CHEDDAR CHEESE PUFFS

1 cup flour
1 teaspoon baking powder
1 cup grated sharp Cheddar cheese
½ cup margarine

¼ teaspoon red pepper
1 teaspoon Worcestershire sauce
3 tablespoons cold water

Cut or blend flour, baking powder, cheese and margarine as you would for a pie crust. Add seasoning and cold water. Form into small balls. Bake in 425° oven for 8-10 minutes on an ungreased cookie sheet. These raw balls can be frozen but thaw before baking.

Yield: 24 walnut size balls   *Virginia Minvielle*

CHEESE BALL

1 pound sharp Cheddar
  cheese
1 pound American cheese
1 small onion
2 cloves garlic
1/4 cup chopped pecans

2 jalapeño peppers
1 pound cream cheese,
  softened
Juice of 1 lemon
Paprika

Put Cheddar cheese, American cheese, onion, garlic, pecans, and jalapeño peppers through meat grinder or food processor. Combine with softened cream cheese and lemon juice. Add additional salt and pepper if desired. Form into a ball and roll in paprika. May be frozen in foil and rolled in paprika after defrosting. Serve with assorted crackers.

Yield: 3 pound ball

CHEESE STRAWS

1 pound sharp Cheddar
  cheese, grated
3 sticks margarine, softened
1/2 teaspoon salt

1 teaspoon red pepper
4 1/2 cups flour (measured
  after sifting once)

Blend cheese and margarine. Then work in flour, salt and pepper. Put through cookie press in strips onto waxed paper on cookie sheet. Mark lengths with spatula. Bake at 250° about 30 minutes or until done. If using a food processor divide recipe in half.

Yield: 5-6 dozen   *Celia Davis*

CRAB BALL

1 (8-ounce) package cream
  cheese, softened
1/2 pound crabmeat, fresh,
  frozen or canned, drained
2 teaspoons onion, chopped
  fine

1 1/2 teaspoons Worcestershire
  sauce
1/2 cup ketchup
2 tablespoons horseradish
1 teaspoon lemon juice
Tabasco pepper sauce to taste

Thoroughly blend first 4 ingredients; form into a ball. Chill 6 to 8 hours or overnight. Combine remaining ingredients for sauce and serve with ball. Spread over crackers.

Yield: 1 large ball   *Nancy Lewis*

CRABMEAT SPREAD

2 cups fresh lump crabmeat
1 (3-ounce) package cream
  cheese, softened
¼ cup mayonnaise
6 ripe olives, minced
Dash of lemon juice

1 tablespoon horseradish
1 clove garlic, crushed
1 teaspoon Tabasco pepper
  sauce
2 tablespoons chili sauce

Mix all ingredients well. Place in mold and chill in refrigerator. Unmold and serve with crackers.

Yield: 2½ cups

Keith E. Courrege

CHICKEN GLACÉ

2 fryers (3 pounds each)
1 onion, quartered
1 carrot sliced
2 stalks of celery, sliced
Salt and pepper to taste
2 envelopes gelatin
1 (3-ounce) package cream
  cheese

½ cup mayonnaise
1 (16-ounce) can black olives,
  pitted and chopped
1 (7-ounce) jar pimento,
  chopped
2 tablespoons minced parsley
2 tablespoons chopped green
  onion tops

Steam fryers in 4 cups of water seasoned with onions, carrots, celery, salt and pepper in a covered heavy pot until tender. Cool, strain and reserve broth. Remove fat, skin and bones and cut chicken into 1-inch pieces. Dissolve gelatin in 4 cups of cool chicken broth. Heat 5 minutes on low fire. Add cream cheese, mayonnaise, olives, pimento, parsley, green onions and stir. Pour into a greased Bundt pan and chill overnight. Remove from pan by inserting a sharp knife around the edge. Dip pan into hot water for the count of five. Invert pan over large platter. To serve, garnish with curly parsley, place butter knife on side. Serve with crackers or melba toast.

Yield: 1 Bundt pan

Juanita Winkle, Bobby Jefferson

CRAB TRIANGLES

1 tablespoon unsalted, sweet
  butter
1 tablespoon flour
½ cup milk
½ teaspoon salt
3 shallots, minced
1½ tablespoons unsalted
  sweet butter
1 cup flaked cooked crabmeat
  or 2 (6½-ounce) cans

1 egg yolk, lightly beaten
1 teaspoon lemon juice
¼ teaspoon freshly grated
  nutmeg
¼ teaspoon freshly ground
  white pepper
5 phyllo leaves
½ cup melted, unsalted, sweet
  butter

Melt 1 tablespoon butter in small sacuepan over low heat; whisk in flour. Cook 1 minute. Whisk in milk. Cook, whisking constantly, until smooth and thickened, 3 to 4 minutes. Stir in salt. Sauté shallots in 1½ tablespoons butter in 9-inch skillet over medium heat until soft, 3 to 5 minutes. Reduce heat to low; stir in white sauce, crabmeat, egg yolk, lemon juice, nutmeg and pepper. Cool. Place phyllo leaves between slightly dampened paper toweling to prevent drying. Brush 1 leaf with melted butter; cut into six 2-inch-wide strips. Place about 2 teaspoons of the filling in top corner of 1 strip; fold corner over to opposite edge, making a triangle. Continue folding (as you would a flag), keeping triangular shape with each fold and brushing with butter as needed. Place on buttered baking sheet. Repeat with remaining phyllo and filling. Heat oven to 400.° Bake until puffed and golden, about 15 minutes. Serve warm.

Yield: 30 triangles   *Sue MacDonough*

Note: Before baking, crab triangles can be frozen, covered, with layers of waxed paper between triangles. Thaw and bake at 350° until puffed and golden, 15 to 18 minutes.

SCANDINAVIAN CRAWFISH

1 pound peeled crawfish tails
½ teaspoon salt
½ teaspoon Tabasco pepper
  sauce
4 tablespoons Dijon mustard

1 teaspoon dry mustard
3 tablespoons sugar
2 tablespoons white vinegar
⅓ cup vegetable oil
3 tablespoons dill weed

Boil crawfish with salt and Tabasco pepper sauce. Drain and chill until icy. Make paste with mustards, sugar, and vinegar. Slowly add oil, beating with a wire whisk until mixture becomes thick. Stir in dill, pour over crawfish and serve with crackers.

Yield: 2½ cups   *Maureen Doerle*

EGGPLANT ANTIPASTO

3 cups eggplant, peeled and
  cubed
1 cup bell pepper, chopped
1 medium onion, chopped
2 cloves garlic, chopped
1/2 cup Plaginol olive oil
1 teaspoon salt

1 (6-ounce) can tomato paste
1/4 cup chopped mushrooms
1/4 cup water
1/2 cup chopped pimento
  stuffed olives
1 1/2 teaspoons sugar
1/2 teaspoon oregano
Red pepper to taste

Combine first 5 ingredients in skillet. Cook and stir 10 minutes. Add remaining ingredients and mix well. Cover and simmer until vegetables are tender. Chill. Good to serve with crackers as an appetizer, or serve hot as a vegetable dish.

Yield: 4 cups

Yolanda V. Trahan

FESTIVE HAM BALLS

1 pound lean cooked ham,
  cubed
1 green onion, cut into equal
  lengths
2-3 sprigs parsley
1 egg
1 cup soft bread crumbs

Salt to taste
1/2 teaspoon prepared mustard
1/2 cup homemade or bottled
  barbecue sauce
1 (10-ounce) jar apricot-
  pineapple jam

Place ham, green onion, parsley in work bowl of food processor fitted with metal blade. Process with a few short on/offs. Add egg, bread crumbs, salt and mustard. Process with a few short on/offs until well combined. Shape mixture into 1-inch balls. Arrange balls on a rack in broiler pan. Bake 15 minutes in 350° oven until lightly browned.

In a large skillet combine barbecue sauce and apricot-pineapple jam. Stir over medium heat until well blended. Add cooked ham balls; heat until bubbly. Serve hot in stovetop casserole or spoon into chafing dish.

Yield: 35-40 appetizers

Shara Viator

HIDDEN TREASURES

2 cups mayonnaise
1/2 cup horseradish, drained
1/2 teaspoon monosodium
  glutamate
2 teaspoons dry mustard
2 teaspoons lemon juice
1/2 teaspoon salt
1 pound shrimp (cleaned and
  cooked)

1 pint size basket cherry
  tomatoes, whole
1 (6-ounce) can pitted black
  olives, drained
1 (8-ounce) can water
  chestnuts, drained and cut
  into chunks
1 (6-ounce) can button
  mushrooms, drained
1/2 head cauliflower, bite size
  pieces

Mix mayonnaise with seasonings. Add next 5 ingredients. Refrigerate. Add cauliflower just before serving.

Yield: 10 servings   *Kitty Schwing*

JEZEBEL SAUCE

1 (16-ounce) jar pineapple
  preserves
1 (16-ounce) jar apple jelly

2 tablespoons Dijon mustard
1 (5-ounce) jar horseradish
1 (2-ounce) tin of dry mustard

Mix all ingredients. Pour a small amount sauce over a block of soft cheese or cream cheese. Serve with crackers. Remainder of sauce keeps indefinitely in refrigerator.

Yield: 4 1/2 cups   *Sherry Landry*

MAUREEN'S CHEESE

2 pounds Brie or Camembert
  cheese (unpeeled)

1 1/2 sticks butter
1 (4-ounce) package almonds

Clarify butter. Add almonds to butter and heat over medium heat until almonds turn golden. Pour mixture over cheese. Heat in microwave until cheese begins to puff, but crust does not break (about 1 to 1 1/2 minutes). Serve with crackers.

Maureen Doerle

PASTELLITOES
(Venezuelan Meat Appetizer)

1 (8-ounce) filet mignon
2 lean pork chops
Olive oil
1 onion (medium to large), chopped
1/2 cup celery, chopped
1/4 cup bell pepper, chopped
1 clove garlic, chopped

1 large tomato, peeled and seeded
1/2 cup green olives, chopped
1/4 cup raisins
1 tablespoon capers
1/2 jalapeño pepper, chopped
1 teaspoon Achote or Amato seeds

Boil filet and pork chops till tender, save liquids. Fry onion in small amount of olive oil until the onion is wilted; add celery, bell pepper, garlic and tomato. Cook at least 30 minutes on a slow fire.

Cut meat very fine and add to vegetables. Cook again on slow fire for 30 minutes adding liquid from meat as needed. Season highly. Add raisins, olives, capers and jalapeño.

Fry in 1 tablespoon olive oil, one teaspoon Achote or Amato seeds (cover pan because seeds pop). When oil is deep red, strain seeds and pour oil into the meat mixture.

Allow mixture to cool. If oil separates, add 1 tablespoon of corn-starch or flour and stir.

Cut 3-inch rounds of your favorite pie pastry and place a teaspoon of mixture on one side, fold over and seal. Bake at 400° for a few minutes. These may be frozen.

Lucille B. Minvielle

PEPPERED PECANS

1/2 pound butter
1/2 cup Worcestershire sauce

1 1/2 pounds shelled pecan halves
Salt and cayenne pepper

Melt butter in a baking pan and add Worcestershire sauce and mix well. Add pecans, stir well. Place in 250° oven and bake slowly, stirring every few minutes until the pecans have absorbed all of the liquid. Remove from the oven and sprinkle with salt and cayenne pepper. Stir again.

Yield: 1 1/2 pounds

Mrs. Sam Broussard

STUFFED MUSHROOM CAPS

1 onion, chopped
1 bell pepper, chopped
1 rib celery, chopped
1 stick butter
1 pound cooked crabmeat
1/4 cup lemon juice
2 tablespoons onion tops, chopped

2 tablespoons parsley, chopped
1 cup bread crumbs
Dash Worcestershire sauce
Dash Tabasco pepper sauce
Salt and pepper to taste
12 large mushroom caps, cleaned

To make dressing, sauté onions, bell pepper and celery in butter until soft. Add crabmeat and lemon juice, simmer for 10 minutes. Add onion tops, parsley, bread crumbs, Worcestershire, Tabasco, salt and pepper and cook for about 5 minutes. Stir often; do not let stick. Cool dressing and stuff mushroom caps. Bake at 350° for 7 minutes.

Yield: appetizers for 6   *Alex and Gigi Patout*

RIPE OLIVE CURRY

2 (4½-ounce) cans ripe olives, chopped, drained
1 cup chopped green onions
1 cup mayonnaise

3 cups sharp cheese, grated
½ teaspoon salt
½ teaspoon curry powder
3 English muffins

Mix all ingredients and place on cut side of toasted, buttered English muffin. Broil until cheese melts and browns. Cut into fourths and serve hot. Or, place 1 teaspoon mixture on a Triscuit and heat in microwave or oven until cheese is melted.

Yield: 4 cups   *Ellen Minvielle*

TOAST CUPS

Many appetizers are served in patty shells. Toast cups are an inexpensive, easy-to-prepare substitute. One 22-oz. loaf of bread will make 80 cups. Cut crusts from bread. Cut each slice into 4 squares. Use a muffin pan that makes 12 small one-inch muffins. Press into cup with thimble or small round bottle such as food coloring bottle. Place in a 250° oven and bake approximately 1 hour or until dry throughout. Can be stored in tightly covered container for several weeks.

SHRIMP DE JONGHE

2 cups peeled shrimp
Salt, red and black pepper
1 medium onion
1 stalk celery
1 lemon, halved
½ pound butter

4 green onions, finely chopped
1 bunch parsley, chopped
Juice of one lemon
1 cup fresh bread crumbs
1 teaspoon Worcestershire
  sauce
Tabasco pepper sauce to taste

Boil shrimp in water seasoned with salt, red and black pepper, onion, celery, and lemon. Cook until shrimp turn pink and remove. Melt butter and mix with rest of ingredients. Pour over shrimp. Heat until warm when ready to serve. Serve with crackers or melba toast.

Yield: 3 cups   *Celia Davis*

SHRIMP CANAPES

1 pound raw shelled shrimp
1 (5½-ounce) can water
  chestnuts
¼ cup minced onion
2 teaspoons salt

1 teaspoon sugar
1 tablespoon cornstarch
1 egg
12 slices sandwich bread,
  crusts removed

Grind raw shrimp and water chestnuts. Mix with onion, salt, sugar and cornstarch. Beat an egg well and stir into the shrimp mixture. Put on top of bread. Cut bread into 4 squares. Heat fat to 375° and fry mixture side down till edges brown. Then fry other side. (Can be done day before and refrigerated. Just before party, put into oven and warm.)

Yield: 48 squares   *Susie Pharr*

MARINATED VEGETABLES
(Low Calorie)

1 (10½-ounce) can chicken
  broth
1½ cups sliced carrots
1 cup cauliflower florets
1 cup broccoli florets

1 cup zucchini, sliced
¼ cup wine vinegar
1 cup yellow squash, sliced
1 envelope (0.6-ounce) Italian
  salad dressing mix

Heat broth to boiling point in large saucepan. Add carrots, broccoli, and cauliflower. Simmer 2 minutes. Cool and stir in squash, vinegar and salad mix. Chill 6 hours or more, stirring occasionally.

Yield: 6-8 cups   *Celia Davis*

SMOKED OYSTER LOG

1 (8-ounce) package cream
  cheese
2 tablespoons mayonnaise
1 teaspoon Worcestershire
  sauce
Salt, red pepper, and Tabasco
  pepper sauce to taste

1 clove garlic, minced
1 (3.66-ounce) can of smoked
  oysters, drained and
  chopped
2 tablespoons minced parsley
  or green onion tops

Combine softened cream cheese and mayonnaise. Blend well. Stir in seasonings. Spread 1/4 inch thick on waxed paper. Chill at least 30 minutes. Next spread oysters on cream cheese mixture and roll up jelly roll fashion. Roll log in parsley or green onion. Chill overnight. Cut in 1/2-inch slices and serve with crackers. Variation: mix oysters with cream cheese mixture and seasonings; shape into a log instead of jelly roll.

Yield: about 2 dozen
Ellen Minvielle

SPINACH BALLS

2 (10-ounce) packages
  chopped frozen spinach,
  cooked and well drained
3 cups herb seasoned stuffing
  mix
1 large onion, finely chopped
6 well beaten eggs
3/4 cup melted margarine

1/2 cup Parmesan or Romano
  cheese
1 tablespoon black pepper
1 1/2 teaspoons garlic salt
1 large pod finely chopped
  garlic
1 teaspoon poultry seasoning
  or thyme
1 teaspoon celery salt

Combine all ingredients, shape into small balls. Put on lightly greased cookie sheet. If put in refrigerator for a few hours, mixture is easier to make into balls. Bake for 15 to 20 minutes in 325° oven. After being put on cookie sheet, these can be put into freezer and when frozen, put into plastic bags to be kept until needed. Then place on cookie sheet as above and bake.

Yield: 100 balls
Beverly Shea

TIROPITES
(Cheese Triangles)

1 pound cottage cheese	4 whole eggs
1 pound Feta cheese	1 pound phyllo
1 pound Ricotta cheese	1 pound unsalted butter,
1 pound soft cream cheese	melted

Blend together cheeses and eggs. Brush one sheet of phyllo with butter (use a good paint brush). Fold over in half. Brush again with butter. Cut into 1½-inch strips. Place ½ teaspoon of filling at the end of each strip. Fold over into triangles (as folding a flag). These may be frozen. Bake at 375°F until brown (12 to 15 minutes if thawed; 5 minutes longer if frozen).

Yield: 10-12 dozen   *Evelyn Foti*

ARTICHOKE DIP

1 (14-ounce) can plain hearts of artichoke	1 cup mayonnaise
	½ cup Parmesan cheese
1 (6-ounce) jar marinated hearts of artichoke	Red pepper to taste

Drain plain artichokes. Reserve oil from marinated artichokes. Chop artichokes. Add mayonnaise, reserved oil and seasonings. Blend. Serve with melba rounds.

Yield: 3 cups   *Beverly Shea, Joan Wilson*

Note: May be used as a topping for vegetables.

HOT CHICKEN DIP

1 (10½-ounce) can cream of mushroom soup	1 (8-ounce) package cream cheese
2 (5-ounce) cans chunky, white chicken	2 (½-ounce) packages slivered almonds
1 tablespoon lemon juice	Tabasco pepper sauce to taste

Toast almonds. Mix all ingredients. Heat and serve on crackers or in miniature tart shells.

Yield: 3 cups   *Evelyn Sexton*

CRABMEAT DIP

2 pounds crabmeat
2 sticks margarine
4 cups chopped onions

1 cup chopped celery
1 cup chopped bell pepper

Clean crabmeat and set aside. Melt margarine, add vegetables; sauté together until very tender and slightly brown. Stir in the following:

1¼ cups plain flour
4 (10½-ounce) cans cream of mushroom soup
2 tablespoons Teriyaki sauce

4 (13-ounce) cans evaporated milk
2 tablespoons Worcestershire sauce
Salt, red and black pepper

Sauce should be very thick and smooth. When heating for serving, add crab meat.

Yield: 125 servings

Juanita Winkle

CRAWFISH OR SHRIMP DIP

2 cups chopped onions
1 cup chopped bell pepper
1 cup chopped celery
⅔ cup chopped parsley
⅔ cup chopped onion tops
1 (2-ounce) jar pimento, chopped

1 stick margarine
2-3 pounds crawfish or shrimp, cooked and peeled
2-4 (10½-ounce) cans cream of mushroom soup
Garlic powder, salt and pepper to taste

Sauté first 6 ingredients in margarine until wilted. Add crawfish or shrimp and cook 1 minute. Add soup and cook until seafood is cooked. Season to taste.

Yield: 5-6 cups

Kitty Schwing

CURRY DIP (BASIC)

1 cup mayonnaise
1 teaspoon curry powder
1 teaspoon horseradish
1 teaspoon tarragon vinegar

1 teaspoon minced onion
1 teaspoon Beau Monde
   seasoning
Salt and pepper to taste

Mix well and chill. Serve with raw vegetables.

Variations: 2 teaspoons tarragon vinegar, 2 teaspoons chili sauce and 2 teaspoons chives.

1 tablespoon hot Madras curry powder, 1 tablespoon minced onion, 1 tablespoon tarragon vinegar, and 1 tablespoon horseradish to 1 cup mayonnaise.

1 teaspoon onion flakes in place of minced onion, 2 teaspoons horseradish and 1 tablespoon garlic salt.

Yield: 1 cup   *A Friend of the Shadows*

HOT MUSHROOM DIP

2 pounds fresh mushrooms,
   chopped coarsely
10 green onions, including
   tops, chopped
1/4 cup butter
3 tablespoons flour
2 tablespoons milk

2 cups sour cream
1/2 teaspoon salt
1/4 teaspoon pepper
1/2 teaspoon Tabasco pepper
   sauce
1/2 cup parsley, chopped

Sauté mushrooms and green onions in butter. Stir in flour. Brown lightly. Stir in milk and sour cream. Mixture will thicken quickly. Remove from heat and add seasonings and parsley. Serve in chafing dish with bland crackers (melba toast).

Leftover dip can be thinned with milk, heated, and served as cream of mushroom soup.

Yield: 4 cups   *Jess Musson*

LEMONY SHRIMP DIP

1 ½ (8-ounce) packages
  cream cheese
⅓ cup lemon juice
⅓ cup finely chopped green
  onion
2 tablespoons or more
  prepared horseradish

1 teaspoon seasoned salt
½ teaspoon pepper
1 pound boiled seasoned
  shrimp, chopped and
  peeled
Tabasco pepper sauce to taste

Beat cream cheese until fluffy. Gradually add lemon juice beating well after each addition. Stir in onion, horseradish, salt, pepper, shrimp and Tabasco pepper sauce. Refrigerate to set flavor. Serve with melba rounds.

Barbara Schwing

SPINACH DIP

1 cup sour cream
1 (10-ounce) package
  chopped spinach, thawed
  and squeezed dry

1 cup mayonnaise
1 package Knorr vegetable
  soup (dry)

Mix all of the above and let stand overnight. Serve with chips or vegetables.

Yield: 30 cups

Bea Gordy

Variation: 1 pint sour cream instead of 1 cup. Use Hellmann's mayonnaise or homemade. 1 small onion chopped and 1 small can of water chestnuts drained and chopped. Pepper sauce to taste. Place all of the ingredients in food processor. Serves 20.

Mac Beyt

CHICKEN LIVER PÂTÉ I

1/2 pound chicken fat
2 to 3 shallots, chopped
1/8 teaspoon thyme
1 bay leaf, crushed

1/2 pound chicken livers
1 teaspoon cognac
Salt
Pepper

Melt chicken fat; add shallots, thyme, bay leaf and sauté. Add livers and cook for 1½ to 2 minutes, stirring over medium high heat. Pour into a food processor; using the steel blade, purée until smooth. Then add cognac, salt and pepper. Process for another 10 to 15 seconds. Place in refrigerator and stir every 12 to 15 minutes until thick.

Yield: 2-3 cups

Alex Patout

CHICKEN LIVER PÂTÉ II

1 pound chicken livers
2 medium size onions
1 stick butter or margarine

2 hard cooked eggs
1/2 teaspoon salt
1 teaspoon black pepper

Sauté chicken livers and chopped onions in butter until no pink remains in livers. Chop onions, livers, eggs and stir in salt and pepper; or put in food processor being careful not to overprocess. Chill and serve in lettuce cups for first course or as a spread on melba rounds.

Yield: 3 cups

Celia Davis

TACO DIP

1 cup chopped onion
2 tablespoons butter
1 (10-ounce) can Rotel
   tomatoes, mashed
1/2 teaspoon cumin
1 pound diced Velveeta
   cheese

12 ounces Cheddar cheese,
   cubed
1 (10-ounce) can Wolf's chili
   (without beans)
4 tablespoons taco sauce
1 (4-ounce) can chopped
   green chilies

Sauté onion in butter. Add mashed tomatoes and juice. Add all other ingredients and cook until cheese is melted. Serve with corn chips.

Yield: 3 cups

Millie Brooks

CURRY PÂTÉ

1 (8-ounce) package cream
  cheese, softened
1 cup shredded sharp cheese
½ teaspoon curry powder

2 tablespoons dry sherry
1 cup chopped green onion
1 (10-ounce) bottle chutney,
  drained, chopped

Cream first 4 ingredients. Spread on plate to ½-inch thickness. Top with half of the onions. Top with chutney. Sprinkle with remaining onions. Serve with crackers.

Yield: 3½ cups   *JoAnn Riley*

PORK PÂTÉ

4 pounds pork liver
3 pounds pork meat (filet best)
Salt and red pepper to taste

2 pounds pork fat (from inside)
7 small pods garlic finely
  minced

Grind above ingredients twice. Add water to cover (4¾ cups). Bring to boil; lower heat to simmer. Stir often; cook until fat rises to top (3 hours). Put in pint jars and refrigerate. When serving, mix fat (which rises) back into the mixture with a fork. Serve on crackers or melba toast. Freezes well for about 3 months.

Yield: 8-10 pints   *Mrs. Sam Broussard*
                                        Recipe of Mrs. Luke Bonin

GUMBOS, BISQUES AND SOUPS

The Shadows was built, not as a plantation house, but as a town house. David Weeks, who owned several plantations in the area, bought 4-1/2 arpents (about 4 acres) of land, on the edge of the little town of New Iberia, where he built the splendid home we see today for his wife and children. The Shadows was under construction during 1831-34. Much of the building materials were obtained locally. The bricks for the house were made right on the property from the clay on the banks of the Teche, and much of the wood in the house is native Louisiana cypress. Nonetheless, the steamboat records indicate that a steady flow of other items came from New Orleans and other cities. Construction of the house was entrusted to master builder James Bedell and estate agent Boyd Smith, although all aspects of construction were certainly under David Weeks' watchful eye.

As the house neared completion in the spring of 1834, David Weeks sailed for New Haven, Connecticut, in an effort to recover his failing health. He sent many objects to furnish his home in Louisiana. He was never to see it completed. He died in August of 1834. His wife, Mary Clara, was left with the responsibilities of the family and the plantations.

Gumbos, Bisques and Soups

GUMBOS

How to Make a Roux. 48
Chicken and Okra. 48
Chicken Gumbo Filé with
   Oysters. 49
Seafood and Okra. 50
Shrimp. 49
Shrimp and Okra. 50
Z'Herbes. 51

BISQUES

Corn and Crab. 51
Crawfish and Shrimp. 54
Crawfish Bisque I. 52
Crawfish Bisque II. 53

SOUPS

Cream

Artichoke. 55
Avocado. 55
Carrot. 56
Cauliflower. 56
Eggplant. 56

Mushroom. 57
Mushroom and Artichoke. 57
Potato. 58

Cold

Bloody Mary. 59
Cucumber. 58
Gazpacho. 59
Strawberry. 59
Vichyssoise. 60
Vichyssoise, Spinach. 60
Zucchini, Curried. 61

Hot

Corn Soup, Mama's. 61
Courtbouillon, Daddy's. 63
L'Oignon. 62
Onion, French. 62
Oyster, Lafayette. 64
Pinto Bean. 64
Potato, Hearty Cajun. 65
Turtle I. 65
Turtle II. 66

Refer to additional recipes in "How Men Cook" section.

GUMBOS, BISQUES AND SOUPS

Mealtime in Acadiana was always a special time of the day for the coming together of families. The main meal dinner was usually served at mid-day. Evening time was a light supper.

As an appetizer, soup prefaced almost every dinner. On cold days, soup provided a warm heartiness of meat or seafood. In summer, chilled soups were served, using the fresh garden vegetables and cream from the morning dairy.

As an important part of the meal, soup, gumbo, and bisque utilized left-overs and extended the filling quality of the meal. A serving of cooked rice, as an additional filler, was always added to the bowl of gumbo or bisque.

The Catholicism of Acadiana relied heavily on the seafood of the area for the Friday observance of abstinence from meat. This brought about an almost traditional Friday dinner of seafood gumbo (shrimp, oysters, or crab) or a bisque of crawfish.

"Gumbo" is an African word which originally meant that the soup was thickened with okra. Gumbo filé is a powder made from ground sassafras leaves and used for thickening gumbo after it is cooked. Gumbo filé is sprinkled on top of the gumbo in the serving bowl, just before eating. This filé powder was first made by the Choctaw Indians of Louisiana.

"Bisque" is a French word. It usually refers to a thick soup made from seafood.

Every gumbo and bisque begins with a roux (rhymes with shoe). This is a blending of fat and flour which is cooked until a brown color (from light tan to dark caramel) appears. This is up the individual cook, who usually judges the color of the roux according to the color of the gumbo he or she desires. New Orleans' Creole cooks generally prefer a light roux, while Acadians use a dark one. Use equal parts of fat and flour (plus one tablespoon more flour). Cook over low heat, stirring constantly, until the desired color is attained. Then the seasonings and stock are added slowly while blending the roux into these additions. Practice will increase the perfection of a roux. Do not let burn. This roux is actually the thickening agent which makes the gumbo rich and flavorful.

ROUX

What is a roux? It is a mixture of oil and flour that is browned to a desired color. A roux is used to thicken many of the area recipes. Not only is it a thickening agent, but its distinct flavor imparts a special taste to the food, as a result of the browning of the flour.

1 cup oil
1 cup plus 1 tablespoon flour
1 large onion, chopped
½ bell pepper, chopped
    very fine

3 ribs celery, chopped
    very fine
2 cloves garlic, chopped
    very fine

Mix oil and flour together in a 2-quart heavy pot. Cook over low heat, stirring constantly until the roux becomes a rich, dark, reddish brown. Add onions, bell pepper, celery and garlic and sauté until they are all tender. This may be stored in a jar in the refrigerator for use as recipes require. It may also be frozen.

CHICKEN AND OKRA GUMBO

1 (3-pound) young chicken
3 large tablespoons vegetable
    shortening
2½ pounds okra
2 tablespoons flour
2 large onions, cut fine

1 bell pepper, chopped fine
3 cloves garlic, cut fine
3 tomatoes or 1 small can
2 ears tender corn, cut from cob
1 red hot pepper
2 tablespoons vinegar

Disjoint the chicken, season with salt and pepper and put in skillet where one tablespoon of vegetable shortening has melted. Fry until deep brown. Cut the okra in thin round slices. Put other tablespoon of vegetable shortening in a heavy skillet and melt; place the okra in this. Fry until well dried out, about 10 minutes, stirring constantly. In a deep pot, put the remaining spoonful of vegetable shortening and let it begin to melt. Add the flour and stir to make a dark roux. Onions should be added and fried; then the bell pepper and garlic. Cook 5 minutes. Add okra and stir well. Then add 3 pints of hot water. Put in the fried chicken and add salt and red pepper. Let cook for 1 hour. Add tomatoes and corn cut from the cob. Let cook another hour and add 2 tablespoons vinegar just before serving.

Yield: 6 servings   *Old Weeks Family recipe*

CHICKEN GUMBO FILÉ WITH OYSTERS

1 (3-pound) chicken,
   disjointed
Salt and red pepper
2 tablespoons vegetable
   shortening
2 tablespoons flour
2 large onions, cut very fine

2 tablespoons minced celery
1 bell pepper, minced
2 cloves of minced garlic
2 dozen large oysters, with
   liquid
½ tablespoon filé powder

After disjointing the chicken, rub with salt and red pepper. Put 1 tablespoon vegetable shortening in skillet and when it gets very hot, place chicken pieces in and fry until very brown. Put another tablespoon of vegetable shortening in a deep pot and add 2 tablespoons flour and make a very dark roux. Then add onions and cook five minutes. Add celery, bell pepper, and garlic. Put the fried chicken in the pot with the roux and add three pints of warm water. Cover the pot and cook on a slow fire, 1½ hours or until the chicken is tender. Then add the liquid from the oysters. Cut the oysters in half and add to the gumbo. Cook for 5 minutes. Take off of the fire and add ½ tablespoon powdered filé. Stir well and serve over boiled rice.

Yield: 6 servings   *Old Weeks Family recipe*

SHRIMP GUMBO

1 pound raw shrimp, peeled
1 tablespoon bacon drippings
1 bunch green onions
2 cups chopped okra
1 cup tomatoes chopped

6 cups chicken stock
1 pod red pepper
1 green pepper
1 bay leaf
1 tablespoon filé

Heat bacon drippings in saucepan. Clean green onions, reserving 1 cup of the green tops. Chop onions and sauté with okra in bacon drippings for 10 minutes. Add tomatoes and cook for 5 minutes. Add stock, peppers, green onion tops, bay leaf and pinch of salt. Bring to boil and cook about 1½ hours. Add shrimp, cover with tight fitting lid and cook slowly for 10 minutes. Just before serving add filé. Serve with cooked rice.

Yield: 6-8 servings   *Penny Fenton*

SEAFOOD AND OKRA GUMBO

1 pound fresh okra
1 tablespoon vegetable oil
1 large onion, chopped fine
1 bell pepper, chopped fine
3 large fresh tomatoes

1 pound peeled shrimp
1 dozen boiled crabs, shells
   removed and cleaned, and
   broken in half
Fresh, flat-leaf parsley, minced

Cut fresh okra in slices and fry in pan with vegetable shortening. Watch closely so that the okra does not stick. When okra is dry, add onion and bell pepper and tomatoes. Let cook for about 5 minutes. Add peeled shrimp. When pink in color, shrimp are cooked. Crab halves are then added. Add 4 cups of hot water. Salt and pepper to taste. Let cook slowly for about an hour. Sprinkle minced parsley on top. If gumbo is too thick, add a little more hot water. Serve over cooked long-grain rice.

Yield: 6-8 servings   *Mrs. John F. Roth*

GUMBO 1—Top p50

SHRIMP AND OKRA GUMBO

3 pounds fresh shrimp, heads
   left on
1 gallon water
½ cup vegetable oil
5 pounds fresh okra, cut into
   thin rings
2 onions, chopped
2 bell peppers, chopped
2 stalks celery, chopped
2 (15-ounce) cans whole
   tomatoes

1 teaspoon vinegar
1 cup dark roux (see basic
   recipe for roux on page 48)
2 tablespoons salt
2 tablespoons red pepper
1 tablespoon black pepper
1 tablespoon white pepper
4 or 5 dashes Tabasco pepper
   sauce
3 cups cooked rice

Shrimp Stock: peel and devein the shrimp. Place the heads and peelings in a stock pot and add water and let reduce to 1 quart. Strain and set aside. Heat oil and smother okra with onion, bell pepper, celery and tomatoes. Add vinegar. Cook over medium low fire until okra is tender, approximately 45 minutes. Add shrimp stock, roux and seasonings. Let simmer for at least 1½ hours. This may be done the day before, but do not add the shrimp until 10 minutes before serving. Serve over cooked rice in a gumbo bowl.

Yield: 6 servings   *Gigi and Alex Patout*

Z'HERBES GUMBO

1 pound pickled pork
1 cabbage
2 large bunches fresh spinach
1 bunch turnip tops
1 bunch mustard greens
1 heaping tablespoon
   vegetable shortening

2 tablespoons flour
2 large onions, chopped
4 cloves garlic, chopped
2 tablespoons vinegar
1 pod hot red pepper, chopped
Salt and pepper to taste

Cover salt meat with water to boil until tender (salt meat and pickled pork are the same). At the same time, break up the cabbage, stem spinach, turnip tops and mustard greens and put them in the pot with enough water to cover. When the greens are cooked to tenderness, place in a colander and drain. After well drained, chop very fine. Place a deep iron pot on the fire. When it is hot, add the vegetable shortening and stir in the flour slowly to make a dark roux. Add chopped onions and garlic and brown. Put in the chopped salt meat and add the greens. Allow to cook 5 minutes, stirring all the time. Add 1½ quarts of water and let cook slowly until it becomes a thick purée. Put in vinegar, a pod of red pepper broken up and salt to taste. Serve with grits.

Yield: 6 servings

Patti Weeks Torian
Old Weeks Family recipe

Note: For a meatless dish, put in the pot a heaping tablespoon of butter in place of the pork; when ready to serve, add another tablespoon of butter. In this way, the meat may be omitted without losing the richness of the dish.

CORN AND CRAB BISQUE

1 stick butter
2 tablespoons flour
½ cup chopped onions
1 pound white crabmeat
1 quart milk
1 (16-ounce) can cream style
   white corn
1 (10½-ounce) can cream of
   potato soup, undiluted

½ teaspoon Accent
½ teaspoon Worcestershire
   sauce
Pinch mace
Tabasco pepper sauce to taste
¼ cup grated cheese
¼ cup chopped parsley
¼ cup chopped shallots

Melt butter, add flour, blend thoroughly, then add onions. Cook slowly on low fire for 10 minutes. Add crab meat, milk, cream style corn, potato soup, Accent, Worcestershire sauce, mace, and Tabasco pepper sauce. Cook slowly for 15 to 20 minutes. Just before serving, add cheese, parsley and shallots.

Yield: 2½ quarts

Michael "a catering experience"

CRAWFISH BISQUE I

GUMBO

2 gallons crawfish stock
1 ½ cups flour
1 cup oil
3 onions, chopped
2 bell peppers, chopped

2 stalks celery, chopped
2 (2-ounce) containers
crawfish fat
Salt, pepper and Tabasco
pepper sauce to taste

Crawfish Stock: When crawfish heads have been saved from a crawfish boil, add these to 3 gallons water and cook for about 1 hour. Reduce to 2 gallons. Remove heads from water and set aside for stuffing. When using live crawfish, scald for 2 minutes to kill. Separate heads from tails; peel tails. Boil heads and peelings in 3 gallons water; reduce to 2 gallons. Remove and set aside heads; discard peelings.

Make a dark roux with the flour and oil until it is a chocolate color. Remove from heat and cool. To the stock, add the vegetables; when it boils again, add the cooled roux slowly and the crawfish fat. This gumbo will not be thick as the stuffed heads added later will thicken gumbo. Adjust seasonings with salt, pepper and Tabasco. The heads will have flavored the stock, season carefully.

STUFFED HEADS

1 pound butter
½ gallon chopped onions
1 quart chopped bell pepper
1 quart chopped celery
2 (2-ounce) containers
crawfish fat
2 tablespoons salt
2 tablespoons white pepper
2 tablespoons red pepper

2 pounds chopped crawfish
tails
2 cups bread crumbs
½ cup chopped green onion
tops
½ cup chopped parsley
Tabasco pepper sauce to taste
50 to 60 cleaned crawfish
heads
Flour to dredge stuffed heads

In melted butter, sauté the onions, bell pepper and celery. Cook about 45 minutes until vegetables are extremely tender. Add the crawfish fat and cook for 15 minutes. Add the salt, white and red pepper and crawfish tails; cook for 5 minutes. Add bread crumbs, green onion tops and parsley. Cool. Stuff heads with dressing mixture and roll in flour and place on a baking sheet. Bake at 350° for 30 to 45 minutes. May be prepared a day or two ahead of adding to gumbo.

CONTINUED...

BISQUE

2 pounds peeled crawfish tails	1 cup chopped parsley
1 cup chopped green onion tops	

Add stuffed heads and crawfish tails to boiling gumbo. Cook for 20 minutes. Add chopped onion tops and parsley. Serve over rice.

Yield: 12 servings   *Alex Patout*

CRAWFISH BISQUE II

STUFFED HEADS (make this first)

1½ pounds peeled crawfish tails, reserve fat	¼ cup cooking oil
	Salt, red and black pepper to taste
3 cups toasted French bread crumbs	¼ pound butter
3 onions, chopped fine	½ cup chopped parsley
1 cup celery, chopped fine	½ cup chopped green onions
1 bell pepper, chopped fine	50 to 60 crawfish heads, cleaned
3 cloves garlic, minced	

Put bread crumbs in bowl. Pour fat over and toss well. Chop crawfish. Sauté onions, celery, bell pepper and garlic in cooking oil in heavy pot until very tender. Add the chopped crawfish. Cook 5 minutes more. Add moistened bread crumbs. Season with salt, red pepper, and black pepper to taste. Add butter, parsley and green onions. Mix well. Take off burner and allow to cool. Fill dried crawfish heads. Save some of dressing (about 1 cup) to put into gumbo later. Roll heads in flour. Put on cookie sheet and bake about 30 minutes at 350°

GUMBO

1½ pounds peeled crawfish tails	½ cup chopped celery
	1 cup chopped green onions
Salt, red and black pepper	2 tablespoons chopped bell peppers
1 cup flour	
1 cup oil	Reserved fat
1 cup chopped onions	2 tablespoons parsley

Put crawfish tails in a bowl and season well with salt and pepper. Make a roux with flour and oil. Cook until the color of peanut butter. Do not let this burn or overcook. Stir well over low heat. Add the chopped onions, celery, ½ cup green onions and bell peppers and stir well. Cook until tender. Add crawfish fat and mix well. Add crawfish, mix gently and heat thoroughly. Add 2 quarts water and bring to a boil. Add the dressing you saved from the heads, simmer about an hour. Stir often. Correct seasonings. Add remaining green onions and parsley. When ready to serve, add stuffed heads and heat. Serve in gumbo bowls with rice.

Yield: 8 servings   *Scotty Broussard*

CRAWFISH AND SHRIMP BISQUE

STUFFING

2 pounds raw shrimp, peeled, deveined and chopped
2 pounds raw crawfish tails, chopped
¾ cup minced onion
¼ cup minced celery
2 cloves garlic, minced

1 teaspoon Creole salt seasoning
2 tablespoons minced parsley
4-5 slices stale French bread
1 egg
Cleaned, scalded crawfish heads

Sauté shrimp and crawfish in a little cooking oil. Add onion, celery, garlic and sauté till onions are wilted and transparent. Add seasoning and parsley. Lightly salt mixture to taste. Dip each slice of stale bread in a little water and add one slice at a time to the mixture. Stir lightly until the bread breaks up into the mixture. Repeat until all slices have been added. Let cook 3 minutes over low to medium heat. Break the egg over the mixture and quickly stir the egg around until completely mixed into the shrimp-crawfish mixture. Remove from heat and set aside. When cooled, fill each crawfish head with a little stuffing, packing well. Place the stuffed heads in the freezer for about 15 minutes. Add the heads to the bisque.

BISQUE

4 cups crawfish stock or 4 cups hot chicken broth
1 cup minced onion
¼ cup minced celery
1 clove garlic, minced

1 bay leaf, crushed
3 tablespoons flour
3 tablespoons cooking oil
4 cups hot water
1 (6-ounce) can tomato paste

Crawfish stock is made only if boiled crawfish have been served and the carcasses are placed in a colander in a pot of water and boiled for 15 minutes. Discard crawfish carcasses and retain stock. This is usually highly seasoned from the seasoning used in the boiling of the crawfish.

Sauté onions, celery, garlic and bay leaf in a little oil. Sprinkle flour over this and stir thoroughly. Add remaining oil and mix well. Stir to make a dark roux (about the color of chocolate). Begin adding ½ cup of stock slowly, stirring with each addition. Continue until all stock has been added. Add tomato paste. Add 4 cups of the water. Stir well. Cook 1 hour over gentle heat. If the bisque is too thick, add a little more water, about 1 cup and stir. If right consistency, add heads and simmer for additional 10 minutes. Bisque should be thicker than soup. Serve in bowls over cooked rice.

Yield: 10 servings

A Friend of the Shadows

CREAM OF ARTICHOKE SOUP

1 medium onion, finely
   chopped
2 tablespoons butter
2 tablespoons flour
1 1/2 cups fresh chicken stock
1/2 cup dry white vermouth

1 (8 1/2-ounce) can artichoke
   hearts, rinsed, drained and
   chopped
1 1/4 cups light cream
Salt and pepper to taste
Sour cream
4 tablespoons finely minced
   parsley

Cook onion in butter until soft. Add flour and stir for 2 minutes. Remove from heat. Add chicken stock, vermouth, 1 cup of the artichoke hearts, and 2 tablespoons parsley. Cook over moderate heat, stirring for 5 minutes. Purée in the blender, return to saucepan, add light cream, the remaining chopped artichokes, salt and pepper. When ready to serve, top with a spoonful of sour cream and chopped parsley. May be served hot or cold.

Yield: 4-6 servings

Cathy Kwong

CREAM OF AVOCADO SOUP

3 large ripe avocados, peeled,
   seeded and diced
1 1/2 cups heavy cream
6 cups chicken broth

1 teaspoon salt
3 drops Tabasco pepper sauce
3 tablespoons fresh chives

Purée the diced avocados and cream in a blender for 30 seconds. In a 3-quart saucepan, bring the broth to a boil over high heat; reduce to a simmer; add purée, salt and Tabasco pepper sauce to taste. Stir lightly, until well blended. Remove from heat, place in a bowl and refrigerate several hours. When ready to serve, sprinkle with chives.

Yield: 1 quart

A Friend of the Shadows

Note: Chicken broth may be made from chicken-flavored bouillon cubes dissolved in boiling water. Use 6 cubes dissolved in 6 cups boiling water.

CREAM OF CARROT SOUP

2 tablespoons butter
¾ cup chopped onions
3 cups chopped carrots
1 quart chicken stock

2 teaspoons tomato paste
2 tablespoons raw rice
½ cup heavy cream
Salt and pepper to taste

Cook onions in butter until soft. Add carrots, chicken stock, tomato paste, and rice. Simmer, uncovered, 30 minutes. Purée the soup in blender. Stir in cream and salt and pepper to taste. May be served hot or chilled. Use a carrot curl as garnish.

Yield: 1 quart   *Manon Hunter*

CREAM OF CAULIFLOWER SOUP

½ stick butter
¼ cup flour
½ onion, chopped
2 carrots, grated
1 head cauliflower, broken up

2 quarts chicken stock
3 cups Half & Half (whole milk
    is acceptable)
Salt, pepper, thyme and
    Tabasco pepper sauce
    to taste

Melt butter. Add flour and mix well. Add onions and carrots and sauté until tender. Add cauliflower and stock and simmer till cauliflower is tender. Add Half & Half, seasonings and heat.

Yield: 6-8 servings   *Carla I. Mouton*

Note: Do not use a very rich stock as it will overpower the cauliflower.

CREAM OF EGGPLANT SOUP

½ stick butter
2 onions, chopped
3 ribs of celery, chopped
1 eggplant, peeled and diced
2 potatoes, peeled and diced

1½ quarts chicken stock
1 quart Half & Half (or milk)
½ teaspoon thyme
Salt and pepper

Melt butter. Add all vegetables. Sauté until potatoes are tender. Add stock and simmer until soup begins to thicken. Add Half & Half and heat. Add seasonings and simmer until flavors mingle.

Yield: 6-8 servings   *Carla I. Mouton*

CREAM OF MUSHROOM SOUP

3 tablespoons butter
3 tablespoons flour
1½ cups Half & Half
1 cup minced fresh mushrooms
(use processor)

½ teaspoon garlic powder
1 teaspoon salt
½ teaspoon pepper

Melt butter, add flour and cook for 3 minutes. Remove from heat, beat the Half & Half into the mixture with a wire whisk. Add mushrooms, garlic powder, salt and pepper. Return to heat; bring to a boil; lower heat and cook until thick.

Yield: 12 ounces   *Mac Beyt*

Note: This may be used as a substitute for one (10½-ounce) can of undiluted cream of mushroom soup.

CREAM OF MUSHROOM AND ARTICHOKE SOUP

2 cups evaporated milk
2 tablespoons flour
1 cup water
3 tablespoons butter
1 (8½-ounce) can artichoke
hearts, rinsed, drained and
diced
4 shallots, tops and bottoms
finely chopped

1 cup fresh mushrooms,
washed and sliced (reserve
some for garnish)
2 cloves garlic, minced
2 tablespoons grated
Parmesan cheese
1 tablespoon parsley, minced
(flat, broad leaf parsley)

Mix 1 cup milk with flour and mix 1 cup milk with water. Sauté diced artichoke hearts, shallots, mushrooms and garlic in 3 tablespoons butter or margarine until wilted. Reduce heat and add milk and flour mixture, stirring constantly. When mixture begins to thicken, very slowly add the milk and water mixture, stirring very lightly. Simmer about 5 minutes. If mixture becomes too thick, add a little warm water, just to keep mixture from sticking to bottom of saucepan. Simmer another 5 minutes and then season to taste. Add cheese and parsley. When ready to serve, roll reserved mushroom slices in paprika and place on top.

Yield: 1 quart   *A Friend of the Shadows*

CREAM OF POTATO SOUP

2½ cups mashed potatoes, firmly packed
3 cups milk, or 1½ cups evaporated milk plus 1½ cups water
3 tablespoons butter
½ teaspoon Tabasco pepper sauce
1 teaspoon grated raw onion
Salt and pepper to taste
2 tablespoons finely diced ham—per serving
2 tablespoons grated cheese— per serving

Place potatoes in heavy saucepan. Gradually add milk, blending constantly. Beat with a wire whisk until thoroughly blended and mixture is smooth. Place over low heat. Stirring frequently, heat just to boiling point. Add butter, Tabasco pepper sauce, onion and salt and pepper. Blend thoroughly. Serve hot. Garnish with ham and cheese.

Yield: 6-7 cups   *Mrs. Paul W. Worden*

COLD CUCUMBER SOUP

2 large cucumbers, peeled, seeded, cubed
1 bell pepper, chopped
½ cup chopped onion
3 cups chicken stock, homemade
1 cup sour cream (reserve 4 teaspoons for garnish)
1 tablespoon parsley, chopped
½ teaspoon fresh dill, finely chopped or
¼ teaspoon dried dill
Salt and freshly ground pepper to taste

Place cucumbers, bell pepper, onion and chicken stock in large pan. Simmer covered for 20 minutes. Strain vegetables, reserving stock. In food processor or blender, process the cooked vegetables. Add the sour cream, parsley, dill and stock, keeping the machine running. (This may have to be done in 2 parts so that it will not spill out of processor.) Strain. Season to taste and chill. (Cubed raw cucumbers may be added at the end for crunch.) Garnish with sliced cucumbers, sour cream dollops and chopped dill.

Yield: 4 servings   *Nancy Lewis*

Note: 8 stalks of asparagus may be substituted for the cucumber.

BLOODY MARY SOUP

2 tablespoons olive oil
1 tablespoon red wine vinegar
1 clove garlic, minced
1 quart Mott's Clamato Juice
Tabasco pepper sauce to taste
Juice of 1 lime
1 bell pepper, chopped fine
½ cup chopped Spanish olives

1 red Bermuda onion,
    chopped fine
4 peeled tomatoes, chopped
    fine
1 cucumber, chopped fine
2 tablespoons parsley
Salt, black (freshly cracked)
    cayenne pepper to taste

Mix all ingredients and chill overnight. Before serving as chilled soup, add 1½-ounces vodka to each serving.

Yield: 6 servings

Bryan N. Richard

GAZPACHO

1 cup cold water
2 tablespoons olive oil
1 tablespoon vinegar
1 slice of bread, crumbled
1 large tomato, peeled and
    chopped

1 small cucumber, chopped
1 small bell pepper, chopped
Salt to taste
½ cup milk
1 clove of garlic, minced

Put all ingredients in large bowl. Mix and chill. Serve cold.

Yield: 1 quart

Susie Pharr

STRAWBERRY SOUP

1½ cups water
1 cup red wine
½ cup sugar
Juice of 2 lemons
Pinch cinnamon

1 quart fresh strawberries
    puréed
½ cup whipped cream
¼ cup sour cream

Combine water, wine, sugar, lemon juice and cinnamon. Boil, uncovered, for 15 minutes stirring occasionally. Add strawberries and simmer 10 minutes, stirring frequently. Refrigerate until cold. When ready to serve, mix creams, add to soup and serve.

Yield: 2 quarts

Carla I. Mouton

VICHYSSOISE

4 green onions
1 medium onion, chopped
2 tablespoons butter
5 medium raw potatoes,
    peeled and sliced

5 cups ham or chicken broth
Salt and red pepper to taste
2 cups milk
2 cups light cream
Sour cream

Wash and slice white part of green onions. In large soup pot, sauté green onion bottoms and onion in butter until just tender. Add sliced potatoes, ham broth and salt and pepper. Boil until potatoes are soft. Press through a fine sieve. Scald the milk and light cream. Add the potato purée and heat, do not boil. Chill in refrigerator. Adjust seasonings.

To serve, float the sour cream on top and add finely chopped green onion tops.

Yield: 3 quarts

Juanita Winkle

SPINACH VICHYSSOISE

¼ cup butter
4 leeks, white part only
¼ cup chopped onion
2 large Idaho potatoes, peeled
    and sliced
1 carrot, sliced

4 cups chicken broth
1 teaspoon salt
1 pound fresh slightly cooked
    spinach
2 cups Half & Half, or milk

Melt butter. Sauté leeks and onion at medium heat until yellow, not brown. Add potatoes, carrot, chicken broth and salt. Cover and simmer until potatoes and carrot are soft. Cool. Put potato mixture in blender with 1 cup cooked spinach. Add Half & Half, season to taste with salt and pepper and chill. Purée remaining spinach and season to taste. Serve in very cold bowls with a spoonful of the puréed spinach swished on top. If potato mixture becomes too dry during cooking, add more chicken broth.

Yield: 1 quart

Manon Hunter

CURRIED ZUCCHINI SOUP

6 tablespoons butter
2 pounds zucchini, cut in
   1-inch lengths
1 cup minced shallots or onion
1 tablespoon curry

1 tablespoon ground cumin
2 cups chicken broth
3 cups buttermilk
Salt and pepper to taste

Sauté zucchini with 1 cup minced shallots or onion in 6 table-spoons butter, until soft. Add 1 tablespoon each, curry and ground cumin. Cook and stir for 2 minutes. Stir in 2 cups chicken broth. Purée mixture in processor. Transfer to large bowl and stir in 3 cups of buttermilk. Chill for 4 hours. If too thick, thin with a little more broth or buttermilk. Serve with a garnish in chilled bowls.

Yield: 6 servings
Martha Coons

MAMA'S CORN SOUP

12 ears of corn, shucked and
   cleaned
2 quarts water
2 pounds pickled pork, cut into
   pieces (not salt pork)
2 tablespoons oil
2 tablespoons flour
3 large onions, chopped

1 bell pepper, chopped
2 stalks celery, chopped
2 cloves garlic, minced
3 large, whole, fresh tomatoes,
   peeled and chopped (you
   may substitute one can of
   whole tomatoes)
Salt and pepper to taste

Cut kernels from cob, scrape milk from cob and reserve. Keep at least 6 of the cobs. Bring water to a boil, add the cobs and pickled pork. Simmer for at least 15-30 minutes to make stock. Heat oil, add flour and stir until roux is a light brown. Add all of the vege-tables except the corn, cook 5-10 minutes. Add corn and milk from cob, cook 5 minutes more. Remove cobs from stock scraping residue from cobs back into the pot as you remove them. Add roux and vegetables to the stock. Cook 30 minutes more. Season to taste, be careful, pickled pork may be a little salty.

Yield: 2 quarts
Virginia Richard Simon

FRENCH ONION SOUP

⅓ cup butter
6 medium yellow onions
2 tablespoons all-purpose flour
7 cups beef stock or beef broth
½ teaspoon salt
¼ teaspoon pepper

¼ cup sherry or white wine
6 slices French bread (1-inch thick), toasted
8 ounces Swiss cheese, sliced thin or grated
¼ cup Parmesan cheese

In a heavy 5-quart saucepan or Dutch oven, heat the butter. Add onions. Sauté, stirring frequently, over low heat, until golden brown—about 20 minutes.

Stir in flour. Cook, stirring, to brown flour slightly. Gradually add beef stock, stirring. Add salt and pepper. Cook over low heat, covered, for 30 minutes. Add sherry.

In six heatproof bowls, place a slice of the French bread. Cover each with Swiss cheese. Pour soup over top. Sprinkle each with Parmesan cheese. Broil just long enough to melt the cheese.

Yield: 6 servings   *Shereen Minvielle*

SOUP A L'OIGNON

24 small white onions
½ cup butter
Sprinkle of sugar
6 cups heavy beef stock (canned is acceptable)

½ cup Cognac
½ pound Gruyère cheese, grated
6-8 slices toasted rounds of French bread

Peel and slice onions thinly. Heat butter (over a low fire, do not brown) in a large saucepan. Add onions. Sprinkle a little sugar over this. As onions begin to wilt, slowly add beef stock. Cook over a low fire for about 20-25 minutes, stirring frequently. Add Cognac and cover and steam to blend the flavors. Turn off fire. Serve in deep bowls. Place a tablespoon of the grated cheese on top of the soup. Then place the French bread round on top of this and sprinkle another tablespoon of the grated cheese. Serve immediately. Salt and pepper to taste after serving.

Yield: 8 servings   *Glynda Gros*

DADDY'S COURTBOUILLON

1 pound raw shrimp
7 cups water

1 tablespoon instant chicken
   bouillon granules

Peel and devein shrimp. Reserve shrimp. Mix shrimp shells, water and bouillon cubes and boil, covered, about 30 minutes for stock. Drain and reserve stock.

¾ cup bacon fat, cooking oil,
   or combination

¾ cup flour

Cook flour in fat over medium heat, stirring constantly, until chocolate brown in color, making a roux.

1 large onion, chopped fine
½ bell pepper, chopped fine

3 stalks celery, chopped fine
3 cloves garlic, crushed

Add to roux and sauté over medium heat until vegetables are limp.

¼ cup tomato paste

1 cup fresh or canned
   tomatoes, chopped

Add to roux and cook slowly until fat starts to separate from rest.

2 bay leaves
Dash each basil, oregano,
   thyme, allspice and
   monosodium glutamate

1 tablespoon Worcestershire
   sauce
1½ teaspoons sugar
½ cup red wine
7 cups reserved shrimp stock

Add all to above and cook until thick and smooth.

1½-2 pounds catfish fillets
Reserved peeled shrimp
½ cup chopped green onion
   tops

¼ cup chopped parsley
Salt and pepper to taste

Cut catfish fillets into bite size pieces. Add these and other ingredients to above and simmer gently about 10-15 minutes. Turn off heat, cover and let stand. The longer it stands, the better the flavor.

Yield: 10-12 servings   *Keith Courrege*

OYSTER SOUP LAFAYETTE

1 tablespoon butter
1 heaping tablespoon flour
3 green onions (shallots)
1 sprig celery
2 cloves garlic

2 dozen oysters and 1 pint
    liquid
Salt and red pepper
2 eggs
½ cup minced parsley

Melt the butter and stir in the flour carefully to make a light roux. Add the onions, celery, and garlic, all chopped fine. Cut oysters in 3 pieces; add salt and red pepper. Pour oysters and the liquid into the roux. Cover, let cook 3 minutes. Beat the eggs lightly and slowly pour the soup into them, whipping the entire time. A golden color is the result. Sprinkle with parsley and serve.

Yield: 4 servings

Mrs. Walter Torian
A Weeks Family recipe

Note: 1 teaspoon of cold water in the eggs will prevent them from curdling.

Lessen the amount of liquid used and a delicious stew, instead of soup, results.

PINTO BEAN SOUP

½ cup chopped onion
3 tablespoons butter
1 (15-ounce) can Trappey's
    pinto beans w/bacon

2½ cups chicken stock
Garlic salt
½ cup tomato juice
Salt and pepper to taste

Cook onion very slightly in butter. Put in blender and add beans, chicken stock and seasoning. Blend well. Add tomato juice. Heat and serve. Garnish with sliced hard boiled egg.

Yield: 6 servings

B. F. Trappey's Sons, Inc.

HEARTY CAJUN POTATO SOUP

½ cup salad oil
½ cup flour
1 large onion
½ cup celery
2 teaspoons paprika
8 medium potatoes, peeled
   and cubed

1 quart water, hot
1 clove garlic, chopped
1 pound ham hocks
1 pound cubed ham or smoked
   sausage
1 cup sour cream
Salt and pepper to taste

Cook oil and flour until it turns golden (light roux). Add onion, celery, paprika and cook until wilted. Add potatoes and brown. Add hot water, garlic, ham hocks, ham or sausage, salt and pepper to taste. Simmer until potatoes are tender. Add sour cream and simmer until heated through.

Yield: 2½ quarts

Mrs. Joe Mouton

TURTLE SOUP I

4 pounds turtle meat
2 gallons water
¼ cup flour
⅓ cup oil
1 cup chopped celery
1 cup chopped onion

¼ cup chopped bell pepper
1 (8-ounce) can tomato sauce
1 tablespoon tomato paste
12 cloves (tied in cloth bag)
Salt and pepper to taste
4 hard boiled eggs

Boil meat until tender in two gallons of seasoned water. Reserve stock. Length of time varies with age of turtle (several hours).

Make a roux of the oil and flour until brown in color. Add celery, onion, and bell pepper and sauté a few minutes, then add tomato sauce and tomato paste. Combine with the turtle meat and stock. Place bag of cloves into this and simmer at least another 1½ or 2 hours. As each bowl is served, place a slice of lemon and several slices of hard boiled eggs in each plate. Add 1 tablespoon of sherry to each bowl, if desired.

Yield: 8-10 servings

Mrs. Donald Pavy

TURTLE SOUP II

6-10 pounds cleaned turtle meat

6 quarts water
3 tablespoons vegetable shortening

Boil meat in 6 quarts water and skim as meat boils. When meat has cooked about one hour, strain through cheese cloth, keeping stock. Stock should be about one gallon. Allow stock to continue boiling after straining. When cool enough to handle, cut meat into small pieces.

Sauté turtle meat in vegetable shortening until well fried. Set aside.

2 cups flour
2 tablespoons vegetable shortening

2 sticks butter

Make a roux with the above 3 ingredients. Cook until roux is medium brown.

10 medium onions, minced
4 bell peppers, minced
2 pods garlic, minced

2 hot peppers, minced
6 ribs celery, chopped
1 (15-ounce) can tomato sauce

Add all, except tomato sauce, to the roux. Stir well and cook until all are tender. Add tomato sauce and blend well. Add all to stock, along with the next two ingredients:

4 (10-ounce) cans beef bouillon
1 bag spices (crab boil)
Salt, pepper, Worcestershire and Tabasco pepper sauce to taste

6 hard boiled eggs (separate whites and yolks)
1 cup chopped onion tops
1 cup minced parsley
Sherry

Bring to a boil. Do not boil too long or soup will get too spicy. Add meat. When boiling begins again, add salt, pepper, Worcestershire sauce and Tabasco pepper sauce to taste. Do not salt too heavily as bouillon is salty. Allow to simmer about 1½ to 2 hours. If it gets too thick, add water. About ½ hour before the end of the cooking time remove bag and add 6 hard boiled egg yolks, which have been sieved and onion tops and parsley. When ready to serve, add chopped egg whites and 1 tablespoon sherry to each serving bowl. This makes a large amount. Suitable for freezing.

Yield: 10-12 servings   *Eugene Patout*

Note: If crab boil is not available, make a cheese cloth bag of bay leaves, oregano, and allspice.

SALADS, SALAD DRESSINGS
AND SAUCES

The photograph shown above depicts detail from an 1861 egg tempera painting of The Shadows-on-the-Teche. The artist, Adrien Persac, was a surveyor and mapmaker who painted many of the great homes of southern Louisiana. Note that in the early days, the structure was whitewashed to look like marble and to reflect the Greek Revival architecture of the house. Figures of people and horses are cut-outs from Godey's Ladies' Book, a popular periodical of the day.

When the National Trust restored the house, the fence was missing. The Federal troops had used the wood in the fence for firewood during the period of time they occupied the house during the War Between the States. The painting done by Persac provided the National Trust with authentic, accurate information for duplicating the original fence.

Adrien Persac painted the rear view of the house as well as the front. One reason for this is that the bayou was as heavily traveled as Main Street, and often homes during this period faced the bayou rather than the street. From this rendering of the rear view, we know that the back porches had been enclosed by 1861. When the home was restored, the porches were re-opened, as we see on the back cover, according to the original plan.

Salads, Salad Dressings and Sauces

SALADS

Artichoke
Artichoke I................. 69
Artichoke II................ 69
Hearts of Artichoke.......... 69

Avocado
Guacamole................ 70
Molded.................... 70

Bean
Charlotte's Mexican Medley.... 71
Spanish................... 71

Carrot
Fourteen Karat Ring Mold...... 72
Piquant Carrot.............. 71

Fruit
Champagne................ 72
Frozen.................... 72
Greek Grape................ 73
Strawberry Delight........... 73
Yum-Yum.................. 73

Green
Caesar.................... 74
Cucumber Ring.............. 74
Oriental, Make Ahead......... 75
Pickled Garden.............. 75
Seven Layer................ 76
Vegetable Bowl, Marinated..... 76

Potato
Delicious.................. 77
Dilled Hot.................. 77

Poultry and Game
Cobb..................... 77
Country Fair................ 78
Curried.................... 78
Duck, Wild................. 79

Sauerkraut
Kraut..................... 80

Seafood
Salad..................... 79

Spinach
Captain's.................. 81
Fairmont................... 80
Indian..................... 80
Spinach................... 81

Tomato
Asheville.................. 82
Aspic..................... 82
Cucumber.................. 82
Spaghetti.................. 83

SALAD DRESSINGS
California Blue Cheese.......... 83
Citrus..................... 83
Mayonnaise, Garlic............ 84
Mayonnaise, Never Fail
  Homemade................ 84
Pastoral................... 85
Plantation Club.............. 85
Poppy Seed................. 84

SAUCES
Barbeque, Brown's Texas........ 86
Cajun Mustard................ 87
Cheese, Welsh Style........... 87
Hollandaise................. 87
Hollandaise for Food Processor... 88
Jalapeño, Hot................ 88
Joyce's Special Seasoning....... 88
Newburg................... 89
Red, Old Country............. 89
Remoulade................. 89
Piquante................... 90
Piquante, Variations.......... 90
Seafood, White Wine.......... 92
Tartar, Fisherman's........... 92
White—Thin, Medium and Thick... 91
Zippy..................... 92

Refer to additional recipes in "How Men Cook" section.

ARTICHOKE SALAD I

6 small artichokes or 4
  large ones
2 envelopes Knox gelatin
2 cans beef consommé
2 hard-boiled eggs finely
  chopped

½ cup chopped celery
½ cup ripe olives, finely
  chopped
Salt and pepper

Boil artichokes. When tender and cool, scrape meat from leaves and cut up hearts. Soften gelatin in a little of the consommè. Then heat remaining consommé and add to gelatin. Fold in eggs, celery, olives, artichoke meat and salt and pepper. Butter a mold and pour in. Refrigerate until set.

Yield: 6 cups   *Mrs. Provost Minvielle*

ARTICHOKE SALAD II

2 (8½-ounce) cans water-
  packed artichoke hearts
1 (5½-ounce) can drained
water chestnuts, sliced thin
8 large fresh mushrooms,
  sliced

6 green onions, chopped
6 tablespoons olive oil
2 tablespoons wine vinegar
1 tablespoon mayonnaise
Salt and pepper to taste

Rinse artichoke hearts, drain and put in salad bowl. Place sliced water chestnuts on top of artichoke hearts and add mushrooms and green onions.

Make dressing with the remaining ingredients. Mix well and pour over salad. Let marinate at least overnight.

Yield: 6-8 servings   *Rose Mary Brooks*

HEARTS OF ARTICHOKE SALAD

4 (14-ounce) cans artichoke
  hearts, drained and rinsed
1 small bottle Italian salad
  dressing, or favorite
  home recipe

3 tablespoons mayonnaise
Crushed garlic to taste
½ (3½-ounce) jar capers,
  drained

Combine all ingredients and let marinate in refrigerator for at least 3 days.

Yield: 6-8 servings   *Rose Mary Brooks*

GUACAMOLE SALAD

2 avocados
1 small tomato, peeled
  and chopped
1/4 cup finely chopped onion

2 tablespoons green chilies,
  chopped
1 tablespoon lemon juice
3/4 teaspoon salt

Peel avocados and mash with a fork. Blend in the rest of the ingredients. This can be served as a salad over shredded lettuce or as a dip with tortilla chips.

Yield: 4 servings

A Friend of the Shadows

Note: Keep seed to use in storing leftovers to avoid discoloration.

MOLDED AVOCADO SALAD

1 1/2 to 2 tablespoons gelatin
1/2 cup cold water
1 1/4 cups hot water
4 ripe avocados
4 tablespoons lemon juice
2 teaspoons salt

1 teaspoon cayenne pepper
3 tablespoons grated onion
1 tablespoon sugar
3/4 cup mayonnaise
1/2 cup diced celery

Dissolve gelatin in cold water; add hot water. Process the avocados and lemon juice until smooth; add gelatin mixture, salt, pepper, onion and sugar. Refrigerate until almost congealed. Fold in mayonnaise and celery. Place in an oiled mold and refrigerate until set. Remove mold before serving.

SAUCE
1 pint sour cream
1/2 cup ketchup
2 tablespoons Worcestershire
  sauce
1/2 tablespoon grated onion
1 teaspoon salt

2 tablespoons horseradish
1 teaspoon paprika
1 tablespoon lemon juice
1/4 teaspoon dry mustard
1 pound cooked shrimp

Mix well and refrigerate. Pour over molded salad and serve.

Yield: 12 servings

Julaine Porter

Note: This sauce may also be served as a remoulade sauce over shrimp or crabmeat.

CHARLOTTE'S MEXICAN MEDLEY

1 (15¼-ounce) can kidney
  beans, drained
1 head lettuce, torn
8 ounces sharp Cheddar
  cheese, grated
½ onion, grated

½ bell pepper, chopped
1 (8-ounce) bag corn chips,
  crumbled
1 (8-ounce) bottle Catalina
  salad dressing
Tabasco pepper sauce
  to taste

Mix all ingredients in large bowl and serve chilled.

Yield: 10-12 servings   *Charlotte Guinn*

SPANISH BEAN SALAD

1 (15¼-ounce) can red kidney
  beans
1 (16-ounce) can cut green
  beans
1 (16-ounce) can cut
  wax beans

1 cup thinly sliced red onions
½ cup pimento-stuffed
  olives, halved
⅓ cup sugar
½ cup vinegar
¼ cup salad oil

Drain kidney beans and rinse well with cold water. Drain other beans and combine all beans with onion and olives. Mix sugar, vinegar and salad oil and pour over beans, stirring slightly. Chill one day before serving and serve over crisp salad greens.

Yield: 5 cups   *Barbara Schwing*

PIQUANT CARROT SALAD

8 medium carrots peeled and
  cut into strips
1 medium onion cut into rings
1 small bell pepper cut
  into rings
¼ cup white wine vinegar
3 tablespoons sugar

½ teaspoon Dijon mustard
3 tablespoons salad oil
1 tablespoon catsup
½ teaspoon seasoned salt
½ teaspoon celery seed
½ teaspoon Worcestershire
  sauce

Cook carrots covered in 1 inch boiling salted water about 5 minutes or until just tender. Drain thoroughly. In bowl, layer carrots, onions and pepper rings. In small jar combine remaining ingredients, shake well and pour over carrot mixture. Cover and chill at least 4 hours. Stir several times and serve.

Yield: 4-6 servings   *Grace Shaw*

FOURTEEN KARAT RING MOLD

1 envelope unflavored gelatin
1/3 cup sugar
1/4 teaspoon cinnamon
1/4 cup cold water
3/4 cup boiling water

1 (8-ounce) carton plain yogurt
1 cup finely grated carrots
1/2 cup drained, crushed
  pineapple
1/2 cup finely chopped pecans

Mix together gelatin, sugar and cinnamon. Add 1/4 cup cold water and let stand 5 minutes. Add 3/4 cup boiling water. Stir until gelatin is dissolved. To this add the yogurt, stirring until smooth. Chill until slightly thickened. Add the carrots, pineapple and pecans. Pour into oiled, 9-inch ring mold and chill until firm.

Yield: 4-5 servings

Teri Curtis

CHAMPAGNE SALAD

1 (8-ounce) package cream
  cheese
3/4 cup sugar
1 (151/4-ounce) can crushed,
  drained pineapple

1 (10-ounce) package frozen
  strawberries
1/2 cup chopped nuts
1 (8-ounce) carton
  whipped topping

Soften and blend cream cheese and sugar. Mix pineapple, strawberries and nuts. Add whipped topping. Combine with cheese mixture. Place in oiled, 9 x 13 pan. Freeze several hours or overnight.

Yield: 15-20 servings

Millie Swatloski

FROZEN FRUIT SALAD

21/2 cups sour cream
21/2 tablespoons lemon juice
3/4 cup sugar
1/8 teaspoon salt
1 cup drained, crushed
  pineapple

1/2 cup chopped maraschino
  cherries
1 large banana, diced
1/2 cup chopped walnuts
12 lettuce leaves

Mix sour cream, lemon juice, sugar and salt in a large bowl. Stir in fruits and nuts. Pour into 12 21/2-inch muffin tins lined with baking cups. Freeze for several hours. Serve on salad greens.

Yield: 12 servings

Jean Ostrich

GREEK GRAPE SALAD

1 large red onion, sliced thin
1 teaspoon sugar
1 cup halved seedless green
   grapes
1 cup seeded Tokay (red)
   grapes

2 oranges, sectioned
1 cup crumbled Feta cheese
1 bunch Romaine lettuce
4 tablespoons olive oil
Lemon juice
Salt and pepper

Slice onion and let stand in bowl of ice water with sugar for 10 minutes. Drain well. Add next 6 ingredients, mix well. Add lemon juice, salt and pepper to taste.

Yield: 4-6 servings

Julaine Porter

STRAWBERRY DELIGHT SALAD

1 (6-ounce) package
   strawberry Jello
1 cup boiling water
2 (10-ounce) packages
   frozen strawberries

1 (20-ounce) can crushed
   pineapple, drained
1 cup chopped pecans
1 (8-ounce) carton sour cream
1 (8-ounce) package cream
   cheese

Stir Jello in boiling water, add strawberries and juice, pineapple and pecans. Pour ½ mixture into a 9 x 13 x 2-inch pan and chill. Beat sour cream and cream cheese until soft and spread over jellied mixture. Chill until firm.

Yield: 12 servings

Carol Haik
Matilde Smith

YUM-YUM SALAD

2 cups crushed pineapple
½ cup sugar
2 envelopes gelatin in
   1 cup water

Juice of 1 lemon
1 (8-ounce) container
   Cool Whip
1 cup grated mild Cheddar
   cheese

Put gelatin soaking in water. Cook sugar, lemon juice and pineapple to boil; then add gelatin and bring to another boil. Then cool. Combine Cool Whip to mixture in large bowl and add grated cheese. Place mixture in flat 1 quart casserole. Refrigerate overnight.

Yield: 6-8 servings

Odette Voorhies

CAESAR SALAD

1 clove garlic
½ cup oil
3 tablespoons lemon juice
2 teaspoons Worcestershire
    sauce
½ teaspoon salt

¼ teaspoon pepper
8 anchovy filets
2 heads Romaine lettuce
2 eggs, lightly beaten
½ cup Parmesan cheese
¼ cup crumbled blue cheese
2 cups garlic croutons

Crush garlic and cover with oil. Refrigerate, covered for 30 minutes. Combine lemon juice, Worcestershire sauce, salt, pepper, anchovies and crush in bottom of salad bowl. Tear lettuce in bite size pieces and add to the salad bowl. Drain oil from garlic, add to the slightly beaten eggs and pour over the lettuce. Add cheeses and croutons. Toss and serve.

Yield: 8-10 servings

Hattie Kenworthy

CUCUMBER SALAD RING

2 envelopes gelatin
2 tablespoons sugar
1 teaspoon salt
⅔ cup water
1 (8-ounce) package cream
    cheese, softened

2 tablespoons lemon juice
3 tablespoons grated onion
¼ cup chopped parsley
2 cups peeled, seeded, grated
    and drained cucumbers
1 cup mayonnaise

Mix gelatin, sugar and salt and soften in ⅔ cup of water. Heat until boiling to dissolve. Stir in the remaining ingredients, pour into oiled 5-cup mold and refrigerate until firm.

Yield: 8-10 servings

A Friend of the Shadows

MAKE AHEAD ORIENTAL SALAD

1 (17-ounce) can tiny peas, drained
1 (12-ounce) can whole kernel white corn, drained
1 (4-ounce) jar pimento, drained and sliced
1 large onion, thinly sliced
1 (16-ounce) can bean sprouts, drained
2 (5-ounce) cans sliced water chestnuts, drained
1 large bell pepper, thinly sliced
1 cup diced celery
1 cup salad oil
1 cup salad oil
1 cup sugar
1/2 cup vinegar
1 cup water
Salt and pepper to taste

Combine all vegetables in large bowl. Blend remaining ingredients and pour over vegetables. Cover and chill 24 hours. Drain before serving.

Yield: 10-12 servings

Virginia LaSalle

PICKLED GARDEN SALAD

1/2 head cauliflower, cut in flowerets and sliced
2 stalks celery, cut in 1-inch pieces
1 (4-ounce) jar pimentos, drained and diced
3/4 cup wine vinegar
1/2 cup olive oil
1 teaspoon salt
1/2 teaspoon pepper
2 carrots, pared and cut in 1-inch strips
1 bell pepper, cut in 1-inch pieces
1 (3-ounce) jar pitted green olives, drained and diced
2 tablespoons sugar
1/2 teaspoon oregano
1/4 cup water

In large skillet combine all ingredients with 1/4 cup water. Bring to a boil, stirring occasionally. Reduce heat and simmer covered for 5 minutes. Cool and then refrigerate 24 hours. Drain well and serve.

Yield: 8 servings

Sue Dauterive

SEVEN LAYER SALAD

1 (16-ounce) package fresh
   spinach
8 hard cooked eggs
1 medium head lettuce
1 purple onion
1 pound bacon

1 (16-ounce) can sweet peas,
   beets or string beans
1½ cups mayonnaise
1 (8-ounce) package cream
   cheese, softened
1 (4-ounce) package shredded
   Cheddar cheese

Wash and break spinach into bite size bits and line bottom of 9 x 13 inch pan. Slice eggs and place on top of spinach. Break lettuce into bite size pieces and place on top of eggs. Slice onion very thin and place on top of lettuce. Cook bacon crisp and crumble over onions. Add remaining vegetables one layer at a time. Mix mayonnaise and cream cheese and spread over top. Sprinkle with Cheddar cheese.

Yield: 20 servings

Susie Pharr
Betty LeBlanc

Note: You may add any vegetables you like—zucchini, squash, cucumber, asparagus, etc.

MARINATED VEGETABLE BOWL

½ cup corn oil
1 cup vinegar
1 cup sugar
1 teaspoon salt
1 cucumber, sliced
1 (16-ounce) can French
   style green beans, drained
1 (17-ounce) can petit pois
   peas, drained
1 purple onion, sliced

3 to 5 stalks celery, chopped
1 green pepper cut into
   half rings
1 red sweet pepper or
   1 (2-ounce) jar pimento,
   chopped
2 (14-ounce) cans artichoke
   hearts, drained and
   quartered

Mix corn oil, vinegar, sugar and salt. Pour this over vegetables and marinate for 48 hours. Drain before serving.

Yield: 25 servings

Mary Ann St. John

DELICIOUS POTATO SALAD

5 cups potatoes, boiled,
   peeled and chilled
3 eggs, boiled, peeled
   and chilled
¼ cup finely chopped onion
1 (2-ounce) jar chopped
   pimento

½ teaspoon pepper
¼ cup chopped sweet pickle
   relish
½ tablespoon prepared
   mustard
1 teaspoon salt
1 cup mayonnaise

Using medium grater, grate potatoes and eggs. Mix remaining ingredients and add to the grated potatoes and eggs. Refrigerate.

Yield: 8-10 servings

Cathi Gibbens
Juanita Winkle

DILLED HOT POTATO SALAD

4 slices bacon, cut up
½ cup chopped onion
½ cup chopped celery
½ cup chopped dill pickles,
   drain, reserve liquid
4 large potatoes, cooked,
   peeled and cut into
   thick slices

¾ cup dill pickle liquid
1½ tablespoons sugar
½ teaspoon caraway seeds
½ teaspoon dry mustard
½ teaspoon salt
1 tablespoon parsley

In large skillet cook bacon pieces partially. Add onion, celery and pickles. Cook 3 to 5 minutes. Stir in potatoes and remaining ingredients. Cover and cook about 10 minutes stirring and lifting occasionally with a pancake turner. Garnish with parsley. Serve hot with ham or smoked sausage.

Yield: 6 servings

Barbara Schwing

COBB SALAD

½ head lettuce
½ bunch watercress
1 small bunch chicory
½ head romaine lettuce
2 tomatoes
2 tablespoons chives
3 cups cooked chicken, diced

6 slices bacon, cooked and
   crumbled
1 avocado, sliced
3 hard boiled eggs, chopped
½ cup crumbled Roquefort
   cheese
½ cup vinaigrette dressing

Chop greens into fine pieces. Peel, seed and chop tomatoes. Add chives. Arrange tomatoes and chives, chicken, bacon, avocado, and eggs in narrow strips over greens and sprinkle with cheese. Just before serving, toss with dressing.

Yield: 4-6 servings

Phyllis Peterson

COUNTRY FAIR CHICKEN SALAD

2 (5 to 7 pound) hens
Salt, red and black pepper
Garlic powder and Tabasco
  pepper sauce to taste
1 bunch celery, chopped
1 bell pepper, chopped
1 (8-ounce) jar small stuffed
  olives, chopped

6 eggs, cooked and chopped
1 (9½-ounce) jar Cross and
  Blackwell chow chow,
  chopped
3 cups Hellmann's
  mayonnaise
Zatarain's Creole mustard
  to taste

Boil hens in water seasoned with salt, pepper, garlic powder and Tabasco pepper sauce; this should be highly seasoned. Cook until tender; cool. Cut into small chunks; do not use food processor or meat grinder to cut chicken. Add celery, bell pepper, olives and eggs. Blend chow chow with mayonnaise and mustard in a separate bowl and season to taste. Mix with chicken.

Yield: 30 servings

Dianne Landry

Note: Turkey may be used in place of chicken.

CURRIED CHICKEN SALAD

3 (2½ to 3 pound) fryers
  boiled with onions, celery
  and salt
3 cups mayonnaise
2 teaspoons soy sauce
1 tablespoon curry powder

5 hard boiled eggs, diced
2 cups diced celery
3 (5½-ounce) cans water
  chestnuts, diced
2 cups sliced almonds, toasted

Bone chicken. Remove and discard skin. Dice chicken meat. Blend mayonnaise, soy sauce and curry powder. Mix with chicken, eggs, celery, and water chestnuts. Fold in toasted almonds.

Yield: 12 servings

A Friend of the Shadows

WILD DUCK SALAD

6 wild teal ducks
Water to cover
4 stalks of celery
2 large onions quartered
2 tablespoons of salt
1 teaspoon pepper
2 bay leaves
2 sprigs of parsley

½ cup chopped green onions
¾ cup chopped celery
½ cup finely chopped chutney
Mayonnaise to desired
  consistency
Tabasco pepper sauce
  to taste

Place ducks in large pot and boil with first 7 ingredients. Simmer for 1 hour or until tender. Skin, debone and chop meat. Refrigerate. When cold, mix with green onions, celery, mayonnaise, Tabasco pepper sauce and chutney. May be served as a salad or with crackers as an hors d'oeuvre.

Yield: 4 servings

Judy McIlhenny

SEAFOOD SALAD

1 pound peeled shrimp, boiled
  in shrimp boil and chopped
1 (6-ounce) can crabmeat,
  drained
3 stalks celery, chopped
5 hard boiled eggs
1 (3-ounce) package cream
  cheese, softened

Mayonnaise
Catsup
Salt
Pepper
½ teaspoon garlic powder
½ teaspoon Tabasco pepper
  sauce

Place seafood and celery in large bowl. Mash egg whites with fork and add to seafood. In another bowl, mash egg yolks and add softened cream cheese and enough mayonnaise and catsup until mixture is of desired pink color. Add salt, pepper, garlic powder and Tabasco pepper sauce. Add this mixture to seafood, adding more mayonnaise to desired consistency. This may be placed in large mold or individual ramekins. Chill overnight, remove from mold and place on lettuce leaves. Surround with quartered tomatoes and hard boiled eggs. Served with crackers, this is perfect for a summer luncheon.

Yield: 6 servings

Shirlyn Laborde

KRAUT SALAD

1 (16-ounce) can sauerkraut
2 cups sugar
⅔ cup vinegar

2 cups chopped celery
½ cup chopped green peppers
¼ cup chopped onions

Drain, rinse and drain sauerkraut. Bring sugar and vinegar to a boil. Cool. Mix sauerkraut, celery, onions and green pepper and pour syrup over all. Refrigerate 24 hours before serving. Keeps for a long time in refrigerator.

Yield: 10 servings   *A Friend of the Shadows*

FAIRMONT SPINACH SALAD

4 strips of bacon, crisp and
    crumbled
2 tablespoons bacon drippings
⅓ cup olive oil
1 tablespoon Dijon mustard
3 tablespoons Worcestershire
    sauce

2 tablespoons brown sugar
⅓ cup red wine
5 large handsful of fresh
    spinach, washed, drained
    and torn into bite size
    pieces
Seasoned salt

Fry bacon. Remove and set aside. Add olive oil and remaining ingredients except spinach to bacon drippings. Heat and pour sauce over spinach to wilt. Add bacon and garnish with 6 cherry tomatoes if desired.

Yield: 3-4 servings   *A Friend of the Shadows*

INDIAN SPINACH

¼ cup white wine vinegar
¼ cup salad oil
2 tablespoons chutney,
    chopped
2 teaspoons sugar
½ teaspoon salt
½ teaspoon curry powder
1 teaspoon dry mustard

8 cups fresh spinach
1½ cups chopped unpared
    apple
½ cup golden raisins
½ cup peanuts
2 tablespoons sliced
    green onion

In a screw top jar, combine the first 7 ingredients. Cover, shake and chill. When ready to serve, place clean, torn spinach in large salad bowl. Top the spinach with the apples, raisins, peanuts and onion, pour dressing over this and toss.

Yield: 6-8 servings   *Maureen Doerle*

SPINACH SALAD

1 cup oil (not olive oil)
7 tablespoons red wine
    vinegar
4 tablespoons sour cream
1½ teaspoons salt
½ teaspoon dry mustard
2 tablespoons sugar
2 tablespoons chopped fresh
    parsley

2 cloves garlic crushed
2 (12-ounce) bags of spinach.
    washed, dried, with stems
    removed
5 hard boiled eggs, chopped
1 pound bacon, cooked
    and crumbled

Six hours before serving, mix the first 8 ingredients to make dressing. Just before serving salad put layer of spinach into a large bowl. Add some of the chopped eggs and crumbled bacon and pour a little of the dressing over this. Repeat using the rest of the spinach, bacon, eggs and dressing. Toss well and serve.

Yield: 8-10 servings

Millou Roy

CAPTAIN'S SALAD

1 quart lettuce
1 quart fresh spinach
½ cup small sweet onion
    rings
3 tablespoons sesame seeds,
    toasted
1 teaspoon salt
¼ teaspoon pepper

½ teaspoon dry mustard
3 tablespoons vinegar
3 tablespoons honey
½ cup vegetable oil
3 tomatoes peeled and cut
2 cups herb-seasoned
    croutons

Trim and wash greens, and tear into bite size pieces. Add onion rings and sesame seeds. Toss and refrigerate until time to serve. Combine salt, pepper and mustard in small bowl. Stir in vinegar and honey and slowly add oil while beating with mixer or rotary beater. Refrigerate. When ready to serve, toss greens, tomatoes and croutons with salad dressing.

Yield: 8-10 servings

Maureen Doerle

Note: Spinach only may be used instead of the lettuce/spinach combination.

ASHEVILLE SALAD

1 (10½-ounce) can tomato
soup
2 (3-ounce) packages of
cream cheese
2 envelopes gelatin softened
in ½ cup cold water

½ cup olives, chopped
1½ cups chopped celery
1 cup chopped bell pepper
1 cup mayonnaise

Bring soup to a boil, add cheese, stirring until dissolved. Add gelatin. When mixture is nearly cool, add other ingredients and mold as desired. Molded in a ring, center can be filled with shrimp salad.

Yield: 4-6 servings

The Weeks Family

TOMATO ASPIC

1 (3-ounce) package lemon
Jello
1 envelope plain gelatin
4 cups V-8 juice
¼ teaspoon ground cloves

4 tablespoons vinegar
1 tablespoon Worcestershire
sauce
¾ cup diced celery (optional)
1 cup sliced olives (optional)

Dissolve Jello and gelatin in hot V-8 juice. Add cloves, vinegar and Worcestershire sauce. When this begins to thicken, add the celery and sliced olives. Pour into mold and chill until set. This may be served with asparagus tips as a garnish.

Yield: 4-6 servings

Lucille Barrow Minvielle

TOMATO AND CUCUMBER SALAD

3 to 4 tomatoes, sliced
1 to 2 cucumbers, sliced
¼ bell pepper, chopped
1 green onion, chopped
1 teaspoon Accent

½ teaspoon basil
2 tablespoons salad oil
1 tablespoon vinegar
Salt and pepper to taste

Combine vegetables in salad bowl. Combine remaining ingredients and pour over vegetables. Chill until serving time.

Yield: 6 servings

Ann Morrow

TOMATO-SPAGHETTI SALAD

2 cups chopped tomatoes,
   canned tomatoes may be
   substituted if fresh not
   available
1 teaspoon oregano
6 to 8 cloves garlic, minced

2 tablespoons olive oil
2 teaspoons Italian seasonings
Salt and pepper to taste
12-ounce package very
   thin spaghetti, cooked
   according to directions

Mix all above ingredients and allow to marinate in refrigerator for several hours before serving, or a marinade may be made of all ingredients except spaghetti. This may be stored in the refrigerator and used over freshly cooked spaghetti and served immediately.

Yield: 4-6 servings
Sylvia Conrad

CALIFORNIA BLUE CHEESE DRESSING

4 ounces blue cheese
4 or 5 drops of Tabasco
   pepper sauce

1 tablespoon onion, grated
1 cup mayonnaise
¼ cup dry white wine

Crumble cheese, add other ingredients and chill. Serve over vegetables or tossed salad.

Yield: 1¾ cups
Irene Young

CITRUS DRESSING

¼ cup mayonnaise
¼ cup sour cream
3 tablespoons fresh orange
   juice

1 teaspoon grated orange rind
1 teaspoon sugar
¼ teaspoon salt

Combine all ingredients in small bowl, mix and chill. Use on tossed salads.

Yield: 4 servings
Janice Holley

GARLIC MAYONNAISE

4 egg yolks
½ teaspoon dry mustard
½ cup of cut onion tops or
   green onions
3 cloves garlic

1 teaspoon salt
5 to 6 drops Tabasco pepper
   sauce
4 cups oil

Using steel blade of a food processor, put all ingredients in except oil. Process for 10 seconds. Then add small stream of oil while processor is running. Too much oil at one time will "break" the mixture.

Yield: 1 quart

Gigi and Alex Patout

NEVER FAIL HOMEMADE MAYONNAISE

2 hard boiled egg yolks
2 raw egg yolks
2 cups salad oil

2 tablespoons lemon juice
Dash of Tabasco pepper sauce
1 teaspoon salt

In small mixing bowl of blender or electric mixer mash the boiled egg yolks, add raw egg yolks and mix well. Slowly add half of the oil and lemon juice and beat at high speed. Add salt, Tabasco pepper sauce and remaining oil.

Yield: 3 cups

Juanita Winkle

POPPY SEED DRESSING

⅔ cup sugar
⅓ cup honey
¼ teaspoon salt
1 teaspoon dry mustard
1 tablespoon lemon juice

5 tablespoons vinegar
1 tablespoon grated onion
2 teaspoons poppy seed
1 cup salad oil

Using a blender, mix together all ingredients except salad oil. Add salad oil slowly. Store in covered container.

Yield: 1 pint

A Friend of the Shadows

SALAD DRESSING PASTORAL

2 hard boiled eggs
2 cloves minced garlic
3 tablespoons olive oil
1 stalk of celery, minced
Salt and red pepper

3 tablespoons tarragon
  vinegar
Lettuce
1 teaspoon powdered sugar
½ teaspoon paprika

Mash the egg yolks with the minced garlic. Add the olive oil slowly, then the minced celery, salt and pepper. Thin with the vinegar. Shred the lettuce in a chilled salad bowl and toss with dressing. Chop the egg whites very finely and sprinkle over this, following with the powdered sugar and paprika.

Yield: 4 servings   *Mrs. Walter Torian*

Note: The breath of the Arctic must blow on the ingredients, everything thoroughly chilled.

PLANTATION CLUB SALAD DRESSING

2 cups mayonnaise
1 cup French dressing
¼ cup grated Parmesan
  cheese
½ tube anchovy paste
  (optional)

⅛ teaspoon garlic powder or
  1 clove garlic, minced
2 tablespoons sugar
1½ cups sour cream

Combine all ingredients and mix well for a tossed salad. Keep refrigerated.

Yield: 48 servings   *Lucille Barrow Minvielle*

BROWN'S TEXAS BARBEQUE SAUCE

4 to 6 pounds beef suet, ground
6 pounds margarine
1 quart vinegar
25 ounces lemon juice
36 ounces prepared mustard
3 ounces garlic powder
3 ounces onion powder
3 ounces chili powder

2 (16-ounce) boxes dark brown sugar
126 ounces catsup
210 ounces tomato sauce
30 ounces Worcestershire sauce
Salt, red and black pepper to taste
¼ cup Tabasco pepper sauce or to taste

Wide mouth canning jars, rings, lids—preferably quart size
These jars need to be sterilized in dishwasher just prior to cooking

Render suet either in microwave or 500° oven. Strain (when melted) into a large 6 gallon pot. Add margarine to suet and place on medium heat. To prevent dry ingredients from lumping when added to liquid: in food processor or blender, combine small amounts of vinegar or lemon juice with mustard, garlic and onion powder and brown sugar. This may take 3 or 4 batches to complete. Add to pot. Add all other ingredients by rinsing out bottles and cans with small amounts of water to clean the bottle or can. This water will amount to approximately ½ to 1 gallon. (DO NOT MAKE SAUCE TOO THIN BY ADDING TOO MUCH WATER.) Add salt, pepper and Tabasco pepper sauce to taste. Bring to a boil and let cook for 5 minutes, stirring to prevent sticking. Not necessary to cook down unless too much water added earlier.

Can in sterilized wide mouth jars. The sauce should be very hot when placed in jars. Place lids (flat top with rubber ring) in pan with water to cover and bring to a boil; remove from heat. When jar is filled, cover the jar with lid and secure with ring by turning as tightly as possible. When jars have cooled, check the flat lid by pressing in middle of lid with forefinger. If lid is loose, or gives under your pressure, tighten ring and set aside to recheck. Tighten all rings and store only when properly sealed. If any lids refuse to seal, it may be necessary to use water bath treatment to properly seal, or these jars may be frozen instead. Refer to an authoritative canning guide for water bath treatment.

Great on hamburgers, chicken, brisket, leftover meats, hot dogs, and dunking most anything. If using on outdoor grill, open jar, stir and reheat. When using on inside stove, one may prefer to discard the fat layer that covers top. Will keep indefinitely in refrigerator after opening.

This was developed by my parents and a friend during many years of cooking together in Andrews, Texas.

Yield: Approximately 6 gallons
    May be reduced

Sherry B. Landry

CAJUN MUSTARD SAUCE

1 (2-ounce) can of dry mustard
⅓ cup sugar
¼ cup cider vinegar
1 teaspoon lemon juice

¼ cup salad oil (not olive oil)
1 teaspoon Worcestershire
  sauce

In a small mixing bowl beat together all the ingredients until well blended. Pour into a screw top jar and cover tightly. Refrigerate a few days before using.

Yield: ¾ cup sweet, hot mustard   *Juanita Winkle*

WELSH STYLE CHEESE SAUCE

2 cups medium white sauce
  Recipe for white sauce
  is on page 91

2 cups shredded cheese
  (Mozzarella, Swiss,
  Cheddar or hot pepper
  cheese)

Start with the medium white sauce and add the cheese, stirring on low fire until cheese melts. Add some extras for interest such as chopped pimentos, canned green chilies, snipped parsley or sliced mushrooms. Heat thoroughly and serve on toasted English muffins, corn bread, toast, sliced tomatoes or boiled potatoes.

Yield: 3 cups   *A Friend of the Shadows*

HOLLANDAISE SAUCE

1 cup butter
4 egg yolks, slightly beaten

2 tablespoons lemon juice
⅛ teaspoon cayenne pepper

Divide butter in half. Put half in a small, heavy saucepan with the egg yolks and lemon juice. Hold pot over low fire and stir constantly until butter is melted. Add remaining butter and stir until thick. Remove and add pepper. Serve at once. If sauce curdles, beat in 1 tablespoon cream.

Yield: 1 cup

HOLLANDAISE SAUCE FOR FOOD PROCESSOR

¼ pound butter, melted
3 egg yolks

2 tablespoons lemon juice
⅛ teaspoon cayenne pepper

Place melted butter and all other ingredients in processor or blender. Using the plastic blade, process until sauce is thick, approximately 2 to 3 minutes. It takes a little longer in processor than in blender.

Yield: 1 cup

JALAPEÑO HOT SAUCE

½ cup chopped jalapeño
   peppers
3 cups chopped onions
3 cloves chopped garlic
1 chopped bell pepper
   (optional)

1 teaspoon salt
1 teaspoon black pepper
½ cup salad oil
2 (10½-ounce) cans
   condensed tomato soup
1½ cups water

Mix all and bring to a boil for 30 minutes. Pour into jars and refrigerate.

Yield: 8 cups

Kathy Uncapher

JOYCE'S SPECIAL SEASONING

20 each cayenne peppers,
   Tabasco peppers, and
   jalapeño peppers or
   an equal amount of any
   hot peppers

3 tablespoons white vinegar
1 teaspoon salt

Put the ingredients in blender or food processor and blend until smooth. Add more vinegar if the mixture is too thick. Use this seasoning sparingly in any dish calling for pepper. Store in jars in the refrigerator.

Yield: 1 pint

Joyce Indest

NEWBURG SAUCE

2 tablespoons butter
2 tablespoons flour
2 cups light cream
2 egg yolks

1 tablespoon sherry
1 tablespoon brandy
1 teaspoon dry mustard
Salt and pepper to taste

In top of double boiler, melt the butter, add the flour and cook for about 2 minutes. Gradually add cream and well beaten egg yolks, sherry, brandy, dry mustard, salt and pepper. Add any cooked seafood, leftover chicken or turkey to sauce.

Yield: 2½ cups   *Ollie Vidrine*

OLD COUNTRY'S RED SAUCE

3 tablespoons olive oil
3 cloves finely chopped garlic
1 (6-ounce) can tomato paste

¾ cup water
3 rounded tablespoons sugar
Salt and pepper to taste

Pour oil in pan and brown garlic, add tomato paste and cook a few minutes. Pour in water, bring to a boil, turn heat down to low, add sugar, salt and pepper, cover and cook for an hour. Pour this over ½ pound of cooked spaghetti.

Yield: 2 cups   *Carolyn Sorci*

Note: This is a basic red sauce to be used for chicken or meatball spaghetti, or to pour over a roast. With these dishes one may double the recipe and add a can of whole tomatoes.

REMOULADE SAUCE

½ teaspoon dry mustard
½ teaspoon Tabasco pepper
   sauce
1 tablespoon chopped celery
1 tablespoon chopped green
   onion

1 tablespoon chopped parsley
2 tablespoons horseradish
1 tablespoon Worcestershire
   sauce
⅔ cup catsup

Combine all ingredients and store in refrigerator. Use on meat, fish, shrimp and salads.

Yield: 1 cup   *Linda Young*

SAUCE PIQUANTE

2 tablespoons salad oil or
   bacon drippings
¼ cup flour
1 cup chopped onion
1 cup chopped celery
1 cup chopped bell pepper
1 cup water

½ teaspoon brown sugar
1 (16-ounce) can tomatoes
   or 2 (8-ounce) cans tomato
   sauce
1 (6-ounce) can tomato paste
1 teaspoon Tabasco pepper
   sauce

Make a roux—heat oil in skillet and gradually add flour. Stir constantly while lightly browning the flour. Add onion, celery and green pepper and cook until soft. Stir in remaining ingredients. Heat to a boil. Cover, reduce heat to simmer and cook about 20 minutes.

Sauce Piquante Variations

Shrimp—Add 2 cups cleaned raw shrimp and ½ lemon, sliced thin, to the Sauce Piquante. Simmer about 20 minutes. Serve with rice. If canned shrimp are used, precook sauce for 30 minutes, then add shrimp. Heat thoroughly and serve. Yields 4-6 servings.

Baked Fish—Choose a 4 to 5 pound fish such as redfish, red snapper or channel bass. Rub fish inside and out with Tabasco pepper sauce and salt. Place in a long oven-proof baking dish. Crumble a bay leaf over the fish and add a sliced lemon. Top with full recipe of Sauce Piquante. Bake at 350° (moderate oven) about 45 minutes, basting occasionally. Yields 6-8 servings.

Courtbouillon—Use a 4 to 5 pound fish. Prepare Sauce Piquante using 2 teaspoons salt, ½ teaspoon Tabasco pepper sauce and 3 cups water. Add the fish head and tail during the simmering period. Then remove head and tail; add remainder of fish and cook 15 minutes longer. Serve with rice. Yields 6-8 servings.

Chicken—Disjoint large chicken (4½ to 5 pounds). Sprinkle with Tabasco pepper sauce and salt. Brown in 3 tablespoons salad oil or shortening. Remove chicken and prepare Sauce Piquante recipe, adding ½ teaspoon oregano. Add chicken to sauce. Cover and cook until chicken is tender, 1 to 2 hours. Add ½ cup of red wine 5 minutes before serving. Serve with rice or spaghetti. Yields 6 servings.

Grillades—Similar to Swiss Steak—Cut a large beef round (1 inch thick, about 2 pounds) into serving pieces or allow 1 shoulder chop per serving. Spread with Tabasco pepper sauce and salt. Proceed as for Chicken Sauce Piquante, omitting oregano. Yields 4 servings.

CONTINUED...

Meat Loaf—Pour 2 cups of Sauce Piquante (½ recipe) over your favorite meat loaf for 4 servings. Bake at 350° (moderate oven) about 50 minutes. Use sauce to baste loaf.

Salmon—To 2 cups of Sauce Piquante add 1 can (16 ounce) salmon plus 1 tablespoon capers. Heat for 10 minutes and serve on toast or noodles. Yields 4-6 servings. Tuna may also be used.

Alligator—Cube 2 pounds raw, lean alligator meat. Brown in ½ cup cooking oil. Remove alligator meat and prepare Sauce Piquante recipe. Add alligator meat to sauce. Cover and cook about 1 hour.

A Friend of the Shadows

BASIC WHITE SAUCE—THIN, MEDIUM AND THICK

THIN WHITE SAUCE

1 tablespoon butter or margarine	1 cup milk
	½ teaspoon salt
1 tablespoon flour	Pepper to taste

MEDIUM WHITE SAUCE

2 tablespoons butter or margarine	1 cup milk
	½ teaspoon salt
2 tablespoons flour	Pepper to taste

THICK WHITE SAUCE

4 tablespoons butter or margarine	1 cup milk
	½ teaspoon salt
4 tablespoons flour	Pepper to taste

In a heavy saucepan melt butter, add flour and cook over low heat, stirring constantly until the mixture is smooth. Add milk, salt and pepper. Stir until smooth again.

There are many variations to this basic sauce recipe. You may use cream or Half and Half in place of milk or you may use stock of vegetables, seafood, meat or poultry in place of some of the milk. Grated cheese may also be added to make the sauce richer.

Yield: 1 cup

WHITE WINE SEAFOOD SAUCE

1 stick butter
1 small, finely chopped
   white onion
1/4 cup finely chopped
   bell pepper
1 small stalk celery,
   finely chopped

1/2 clove garlic, finely chopped
3 heaping tablespoons flour
1 quart milk, not evaporated
Salt and pepper to taste
3 tablespoons sherry wine

Sauté vegetables in butter until clear and well cooked. Add flour and mix well. Add milk and cook over low heat until smooth and thick, stirring constantly. Blend this in food processor with salt, pepper and sherry, and pour over fish or shrimp and bake. (Cook shrimp a little before putting sauce over them.)

Yield: 5 cups

Susie Pharr

FISHERMAN'S TARTAR SAUCE

1 cup mayonnaise
2 tablespoons dill pickles,
   finely chopped
2 tablespoons onions,
   finely chopped
2 tablespoons olives,
   finely chopped

2 tablespoons green onions,
   finely chopped
1 teaspoon lemon juice
Dash of pepper
1/4 cup sour cream
   (optional)

Combine all ingredients, mix well and chill.

Yield: 2 cups

A Friend of the Shadows

ZIPPY SAUCE

1 cup finely chopped onion
1/3 cup salad oil
1 1/2 cups catsup
1/2 cup water
1/2 cup lemon juice

1/4 cup sugar
1/4 cup Worcestershire sauce
2 1/2 teaspoons salt
1/2 teaspoon pepper
5 drops Tabasco pepper sauce

Cook onions in hot salad oil until soft and golden. Add remaining ingredients and simmer 15 minutes. Cool and store in refrigerator. For a more tart sauce, use more lemon juice. For a hotter sauce, use more Tabasco pepper sauce.

Yield: 1 quart

A Friend of the Shadows

VEGETABLES

Circa 1870

The War Between the States is over, the Federal troops have left, and the Weeks family are rebuilding their lives. During the war, the house had been occupied by Union soldiers. It was common for generals and other top ranking officials to set up their headquarters in the finest homes.

Major General Nathaniel Banks, Commander of the Department of the Gulf, entered New Iberia with his troops in October 1863 and occupied the Shadows. General Banks had Mrs. Moore (Mary Clara Weeks, now remarried) and her household occupy the upper portion of the building, while the general and his staff used the lower floor.

Mary Clara Conrad Weeks Moore died at the Shadows in 1863, during the occupation of her beloved home. She had been its owner for 30 years. It is sad that she left it in the hands of others and did not know it would someday be restored to its former glory.

Vegetables

Artichoke
Asparagus. 95
Dressing Casserole. 95
Florentine. 96
Spinach Cheese Casserole. 96
Stuffed. 97
Bean
Green, Casserole. 97
Green, Medley. 98
Lima, Bake, Super. 98
Red, Creamy. 99
Beets
Chinese. 99
Broccoli
Casserole. 98
Tangy Marinated. 99
Cabbage
Casserole. 100
Casserole—Meatless. 101
Rolls. 100
Carrots
á L'Orange. 101
Cauliflower
Broccoli Bake. 102
Broccoli, Casserole, Mary's. 102
Holiday. 103
Swiss, Baked. 103
Wild Rice. 104
Corn
Fritters. 104
Indian. 104
Maque Choux. 105
Pudding. 105
Eggplant
Casserole I. 105
Casserole II. 106
Casserole III. 106
Caviar. 107
Dressing, Alex's. 107
Mirliton
(Vegetable Pear), Casserole. . . . 108
Mushroom
Asparagus. 108

Mustard Greens
Smothered. 109
Okra
Bacon Casserole. 109
Creole. 110
Tomatoes, Smothered. 110
Peas
English, Casserole. 111
Potatoes
Casserole. 111
Casserole, Cheese. 112
Cheddar Cheezy Hash Brown. . . 112
Puffs. 113
Soufflé. 113
Spinach
Creamed, Mert's. 114
Pie. 114
Rice. 115
Squash
Acorn or Butternut, Baked. 113
Spaghetti, Stuffed. 115
Yellow Squash
Casserole I. 116
Casserole II. 117
Casserole III. 117
Carrot. 116
Green Chili. 116
Stuffed. 118
Summer. 118
Tomatoes. 119
Tomato
Casserole I. 119
Casserole II. 120
Turnip
Puff. 121
You Can't Believe It's Turnips. . . . 120
Yam
Bourbon Casserole. 121
Pineapple. 122
Super. 122
Zucchini
Vegetable Pie. 122

Refer to additional recipes in "How Men Cook" section.

ARTICHOKE ASPARAGUS

2 tablespoons margarine
2 tablespoons flour
2 tablespoons asparagus
   juice
1 cup Half & Half
¾ pound sharp Cheddar
   cheese
1 (14-ounce) can artichoke
   bottoms, drained

2 (14½-ounce) cans asparagus
2 hard boiled eggs
1 (4-ounce) package sliced
   almonds
1 (4-ounce) can mushrooms,
   drained
½ teaspoon paprika
Salt and pepper to taste

Begin by melting cream sauce with margarine and flour. Thin with asparagus juice and cream. Add cheese and melt. Layer artichokes, asparagus, eggs, almonds, and mushrooms in 2 layers. Add salt and pepper to taste and sprinkle with paprika as you go. Pour half of sauce over each layer. Bake in a 350° oven for 40 minutes.

Yield: 8-10 servings   *Curtis Thomas*

ARTICHOKE DRESSING CASSEROLE

2 (14-ounce) cans artichoke
   hearts (reserve liquid)
1 (1 pound 8-ounce) box
   Italian bread crumbs
½ cup olive oil

Juice of 2 lemons
2 cloves garlic, minced
1 cup Romano cheese, grated
Salt and pepper

Mix artichoke juice, crumbs, olive oil, and lemon juice. Mash artichokes thoroughly and add to above mixture, add cheese and garlic. Blend well. Bake in a 350° oven for 20 minutes. Fills a 2½-quart casserole.

Yield: 6-8 servings   *Barbara G. Barton*

✓

ARTICHOKES FLORENTINE

4 large fresh artichokes
2 (10-ounce) packages frozen
  chopped spinach
4 tablespoons butter, melted
3 tablespoons flour

¾ cup warm milk
1 tablespoon white wine
  (optional)
Parmesan cheese
Nutmeg

Place the fresh artichokes in boiling salted water, upside down and snug in the pot, and cook until the stems are fork-tender. As a courtesy to your guests, prior to cooking, trim the thorn from each leaf with scissors. After the artichokes are tender, invert on paper towel to drain. As you do, lightly smash open the artichoke to make the center easy to reach when cooled. While the artichokes are cooling, cook spinach according to package directions. Drain and set aside. Slowly stir flour into melted butter. Gradually add milk and wine and stir over low heat until mixture is well blended.

When artichokes are cooled, pull out center thorny part and the choke. This leaves a little "well" in the center of the artichoke. Fill this "well" with cooked spinach, a pat of butter, a large serving spoon of the white sauce, and a dash of paprika for color. Sprinkle with Parmesan cheese and a hint of nutmeg on top. Place under broiler for barely 3 minutes.

Yield: 4 servings   *Carol Ann Roberts Dumond*

ARTICHOKE SPINACH CHEESE CASSEROLE

1 (8½-ounce) jar marinated
  artichoke hearts, drained
2 (10-ounce) packages frozen
  chopped spinach, thawed
1 (8-ounce) package of cream
  cheese

2 tablespoons softened butter
  or margarine
4 tablespoons milk
Pepper to taste
½ cup grated Parmesan
  cheese

Put artichoke hearts in medium casserole. Squeeze spinach dry. Arrange evenly over artichoke hearts. Beat cream cheese and butter until smooth, gradually add milk. Spread over spinach, add pepper. Sprinkle with Parmesan cheese. Cover and refrigerate for 24 hours. Bake covered in a 350° oven for 40 minutes. Uncover and bake another 10 minutes.

Yield: 6 servings

STUFFED ARTICHOKES

8 artichokes
2 pounds bacon
3 or 4 medium onions,
  chopped
¼ teaspoon garlic powder
6 or 7 hard boiled eggs
  mashed fine

2 (24-ounce) cans Italian
  bread crumbs
1½ cups grated Romano
  cheese
Chopped onion tops and
  parsley

Clip points off artichokes. Cut stems so they will lie flat. Fry bacon crisp and keep drippings. Set bacon aside. Sauté onions and garlic powder in bacon drippings. Turn fire off and add rest of ingredients. Mix well and add salt and pepper to taste. Then stuff artichoke leaves. Steam well until leaves pull out easily. You can tie them together with any kind of heavy string to keep them from falling apart. Let cool before taking string off and they will stay together.

Yield: 8 servings   *Kathy Musso Romero*

GREEN BEAN CASSEROLE

3 tablespoons vegetable oil
2 tablespoons flour
1 medium onion, chopped
3 (15-ounce) cans French style
  green beans, drained
1 tablespoon sugar
½ cup cream of mushroom
  soup

½ cup shredded Cheddar
  cheese
½ cup slivered almonds
Salt and seasonings to taste
¼ cup bread crumbs
Butter for topping

Make roux of oil and flour. Sauté onions in roux, add beans and sugar. Cook for 10 minutes; add soup, cheese and almonds. Season to taste. Pour into pyrex dish, sprinkle bread crumbs and dot with butter. Bake for 30 minutes in a 350° oven.

Yield: 8-12 servings   *Mrs. Leonce J. Broussard*

Note: ½ recipe cream of mushroom soup may be used, page 57.

GREEN BEAN MEDLEY

2 (9-ounce) packages frozen
French style green beans
1 (16-ounce) can bean sprouts,
drained and rinsed
1 (8-ounce) can water
chestnuts, drained and
sliced

1 (10½-ounce) can condensed
cream of mushroom soup,
undiluted
1 tablespoon Worcestershire
sauce
½ teaspoon salt
Bread crumbs

In a large pan cook beans according to directions; drain well. Stir in bean sprouts, water chestnuts, soup, Worcestershire sauce, and salt. Top with bread crumbs. Bake at 350° for 15 minutes in medium casserole.

Yield: 6 servings   *A Friend of the Shadows*

Note: 1 recipe cream of mushroom soup may be used, page 57.

SUPER LIMA BEAN BAKE

½ bell pepper, chopped
1 large onion, sliced
4 slices bacon
1 (10½-ounce) can tomato
soup, condensed

2 (10-ounce) packages frozen
lima beans
Buttered bread crumbs

Brown onion in drippings from bacon which has been cooked crisp. Add chopped bell pepper and tomato soup. Cook lima beans according to package directions. Drain and add to tomato mixture. Add crumbled bacon and place in casserole and sprinkle with bread crumbs. Bake at 350° for 35 minutes.

Yield: 8 servings   *Curtis Thomas*

BROCCOLI CASSEROLE

2 (10-ounce packages frozen,
chopped broccoli
1 cup mayonnaise

1 cup shredded Cheddar
cheese
2 eggs, slightly beaten
2 large onions, chopped

Cook broccoli for 5 minutes. Drain. Mix together mayonnaise, cheese, eggs and onions. Fold broccoli into mixture. Top with crushed cracker crumbs or buttered bread crumbs. Bake in 350° oven for 45 minutes.

Yield: 6 servings   *Flo Piccione*

TANGY MARINATED BROCCOLI

3 bunches fresh broccoli
1 cup cider vinegar
1 tablespoon sugar
1 tablespoon dried dill weed
1 teaspoon salt

1½ cups vegetable oil
1 teaspoon pepper
1 teaspoon garlic powder
Lemon slices

Trim off broccoli leaves. Remove stalks and reserve for another use. Separate broccoli into flowerets and wash thoroughly. Drain and place in a large shallow container; set aside. Combine next 7 ingredients, mixing well; pour over broccoli. Toss gently to coat. Chill 24 hours, covered, stirring several times. Garnish with lemon slices. Serve cold.

Yield: 10-12 servings

Barbara G. Barton

CHINESE BEETS

3 (16-ounce) cans beets
   (whole or cut)
1½ cups beet juice
1 cup sugar
2 tablespoons cornstarch
1 cup vinegar

24 whole cloves
3 tablespoons catsup
3 tablespoons cooking oil
1 dash of salt
1 teaspoon vanilla

Mix sugar and cornstarch in a large skillet. Add vinegar, cloves, catsup, oil, salt, vanilla and beet juice. Cut beets to bite size pieces and add to pan. Cook over medium heat 3 or 4 minutes, stirring constantly until mixture thickens.

Yield: 8-12 servings

CREAMY RED BEANS

1 pound red kidney beans
   (soak overnight in water
   to cover)
4 tablespoons fat or drippings
1 large onion, minced
1 ham hock or ham slice

1 bell pepper, finely diced
2 bay leaves
2 sprigs thyme
Salt to taste
Tabasco pepper sauce
4 cups water

Drain beans well. Melt fat in large covered pot and sauté onion. Add beans and remaining ingredients. Cover and cook over low heat approximately 4 hours, stirring occasionally. Serve over rice accompanied with smoked sausage. This may also be cooked in a pressure cooker at 15 pounds pressure for 1½ to 2 hours.

Yield: 8 servings

Judy McIlhenny

CABBAGE ROLLS

½ pound ground pork
½ pound ground beef
2 cups raw rice
Salt
Pepper, red and black
Melted butter or margarine

1 large head of cabbage
Ham or beef bones
Juice of 2 or 3 lemons
1 bell pepper, chopped
2 pods garlic, minced
1 (8-ounce) can tomato sauce

Brown the pork and beef. Mix meats with rice, salt, pepper, and butter in a large pot. Add garlic and bell pepper. Remove cabbage leaves and wilt in boiling water. Drain. Put about 1 tablespoon dressing mix into each leaf at core end. Roll once. Tuck the ends of the leaves in and continue rolling so that the meat will not come out.

Line bottom of another pot with ham bones or beef bones. Layer cabbage rolls over bones. Make a sauce of 1 cup water, 1 (8-ounce) can tomato sauce, 2 tablespoons lemon juice and salt to taste. Pour over cabbage rolls and cook for 1 hour and 45 minutes on top of stove on low heat.

Yield: 8-10 servings   *Harriet Shea*

CABBAGE CASSEROLE

1 pound ground meat
1 tablespoon salt
2 tablespoons sugar
1 teaspoon allspice, ground

¼ teaspoon each of black and
    red pepper
1 small cabbage, chopped
Bread crumbs

Brown ground meat, add seasonings and cabbage; cook about 15 minutes. Place in casserole dish. Top with bread crumbs and bake at 350° about 30 minutes.

Yield: 4 servings   *Mrs. Flo Piccione*

Variation I: Add 1 cup cooked rice and 1 (8-ounce) can tomato sauce.

Variation II: Add 1 cup cooked rice and 1 package of Taco seasoning.

CABBAGE CASSEROLE—MEATLESS

2 medium cabbages
¼ cup butter
2 onions, chopped
1 bell pepper, chopped
3 cloves garlic, minced

½ pound grated yellow cheese
1 cup bread crumbs
½ pint of cream
Salt and pepper to taste

Chop cabbage and boil until just tender. Drain. Melt butter, add onion, bell pepper and garlic. Cook until wilted. Add cabbage cheese, ½ cup of the bread crumbs, salt and pepper. Place in casserole, add cream. Cover with remaining bread crumbs. Bake at 350° for 15 minutes.

Yield: 6-8 servings

CARROTS A L'ORANGE

2 large bunches fresh carrots
   (approximately 4 pounds)
1 teaspoon salt
2 tablespoons butter
3 cups water
1 cup sugar

Grated rind and juice of 1
   orange
½ teaspoon orange extract
2 tablespoons cornstarch
   dissolved in ¼ cup water
Orange slices and parsley
   for garnish

Peel and slice the carrots into penny-sized slices. Cook in salted water (just enough to cover) until tender. Drain and add the butter while warm enough to melt the butter. Heat 3 cups water with 1 cup sugar, grated rind and juice of an orange and orange extract until the sugar dissolves. Stir in the cornstarch that has been dissolved, and boil the sauce, stirring until it thickens. Return the carrots to this sauce and warm.

For an adult dinner party, a jigger of Triple Sec in place of the orange extract adds a little zest. To garnish, slice a large orange. Then cut through only half of the slice. Twist the slice to form a slight "curl"; sprinkle with finely minced parsley and place on top of the carrots just before serving.

Yield: 8 servings   *Carol Ann Roberts Dumond*

CAULI–BROCCOLI BAKE

1 head cauliflower
1 (10-ounce) box frozen
    broccoli spears
1 (8-ounce) can mushrooms,
    drained
1/2 cup mayonnaise

1 tablespoon prepared
    mustard
1 cup shredded Cheddar
    cheese or 1/2 cup Cheddar
    and 1/2 cup Mozzarella

Remove leaves, trim head of cauliflower and wash. Cook in boiling, salted water for 12-15 minutes. Drain. Place in center of round ungreased casserole dish. Cook broccoli in boiling, salted water. Drain. Arrange in ring around cauliflower. Sprinkle mushrooms on top of broccoli and dot with butter. Frost cauliflower with mayonnaise and mustard mixed. Top with cheese. Bake for 10 minutes in 375° oven or until cheese bubbles. This may be prepared and refrigerated prior to oven baking.

Yield: 10 servings

Margo LeBlanc

MARY'S CAULIFLOWER AND BROCCOLI CASSEROLE

4 (10-ounce) boxes frozen
    broccoli
4 (10-ounce) boxes frozen
    cauliflower
2 tablespoons butter or
    margarine
2 tablespoons flour

2 cups milk
1/2 cup grated Parmesan
    cheese
1/2 teaspoon salt
1/2 teaspoon Tabasco pepper
    sauce
1 cup grated Velveeta cheese

Cook broccoli and cauliflower according to directions on box. Drain. Melt butter in small pot. Add flour and stir until blended. Add milk, stirring until smooth and thick. Add Parmesan cheese, salt, and Tabasco pepper sauce. Blend well. Arrange broccoli and cauliflower in 3 quart rectangular casserole, and season to taste. Pour sauce over it, and sprinkle with grated Velveeta cheese. Bake for 30 minutes in 350° oven.

Yield: 20-24 servings

Patsy Dauterive

HOLIDAY CAULIFLOWER

1 large head cauliflower
1 (4-ounce) can sliced
   mushrooms, drained
1/4 cup diced bell pepper
1/4 cup butter
1/3 cup flour

2 cups milk
1/2 teaspoon salt
1 cup shredded Swiss cheese
2 tablespoons chopped
   pimento

Break cauliflower into medium size flowerets; cook in boiling water until crisp-tender, about 10 minutes. Drain well and set aside. Sauté mushrooms and green pepper in butter until tender. Blend in flour. Gradually stir in milk. Cook, stirring constantly, over medium heat until mixture is thick. Stir in salt, cheese and pimento. Place half of the cauliflower in a buttered 2-quart casserole. Cover with half of the sauce; add remaining cauliflower; top with sauce. Bake 15 minutes in 325° oven.

Yield: 8 servings

Betty H. Voorhies

BAKED SWISS CAULIFLOWER

1 large head cauliflower
1/2 cup bread crumbs
2 3/4 cups shredded Swiss
   cheese
1 1/2 cups Half and Half
3 egg yolks, beaten

1/4 teaspoon ground nutmeg
1/2 teaspoon salt
1/4 teaspoon pepper
1/4 cup melted butter or
   margarine

Wash cauliflower and discard green leaves, break into flowerets. Cook, covered, 10 minutes in a small amount of boiling, salted water. Place cauliflower in a buttered 1 1/2 quart shallow baking dish. Combine remaining ingredients except butter and pour over cauliflower. Drizzle butter over top. Bake for 15-20 minutes in 350° oven.

Yield: 6 servings

Violeta B. Romero

VEGETABLES

CAULIFLOWER—WILD RICE

1 cup wild rice
½ teaspoon salt
3 cups water
1 head cauliflower
3 tablespoons butter

3 tablespoons flour
2 cups milk
1 cup grated Cheddar cheese
⅓ cup grated Swiss cheese
Bread crumbs

Wash rice well; add to boiling, salted water. Simmer covered for 45 minutes. Drain and place in bottom of large, greased casserole. Separate cauliflower. Boil in salted water until barely tender. Drain. Arrange over rice. In heavy saucepan, blend flour and butter over medium heat. Slowly add milk, stirring to proper consistency for cream sauce. Add cheese, stir until blended. Pour over wild rice and cauliflower. Top with bread crumbs. Bake in 375° oven about 30 minutes or until brown and bubbling.

Yield: 6-8 servings

Jessamine Musson

CORN FRITTERS

1⅓ cups flour
¾ teaspoon baking powder
1 teaspoon baking soda
¼ teaspoon salt
2 tablespoons sugar
1 egg

⅔ cup milk
1 (8¾-ounce) can yellow
 cream style corn
1 (8¾-ounce) can yellow
 drained whole kernel corn
1 quart corn oil for frying

Put dry ingredients in a large bowl. Stir together. In a small bowl, beat egg and milk and stir in both cans of corn. Make a well in the center of flour mixture. Pour corn mixture into well and stir until dry ingredients are moistened. Drop mixture by heaping tablespoons into hot corn oil. Fry at 375° about 4 at a time until golden brown, turning once. Drain on paper. Add oil as needed.

Yield: 1 dozen

Barbara Schwing

INDIAN CORN

6 tablespoons oil
1 large onion, chopped
1 cup creamed corn
Salt and red pepper

2 cups milk
1 cup corn meal
1 egg, beaten

Sauté onion in oil until clear. Add corn and season highly with salt and red pepper. Add milk and stir in corn meal gradually. Remove from heat when thickened and stir in egg. Place in buttered casserole. Bake at 350° until brown, about 40 minutes.

Yield: 6 servings

Eleanor Holleman

MAQUE CHOUX

2 dozen ears fresh sweet corn
2 onions, finely chopped
2 large bell peppers, chopped
4 large overripe tomatoes or
   1 (15-ounce) can whole
   tomatoes

1 stick butter
1 tablespoon salt
2 tablespoons black pepper
Milk

Shave the tops of the kernels off the cob; DO NOT CUT DEEPLY INTO KERNEL. Scrape the cob to extract the milk of the kernel and loosen the remaining pieces of corn. Set aside. Sauté onion, bell pepper and tomato over medium-high fire for about 10 minutes. Add corn and cook until the corn changes color. It loses its milky color and becomes golden. Add salt and pepper; cook for about 5 minutes. It may be necessary to add a little milk and butter to corn if it becomes too dry during cooking.

Yield: 4-6 servings

Gigi and Alex Patout

CORN PUDDING

6 ears of corn
1 teacup sifted flour
1 teaspoon baking powder
1 pinch salt

1 tablespoon sugar
2 teacups sweet milk
4 eggs, beaten separately
4 tablespoons melted butter

Cut the grains of corn down the center of the grain; scrape from cob with a knife into a large bowl. Add flour, baking powder, salt and sugar. Add the milk to these dry ingredients and the well beaten yolks. Add melted butter. Fold in stiffly beaten egg whites. Bake in buttered dish in 400° oven until well done.

Yield: 6-8 servings

Old Weeks Family recipe

EGGPLANT CASSEROLE I

1 medium eggplant
3 slices toasted bread soaked
   in ¼ cup milk
3 tablespoons melted butter
1 small onion, chopped

2 eggs, slightly beaten
Salt and pepper to taste
½ cup shredded Mozzarella
   cheese
2 tablespoons evaporated milk

Peel, slice and boil eggplant in salted water until done. Drain and mash. Soak toast in milk until soft. Melt butter. Sauté onions. Combine all ingredients and put in a buttered 1 quart casserole. Drizzle evaporated milk and cheese on top. Bake at 350° for 35 minutes.

Yield: 6 servings

Mathilde Smith

EGGPLANT CASSEROLE II

1 medium eggplant, chopped
1 medium onion, chopped
1 bell pepper, chopped
½ cup diced celery
2 tablespoons shortening
1 (1-pound) can tomatoes
1 teaspoon salt

1 tablespoon sugar
½ bay leaf
Pinch cloves
Pinch cayenne
2 cups soft bread crumbs
½ cup grated cheese
2 tablespoons butter

Cover eggplant with boiling water to which ½ teaspoon salt has been added. Return to boil, turn off heat, and let stand for 5 minutes. Drain. Meantime, sauté onion, pepper and celery in shortening until soft. Add tomatoes, salt, sugar, seasonings and eggplant. Simmer 10 minutes. Mix with bread crumbs. Turn into 1 quart greased casserole. Sprinkle with cheese and dot with butter. Bake at 350° for 1 hour. May be frozen before baking.

Yield: 6 servings

Ann Morrow

EGGPLANT CASSEROLE III

1 large eggplant
2 tablespoons flour
1 egg, beaten
1 cup Italian seasoned bread
    crumbs
2 tablespoons oil
1 large onion
2 stalks celery
½ bell pepper

1 (1-pound) can tomatoes
1 clove garlic, crushed
Salt and pepper
½ teaspoon thyme
1 cup grated Mozzarella
    cheese
½ cup grated Parmesan
    cheese

Dip peeled, sliced eggplant in flour, then in egg, then in seasoned bread crumbs. Fry in 2 tablespoons oil until brown. Remove to shallow casserole.

Sauté chopped onion, celery, and bell pepper in 2 tablespoons oil until transparent. Add can of tomatoes and juice. Add crushed garlic, salt, pepper, and thyme. Reduce heat and continue cooking until thickened. Pour over eggplant in casserole. Sprinkle with both cheeses and bake in 350° oven for ½ hour.

Yield: 6 servings

Cathi Gibbens

EGGPLANT CAVIAR

1 large eggplant
½ cup olive oil
1 large onion, chopped
1 bell pepper, chopped
1 clove garlic, minced

2 fresh tomatoes, peeled,
   seeded and chopped
Salt and red pepper
2 tablespoons dry white wine

Put whole eggplant in 400° oven and bake until soft (about 1 hour). Sauté chopped vegetables in olive oil until tender but not brown. Peel and chop eggplant. Mix with tomatoes. Add sautéed vegetables, salt, pepper and white wine. Mix well and continue to cook gently until mixture is fairly thick. Cool and place in refrigerator. Serve chilled with thin slices of rye or pumpernickel bread.

Yield: 2 cups
Juanita Winkle

ALEX'S EGGPLANT DRESSING

1 pound raw shrimp
¾ pound butter
3 medium-large onions, finely
   chopped
2 bell peppers, finely chopped
1 stalk celery, finely chopped
4 large eggplants
¾ teaspoon cayenne
¾ teaspoon white pepper
¾ teaspoon black pepper

Salt to taste
3 dashes hot pepper sauce
¼ teaspoon dried thyme
¼ teaspoon dried basil
¼ teaspoon dried oregano
½ pound crab meat
¼ cup each chopped green
   onion and parsley
1 cup oil, approximately

Peel shrimp; set aside. Cover shells with 2 cups water; boil to reduce to 1 cup. Strain; set stock aside. Heat butter in large skillet; add onion, peppers and celery. Cook slowly, 15 minutes, until mixture is very soft. Peel and cut 2 eggplants into ¾-inch cubes; place in saucepan with water to cover half of the eggplant. Cook until eggplant is tender, about 7 minutes; drain to remove as much water as possible; purée. Add eggplant, stock and seasonings to sautéed vegetables; cook over medium-low heat about 20 minutes. Add shrimp; cook 7 to 10 minutes over moderately high heat until shrimp are pink. Add crab meat; heat thoroughly. Stir in green onion and parsley. Peel and slice remaining eggplant in 12 ½-inch thick slices. Brown in hot oil. Repeat until all slices are done. Drain. Serve dressing over slices of fried eggplant.

Yield: 6-8 servings
Alex Patout

MIRLITON CASSEROLE
(Vegetable Pears)

5 to 7 medium mirlitons
2 medium onions, chopped
1 bell pepper, chopped
1 celery stalk, chopped
2 cloves garlic, minced
½ stick butter
3 tablespoons olive oil
Salt and pepper to taste
1 pound peeled and deveined
  shrimp

½ pound ground meat
1 (6-ounce) can mushroom
  gravy
1 whole tomato, chopped
½ teaspoon Tabasco pepper
  sauce (more if desired)
Seasoned bread crumbs
1 cup Parmesan cheese,
  grated

Cut mirlitons in quarters and parboil until tender. Drain, peel and cut in small cubes; cook about 20 to 25 minutes, with garlic, half of the onions, bell pepper and celery. Sauté raw shrimp and ground meat with remainder of vegetables in a little olive oil. Cook for 20 minutes. Salt and pepper to taste; add can of gravy. Combine with mirliton mixture, add chopped tomato and Tabasco pepper sauce, cook for 15 minutes. Check seasonings, adjust to taste. Use a 10-inch casserole dish, sprinkle some bread crumbs on bottom, empty all ingredients into casserole and top with bread crumbs, cheese, and pats of butter. Cover and bake for 40 to 45 minutes in 350° oven. Remove cover during the last 5 to 10 minutes of cooking.

This dish can be frozen; just defrost and put in oven when ready to serve.

Yield: 8-10 servings

MUSHROOMS AND ASPARAGUS

6 tablespoons butter
3 tablespoons flour
1 (16-ounce) carton sour cream
2 teaspoons salt
2 teaspoons prepared mustard
1 teaspoon lemon juice
2 pounds fresh mushrooms,
  cleaned

1 pound fresh asparagus,
  blanched and sliced in
  2-inch pieces (green beans
  may be substituted)
1 bunch green onions,
  chopped
¼ cup chopped parsley

Melt butter and add flour. Cook 1 to 2 minutes. Add rest of ingredients and mix. Pour into a 3-quart dish and cover and microwave 20 to 25 minutes, stirring often, until mushrooms are tender. Can be made ahead of time and refrigerated until ready to cook. For conventional oven cook at 350° for 1 hour.

Yield: 8 servings   *A Friend of the Shadows*

MUSTARD GREENS, SMOTHERED

2 bunches mustard greens
1 medium onion, chopped
2 tablespoons oil
Salt and pepper

1 package hamhocks (may be
  smoked)
or leftover ham pieces
or bacon
or salt pork

Wash greens in lots of water. Remove thick stem and tear leaf into pieces. Meanwhile boil 1 gallon water. Submerge greens and boil for 10 to 15 minutes. Drain in colander. Sauté whichever meat you use in a large skillet. If using salt pork, be sure to boil it first for 15 minutes. When meat is browned, add onion and cook 5 minutes. Add well-drained greens to skillet. Stir and cover pot and cook slowly for 45 minutes. Add salt and pepper to taste.

Yield: 4 servings

Mac Beyt

OKRA—BACON CASSEROLE

1½ pounds small young fresh
  okra
3 fresh tomatoes, chopped
1 medium onion, chopped

½ bell pepper, chopped
5 strips bacon
Salt and pepper to taste
Tabasco pepper sauce to taste

Slice okra into thin rounds. Grease a 2½-quart casserole. Place layers of okra, tomatoes, onion and bell pepper. Season each layer with salt, pepper and Tabasco pepper sauce to taste. Lay bacon overlapping on top. Bake for 1½ hours at 350.°

Yield: 6-8 servings

A Friend of the Shadows

Note: 2 (10-ounce) packages frozen okra thawed may be substituted for fresh okra; bake for 1 hour.

CREOLE OKRA

2 pounds okra, sliced
Bacon drippings
1 green pepper, chopped
1 large onion, chopped
1½ cups cooked ham,
    chopped (shrimp may be
    substituted)
2 ribs celery, chopped

1 (28-ounce) can peeled
    tomatoes (3 to 4 fresh
    tomatoes)
¼ teaspoon thyme
1 bay leaf, crumbled
2 cloves garlic
1½ tablespoons chopped
    parsley
Salt and pepper to taste
Tabasco pepper sauce

Fry okra in drippings. Add green pepper, onion, celery and ham. Cook until tender; add tomatoes and seasoning. Cover and simmer slowly about 45 minutes.

Yield: 6-8 servings

Nancy Lewis

SMOTHERED OKRA AND TOMATOES

10 pounds okra
3 onions, chopped
8 fresh tomatoes, peeled,
    seeded and chopped (or
    2 (16-ounce) cans whole
    tomatoes, drained)

2 cloves garlic, diced
1 cup cooking oil

Wash and dry okra and remove stems and run through processor or slice very thin. Heat oil in large pot (never cast iron pot). Add all ingredients at one time. Stir thoroughly, lower fire and cover pot. Stir frequently. It is cooked when okra is no longer slimy. Season with salt and pepper. This may be cooked in a heavy roaster in the oven at 250° for 3 hours. Remove cover for last half hour. This freezes well and may be used as a base for okra gumbo.

Yield: 8-10 servings

Mac Beyt

ENGLISH PEA CASSEROLE

3 cups frozen peas
1 stick margarine
½ cup celery, chopped
½ cup bell pepper, chopped
½ cup onion, chopped

1 recipe cream of mushroom
  soup page 57
1 cup sliced water chestnuts
6 to 8 Ritz crackers, crushed

Sauté celery, pepper, and onion in margarine. Mix soup with peas and water chestnuts and combine with sautéed vegetables. Place in 2 quart baking dish. Cover top with crushed Ritz crackers or toasted bread crumbs. Bake at 350° for 30 minutes.

Yield: 6 servings   *Nancy S. Vita*

Note: 1 (10¾-ounce) can cream of mushroom soup may be substituted.

POTATO CASSEROLE

5 to 6 medium potatoes, grated
1 to 2 tablespoons bacon
  drippings
1 (3-ounce) package cream
  cheese
½ pint sour cream

Salt and pepper to taste
1 (10¾-ounce) can cream of
  chicken soup, undiluted
3 to 6 ounces Cheddar cheese,
  shredded

Brown potatoes in bacon drippings. Add rest of ingredients except Cheddar cheese. Put in casserole dish. Top with cheese. Bake for 30 minutes in 350° oven.

Yield: 6 servings   *Virginia Lee Minvielle*

Variation: Add 1 cup finely chopped green pepper or onion or both.

CHEESE AND POTATO CASSEROLE

6 to 8 potatoes, boiled
1 ½ cups sour cream
8 ounces Gruyere cheese,
  grated
2 small onions, finely chopped

3 tablespoons chopped chives
Salt and pepper
Bread crumbs
Butter

Thinly slice peeled potatoes. Mix sour cream, cheese, onions and chives together, alternate layers of potatoes and sour cream mixture in a large buttered casserole. Salt and pepper each layer of potatoes and end with sour cream mixture. Top with bread crumbs and dot with butter. Cover the casserole with a buttered cover; may be refrigerated at this point. Bake 30 minutes at 350° or until brown and bubbly.

Yield: 6 servings

Barbara Schwing

CHEDDAR CHEEZY HASH
BROWN POTATOES

1 (2-pound) package frozen
  hash brown potatoes,
  thawed
Salt and pepper to taste
1 stick margarine
1 recipe cream of mushroom
  soup page 57

8 ounces sour cream
½ onion, chopped
8 ounces sharp Cheddar
  cheese, grated
2 cups corn flakes, crushed

Spread thawed hash brown potatoes in greased 9 by 13-inch baking dish. Sprinkle with salt and pepper. Melt margarine in saucepan; add mushroom soup, sour cream, onion and grated cheese. Spread soup mixture over top of potatoes. Sprinkle with corn flake crumbs. Bake at 300° for 45 minutes to 1 hour.

Yield: 8 servings

Shara Viator

Note: 1 (10½-ounce) can cream of mushroom soup may be substituted.

Variation: Substitute 2 cups chicken stock for the soup and green onions for onion.

POTATO PUFFS

½ cup sifted flour
1½ teaspoons baking powder
¼ teaspoon salt

2 eggs, well beaten
1 cup mashed potatoes
Dash of pepper

Sift all dry ingredients together. Combine with the remaining ingredients and mix. Drop by teaspoons into deep fat heated to 375° Fry until golden.

Yield: 18 puffs   *Ollie Vidrine*

Variation: Make larger balls and put them on a baking sheet and bake instead of frying. Before baking, make large indentations in balls in order to form cup for creamed peas. Best if served immediately.

POTATO SOUFFLÉ

6 boiled potatoes
1 stick butter
Salt, red and black pepper
  to taste
2 carrots, shredded and boiled
  in 2 tablespoons water for
  5 minutes

2 eggs, well beaten
½ pint sour cream
¾ cup grated cheese of choice
(¼ cup inside; ½ cup on top)

Cream potatoes with butter and seasonings. Add remaining ingredients and mix well. Place in a deep soufflé dish that has been buttered well and cover with grated cheese. Bake in 250° oven for 30 minutes until puffed and cheese on top is melted.

Yield: 8 servings   *Sherry Landry*

BAKED ACORN OR BUTTERNUT SQUASH

Acorn or butternut squash
Butter

Brown sugar
Cinnamon

Cut squash in half and remove seeds. In each half put 1 to 2 tablespoons butter, 1 to 2 tablespoons brown sugar and sprinkle with cinnamon. Bake at 375° for about 1½ hours or until soft when pricked with fork. Children love this dish. Serve ½ squash per person.

Yield: 1 squash equals 2 servings   *Sonja Klein Viator*

MERT'S CREAMED SPINACH

4 (10-ounce) package
   frozen chopped spinach
1 (8-ounce) package cream
   cheese
1 stick butter
1/4 cup Parmesan cheese
1 tablespoon fresh lemon juice
1 (8-ounce) carton sour cream

1/4 teaspoon onion powder
1/4 teaspoon salt
1/4 teaspoon celery salt
1/8 teaspoon red pepper
1/2 teaspoon garlic salt
2 tablespoons Parmesan
   cheese
Italian seasoned bread crumbs

Cook spinach as directed on package. Cream together cream cheese and butter; mix all ingredients except bread crumbs and Parmesan cheese. Place in a shallow casserole dish. Top with bread crumbs and Parmesan cheese and dot with 3 tablespoons butter. Bake at 350° for 40 to 50 minutes.

Yield: 8-10 servings   *Yolanda Trahan*

Optional: 1 (10-ounce) package frozen cooked artichoke hearts or 1 (14-ounce) can hearts of artichokes, drained, may be added.

SPINACH PIE

1 pound fresh spinach
1 bunch green onions, finely
   chopped
3 tablespoons minced parsley
Olive oil
1/2 teaspoon dill (optional)
3 eggs, beaten

1/3 pound crumbled Feta
   cheese
Salt
5 phyllo pastry leaves, cut in
   half crosswise
2 tablespoons melted butter

Wash the spinach, cut off the stems, dry completely with towels, and chop. Brown the onions in 2 tablespoons olive oil until tender. Combine spinach, parsley, dill, beaten eggs and cheese; add cooked onions; season with salt lightly and mix well. Grease an 8 x 12-inch baking pan and line with 5 of the phyllo sheets, brushing each sheet with the melted butter combined with 1 tablespoon olive oil. Spread the spinach mixture over the phyllo, and top with remaining sheets of phyllo, brushing each again with the butter and oil. Brush the top sheet, and bake at 350° for 45 minutes. Cool and cut into squares. This may be served hot or cold, as an appetizer in small squares, as a vegetable side dish in larger squares.

Sue Mac Donough

SPINACH AND RICE

1 pound fresh spinach or 2 (10-
   ounce) packages of frozen
   spinach, thawed
1 medium sized onion
   chopped or 2 bunches
   green onions chopped
1/3 cup olive oil

1 1/2 cups water
2/3 cup rice
1/2 teaspoon dry dill weed
Salt and pepper to taste
Dash of Tabasco pepper sauce
Juice of 1/2 lemon

Wash fresh spinach several times, drain well and chop, or thaw frozen spinach, squeeze as much liquid from this as possible and chop coarsely. Sauté onions in olive oil until soft. Add spinach to onions and simmer slowly until wilted. Add water, bring to boiling point, and stir in rice and seasonings. Cover and simmer for 15 minutes, or until rice is soft and liquid is absorbed. Add juice of half lemon before removing from fire. Stir well and keep covered until time to serve. This may be served hot or at room temperature.

Yield: 4 servings *Mary H. Kapsos*

STUFFED SPAGHETTI SQUASH

1 spaghetti squash
5 to 6 zucchini squash
1 large onion
2 cloves garlic

1 1/2 cups grated cheese of
   choice
1 (8-ounce) can tomato sauce
Salt and pepper to taste
Tabasco pepper sauce to taste

Bake spaghetti squash in oven for 50 to 60 minutes, depending on age of squash. While squash is baking, grate the peeled zucchini squash, onion, garlic and cheese. Place in large bowl with the tomato sauce. Remove spaghetti squash from oven and cool to touch; cut in half and remove seeds; scrape meat from squash and place in bowl with other ingredients. Mix thoroughly and stuff into spaghetti squash shells. Bake at 375° about 30 minutes. This is a low calorie main dish.

Yield: 8-10 servings *Sonja Klein Viator*

SQUASH—CARROT CASSEROLE

2 dozen round buttery crackers
1 (8-ounce) package cream
  cheese, softened
2 (10¾-ounce) cans cream of
  chicken soup, undiluted
2 eggs, beaten
½ cup butter or margarine,
  melted

8 cups (about 2½ pounds)
  sliced yellow squash,
  cooked
6 small carrots, grated
1 cup finely chopped onion
1 cup herb-seasoned stuffing
  mix

Place crackers in a greased 13 x 9 x 2-inch baking dish. Set aside. Combine cream cheese, soup, eggs, and butter; beat well. Stir in squash, carrot, and onion. Spoon into prepared baking dish; sprinkle with stuffing mix. Bake for 30 to 40 minutes.

Yield: 10 servings   *A Friend of the Shadows*

GREEN CHILI SQUASH

2 pounds yellow squash
1 small onion, chopped
1 (4-ounce) can green chilies
  or jalapeños, chopped

½ pound grated Cheddar
  cheese
Bread crumbs

Wash and slice yellow squash. Cook with onion until all liquid is gone. Add green chilies and cheese. Pour into casserole and top with bread crumbs. Bake at 350° until bubbly.

Yield: 6 servings   *A Friend of the Shadows*

SQUASH CASSEROLE I

2 pounds yellow or white
  squash
1 large onion, sliced
1 stick butter
1 (10¾-ounce) can cream of
  chicken soup

1 cup sour cream
1 cup herb seasoned stuffing
  mix
Salt and pepper to taste
½ cup grated cheese

Cook squash and onion in boiling water. Drain and mash fine. Mix with other ingredients. Place in buttered casserole and bake about 20 minutes at 350°F. Sprinkle some of the stuffing mix and grated cheese on top before baking.

Yield: 6-8 servings   *Adele Wormser*

SQUASH CASSEROLE II

8 yellow squash
1 large onion, chopped
½ bell pepper, chopped
Garlic to taste
Green onion tops, chopped
1 stick margarine
1 cup grated cheese

1 teaspoon Worcestershire
  sauce
¼ teaspoon Tabasco pepper
  sauce
1½ to 2 cups bread crumbs
Grated cheese to garnish

Boil squash until tender. Drain and chop. Sauté chopped ingredients in margarine. Mix with drained squash, seasonings, bread crumbs and cheese. Place in buttered casserole. Sprinkle with grated cheese. Bake at 350° for 30 minutes.

Yield: 6-8 servings   *Carolyn Sutton*

YELLOW SQUASH CASSEROLE III

1½ to 2 pounds yellow squash
1 carrot, grated
1 large onion, finely chopped
3 tablespoons chopped green
  pepper
1 (10¾-ounce) can cream of
  chicken soup
½ pint sour cream
1 (4-ounce) jar pimentos,
  drained and sliced
1 (8½-ounce) can water
  chestnuts, drained

1½ cups Pepperidge Farm
  Herb Stuffing mix
¾ stick margarine
8 ounces grated cheddar
  cheese
Seasoned pepper
Worcestershire sauce
Cayenne pepper
Salt
Parsley

Cook squash until tender, about 12 minutes, in salted water. Drain well and mash with spoon. In large bowl mix squash, carrot, onion, green pepper, soup, sour cream, pimentoes and water chestnuts. Add one cup of buttered dressing mix. (Melt butter and mix well with all the stuffing mix.) Add half grated cheese. Add seasoned pepper, Worcestershire sauce, cayenne pepper, salt and parsley to taste. Pour into a 2-quart greased baking dish and cover with remaining cheese and stuffing mixture. Bake at 350° for 30 minutes.

Yield: 8 servings   *Nancy Lewis*

STUFFED SQUASH
(A Main Dish)

8 to 10 medium yellow or white squash

Boil 6 medium yellow squash (or small white ones) for about 5 minutes. Remove from water; cool enough to handle. Cut a thin slice off top of squash. Carefully scoop out pulp, leaving a ½-inch shell. Set shells aside until ready to stuff.

STUFFING

**4 cups sliced squash
(from the remaining squash)
1 tablespoon margarine
1 pound ground meat
1 large onion, finely chopped
2 cloves garlic, minced
½ cup chopped celery
2 tablespoons finely chopped
bell pepper**

**Salt and pepper to taste
4 slices bread, soaked in water
(or 1 cup cooked rice)
1 cup shredded sharp cheese
1 teaspoon Worcestershire
sauce
1 egg, slightly beaten
Buttered bread crumbs**

Cook sliced squash until tender in just enough water to prevent scorching, drain. Mix in scooped squash from shells.

Brown ground meat in margarine in skillet. Stir in onion, garlic, celery, bell pepper, salt and pepper. If bread is used, squeeze out excess water. Add bread (or rice), squash, cheese and Worcestershire sauce to meat. Remove from heat, stir in egg.

Fill squash shells, top with buttered crumbs and bake at 350° for about 20 minutes.

Yield: 6 servings

SUMMER SQUASH CASSEROLE

**2 to 2½ pounds yellow squash,
sliced
½ cup sour cream
¼ cup melted butter
2 green onions, minced,
including tops**

**Salt and pepper to taste
½ cup buttered bread crumbs
¼ cup grated Parmesan
cheese**

Cook squash in boiling, salted water for 15 to 20 minutes, or until tender. Drain and cool. Add sour cream, butter, green onions, salt and pepper. Place in a casserole, lightly greased. Top with bread crumbs and cheese. Bake at 350° for 10 to 15 minutes.

Yield: 4-6 servings   *A Friend of the Shadows*

SQUASH AND TOMATOES

1 pound yellow squash, sliced
thin
1 stick margarine
Salt and pepper
1 bell pepper, chopped
1 (16-ounce) can tomatoes,
drained and mashed

½ pound grated Cheddar
cheese
1 recipe homemade cream of
mushroom soup page 57,
or 1 (10½-ounce) can
cream of mushroom soup
1 cup buttered cracker crumbs

Grease oblong 9 x 13-inch casserole with ½ stick margarine. Melt other ½ stick for cracker crumbs. Place sliced squash, salt and pepper in casserole and rest of ingredients in order given. Top with buttered cracker crumbs. Cover with foil. Bake for 1 hour and 15 minutes in 350° oven.

Yield: 4-6 servings   *Betty H. Voorhies*

TOMATO CASSEROLE I

1 pound ground beef
5 slices rye bread
3 cubes instant beef bouillon
3 cups hot water
1 onion chopped
1 bell pepper chopped
1 pint Ragú Thick and Zesty
sauce

1 (10-ounce) can Rotel
tomatoes
3 (8-ounce) cans stewed
tomatoes
2 packages Mrs. Savoie's
cooked dressing mix
1 cup bread crumbs

Cook ground meat until brown. Soak five slices rye bread in broth made with bouillon cubes. In another pot sauté onion and bell pepper in small amount of oil. Add Ragú sauce, Rotel tomatoes. Add stewed tomatoes. Cook about 30 minutes, add meat and dressing mixture and season. Cook 1 hour, stirring often. Add soaked rye bread and cook again until the right consistency for a casserole. Put in baking dish, sprinkle with crumbs and bake at 350° for 10 minutes. Serve hot. This freezes well.

Yield: 18 servings   *Mildred W. Dauterive*

Note: If Mrs. Savoie's dressing mix is not available substitute 1 pound chicken livers and 1 pound chicken gizzards, ground and cooked with 1 chopped bell pepper, 1 chopped onion and 1 clove garlic minced.

VEGETABLES

TOMATO CASSEROLE II

6 large very ripe tomatoes
¼ teaspoon sugar
½ pound ground beef
2 onions, chopped
2 bell peppers, chopped

1 rib celery chopped
2 cloves garlic, minced
Salt and pepper to taste
2 cups bread crumbs

Mash tomatoes in food processor and add sugar. Brown beef and pour off fat. Add chopped onions, bell peppers, celery and garlic to beef. Simmer until vegetables are tender. Add mashed tomatoes and simmer slowly for about 1 hour. Season to taste. Add 1¾ cups bread crumbs to mixture. Pour into buttered casserole, sprinkle remaining bread crumbs on top. Bake at 300° for 30 minutes. This dish freezes very well.

Yield: 6 servings

Mrs. Eugene (Ann) Patout

YOU CAN'T BELIEVE IT'S TURNIPS

8 medium turnips
1 stick butter
1 large onion, chopped
2 (5¾-ounce) Dawn Fresh
    mushroom steak sauce

1 tablespoon sugar or equiva-
    lent of sugar substitute
Salt and red pepper to taste
1 cup green onion tops,
    chopped
¼ cup bread crumbs

Peel and dice turnips; melt butter in Dutch oven. Add turnips, onion, sauce, sugar, salt and pepper. Simmer for 1 hour stirring often to prevent sticking. Add green onions and continue cooking for 10 minutes. Place in casserole and sprinkle with bread crumbs. Place under broiler for 5 minutes or until brown.

Julie Harris

Note: If turnips are not fresh, young turnips, more sugar may be needed.

Variation: Sauté one pound ground meat (beef or pork) and add to dutch oven; before adding to casserole, mix into mixture 1½ to 2 cups soft French bread crumbs. This is a turnip dressing.

TURNIP PUFF

4 cups mashed cooked turnips
2 cups soft bread crumbs
½ cup melted margarine
2 tablespoons sugar

1 teaspoon salt
½ teaspoon pepper
4 eggs slightly beaten
2 teaspoons margarine

Mix the above and spoon into greased casserole. Brush the top with melted butter or margarine. Bake at 275° for ½ hour.

Yield: 6-8 servings

Curtis Thomas

YAM/BOURBON CASSEROLE

3 (17-ounce) cans Trappey's
  yams
½ cup brown sugar
Rind of one large orange,
  grated

½ cup fresh orange juice
⅓ cup bourbon whiskey or
  sherry
½ stick butter
1 teaspoon salt

Place yams in a buttered casserole (1 layer thick), sprinkle with sugar, add orange juice, rind, and bourbon or sherry. Dot with butter, cover and bake at 350° for 45 to 50 minutes until all the juice has cooked into the yams.

Yield: 6-8 servings

B. F. Trappey's Sons, Inc.

Note: This recipe can also be used by mashing the yams before putting into casserole, mixing the butter, sugar, rind, orange juice and bourbon or sherry together.

YAMS WITH PINEAPPLE

1 (17-ounce) can of yams or
   5-6 medium boiled yams
½ stick margarine
½ cup sugar
Dash of salt

1 (8-ounce) can crushed pineapple, drained, reserve juice
½ cup raisins
½ cup chopped pecans
Marshmallows

Drain can of yams or peel fresh ones. Beat with mixer. Add margarine, sugar, salt, and pineapple juice. Fold in pineapple, raisins and pecans. Put in a casserole and bake at 350° for 30 minutes. Top with marshmallows and return to the oven to brown.

Yield: 4-6 servings   *Mrs. Leonce J. Broussard*

SUPER YAMS

8 medium cooked yams, cut in
   1 to 1½-inch slices
5 tablespoons brown sugar

2 ounces dark crème de cacao
1½ cups honey
¼ cup chopped pecans

Place yams in baking dish. Sprinkle with brown sugar, and then add crème de cacao and honey. Bake at 425° for 15 to 20 minutes.

Yield: 8 servings   *Keith Courrege*

VEGETABLE PIE

1 deep dish pie crust (frozen)
1 eggplant, about 1 pound, cut
   into cubes
1 medium onion, chopped
1 clove garlic, minced
¼ cup butter or margarine
1 teaspoon salt

1 small zucchini, sliced
⅔ cup of evaporated milk
1 egg
3 cups grated Mozzarella
   cheese
Dash red pepper

In a large skillet, sauté eggplant, onion and garlic in butter until tender. Stir in seasonings. Cover sides and bottom of frozen crust with sliced zucchini. Spoon in cooked vegetables. Meanwhile combine evaporated milk and egg. Stir cheese into milk mixture. Pour over vegetables. Bake in a 350° oven on a cookie sheet until crust is lightly browned, about 30-35 minutes.

Yield: 6 servings   *Eleanor Holleman*

EGGS, CHEESE, GRITS, PASTA, RICE AND RICE DRESSINGS

Circa 1907

William Frederick Weeks, grandfather of Weeks Hall, was the second owner to occupy the house. William Frederick had two daughters, Lily and Harriet (called "Pattie").

Pattie Weeks Torian is shown in this photograph in the fashionable "Turkish Corner" of the parlor at the Shadows. Lily married Gilbert Hall and named her only son William Weeks Hall. Pattie and Lily were part of the third generation of the Weeks family to occupy the house.

William Weeks Hall was the fourth generation of his family to own the house. He had inherited his mother's, Lily's, share of the house in 1919. He bought his Aunt Pattie's share in the family home for $7,500.00 in 1919. He returned to the Shadows in 1922—after his service in World War I and the completion of his art studies in Paris. At this time he began the restoration under the direction of his friend, New Orleans architect Richard Koch.

Eggs, Cheese, Grits, Pasta, Rice and Rice Dressing

CHEESE
Fondue. 131
Pie, Mexican. 130

EGGS
Baked. 125
Breakfast Casserole. 125
Casserole, Cheese and Bread. 125
Crab in Brandy Cream Sauce. 126
Creole. 126
For Supper. 127
Plantation. 128
Quiche, Crustless. 127
Quiche, Shadows Service
    League. 127
Ranchero. 128
Shrimp Soufflé with Sauce. 129
Toast, Orange French. 130

GRITS
Baked. 131
Couche Couche, Mère's. 132
Garlic Cheese. 131

PASTA
Artichoke Casserole, Noodle. 132
Chicken-Spinach Noodle
    Casserole. 133
Crawfish. 133
Lasagne. 134

Lasagne, Chicken. 135
Olive Oil Spaghetti. 134
Parmesan Primavera. 137
Salad. 135
Spaghetti with Green Sauce. 137
Spinach Fettuccine. 136
Spinach Noodle Ring. 136
Vermicelli Vinaigrette. 138

RICE
Casserole, Mushroom. 138
Casserole, Seafood. 139
Casserole, Wild. 139
Casserole, Wild and Oysters. 140
Curried. 140
Green. 141
Jambalaya. 141
Jambalaya, Black-Eyed Pea. 142
Jambalaya, Chicken. 142
Jambalaya, Chicken and
    Sausage. 143
Vegetable. 143

RICE DRESSING
Cajun I. 144
Cajun II. 145
Oyster. 145
Shrimp and Oyster. 146

Refer to additional recipes in "How Men Cook" section.

BAKED EGGS

1 stick butter
12 eggs
¾ cup milk

1 (16-ounce) carton small curd
   cottage cheese
8 slices Cheddar cheese

Melt butter in 9 x 12 baking dish in 350° oven. Beat eggs, add milk and cottage cheese, blending well. Pour into baking dish over melted butter. Bake 15 minutes, then top with cheese slices. Bake until cheese melts and eggs are solid, about 10 minutes.

Yield: 6-8 servings   *A Friend of the Shadows*

BREAKFAST CASSEROLE

12 slices white bread, buttered
2 (12-ounce) packages
   smokies sausage
½ pound Velveeta or Cheddar
   cheese

6 eggs, well beaten
1 quart milk
1 teaspoon salt
Pepper to taste
1 teaspoon dry mustard

Break up bread into oiled 9 x 13 ovenproof dish. Add sausage and cheese that has been cut into bite size pieces. Add milk to eggs and beat well. Add salt, pepper and mustard and pour over bread, sausage and cheese. Refrigerate overnight. If time is short, let the mixture sit long enough for the bread to soak up the egg and milk mixture. Bake, uncovered for 1 hour in 350° oven. Reheats beautifully in microwave.

Yield: 10-12 servings   *Curtis Thomas*

EGGS, CHEESE AND BREAD CASSEROLE

8 slices of bread, crust
   removed
3 cups of grated Cheddar
   cheese

4 eggs
2 cups milk
1 teaspoon dry mustard
½ teaspoon salt and pepper

Butter bread and in a buttered 9 x 9 baking dish alternate layers of bread and cheese. Mix the eggs, milk, mustard, salt and pepper. Pour over bread and cheese. Cover and let stand for 2 hours, or refrigerate overnight. Bake at 350° for 45-60 minutes.

Yield: 4-6 servings   *Mac Beyt*

EGGS AND CRAB IN BRANDY CREAM SAUCE

3 tablespoons butter
3 tablespoons green onions, finely chopped
3 tablespoons flour
1½ cups Half & Half
2 tablespoons brandy
1 teaspoons lemon juice
Salt and red pepper to taste

Grated nutmeg, to taste
8 tablespoons butter
1 pound cleaned crabmeat
⅛ teaspoon red pepper
Salt to taste
8 eggs
½ teaspoon paprika

Melt 3 tablespoons butter over moderate heat; when foam subsides, add onion and sauté until soft. Add flour and mix well. Whisk in Half & Half slowly. Cook, whisking constantly, until mixture boils and is thick and smooth. Reduce heat to low and simmer 2 or 3 minutes more. Warm brandy in separate pan; ignite and shake pan back and forth until flames subside. Stir in brandy, lemon juice, salt, pepper and nutmeg. Remove from heat, cover pan to keep warm. Melt 6 tablespoons butter; add crabmeat and toss gently to coat. Add salt and pepper. Place in a 10-inch round oven proof dish. Cover to keep warm. Poach eggs according to personal taste. Arrange eggs on top of crabmeat and spoon sauce over all. Sprinkle with paprika for color. Add remaining butter, cut into bits. Bake at 450° for 10 minutes.

Yield: 4 servings

Carla Mouton

EGGS CREOLE

4 slices toast or toasted English muffins

8 slices bacon, cooked
4 poached eggs

Place 1 piece of toast on each plate; put 2 slices bacon on top; place 1 poached egg on top. Cover with Creole sauce.

CREOLE SAUCE
½ cup chopped onion
½ cup chopped bell pepper
½ cup diced celery
2 tablespoons olive oil
2½ cups canned tomatoes

2 teaspoons salt
1 teaspoon pepper
2 teaspoons sugar
2 teaspoons chopped parsley

Sauté onion, bell pepper and celery in oil until soft; add all remaining ingredients and cook over low heat until thick. (If in a hurry, thicken with a little cornstarch.)

Yield: 4 servings

Mac Beyt

EGGS FOR SUPPER

1 (10-ounce) box frozen
  spinach
¼ cup butter
1 clove garlic
6 eggs

3 tablespoons cream
Salt and pepper
6 English muffins, split and
  toasted

Cook spinach and drain and squeeze dry. Melt butter with the clove of garlic. Remove garlic. Add the spinach; add the eggs which have been mixed with the cream, and add the seasonings. Cook over low heat until creamy. Serve on split, buttered and toasted English muffins. If you like anchovies, you can add a little anchovy paste to the butter for the muffins.

Yield: 3-6 servings   *Mac Beyt*

CRUSTLESS QUICHE

2 (7-ounce) cans jalapeno
  peppers

1 pound New York sharp
  cheese, grated
12 eggs

Remove seeds from peppers, chop peppers and sprinkle on bottom of a 9 x 13 greased dish. Sprinkle cheese over peppers. Beat eggs and pour over cheese. Bake in 300° oven about 35 minutes or until inserted knife comes out clean. May be cut in small squares and used as an hors d'oeuvre.

Yield: 10-12 servings   *Susie Pharr*

SHADOWS SERVICE LEAGUE QUICHE

1 cup milk
4 eggs
¾ teaspoon salt
Red pepper to taste

2 cups Swiss cheese, shredded
2 tablespoons flour
1 cup chopped ham
9-inch pie shell

Mix milk, eggs, salt and pepper. Toss together cheese and flour. Add milk mix to cheese mix, a little at a time. Add ham and mix well. Pour into 9-inch pie shell and bake in 350° oven about 1 hour or until inserted knife comes out clean. When finished cooking, do not cover, as crust will get soggy.

Yield: 6-8 servings

Note: 1 cup crab meat or 1 cup cooked chopped shrimp may be substituted for the ham.

PLANTATION EGGS

3 (10-ounce) packages frozen
  chopped spinach
8 strips bacon
1 cup cubed ham
1 stick butter, divided
1 cup flour
4¼ cups milk
1 medium onion, chopped

Salt, freshly ground pepper
  to taste
Tabasco pepper sauce to taste
18 eggs
1½ cups evaporated milk
½ cup French fried onion
  rings, crushed (optional)
½ cup grated cheese
  (preferably Monterrey Jack)

Cook spinach according to directions on package. Drain well. Quarter bacon and fry until crisp; remove from pan and set aside. Fry ham in bacon drippings for 2 minutes. Remove from pan and place with bacon. Add 4 tablespoons butter to drippings and melt. Sauté onion in drippings until wilted. Add flour and mix well with drippings. Cook five minutes and add milk stirring until sauce is thick and smooth. Add spinach, salt and pepper and Tabasco pepper sauce; mix well. Remove from heat. Melt ½ stick butter in another large skillet. Beat eggs and evaporated milk together with pepper. Scramble in butter until lightly set. Butter 9 by 13 oven-proof baking dish. Spread half of eggs in bottom of dish and layer half of bacon and ham over eggs. Cover with half of the spinach mixture. Repeat these layers once more. Top with onion rings and cheese. Refrigerate overnight! Bake at 275 degrees for 1 hour. (Allow casserole to come to room temperature before baking.)

Yield: 12-14   *Nancy Lewis*

EGGS RANCHERO

2 tablespoons butter
1 (28-ounce) can stewed
  tomatoes or 2 (17-ounce)
  cans stewed tomatoes
8 eggs
Basil

Oregano
Salt and pepper
Seasoned bread crumbs
1½ cups sharp Cheddar
  cheese, grated

Cook tomatoes in butter 10 to 15 minutes on low heat until thickened. Season to taste with salt, pepper, basil and oregano. If not thick enough, add a few seasoned bread crumbs. Spread evenly in a 1½ quart rectangular baking dish. Make 8 pockets; break whole egg into each pocket. Top with bread crumbs; sprinkle evenly with cheese. Bake at 450° for 7 to 10 minutes or to desired firmness.

Yield: 4-6 servings   *Nancy Lewis*

SHRIMP SOUFFLÉ WITH SAUCE

1 pound shrimp	2 teaspoons salt
2 cups water	½ teaspoon red pepper

Cook shrimp by dropping into boiling water; remove pot from fire as soon as shrimp begin to turn pink. Let stand one minute; drain, reserving liquid. Peel when cool enough to handle.

SOUFFLÉ MIXTURE

2 tablespoons butter	1 egg yolk
3 tablespoons flour	5 egg whites, stiffly beaten
¾ cup hot milk	½ cup grated Swiss or
Salt, pepper and nutmeg	Parmesan cheese
to taste	

Cook butter and flour together for 2 minutes. Beat in the hot milk with a wire whisk; add ¼ cup shrimp liquid; add a pinch of nutmeg and the salt and pepper to taste. Bring to a boil, stirring constantly for 1 minute. Remove pot from heat and beat in the egg yolk. Stir in ¼ of the beaten egg whites, then fold in, very carefully, the rest of the egg whites and all but 2 tablespoons cheese. Butter an oven-proof dish about 16 inches long. Spread ¼ mixture in bottom of dish. Spread shrimp over mixture. Heap rest of soufflé mixture over the shrimp. Sprinkle with remaining cheese. Bake at 425° for 15 to 20 minutes until puffed and golden on top. Serve immediately.

SAUCE

4 tablespoons butter	Salt and pepper to taste
5 tablespoons flour	½ teaspoon lemon juice
1 cup hot milk	1 tablespoon tomato paste
¾ cup shrimp liquid	(optional)
¾ cup heavy cream	

Heat butter in saucepan; add flour and cook slowly for 2 minutes. Remove from heat and add hot milk beating hard with a wire whisk. Beat in shrimp stock, half of the cream. Boil 1 minute. Reduce heat to simmer and slowly add more cream if sauce is too thick. The sauce should just coat the spoon. Season carefully with salt, pepper and lemon juice. For color, you may add 1 tablespoon tomato paste to sauce when adding shrimp stock and cream.

Crabmeat or crawfish may be substituted for shrimp.

Yield: 4-6 servings   *Mac Beyt*

ORANGE FRENCH TOAST

8 slices French bread ¾-inch
thick
4 eggs
1 cup milk
2 tablespoons Grand Marnier
(orange liqueur)

1 tablespoon granulated sugar
½ teaspoon vanilla
¼ teaspoon salt
2 tablespoons butter
Confectioners' sugar

In 12 x 8 x 2-inch baking dish, arrange bread in a single layer. Combine eggs, with milk, orange liqueur, sugar, vanilla and salt with rotary beater. Mix well. Pour over bread; turn to coat slices evenly. Refrigerate, covered, overnight. To cook, heat butter in a skillet. Add bread and sauté until golden, about 4 minutes on each side. Sprinkle with confectioners' sugar and serve.

Yield: 4 servings

A Friend of the Shadows

MEXICAN CHEESE PIE

Butter
6 small flour tortillas
½ onion, thinly sliced
1 large tomato, chopped
1 (4-ounce) can diced green
chili peppers
3 eggs
3 tablespoons flour

1 teaspoon salt
½ teaspoon baking powder
½ cup milk
1 cup shredded Cheddar
cheese
1 ripe avocado, seeded and
sliced lengthwise
Mild taco sauce

Butter a round baking dish. Line with tortillas, leaving ½ inch extending over top. Place onion, tomato and chili peppers in bottom of dish on tortillas. In bowl beat eggs and mix with flour, salt, baking powder and milk. Fold in cheese. Pour this mixture over ingredients in baking dish. Bake at 350° for 40-45 minutes. Before serving, place avocado slices on top of pie and cut into wedges. Spoon taco sauce over each serving.

Yield: 6 servings

Millie Brooks

CHEESE FONDUE

1 clove garlic
1 cup white wine
1 pound Swiss cheese
  (shredded)

1½ tablespoons corn starch
3 tablespoons sherry
Salt and pepper to taste
French bread, cubed

Rub glass or Corning ware container with garlic. Remove garlic. Heat wine until warm. Do not boil. Add cheese. Cook until cheese melts, then add corn starch which has been dissolved in sherry. Continue cooking until thick and creamy. Keep hot and serve with French bread which has been cut into bite size pieces.

Yield: 4 servings

Susie Pharr

BAKED GRITS

1 cup grits
1 (10½-ounce) can cream of
  chicken soup

1 cup Cheddar cheese,
  shredded
Paprika

Cook grits as directed on package. Remove from heat, add cream of chicken soup, shredded Cheddar cheese and stir well. Put into a greased casserole and sprinkle with paprika. Bake in 300° oven for 1 hour. Freezes well.

Yield: 6-8 servings

A Friend of the Shadows

GARLIC CHEESE GRITS

1 cup grits
4 cups water
1 teaspoon salt
1 roll garlic cheese
1 stick butter

2 eggs, well beaten
¼ cup milk
Salt, pepper and red pepper
  to taste

Cook grits in water with salt according to package directions. Add one roll garlic cheese, cut up, and butter. When cheese and butter have melted, add eggs, milk, salt, pepper and red pepper. Put in a greased 1½ quart casserole and bake 45 minutes to 1 hour in a 350° oven. Jalapeno cheese may be substituted for garlic cheese.

Yield: 6-8 servings

Rosemary Brooks

NOODLE ARTICHOKE CASSEROLE

1 (5-ounce) package of noodles
1 (4-ounce) can stems and
  pieces mushrooms,
  drained
1 (14-ounce) can artichoke
  hearts, drained and sliced

3 ounces Parmesan cheese,
  divided
1 small onion, diced
Parsley
Salt and pepper to taste
1 stick butter, melted

Boil and drain noodles. Mix rest of ingredients with noodles, using ½ of the cheese. Sprinkle remainder of Parmesan cheese on top. Put in 9 x 9-inch casserole and bake in 325° oven for 1 hour.

Yield: 6-8 servings

Rosemary Brooks

MÈRE'S COUCHE COUCHE

1½ cups white corn meal
½ cup flour
2 teaspoons salt
1½ cups very hot water

2 eggs
2 teaspoons baking powder
2 tablespoons oil

Sift together corn meal, flour and salt. Add the hot water to make a light batter. Break 2 eggs into the mixture and beat well. Add the baking powder. Put the oil in a heavy iron skillet. When very hot, pour in the batter, lower the heat, and cover tightly. Cook 5 minutes (until crust is formed at the bottom of the pot). Stir occasionally until cooked, but not dry.

Yield: 4-6 servings

Mildred W. Dauterive

CHICKEN-SPINACH NOODLE CASSEROLE

6 pound hen, cooked,
   deboned and cubed
1 pound spinach noodles,
   cooked
1 cup chopped onion
1 cup chopped bell pepper
1 cup chopped celery
6 tablespoons butter
¾ pound Velveeta cheese,
   grated
2 recipes cream of mushroom
   soup, page 57

1 cup chopped water
   chestnuts
1 cup chopped fresh
   mushrooms
6 shakes Worcestershire
   sauce
1 (5-ounce) jar stuffed olives,
   sliced
Garlic salt to taste
1 (3-ounce) can French fried
   onion rings

Sauté onions, green pepper and celery in butter until golden. Melt cheese with soup and add sautéed vegetables. Combine this mixture with water chestnuts, mushrooms, Worcestershire sauce, olives and garlic salt. Add noodles, chicken and mix well. Place in 4-quart baking dish and top with onion rings and bake at 350° for 30 minutes.

Yield: 16 servings   *Nancy Lewis*

Note: 2 (10½-ounce) cans of soup may be substituted.

CRAWFISH AND PASTA

4 cups of heavy cream
1½ teaspoons thyme
1½ teaspoons basil
Salt and pepper to taste
Tabasco pepper sauce to taste
½ cup chopped green
   onion tops

½ cup chopped parsley
¼ cup Parmesan cheese
1 pound #2 spaghetti, cooked
2 pounds peeled crawfish tails

Pour cream into heavy skillet over high fire. After cream comes to a boil, add thyme, basil, salt, pepper, Tabasco, green onion tops, parsley. Cook for three minutes. Add crawfish tails and cook for 3 minutes. Add pasta and cheese and cook for 2 minutes. Serve in gumbo bowls.

Yield: 6 servings   *Gigi and Alex Patout*

LASAGNE

MEAT SAUCE

1 medium onion, diced
3 cloves garlic, finely diced
2 pounds ground beef
⅓ cup olive oil
1 (8-ounce) can tomato sauce
3 (6-ounce) cans tomato paste
5 cups water

2 tablespoons sugar
1 tablespoon Italian
  seasoning
1 teaspoon oregano
1 (8-ounce) can diced
  mushrooms, drained
Salt and pepper to taste

NOODLE MIXTURE

1 (12-ounce) package
  lasagne noodles
1½ ounces grated
  Romano cheese

3 ounces grated Parmesan
  cheese
2 (12-ounce) packs grated
  Mozzarella cheese

Over medium heat, lightly brown diced onion, garlic and ground beef in olive oil. Add tomato sauce and tomato paste; simmer 5 to 10 minutes with constant stirring. Add 5 cups water, sugar, seasonings, mushrooms, salt and pepper. Mix thoroughly; cook over medium heat 2½ to 3 hours, stirring frequently until sauce is thick and tasty. (Optional: Decrease water to 1½ to 2 cups, pour mixture into a crock pot and cook overnight on low.) Boil noodles until half cooked, drain and separate quickly to prevent sticking. Cover the bottom of 8 x 10-inch pan with a thin layer of meat sauce to prevent sticking. Then place a layer of noodles. Add a layer of meat sauce; sprinkle a nice layer of the three cheeses. Repeat two or three times. Bake at 375° for 30 minutes.

Yield: 8-10 servings   *Kathleen Haik*

OLIVE OIL SPAGHETTI

1¾ cups olive oil
4 cloves finely chopped garlic
1¾ cups water
Salt and pepper (black or red)
  to taste

1 pound cooked spaghetti
½ cup grated fresh Romano
  cheese

Pour oil into saucepan, heat and brown garlic. Add water, salt and pepper and bring to a boil. Turn heat to low, cover and cook until almost all water is gone. The last 10 minutes remove cover and let it cook down.

Pour over cooked and drained spaghetti and top with fresh grated Romano cheese.

Yield: 8 servings   *Carolyn Sorci*

CHICKEN LASAGNE

8 ounces lasagne noodles
1 (10½-ounce) can cream of
   chicken soup
⅔ cup milk
½ teaspoon salt
½ teaspoon poultry seasoning
2 (3-ounce) packages cream
   cheese, softened
1 cup creamed cottage cheese

⅓ cup sliced green stuffed
   olives
⅓ cup chopped onions
⅓ cup chopped green pepper
¼ cup minced parsley
3 cups diced cooked chicken
   or turkey
1½ cups soft buttered bread
   crumbs

Cook noodles in boiling water for 15 minutes. Drain and rinse in cold water. Mix soup, milk and seasonings; heat. Beat the cheeses together. Stir in next four ingredients. Place half of the noodles in a 13 x 9 x 2-inch pyrex pan, spread with half the cheese mixture, half the chicken and half the heated soup and milk mixture. Repeat the layers. Top with the buttered crumbs. Bake for 30 minutes at 375° or until heated.

Yield: 8 servings

Phyllis Peterson

PASTA SALAD

12 ounces vermicelli (cooked
   and drained)
1 stalk celery, chopped
1 (4-ounce) jar pimentos,
   drained
1 medium onion, grated

1 small bell pepper, chopped
2 to 3 cups mayonnaise
Salt and pepper to taste
2 ounces jalapeno peppers,
   drained, or to taste

Mix all of above ingredients together. Serve cold. Best made 24 hours ahead of time.

Yield: 6-8 servings

Jean Ostrich

SPINACH FETTUCCINE

SPINACH FETTUCCINE

1 (10-ounce) package frozen
  spinach
1 (8-ounce) package medium
  egg noodles
2 tablespoons chopped onion
1 clove garlic, crushed

1 tablespoon butter, melted
¼ cup butter or margarine
½ cup whipping cream
1 cup grated Parmesan cheese
Coarsely ground black pepper

Drain spinach in a colander; place on paper towels and press until barely moist. Cook noodles and drain well. Sauté onion and garlic in 1 tablespoon butter until tender: stir in spinach. Cover and simmer 3 minutes.

Add ¼ cup butter to warm noodles, tossing gently, until butter melts. Add spinach mixture, whipping cream and cheese; toss gently. Sprinkle with pepper.

Yield: 8 servings

Barbara Schwing

SPINACH NOODLE RING

1 (8-ounce) package medium
  noodles
2 (10-ounce) packages frozen
  chopped spinach

1 large onion, chopped
½ cup margarine
3 eggs, beaten
½ cup sour cream

Cook noodles and cook spinach according to package directions. Drain well and mix together. Sauté onion in margarine and add to noodle mixture. Add eggs and sour cream. Pour into buttered ring mold. Place mold in pan of water. Bake in 350° oven for 45 minutes. Serve with sautéed mushrooms in center of mold.

Yield: 6-8 servings

A Friend of the Shadows

PARMESAN PRIMAVERA

1 cup of 1-inch broccoli pieces
1/2 cup fresh mushroom slices
2 tablespoons margarine
7 ounces fettucini, cooked and
  drained

2 cups chopped tomatoes
1/2 cup grated Parmesan
  cheese
1/4 teaspoon oregano leaves
1/4 teaspoon basil leaves

Sauté broccoli and mushrooms in margarine. Toss with fettucini and combined remaining ingredients; heat thoroughly. Sprinkle with additional cheese, if desired.

Yield: 6 servings   *Barbara Schwing*

SPAGHETTI WITH GREEN SAUCE

1 (16-ounce) package fine
  spaghetti, cooked
  according to directions
2 tablespoons whole basil
2 tablespoons parsley
1/4 cup butter
1/2 teaspoon pepper

1 (8-ounce) package cream
  cheese
1/3 cup grated Parmesan
  cheese
1/4 cup olive oil
1 clove garlic, minced
2/3 cup boiling water

Add chopped parsley and basil to butter. Blend in cream cheese, olive oil, garlic and pepper. Cream well. Add boiling water when ready to serve. Serve over spaghetti. Serve with meat as side dish and salad of your choice.

Yield: 8 servings   *Terrence Knight Benoit*

VERMICELLI VINAIGRETTE

4 ounces broken vermicelli
  or spaghetti
½ cup salad oil
¼ cup red wine vinegar
1 large clove garlic, minced
¼ teaspoon salt
⅛ teaspoon pepper
1 (6-ounce) jar marinated
  artichoke hearts, drained
  and chopped

¼ teaspoon dried basil,
  crushed
1 cup sliced fresh mushrooms
2 tomatoes, peeled, seeded,
  and chopped
½ cup chopped walnuts,
  toasted
2 tablespoons snipped parsley

Cook pasta in boiling salted water. Rinse and drain. In screw-top jar combine oil, vinegar, garlic, salt, the basil and pepper; shake well. Toss about ⅓ cup dressing with the pasta; cover and chill. Toss the remaining dressing with the artichoke hearts and mushrooms; cover and chill. To serve, toss together pasta, artichoke mixture, tomatoes, walnuts and parsley. Serve in a lettuce-lined bowl.

Yield: 8 servings

Barbara Schwing

RICE AND MUSHROOM CASSEROLE

1 medium onion, chopped
½ cup margarine
3 beef bouillon cubes
2 cups boiling water/
  mushroom liquid (save
  liquid from the canned
  mushrooms and add to
  water to equal 2 cups)

1 cup raw rice
1 (8-ounce) can of mushrooms
Chopped parsley
Chopped onion tops (about 3
  tablespoons)

Sauté onion in margarine. Dissolve bouillon in the 2 cups of water/mushroom liquid. In a 1½ quart oven-proof dish, combine the sautéed onions with the raw rice. Add the 2 cups of bouillon mixture and stir. Top with the drained mushrooms, parsley and chopped onion tops. Cover and bake in 325° oven for 40 minutes.

This recipe can easily be doubled. Cooking time should be extended to about 50 minutes. Also freezes well.

Yield: 5 servings

Shereen Minvielle

SEAFOOD RICE CASSEROLE

1 stick margarine
½ bell pepper, chopped
1 stalk celery, chopped
½ onion, chopped
4 green onions, chopped
½ cup parsley, minced
1 (4-ounce) jar pimento
1 recipe, doubled Cream of
   Mushroom Soup page 57

1 cup grated Cheddar cheese
1 (6-ounce) can crab meat, or
  1 package crawfish, or
  1 pound shrimp or a
  combination of all three
2 cups cooked rice
Bread crumbs

Sauté bell pepper, celery, onion, green onions and parsley in margarine. Add pimento, soups, and seafood. Fold in rice and put in casserole and sprinkle with bread crumbs. Bake at 325° about 30 minutes.

Yield: 6-8 servings   *Jackie Turnage*

Note: 1 can cream of mushroom soup and 1 can Cheddar cheese soup may be substituted for sauce.

WILD RICE CASSEROLE

1 cup wild rice
3 cups water
1 teaspoon salt
⅓ cup melted butter
1 finely chopped small onion
1 (4-ounce) small can chopped
   mushrooms, drained

3 stalks celery, finely chopped
1 can consommé or 1 beef
  bouillon cube dissolved in
  1 cup boiling water

Wash the wild rice with water running through the rice in a wire strainer until the water runs clear. Cover the rice with fresh water and soak it several hours or overnight. Heat 3 cups water and 1 teaspoon of salt to boiling. Add rice, cover and simmer slowly for 30-45 minutes until rice is tender but not mushy. Sauté onion, mushrooms and celery in butter, add consomme and combine with the cooked rice in a casserole. Cover and bake 30 minutes at 350°

Yield: 4-6 servings   *Arthur C. Tomlinson*

WILD RICE AND OYSTER CASSEROLE

1 (6-ounce) package wild rice
2½ cups water
1 tablespoon margarine
1 cup sliced fresh mushrooms
2 tablespoons margarine
1 (12-ounce) jar oysters
  (reserve liquid)
3 tablespoons flour

¼ cup oyster liquid
¼ cup Half & Half
¼ cup chopped parsley
¼ teaspoon salt
½ cup sliced celery
2 tablespoons dry sherry
Bread crumbs

Cook contents of wild rice and seasoning packets with water and 1 tablespoon margarine. While rice cooks sauté mushrooms in 2 tablespoons margarine for 5 minutes. Add drained oysters and cook about 5 minutes longer; until edges curl. Stir in flour, then stir in combined oyster liquid and Half & Half. Cook, stirring until thickened and smooth. Add parsley and salt. When rice is cooked, combine with oyster mixture, celery, sherry and mix well. Turn into greased 1½ quart baking dish; sprinkle with bread crumbs. Can be refrigerated at this point or bake at 350° for 20 minutes. Add 15 minutes baking time if refrigerated.

Yield: 6-8 servings

Yolanda Trahan

CURRIED RICE

½ cup chopped onion
1 (4-ounce) can mushrooms,
  reserve liquid
1 stick butter

1 teaspoon curry powder
1 cup consommé
¾ cup rice

Sauté onion and mushrooms with butter. Add curry powder, consommé and rice. Add water to mushroom liquid to make ¼ cup and add to the above. Bring to a boil, stir once. Lower heat to simmer; cover. Cook 20 to 30 minutes.

Yield: 4 servings

Candy B. Romero

GREEN RICE

2 cups Konriko Wild Pecan
   Rice
2 eggs well beaten
½ cup milk
½ cup oil
1 (10-ounce) package frozen
   chopped broccoli

1 pound Velveeta cheese
½ cup chopped onions
1 teaspoon Konriko Creole
   Seasoning
1 recipe Cream of Mushroom
   Soup page 57

Cook rice according to directions. Mix all together and bake at 350° (uncovered) in a casserole which has been oiled. Cook for 50 minutes. Can use more rice and more mushroom soup to serve more people and is still good.

Yield: 4-6 servings   *Sandy Davis*

Note: Canned soup may be substituted.

JAMBALAYA

1 pound shrimp
2 tablespoons lard
1 medium onion
½ bell pepper
2 cloves garlic

1 slice raw ham
1 (8-ounce) can tomato sauce
1½ cups raw rice
Salt and pepper to taste

Cook shrimp; reserve 2 cups of liquid. Have the lard very hot in a frying pan, then put in the onion, bell pepper and garlic, which have been minced very fine. Add shrimp and minced ham, sauté for a few minutes; then add tomato sauce and rice; add shrimp water. Season with salt and pepper. Boil until rice is well done. Serve very hot.

Yield: 6-8 servings   *A Weeks Family recipe*

BLACK-EYED PEA JAMBALAYA

1 pound sausage, sliced
1 medium onion, minced
½ cup bell pepper, minced
2 tablespoons oil
2 cups rice
2½ cups beef broth

1 (15-ounce) can black-eyed
  peas
1 cup cubed ham
½ tablespoon Worcestershire
  sauce

In a medium saucepan cover sliced sausage with water and bring to a boil. Drain and set aside. In a large Dutch oven, sauté onions and bell pepper in oil until onion is transparent. Add rice and simmer until rice begins to fry, then add broth, peas, ham, sausage. Let liquid come to a boil, stir well, add Worcestershire sauce, lower heat, cover and cook for about 30 minutes.

Yield: 8 servings

JoAnn H. Lasserre

CHICKEN JAMBALAYA

Take one 3 pound chicken. Season highly with salt and pepper and rub well with garlic. Joint the chicken and cut into pieces. Put one heaping tablespoon of lard in a deep skillet and fry chicken until it is a golden brown. Remove from fire and have ready one sweet pepper, two large onions and two cloves of garlic. Fry in lard until brown. Wash 1½ cups rice and add to lard and onions, Cook until light brown stirring all the time. Add chicken to rice and enough boiling water to cover, about 1 inch over. After all the water has cooked out, take a fork and lift (gently) the mixture. Add chopped green onions and parsley, also season highly with salt and pepper.

Yield: 8 servings

Note: This recipe has been left exactly as written by Mrs. Weeks.

CHICKEN AND SAUSAGE JAMBALAYA

1 cup onions, chopped
½ cup bell pepper, chopped
¼ cup celery, chopped
4 cups chicken stock
2 cups chicken, cooked, deboned and cubed
2 pounds smoked sausage, bite size

3 cups raw rice
1 teaspoon salt
½ teaspoon red pepper
½ teaspoon black pepper
5 or 6 dashes Tabasco pepper sauce
¼ teaspoon basil
1½ teaspoons thyme

Cook onions, bell pepper and celery in the chicken stock until tender. Add the remaining ingredients and cook in a large dutch oven (black cast iron preferably) on top of the stove over a low fire for 1½ hours. DO NOT RAISE LID UNTIL READY TO SERVE.

Yield: 6-8 servings   *Gigi and Alex Patout*

VEGETABLE RICE

¾ cup chopped onion
1 pound zucchini, thinly sliced
3 tablespoons butter
1 cup whole kernel corn, drained (fresh or canned)

1 cup chopped tomatoes (fresh or canned)
3 cups cooked rice
1½ teaspoons salt
¼ teaspoon pepper
¼ teaspoon ground coriander

Sauté onions and zucchini in butter until tender. Add remaining ingredients. Cover and simmer 15 minutes.

Yield: 6 servings

CAJUN RICE DRESSING I

3 pounds of ground chicken gizzards
2 pounds of ground chicken livers
3 pounds of ground beef
3 pounds of ground pork
2 cups oil
Salt and pepper to taste
2 cups flour
1-2 bunches of celery, finely chopped
5 large onions, finely chopped
5 large bell peppers, finely chopped
2 quarts hot water
15 bouillon cubes (chicken or beef)
5 pounds of long grain rice
¾ bottle Tabasco pepper sauce
2 bunches parsley, chopped
2 bunches green onions, chopped

Sauté meat in ½ cup of oil until brown. Add salt and pepper to taste. In another large pot make a roux with flour and the remaining 1½ cups of oil. Cook until dark brown, stirring constantly. Add finely chopped or ground celery, onions and 3 bell peppers (use food processor if possible). Cook vegetables in roux on low fire, cover pot, stir frequently until vegetables are wilted and soft. Add 2 quarts of hot water. Add bouillon cubes. Add meat mixture and raw rice. Stir and bring to a rolling boil on high heat. Stir once again. Lower heat until mixture is simmering slowly. Cover pot and cook until rice is done (about 1½ hours). Just before serving add Tabasco pepper sauce, parsley, green onions and the remaining 2 chopped bell peppers. Do not cook any longer. Toss gently. Taste for seasonings and correct if necessary.

This Cajun Rice may be frozen for a short period of time.

Yield: 50 servings   *Lona Smith*

CAJUN RICE DRESSING II

1 pound chicken livers
1 pound gizzards
¼ cup vegetable oil
3 onions, chopped
2 bell peppers, chopped
2 stalks celery, chopped
1 tablespoon dark roux
   (see page 48)

3 cups chicken stock
Salt and pepper to taste
½ cup chopped green onion
   tops
½ cup chopped parsley
4 cups cooked rice

In food processor, purée the livers and gizzards until very fine. Heat oil and add livers, gizzards, onions, bell pepper and celery; cook over a medium fire, stirring often for 45 minutes or until the meat is well cooked. Add roux, chicken stock, salt and pepper; cook for another 20 minutes.

When ready to serve, mix hot mixture with the onion tops, parsley and cooked rice. The dressing may be made one to two days ahead of mixing with rice, onion tops and parsley.

Yield: 6-8 servings   *Alex and Gigi Patout*

RICE AND OYSTER DRESSING

3 tablespoons cooking oil
1 large onion, chopped
1½ pounds ground meat
Chicken giblets (optional)
½ cup green onions, chopped

½ cup chopped parsley
1½ cups chopped celery
4 to 5 dozen oysters, drained
3 cups cooked rice, cooled
Salt

Heat cooking oil and brown finely chopped onion. Add ground meat and giblets and cook until brown in color. Add green onions, parsley, celery and salt and cook a little longer. Add oysters and then rice and mix well. Put into turkey to cook or bake in casserole 45 minutes, at 325.°

Yield: 6-8 servings   *A Weeks Family recipe*
                              Submitted by Margaret G. Weeks

Note: My mother never could give me a recipe, so I watched as she made this one year, wrote down the ingredients as she had me chop or get them ready. Thus I had her recipe of many years.

RICE, SHRIMP AND OYSTER DRESSING

1 tablespoon salad oil
1 tablespoon flour
1 tablespoon onion, chopped
1 tablespoon celery, chopped
1½ cups water

3 cups cooked rice
¾ cup shrimp, cooked
¾ cup oysters, drained
2 tablespoons parsley
2 tablespoons onion tops

Make a brown roux with oil and flour. Add onion and celery and the water. Bring to a boil for 10 minutes. Add cooked rice, shrimp, oysters, parsley and onion tops. Stir lightly and let steam for 15 minutes on low fire.

Yield: 6-8 servings

Penny Fenton

MEATS

Circa 1917

When Weeks Hall returned to New Iberia after serving in World War I, the outbuildings at the Shadows were in the state of disrepair shown in the photograph above. The buildings were too far gone to be saved, though they had once been a vital part of life at the Shadows, housing the kitchen, the school, and the slaves.

Kitchens for antebellum houses were commonly separate buildings. This prevented the heat and cooking odors from permeating the main house and also decreased the chance of fire. Two of the original outbuildings at the Shadows were cabins for slaves. The Weekses would have had just enough slaves on the property in town to make up a household staff.

The cistern for storing fresh water was located near the kitchen. The Shadows' original cistern was underground and stored rain water. Both bayou and well water were too dirty for drinking; thus the cleaner rain water was piped down to the cistern from the gutters along the roof and drawn up in a bucket. Later, an above-ground barrel cistern with a spigot replaced the original. The old underground cistern still provides a unique charm for the grounds of the Shadows. It and the original lightning rods still attached to the Shadows are favorites of visitors.

Meats

BEEF
Smothering-Cajun Style 149
Brisket 149
Brisket with Mop Sauce 150
Daube and Potatoes 150
Daube Glacé 151
Dry Fried 151
East Indian Curry 153
Party, with Herb Biscuits 152
Peppered 153
Short Ribs, Sweet and Sour 154
Stew Bake 154
Stew, Daddy's 155
Stroganoff 155

STEAK
Filet, Stuffed Tenderloin 156
Flank, Grilled and Mushrooms 157
Pepper 156
Round, Sauerbraten 157
Round, Smothered with Onions . . . 158
San Marco 158
Sugar 159

GROUND BEEF
Beef in Eggplant Baskets 159
Chili, for Hot Dogs (Shadows) 160
Chili, Missouri 160
Chili, Sante Fe 161
Enchilada Casserole, Green 161
Hot Tamales 162

Kibbie, Baked, Bill Sinee 163
Meatballs and Spaghetti, French
   Style 165
Meatballs, Mamma Vita's 164
Spaghetti, Holiday 165

LAMB
Crown Roast 166
Leg of, with Mustard-Crumb
   Coating 166
Rolled Shoulder of, and Yams 167
Shanks in Red Wine 167

PORK
Chop Casserole 168
Ham Kabobs-Brussels Sprouts 168
Honduras 169

SAUSAGE
Boudin 169
Cajun, Fresh 170
Pedigreed, and Peppers 170
Swiss Loaf 171

VEAL
Daube Glacé (Veal) 171
Osso Bucco 176
Pies with Mushrooms 172
Ragoût with Onions and
   Chestnuts 174
Risotto 173
Scaloppine a la Marsala 175
Scaloppini 175

Refer to additional recipes in "How Men Cook" section.

SMOTHERING—CAJUN STYLE

This is a technique used by most Cajun cooks. The meat may be of your choice; for example: round steak, shoulder steak, 7-steak, chuck and stew meat.

1 black iron Dutch oven is considered necessary for success, but any heavy covered pot may be used.

1 round roast	3 onions, chopped
Salt, red and black pepper	2 bell peppers, chopped
Garlic for stuffing	1 stalk celery, chopped
Flour for dredging	1 cup water
½ cup vegetable oil	

Season roast with salt and pepper; cut pockets in roast and stuff with garlic. Dredge roast in flour and shake off excess. Brown roast on all sides in hot oil. Remove the roast and set aside. Pour off excess oil leaving about 1 teaspoon. Add ½ of the onions, bell pepper, celery mixture and water. Return roast to pot and add the remaining onion, bell pepper, celery mixture on top of roast. Cover and cook over low heat or in a 300° oven.

When is it done? There are many factors to this answer, but this is a nice guide to be used. TASTE! If it is not the tenderest piece of meat you have ever tasted, LET IT COOK SOME MORE!

Yield: 1 roast   *Gigi and Alex Patout*

BRISKET

10 to 12 pounds brisket	1½ cups vegetable oil
Salt, red and black pepper	½ cup fresh lemon juice
Accent	1 cup dry red wine
Garlic salt	2 tablespoons Worcestershire
Dry mustard	sauce
	2 tablespoons dried parsley

Season brisket heavily with salt, red and black pepper, Accent and garlic salt. Coat with dry mustard. Place in marinade of oil, lemon juice, wine, parsley and Worcestershire sauce. Bake in marinade at 225° for 8 to 10 hours, depending on size of brisket, or until fork tender.

Yield: 16 servings   *Dot Broussard*

BRISKET WITH MOP SAUCE

5 to 6 pound brisket, trimmed
of fat
1/3 cup chili powder

1 1/2 tablespoons ground black
pepper
1 tablespoon garlic powder

Coat brisket with chili powder, pepper and garlic powder. Bake at 250° for 8 hours. Baste with mop sauce once every hour.

MOP SAUCE
1 (10 1/2-ounce) can beef
consommé
1 1/3 cups water
3/4 cup Worcestershire sauce
1/3 cup cider vinegar
1/3 cup oil (optional)
1 1/2 teaspoons Accent

1 1/2 teaspoons dry mustard
2 cloves garlic, pressed
1 teaspoon chili powder
1 teaspoon Tabasco pepper
sauce
1 bay leaf
1/2 teaspoon paprika

Mix all ingredients and baste.

Barbeque Grill: pour sauce over brisket in foil-lined pan. Seal the foil well and cook over hot coals at least 3 hours, or until tender.

Yield: 8-10 servings   *A Friend of the Shadows*

DAUBE AND POTATOES

4 to 5 pounds round steak, cut
2 inches thick
Salt
Red and black pepper
2 pods garlic, cut in half

1/3 cup cooking oil
2 cups water
10 red potatoes, 2 inches in
diameter, peeled and
rubbed with salt

Use a black iron Dutch oven of a diameter large enough for the steak to lie flat. Score the meat at 2 inch intervals all around. Make several slits in the meat and stuff with salt, red pepper, and black pepper, followed by pieces of garlic. Heat the oil in Dutch oven and sear the meat on both sides. Add 2 cups water, cover tightly, and lower heat. Cook this way for 3 1/2 hours on a heat high enough for the gravy to bubble around the meat, adding water in small amounts as needed. When the meat is nearly done, (the longer it cooks, the better it tastes) drop the potatoes around the meat and continue cooking until potatoes are tender (approximately 30 minutes). Turn potatoes once during the cooking. This dish takes a long time to prepare and must be checked regularly, but the effort will certainly be worth it at meal time!

Yield: 8-10 servings   *Elma Minvielle*

DAUBE GLACÉ

10 pounds beef, top round
   roast
6 cloves garlic
1 large onion
½ teaspoon whole allspice
Salt, pepper and Tabasco
   pepper sauce, 2 teaspoons
   each (at least)
½ cup vegetable oil

2 large onions
4 stalks celery
2 bell peppers
4 tablespoons chopped
   parsley
4 tablespoons chopped chives
2 envelopes gelatin
1 cup water

Make pockets in roast with a sharp knife. Mince garlic and onion; mix with salt, pepper, allspice and Tabasco sauce. Stuff into pockets in roast. Rub outside of roast with more salt, pepper and Tabasco sauce. Place in refrigerator, covered, overnight. Heat oil in large heavy pot. Add roast and brown well. Add onions, celery and bell pepper. Cook slowly in covered pot until tender; add water as needed to make gravy. Should be done in approximately 2 hours. Remove the roast, cool and slice. Stack in a long, flat glass serving dish.

To make gelatin: Strain gravy. You should have about 2 cups. Add chopped parsley and chives to gravy. Reheat and pour over 2 envelopes gelatin that have been soaking in 1 cup water. If you do not have enough beef gravy, you can dissolve a bouillon cube in enough hot water to make 2 cups gravy. Cool and pour over roast slices. Refrigerate until firm. May be served as an appetizer.

Lanier Simmons

DRY FRIED BEEF

Shred very thin slices of beef against the grain. Marinate with quite a bit of:

Soy sauce
Coarsely chopped green
   onions
Coarsely ground red pepper
Sugar

Dash of salt
Chopped garlic
Chopped fresh ginger
1 teaspoon olive or
   sesame oil

Let this stand for 2 hours or more. Put some cooking oil in pan, pour beef in pan and stir fry until almost dry. When ready to serve, heat meat, add celery or finely shredded carrots or sliced asparagus, stir and serve.

Charlotte Dann

Note: Above recipe may be used substituting pork for beef and green beans (fresh) for celery, carrots or asparagus. This must be cooked for quite awhile.

151

PARTY BEEF WITH HERB BISCUITS

3 pounds lean beef stew meat
(cut into ¾-inch cubes)
¼ cup flour
2 teaspoons salt
¼ teaspoon pepper
3 tablespoons vegetable
shortening
2 large onions, sliced
4 cups hot water
2 beef bouillon cubes

1 (8-ounce) package fresh
mushrooms (sliced)
8 whole cloves (tied together
in cheesecloth bag)
8 whole allspice (tied together
in cheesecloth bag)
8 small onions
2 cups sliced carrots
1 cup sliced celery

Dredge meat in flour, mixed with salt and pepper. Brown meat in vegetable shortening. Slice the 2 large onions and add to the meat with 2 cups of water, bouillon cubes, mushrooms, clove and allspice combination. Cover tightly and cook in a 350° oven for 2 hours; stir occasionally. Add remaining onions, carrots, celery, 2 cups water and 1 teaspoon salt; cover and return to oven for 30 minutes.

HERB BISCUITS
2 cups prepared biscuit mix
½ teaspoon summer savory
2 teaspoons chopped parsley

⅔ cup milk
⅓ cup melted margarine
or butter

Combine biscuit mix, savory and parsley and mix well. Add milk and ¼ cup margarine. Stir just until dry ingredients are moist. Drop by teaspoonsful around edge of cooked stew. Drizzle remaining butter over biscuits. Turn temperature to 400° Allow biscuits to bake and lightly brown, about 20 minutes.

Yield: 6-8 servings

Yolanda V. Trahan

EAST INDIAN BEEF CURRY

1 cup onions, coarsely
   chopped
1/2 cup celery, coarsely
   chopped
1 stick butter
3 to 4 pounds sirloin steak,
   cut into 1/2-inch cubes
2 (6-ounce) cans tomato paste
2 cups applesauce
1 1/2 cups red wine

1 1/2 cups water
2 tablespoons "Hot Madras"
   curry powder (Regular
   curry powder may be
   substituted. However, add
   more than a dash of red
   pepper.)
Dash of red pepper
Salt and pepper to taste

In a large Dutch oven, cook onion and celery in butter until soft. Add meat and cook until brown. Stir in tomato paste, applesauce, wine, water, curry powder and red pepper. Simmer 45 minutes. Serve over cooked, white long grain rice seasoned with saffron. This is better if made a day ahead.

Top with any of the following condiments: Chopped egg, bacon, green onion, chutney, coconut, peanuts, cucumbers in sour cream or bananas.

Yield: 4-6 servings   *Cathy Kwong*

PEPPERED BEEF

This recipe has been used for many occasions held at The Shadows; it has become a favorite.

8-9 pound eye of round roast   **Cracked black pepper**

Cover roast completely with cracked black pepper. Place in a metal pan and bake for 5 minutes per pound at 500.° Turn oven off but do not open oven door. Continue to cook for a total of two hours. Remove and let cool, thinly slice and serve.

Yield: 16-18 servings   *Betsy Holleman*

Option: Puréed garlic may be rubbed on roast before covering with pepper.

SWEET AND SOUR SHORT RIBS

2-3 pounds stew meat or 5
  pounds short ribs
½ cup flour
2 teaspoons salt
Pepper to taste
2 cups sliced onions

2 tablespoons vinegar
2 tablespoons Worcestershire
  sauce
¾ cup catsup
4 tablespoons soy sauce
¾ cup water

Cut meat into 1½ to 2 inch squares. Mix flour, salt, pepper and coat meat. Put in oven proof casserole. Cover with onions. Mix rest of ingredients, pour over. Cover and bake at 300° for 3 hours. Serve with cooked rice or noodles.

Yield: 4-6 servings   *Trish Fletcher*

BEEF STEW BAKE

1½ pounds beef stew meat
2 tablespoons cooking oil
1 (10-ounce) can Franco-
  American mushroom gravy
1 (6-ounce) can tomato juice

¼ cup dry onion soup mix
1 teaspoon horseradish
4 medium potatoes, pared and
  quartered

In a heavy skillet, brown meat in hot oil, drain off excess fat. Add mushroom gravy, tomato juice, onion soup mix and horseradish. Simmer, covered, 5 minutes. Place potatoes in bottom of 2 quart casserole, top with meat mixture. Bake, covered, in a moderate oven (350°) for 1½ hours or until meat and potatoes are tender, stirring once or twice during baking.

Yield: 6 servings   *Charlotte Guinn*

DADDY'S STEW

3 pounds lean stew meat
1 (16-ounce) can diced carrots
1 (15-ounce) can small onions
1 (16-ounce) can tomatoes
1 (16-ounce) can tiny peas
1 (15-ounce) can whole green
   beans
½ cup wine (red or white)

1½ tablespoons of salt and
   pepper or use equal
   amounts of Tony's Creole
   Seasoning
4 tablespoons of tapioca
1 tablespoon brown sugar
½ cup bread crumbs
1 bay leaf
½ cup beef consommé

Drain all vegetables except tomatoes. Mix all ingredients together and bake at 250° for 6 to 7 hours covered.

Can be made in a slow cooker.

Yield: 6-8 servings   *Cathy Gibbens*

BEEF STROGANOFF

13 pounds roast, cut up
2 cups flour
12 onions
Shortening, enough to sauté
   onions and meat
2 (32-ounce) bottles of
   Beefamato
1 (12-ounce) can tomato juice
Bay leaves

½ cup soy sauce
½ cup Worcestershire sauce
Tabasco pepper sauce, salt,
   red pepper and paprika
   to taste
2 cloves garlic, minced
2 pounds fresh mushrooms
3 pints sour cream

Season flour with salt, pepper, paprika and red pepper. Shake meat in flour mixture and brown. Remove meat and sauté onions in the flour and oil mixture left in pot. Add remaining ingredients except mushrooms and sour cream; cook until tender. This should be done a day ahead. When reheating, add the mushrooms. Add the sour cream immediately before serving.

Yield: 30 servings   *Adele Forrest*

STUFFED TENDERLOIN FILET

1 bunch green onions,
  chopped fine
1 pound fresh mushrooms,
  chopped fine
½ stick butter
1 pint fresh oysters, drained,
  cut each into 4 pieces

½ to 1 cup fresh bread crumbs
1 egg
½ cup finely chopped parsley
Salt and pepper to taste
5-6 pound filet mignon
  (whole strip)

BASTING SAUCE
1 stick butter, melted
¼ cup hot English mustard

½ cup brandy

Sauté green onions and mushrooms in ½ stick butter about 5 minutes. Add oysters, cook 5 minutes more, remove from heat and add bread crumbs to make moist dressing. Add egg, parsley, salt and pepper to taste. Cut a deep slit the length of the filet. Stuff with dressing and tie with string. Broil over charcoal or roast in a 500° oven. Baste occasionally. Cook 25 minutes. Let cool to room temperature before slicing.

Yield: 8-10 servings

Ellen Minvielle

PEPPER STEAK

1 pound round steak, cut in
  bite size pieces
2 tablespoons oil
¼ cup chopped onion
1 clove garlic
1 teaspoon salt
Pepper to taste
1 beef bouillon cube

2 cups hot water
1 large bell pepper, sliced
1 (10-ounce) can Rotel
  tomatoes
2 tablespoons corn starch
½ cup cold water
2 tablespoons soy sauce

Brown steak in oil; add onions and garlic. Season with salt and pepper. Dissolve bouillon cube in hot water, add to meat, cover, simmer until meat is tender, 20-25 minutes. Add tomatoes and bell pepper, cook 10 minutes longer. Combine remaining ingredients, stir into meat mixture. Bring to boil. Cook, stirring constantly 15 minutes longer. Serve over rice.

Yield: 4 servings

Jackie Turnage

GRILLED FLANK STEAK AND MUSHROOMS

¾ cup oil
¾ cup soy sauce
½ cup Worcestershire sauce
½ cup wine vinegar
⅓ cup lemon juice
½ cup red wine (optional)
2 tablespoons dry mustard

2 teaspoons salt
1 teaspoon black pepper, coarse ground
1 teaspoon red pepper
2 cloves garlic, crushed and chopped
2 large onions, thinly sliced

Mix all ingredients; place in plastic bag, one gallon size.

6 pounds flank steak (allow ⅓ to ½ pound per person)
2 pounds fresh mushrooms, cleaned

2 tablespoons chopped green onion tops
½ stick butter

Marinate steak in plastic bag for at least 8 hours, turning to coat. Remove steak from marinade and grill on *hot* grill 6 minutes per side for medium to medium rare. Slice thinly on the diagonal. Sauté mushrooms and green onion tops in melted butter until lightly browned. Add remainder of marinade to skillet and serve hot with steak.

Yield: 4 cups marinade, 12 servings   *Sherry Landry*

ROUND STEAK SAUERBRATEN

1½ pounds round steak, ½ inch thick
1 tablespoon oil
1 envelope brown gravy mix
2 cups water (the mix will call for 1 cup, but use 2)
1 tablespoon onion flakes
1 bay leaf

2 tablespoons red wine vinegar
2 tablespoons brown sugar
½ teaspoon salt
¼ teaspoon pepper
½ teaspoon ground or fresh ginger
1 teaspoon Worcestershire sauce

Cut meat in 1 inch squares and brown in oil. Remove meat and add gravy mix and water; bring this to a boil while stirring. Stir in rest of ingredients and return meat to pan; cover and simmer 1½ hours. The gravy may be thickened and served over buttered noodles.

Yield: 4-5 servings   *Curtis Thomas*

SMOTHERED ROUND STEAK
WITH ONIONS

2½ to 3 pounds round steak,
cut into serving-size pieces
Salt
Red pepper
Black pepper

3 tablespoons cooking oil
2 cups coarsely chopped
onions
1½ cups water

Season the steak with the salt, red pepper and black pepper. In a 3 quart black iron Dutch oven, brown the steak in the cooking oil over a medium-high fire. Remove steak from Dutch oven and pour in 1 cup of the chopped onions. Brown onions for about 2 minutes, stirring. Add steak and stir again, distributing onions well. Pour 1½ cups water over meat and cover, reducing heat to a brisk simmer. Simmer the meat for at least 40 minutes (an hour is better) stirring occasionally and adding small amounts of water as needed to keep the meat from drying out. About 5 minutes before serving time, stir in the other cup of onions and raise fire to medium heat. Cook on medium heat until these onions are tender.

Yield: 5-6 servings

Shereen Minvielle

STEAK SAN MARCO

Whole round steak
1 envelope onion soup mix
1 (16-ounce) can peeled
tomatoes with liquid
1 tablespoon oregano

Garlic powder and pepper
to taste
2 tablespoons oil
2 tablespoons wine vinegar

Cut meat in serving size pieces and place in Dutch oven. Sprinkle onion soup mix on top and lay tomatoes with liquid over this. Add remaining ingredients. Cover and simmer over low heat for 1½ hours. Gravy may be thickened and served over rice.

Yield: 4 servings

Curtis Thomas

SUGAR STEAK

4 to 5 inch thick sirloin steak   **Salt and pepper to taste**
2 to 3 cups sugar

Let steak reach room temperature. Pound sugar into steak until heavily coated. Let stand for 1 or 2 hours; continue to coat during that time. It is necessary to have an adjustable grill to prepare steak.

Cook over medium charcoal fire. Place grill close to coals and cook 6 to 7 minutes on first side. Turn, cooking 5 to 6 minutes. BOTH SIDES WILL FLAME AND THIS IS NECESSARY TO SEAL IN JUICES.

Raise grill and cook 25 minutes on each side to produce medium rare steak. Salt and pepper at this time. Slice into ¼ inch servings on a well-and-tree board to capture juices.

Yield: 10-12 servings   *Virginia Kyle Hine*

BEEF IN EGGPLANT BASKETS

2 large eggplants, cut in half   **1 (12-ounce) can tomato sauce**
**   with pulp removed (leave**   **1 teaspoon salt**
**   ½ inch thick wall)**   **½ cup beer**
½ stick margarine   **½ pound Mozzarella cheese,**
1 pound ground beef   **   sliced thin**
1 (1½-ounce) package
**   spaghetti sauce mix**

Cut eggplant pulp into small cubes and cook in margarine until soft and slightly browned, about 8 minutes. Remove eggplant from pan and set aside. Brown beef in same pan. Drain off fat and add eggplant, sauce mix, tomato sauce, salt and beer. Cook over low heat for a few minutes. Place eggplant shells in baking dish. Fill with meat mixture and top with Mozzarella. Bake at 350° for 30-35 minutes.

Yield: 4 servings   *Barbara Schwing*

CHILI

(Used for the Shadows Flea Market as hot dog sauce)

10 pounds ground meat
8 large onions, chopped
6 to 8 stalks celery, chopped
Salt to taste

4 (15-ounce) cans kidney
  beans (reserve 1 can)
4 (16-ounce) cans tomato
  sauce
2 (3½-ounce) jars chili powder

Break up meat in a large pot and add 1 gallon water, bring to a strong boil, then add remaining ingredients and cook down, over a low flame, about 4 to 5 hours, stirring occasionally. Add 1 can mashed kidney beans to thicken chili last 30 minutes of cooking.

Yield: 175 servings as sauce   *Heloise Trahan*

Note: Onions and celery can be placed in processor bowl with tomato sauce and chopped.

MISSOURI CHILI

1 small onion, diced
1 tablespoon butter
2½ to 3 pounds ground beef
1 tablespoon flour
1 (16-ounce) can tomatoes
1 (15-ounce) can kidney beans

2 teaspoons cumin seed
2 teaspoons salt
3½ tablespoons chili powder
1 teaspoon black pepper
1 pint water

Brown onion in butter. Add flour to ground beef. Sauté with onion until meat is well browned. Add tomatoes, beans and seasonings; add 1 pint water. Cover and cook slowly for several hours, stirring occasionally.

Yield: 10-12 servings   *Beverly Shea*

SANTE FE CHILI

1 pound ground beef
1 tablespoon oil
1 (15-ounce) can pinto beans
½ cup chopped onion
Dash red pepper

1 (10½-ounce) can
  condensed tomato soup
1 teaspoon salt
1 teaspoon vinegar
1 to 2 tablespoons chili powder

Brown meat in oil. Add beans with 1 cup liquid. (If not enough liquid in beans, add boiling water to make 1 cup.) Add remaining ingredients. Cover and simmer 30 minutes or longer.

Yield: 4 servings   *Freddie Vanderhider*

GREEN ENCHILADA CASSEROLE

1 pound ground beef
Garlic and pepper to taste
1 (10½-ounce) can cream of
  chicken soup
1 (10½-ounce) can cream of
  mushroom soup

1 (4-ounce) can evaporated
  milk
1 (4-ounce) can chopped
  green chilies
1 package corn tortillas
Shredded Cheddar cheese

Brown beef with garlic and pepper to taste, add soups, milk and chilies. Stir together. Cut tortillas in quarters and line 8 x 8-inch pan. Put half of meat mixture over them, cover again with tortillas, add remainder of meat mixture, cover with cheese. Bake at 350° for 25 minutes.

Yield: 4 servings   *Jackie Turnage*

HOT TAMALES

These are time consuming but well worth the effort.

Soak hot tamale wrappers, (either paper or corn husks) in large bowl of warm water.

BEEF MIXTURE
2½ pounds ground beef
2 onions, chopped
4 cloves garlic
¼ cup white corn meal
4 teaspoons salt

¼ teaspoon red pepper
¼ cup water
1 (12-ounce) can tomato sauce
1 (2½-ounce) can chili powder

CORN MEAL MIXTURE
2 cups white corn meal
¾ teaspoon salt

1 teaspoon black pepper
2 tablespoons chili powder

BROTH
3½ quarts water
4 beef bouillon cubes
Salt to taste

2 to 3 tablespoons chili powder
1 (8-ounce) can tomato sauce

Mix together the beef mixture and set aside. Mix the corn meal and seasonings and place in a large flat dish, such as pie plate.

Take a tamale wrapper from the water, place on the table in front of you. Sprinkle with 1 teaspoon of corn meal mixture. Take a small amount of meat mixture (about ¼ cup) and shape into a cylinder. Roll this in the dry corn meal mixture in the pie plate and place on the tamale wrapper. Sprinkle with about ½ teaspoon of corn meal mixture. Roll tamale wrapper up with meat mixture and corn meal mixture, fold in the sides so the ingredients don't fall out. Layer all of the tamales on a rack in a large steamer and pour boiling broth mixture over stacked tamales. Steam for 1 to 1¼ hours. Can be frozen in boil in bags to be reheated.

Yield: 3-4 dozen   *Barbara Shea*

BAKED KIBBIE
(Kibbie Bill Sinee)

KIBBIE

2 cups cracked wheat
(medium)
4 cups cold water
1 pound heavy beef round
1 small onion, grated
1½ teaspoons salt

1 teaspoon black pepper
½ teaspoon red pepper
½ teaspoon allspice
steak, center cut, trimmed
of all fat and ground twice

Wash wheat the same way you wash rice. Soak wheat in cold water for 1 hour. Drain excess water and squeeze wheat dry of water. In a large bowl mix meat, onion, salt, pepper and spice. Add a small amount of wheat at a time and mix thoroughly. Continue until all is blended thoroughly. Wet hands to mix wheat into meat mixture.

DRESSING

1 pound ground beef
½ cup oil
4 large onions, chopped
1 teaspoon salt

½ teaspoon red pepper
(optional)
½ teaspoon black pepper

Brown meat in oil, add onions and seasonings. Sauté. Remove from fire and add between layers as follows:

Divide kibbie recipe in half. Form the first layer, spreading kibbie evenly in a 9 x 13-inch oiled pan. Spread meat dressing evenly over kibbie layer. Add a second layer of kibbie, spreading evenly over the entire pan. Cut the combined layers into diamond or square-shaped pieces. (This facilitates serving after baking.) Brush the top layer with oil to glaze. Bake at 450° for 15 minutes. Lower oven temperature to 350° and bake for about 30 minutes or until the top is golden brown.

Yield: 10-12 servings   *Mrs. Morris Haik*

Note: Kibbie may be cut into smaller squares and served as an appetizer.

MAMMA VITA'S RED GRAVY
WITH MEAT BALLS

3 large onions, chopped
4 to 5 cloves garlic, minced
1/4 to 1/2 cup vegetable oil
(enough to cover bottom
of medium sized pot)
1 (6-ounce) can tomato paste
2 (18-ounce) cans tomato
paste
1 teaspoon basil, crushed
1 teaspoon oregano, crushed

3 bay leaves
5 to 6 whole allspice
1 tablespoon vinegar
1 teaspoon rosemary, crushed
1 teaspoon thyme, crushed
5 to 6 whole cloves
2 tablespoons sugar
1/2 teaspoon cinnamon
Salt and pepper to taste
1 1/2 to 2 quarts hot water

Cook onions and garlic just until onions begin to wilt. Add tomato paste and stir well. Add seasonings and cook over low heat for 45 minutes to 1 hour, stirring occasionally. Do not let it stick to the bottom of pot. When paste turns a very dark color and oil begins to separate, cook about 30 minutes longer. At this point add hot water, very slowly, at least 1 1/2 to 2 quarts; partially cover and cook at least 6 to 8 hours. You may, at this point, strain your gravy for a nice smooth consistency, cool and refrigerate or freeze. Use for serving over spaghetti, lasagna, veal or eggplant parmigiana. You may also add meat balls or Italian sausage.

Variation: add 1 cup sweet red wine (Mogen David Concord)

MEATBALLS
2 pounds lean ground chuck
1/2 teaspoon oregano
1/2 teaspoon thyme
1/2 to 1 cup seasoned bread
crumbs
Dash of red pepper
2 to 3 cloves garlic, pressed
(or purée)

3 to 4 whole eggs
Salt and pepper to taste
1 to 2 tablespoons each of
finely chopped parsley and
green onion tops
3 tablespoons grated
Parmesan or Romano
cheese

Mix all ingredients well and shape into medium size balls—fry or broil, then place in red gravy.

Yield: 8-10 servings

Yolanda Trahan

FRENCH STYLE MEATBALLS AND SPAGHETTI

1 1/2 pounds ground meat
Garlic powder
Cayenne pepper
Black pepper
Salt
1 egg
1 cup seasoned bread crumbs
1/2 cup cooking oil

3/4 cup flour
1 medium chopped onion
1 medium chopped bell
 pepper
2 cloves garlic, minced
1 (8-ounce) can tomato sauce
Red pepper flakes

Mix first 7 ingredients in a bowl. Roll into meatballs. Brown in Dutch oven in a little oil. Remove, make a roux with the flour and oil, brown until the color of "earth." When roux is done, remove from heat and add onion, bell pepper, garlic, and tomato sauce. Stir. Roux will be so hot it will brown the tomato sauce and wilt vegetables. Add hot water until gravy is a little thicker than you will want to serve it, as the juice from the meatballs will thin the gravy. Season to taste with salt, pepper and red pepper flakes. Return meatballs to gravy. Simmer covered 1 hour. Serve over cooked spaghetti.

Yield: 8 servings

Suzanne O'Neal

HOLIDAY SPAGHETTI

1 cup minced onions
3/4 cup minced green
 onion tops
1 cup sliced mushrooms
3 teaspoons hot shortening
1 pound ground beef

2 teaspoons salt
1 teaspoon sugar
3 1/2 cups cooked tomatoes
Hot, drained, boiled spaghetti
 (8 ounces cooked)
1 cup grated American cheese

Cook onions, onion tops, and mushrooms in shortening until wilted. Add ground beef and cook until browned. Then add and heat salt, sugar, tomatoes and spaghetti. Pour into well-greased 2 quart casserole 8 inches square. Sprinkle with grated American cheese. Bake for 30 minutes at 350°.

Yield: 6-8 servings

Trish Fletcher

Optional: 1 can green peas

CROWN ROAST OF LAMB

Lemon juice
1 (7 to 8 pound) crown roast
    of lamb, all fat removed
Salt and freshly ground pepper
1/2 cup Dijon mustard

2 tablespoons soy sauce
2 garlic cloves, minced
1 teaspoon dried rosemary
    leaves, crumbled
1/4 teaspoon ground marjoram

Preheat oven to 325.° Moisten a paper towel with lemon juice and rub over lamb. Insert meat thermometer into meatiest section of roast, being careful not to touch bone. Place on rack in roasting pan and sprinkle with salt and pepper to taste. Cover tips of bones with foil to prevent burning; crumble additional foil and place in center of roast to help retain shape. Bake until thermometer registers 130° to 135,° depending on desired doneness. Mix remaining ingredients and baste roast periodically.

Yield: 6 servings   *Michael "a catering experience"*

LEG OF LAMB WITH
MUSTARD—CRUMB COATING

1 (6-pound) leg of lamb
2 tablespoons salad oil
1/2 cup Creole-style mustard
2 tablespoons soy sauce
1 clove garlic, minced
1/4 teaspoon ginger

1/2 teaspoon Tabasco pepper
    sauce
1 teaspoon dried thyme
1 tablespoon chopped chives
1/2 cup fine dry bread crumbs

In medium bowl combine oil, mustard, soy sauce, garlic, ginger, Tabasco, thyme and chives. Spread on lamb, then sprinkle with bread crumbs and let stand 1 hour. Place lamb on roasting rack. Roast in 350° oven 1 1/2 hours. Chill after baking. To carve, place on board or platter, meatier side up. Starting from small end of leg, cut parallel slices down to leg bone. Then cut away slices by running carving knife under slices, along leg bone.

Yield: 8 servings   *A Friend of the Shadows*

LAMB SHANKS IN RED WINE

Oil
Lamb shanks (1 or 2 per
   person)
1 clove garlic for each shank
Salt and black pepper
¼ teaspoon Tabasco pepper
   sauce
Rosemary
Red wine

Oil lamb shanks well. Place in a baking dish in a single layer. Purée garlic over them; sprinkle with salt and black pepper. Add ¼ teaspoon Tabasco pepper sauce and strew with a generous amount of rosemary. Pour in a good red wine to a depth of about ½ inch. Bake in a 350° oven for an hour or so, until tender. Turn the shanks at least once during the cooking and baste. Don't cook too long, lest they become dry and stringy.

A Friend of the Shadows

ROLLED SHOULDER OF LAMB AND YAMS

6 pounds boned, rolled
   shoulder of lamb
1 tablespoon cornstarch
½ teaspoon each: salt, ginger
   and cinnamon
8 whole cloves
1 cup water
½ cup honey
2 tablespoons butter or
   margarine
1 teaspoon grated lemon peel
¼ cup lemon juice
1 red apple, cored and thinly
   sliced
3 (17-ounce) cans Bruce's
   Whole Yams, drained
1 lemon, sliced and notched
Coarse ground black pepper
Parsley

Place lamb on rack in shallow roasting pan. Bake slowly in 325° oven 3½ hours; drain off drippings. While lamb is roasting, mix together cornstarch, salt and spices in a saucepan. Blend in water and honey; cook and stir until mixture boils ½ minute. Reserve ¼ cup for lamb. Add butter, lemon peel, lemon juice and apple slices to remaining sauce. Stir and heat until butter melts; pour over yams and lemon slices in shallow baking dish. Bake lamb 30 minutes longer or until meat thermometer registers 175° to 180.° Brush lamb with reserved sauce; sprinkle with pepper. Bake yam casserole with lamb the last 30 minutes. Garnish lamb with parsley and surround with yams, as desired.

Yield: 8 servings

Bruce's Foods

HAM KABOBS—BRUSSELS SPROUTS

3 medium carrots, cut in 1 inch chunks and cooked 12-15 minutes in boiling, salted water
1 pound fully cooked ham, cut in 1 inch cubes

1 (10-ounce) package frozen brussels sprouts, cooked according to package directions

Marinate above ingredients overnight. Next day, thread ham and vegetables alternately on skewers. Broil 5 minutes. Do both sides and brush with more marinade.

MARINADE
½ cup oil
¼ cup red wine vinegar
Black pepper, to taste

1 envelope Italian dressing mix

Yield: 4 servings

Barbara Schwing

PORK CHOP CASSEROLE

6 pork chops
6 tablespoons raw rice
3 tablespoons water
1 tomato, sliced
½ bell pepper, sliced

1 onion, sliced
4 mushrooms, sliced
½ teaspoon oregano
1 (10½-ounce) can consommé

Brown pork chops in skillet; set aside. Place raw rice (not minute rice) in bottom of baking dish. Place chops on top of rice. Pour 1 large kitchen spoon (about 3 tablespoons) of water in skillet, scrape the drippings and then pour it over the chops. Arrange slice of a tomato on each chop, also bell pepper, onion slices and mushrooms (if desired). Sprinkle ½ teaspoon oregano over all. Add one can consommé, cover dish tightly and cook in a 350° oven for 1 hour.

Yield: 6 servings

Margaret Roane

Variation: May be cooked in electric skillet.

PORK HONDURAS

1 boned and rolled pork roast,
  as lean as possible
1 (16-ounce) can tomatoes
1 (8-ounce) can tomato sauce
1 tablespoon cumin

Salt and pepper to taste
½ teaspoon garlic powder
4 tablespoons Worcestershire
  sauce
2 medium onions, sliced

Line a Dutch oven with foil (a big piece as you will have to wrap the meat later). Place roast on foil lining. Mix the tomatoes, sauce, cumin, salt and pepper, Worcestershire sauce and onions, pour over roast and wrap tightly with foil. Seal and cook 50 minutes per pound in a 350° oven. Sauce may be thickened for gravy.

Yield: 6-8 servings   *Curtis Thomas*

BOUDIN

2 pounds lean pork meat
1½ pounds pork liver
1 large onion, whole
½ bell pepper, unchopped
1 stalk celery
2 cloves garlic
1 large onion, chopped
2 bunches green onions,
  chopped (½ cup reserved)

1 bunch parsley, chopped
  (½ cup reserved)
6 cups cooked rice
Salt, black and red pepper
  to taste
Sausage casings, soaked in
  cold water

Simmer in covered pot the pork meat, liver, onion, bell pepper, celery and garlic in water to cover; when meat falls apart, remove meat and reserve strained broth. Discard cooked vegetables. Grind meat, onion, green onions and parsley. Mix ground meat mixture with the reserved ½ cup of green onions and ½ cup parsley and rice. Gradually add broth to make a moist dressing. Season to taste, but this dish is usually highly seasoned. Stuff into casings with sausage stuffer or form into boudin balls and follow recipe on page 324.

Yield: 5 pounds   *Virginia Kyle Hine*

FRESH CAJUN SAUSAGE

4 pounds lean pork (coarsely
  ground)
2 pounds pork suet, ground
  fine
1 tablespoon red pepper or
  to taste
2²/₃ tablespoons salt or
  to taste

2 tablespoons very finely
  minced garlic
2 tablespoons freshly ground
  black pepper
½ cup fresh parsley, minced
1 cup freshly chopped green
  onion tops

Mix all above ingredients. Purchase enough sausage casing to make 6 pounds of sausage. Fill casings with above mixture using a sausage tuffer or a large funnel. Tie ends and refrigerate immediately to avoid spoiling. It may be kept refrigerated 4 or 5 days. If kept any longer, put in freezer. May be cooked according to personal preference.

Yield: 12 servings   *Virginia Kyle Hine*

Variation: May substitute 2 pounds ground venison for 2 pounds of pork. Also, 2 pounds of alligator meat may be substituted for pork.

PEDIGREED SAUSAGE AND PEPPERS

3 large bell peppers, cut into
  large chunks
3 tablespoons olive oil
Salt and freshly ground black
  pepper to taste

1 pound hot Italian sausage,
  sliced
¾ cup dry red wine

Sauté bell pepper in olive oil in a skillet until peppers are soft. Sprinkle with salt and pepper. Remove peppers. Sauté sausage in same pan until browned. Put into 2-quart baking dish; add wine, cover and bake at 350° for 40 minutes. Uncover and add bell peppers, bake 30 minutes longer. Serve immediately on bed of rice or serve in chafing dish as an appetizer.

Yield: 4 servings   *Barbara Schwing*

SWISS LOAF

1 cup dry, seasoned bread
  crumbs
1 cup milk
1 clove garlic, minced
2 sprigs parsley with stems,
  chopped
½ cup chopped onions
½ bell pepper, chopped
½ pound country-style
  sausage
1 egg, beaten
1½ cups diced Swiss cheese
1½ teaspoons salt
1½ tablespoons
  Worcestershire sauce
¼ teaspoon Tabasco pepper
  sauce
1 teaspoon celery salt
1½ pounds ground beef

Mix all above ingredients and shape into 2 loaves. It can be frozen at this point. Bake at 350° for 45-50 minutes.

Yield: 8-10 servings   *Trish Fletcher*

VEAL DAUBE GLACÉ

3 pounds veal roast
1 tablespoon salt
2 tablespoons shortening
6 cups water
1 onion, chopped
1 cup celery, coarsely chopped
1 bell pepper, coarsely
  chopped
2 bay leaves
3 sprigs parsley, minced
1 tablespoon gelatin softened
  in ¼ cup cold water

Rub salt on roast and sear in shortening until dark brown. Pour off all grease; add water and onion; cover tightly and allow to simmer slowly. Cook about an hour; then add the celery, bell pepper and bay leaves. Continue cooking until meat is very tender and can be pulled apart with a fork. Add the parsley, minced fine. Remove from fire and add the gelatin. When cooled, pour into mold and chill. This dish is tastier if prepared the day before serving. Unmold and slice with a very sharp knife.

Yield: 6-8 servings   *This recipe was among a collection
of Mrs. William G. Weeks*

VEAL PIES WITH MUSHROOMS

½ pound clarified butter
½ cup finely chopped onion
1 tablespoon finely chopped
    parsley
1 teaspoon tomato paste
1 teaspoon salt
Freshly ground black pepper
½ cup water

1½ pounds lean boneless veal,
    coarsely ground
8 sheets phyllo dough
1 egg yolk, beaten
4 fresh mushroom caps, each
    about 2 inches in diameter,
    cut crosswise into ⅛-inch
    slices

In a heavy 10 to 12 inch skillet, heat 4 tablespoons of the butter over moderate heat until a drop of water flicked into it sputters instantly. Add the onions and, stirring constantly, cook for 5 minutes, or until they are soft and transparent but not brown. Add the parsley, tomato paste, salt, a few grindings of pepper and ¼ cup of water and bring to a boil over high heat. Drop in the veal, turning the pieces about with a spoon until they are thoroughly moistened. Reduce the heat to low, and simmer partially covered for about 30 minutes, or until the veal is tender and almost all of the liquid in the pan has evaporated. Then increase the heat to high and, stirring constantly, cook briskly until veal browns lightly. Be careful that it does not burn. With a slotted spoon, transfer the veal to a bowl and set it aside to drain. Pour the remaining ¼ cup of water into the skillet and bring to a boil over high heat, meanwhile scraping any brown particles clinging to the bottom and sides of the pan. Set aside.

Preheat the oven to 400.° With a pastry brush, coat a large baking sheet with one tablespoon of the butter. To assemble each veal pie, lay a sheet of phyllo flat and brush the top evenly with about 1 tablespoon of butter. Cover with a second sheet of phyllo, and fold the two in half crosswise to make 4-layered rectangle about 8 inches wide and 12 inches long. Place about ½ cup of the veal in the center of the pastry in a rectangle about 2 inches wide and 4 inches long. Fold one long edge of the phyllo completely across the filling and bring the opposite side over the first fold to make a packet about 2½ inches wide. Brush the top with 1 more tablespoon butter. Turn both ends of the packet up overlapping them slightly, to enclose the filling securely. The finished pie will be about 4½ inches long.

Place the pies, seam sides down, on the baking sheet and brush them with beaten egg yolk. Bake in the middle of the oven for 15 to 20 minutes until the pastry is crisp and delicately browned. Meanwhile, heat the remaining 2 tablespoons of butter in an 8 to 10 inch

CONTINUED...

skillet. Add the mushrooms and cook over moderate heat for 2 minutes, or until they brown lightly. Add the reserved veal cooking sauce and bring to a boil, then reduce the heat to low. Cover and simmer for 5 minutes.

To serve, arrange the pies on a heated serving platter, place a row of overlapping mushroom slices on top of each, and moisten with the sauce remaining in the skillet.

Yield: 4 servings   *Sue McDonough*

VEAL RISOTTO

2 tablespoons butter or
  margarine
1 clove garlic
2 pounds boneless veal, cut
  in 1-inch cubes
1 medium onion, chopped
2 tablespoons catsup
1 teaspoon salt

½ teaspoon Tabasco pepper
  sauce
1 cup water
1 cup bouillon
1 cup uncooked rice
¼ cup grated Parmesan
  cheese

Melt butter in large skillet. Add garlic clove and veal and cook over medium heat until meat is browned on all sides. Remove garlic. Add onion and continue cooking until tender, but not brown. Stir in catsup, salt, Tabasco pepper sauce, water and bouillon; bring to a boil. Cover and cook over low heat 1 hour or until meat is tender. Remove meat and measure liquid, adding water to make 3 cups. Return liquid to skillet and bring to a boil. Add rice, cover and cook 20 to 25 minutes until rice is tender and liquid has been absorbed. Add meat and Parmesan cheese and heat to serving temperature.

Yield: 6 servings   *A Friend of the Shadows*

VEAL RAGOUT WITH ONIONS AND CHESTNUTS

5 tablespoons unsalted butter
4 tablespoons chicken fat or
vegetable oil
3 pounds boned veal shoulder,
trimmed and cut into
1½-inch cubes
Salt and freshly ground
white pepper
All purpose flour
2¼ cups brown chicken stock
16 garlic cloves
2 small yellow onions,
chopped
1 large sprig fresh thyme
or teaspoon dried

2 tablespoons chicken fat or
vegetable oil
1 tablespoon brown sugar
16 to 18 tiny white onions
(fresh or frozen)
16 to 18 peeled fresh
chestnuts
½ cup minced fresh parsley
1 cup whipping cream
1 tablespoon softened
unsalted butter mixed with
1 tablespoon sifted all
purpose flour to make
beurre manié
Minced fresh parsley (garnish)

Heat 2 tablespoons butter with 1 tablespoon fat in heavy large ovenproof casserole over medium-high heat. Add veal in batches (do not crowd) and sauté until nicely browned on all sides, adding more butter and fat as necessary. Return all veal to casserole and season to taste with salt and pepper.

Position rack in center of 350° oven. Sprinkle veal with flour and toss until veal is covered and lightly glazed. Add about 1¾ cups stock, garlic, yellow onions and thyme and blend well. Bring to boil over medium-high heat, stirring frequently to prevent sticking. Cover and bake until meat is tender, about 1½ hours.

Meanwhile, heat 2 tablespoons fat and brown sugar in heavy large skillet over medium-high heat. Add tiny white onions and sauté until nicely browned. Add chestnuts and remaining stock. Reduce heat, cover partially and simmer until tender, about 15 minutes. Remove from heat and set aside.

When veal is done, remove from casserole using slotted spoon. Transfer pan juices with garlic to processor or blender and purée until smooth. Return purée to casserole. Stir in cream and chestnut mixture and bring to boil over medium-high heat. If sauce seems too thin, whisk in beurre manié a bit at a time and cook until sauce coats spoon. Add meat and heat through. Turn into dish or tureen and sprinkle with minced fresh parsley.

Yield: 6-8 servings   *Michael "a catering experience"*

SCALOPPINE A LA MARSALA

2 pounds veal round
1½ teaspoons salt
¼ teaspoon Tabasco pepper
  sauce
½ cup flour

6 tablespoons butter or
  margarine
4 shallots or small white
  onions, sliced
1 cup sliced mushrooms
1 cup Marsala wine

Cut veal into cutlets; pound thin. Mix salt and Tabasco pepper sauce well; spread over meat; roll in flour. Sauté meat over medium heat in butter in heavy skillet until browned on both sides. Set in a casserole or platter in oven to keep warm. Add onions, mushrooms and wine to skillet. Cover and simmer 5 minutes, then season with a final dash of Tabasco pepper sauce. Pour over cutlets and serve at once.

Yield: 6 servings   *A Friend of the Shadows*

Note: Sherry or Madeira wine may be substituted in place of Marsala.

VEAL SCALOPPINI

1 pound veal
Salt to taste
½ cup grated Parmesan
  cheese
½ cup butter
1 clove garlic

½ pound fresh mushrooms,
  sliced
½ cup boiling water
Dash Tabasco pepper sauce
½ cup white wine

Sprinkle veal with salt and coat with grated cheese. Melt 1 tablespoon butter in large skillet. Add garlic and veal and cook over medium heat until brown on both sides. Add butter as needed. Remove meat as it browns. When all meat is browned, remove garlic and discard. Then cook sliced mushrooms and remove. Lower flame, add water and Tabasco pepper sauce, cook and stir until all browned particles are loosened. Add meat and mushrooms and heat thoroughly. Add wine and serve at once.

Yield: 4 servings   *Trish Fletcher*

OSSO BUCCO

Flour for dredging
Salt and pepper to taste
4 to 6 large pieces of veal
  shinbone (shank, round
  or soup meat)
2 tablespoons butter
2 tablespoons olive oil
½ medium onion, finely
  chopped

1 cup grated carrot
1 clove garlic
2 tablespoons chopped
  parsley
¾ cup white wine
2 tablespoons grated lemon
  rind
1 teaspoon crushed rosemary
½ teaspoon dried sage

Flour, salt and pepper the meat. Brown well in oil and butter. Remove from pan. Add chopped vegetables and sauté until limp. Add wine, return meat to pan, add spices. Cover and cook on low heat for 1½ hours or until very tender. Add a little water or chicken broth if it gets too dry.

Osso Bucco means bone with a hole in it. This is a cheap cut of meat that, when cooked in this fashion, is fit for a king.

It is a traditional dish of North Italy and is usually served with Risotto a la Milanese. The bone marrow (cooked) should be spread on a piece of bread to be eaten.

Yield: 4-6 servings   *Adele Guillot*

GAME AND POULTRY

Circa 1920

The streetcar connecting New Iberia with Jeanerette, 12 miles to the southeast, traveled in front of the Shadows. The house can be seen in this photograph in the background behind the small fence. Restoration that started in the 1920's had not yet begun.

The road on which the streetcar ran, today called Main Street, was once part of the Old Spanish Trail. The portion shown in this photograph was used as a cattle trail between Texas and New Orleans. Cattle were driven from the western ranches to the slaughterhouses in the towns along the way. The road was unpaved. In wet weather it was almost impassable. Horses, cattle and horsedrawn vehicles sank in mud. In dry weather, the road was rutty and dusty. By road, it took weeks to reach New Orleans from New Iberia. It is easy to see why early settlers relied on the bayou!

By the 1860's there was a boardwalk in front of the store fronts in town and a raised side-walk in front of the Shadows. However, it was still necessary to walk in the streets to get about town.

Game and Poultry

GAME
  Alligator
    Balls. 179
    Fried. 179
    Sauce Piquante. 180
    Smothered. 179
  Dove
    Étouffée and Rice. 180
    from Toby. 182
    Smothered. 181
  Duck
    Baked Wild. 183
    Canard Pressé (Pressed). 181
    Wild in Sherry Wine. 182
  Frog Legs
    Fried. 183
  Quail
    Stuffed with Sausage. 184
  Rabbit or Squirrel
    Sauce Piquante. 184
  Venison
    Chili and Beans. 185
    Roast. 185
POULTRY
  Chicken
    Almond Casserole. 186
    Artichoke Casserole. 186

    Birthday, Ken's. 187
    Breasts, Crab Stuffed. 188
    Breasts, Supreme, Baked. 189
    Cadien. 190
    Chinese I. 190
    Chinese II. 191
    Chinese Lemon Baked. 189
    Deluxe. 191
    Drambuie. 192
    Dumplings. 192
    Enchiladas, Sour Cream. 193
    Fried, Alice's. 193
    Golden, in Spaghetti. 197
    Hoisin Sauce. 194
    Kiev, Green Chili. 194
    Limas à la Vita. 195
    Oyster Pie. 196
    Poulet Aux Gros Oignons. 195
    Sesame. 196
    Tetrazzini. 197
    Tortilla. 198
  Cornish Hens
    Basted in Secret Sauce. 198
  Turkey
    Goodbye. 199
    Sauce Piquante. 199
    Tortilla. 200

Refer to additional recipes in "How Men Cook" section.

ALLIGATOR BALLS

2 pounds alligator tail, ground
2 teaspoons salt
1 teaspoon red pepper
1 egg, beaten
1/4 cup milk
1/2 cup bread crumbs
Juice of one lemon

1/2 cup chopped onion
2 tablespoons chopped
    parsley
1 cup flour
1 cup corn meal
Cooking oil for deep fat frying

Mix alligator with salt, pepper, egg, milk, bread crumbs, lemon juice, onion and parsley. Shape into small balls. Mix flour and corn meal. Roll balls in mixture and fry in deep fat at 350° until brown.

Yield: 4-6 servings   *Carolyn Carlon*

FRIED ALLIGATOR

1 cup sherry
1/2 cup Italian salad dressing
1/4 cup lemon juice
1 tablespoon lemon pepper
1 teaspoon seasoned salt

1 pound alligator meat, cut in
    small pieces
Flour to dredge
Cooking oil for frying

Combine the first 5 ingredients and marinate alligator in it for 2 hours. Drain meat and dredge in flour. Fry pieces in hot oil for about 15 minutes turning often until brown. Drain and serve hot.

Yield: 4 servings

SMOTHERED ALLIGATOR

2 onions, finely chopped
1/4 cup cooking oil
1 bell pepper, finely chopped
1/2 cup celery, finely chopped
2 pounds alligator meat, cut
    into chunks

1 bay leaf
1/4 teaspoon dried basil
Salt and pepper to taste
1/4 cup finely chopped parsley
1/4 cup finely chopped shallots

Sauté onions in oil until golden brown; add bell pepper and celery and sauté until tender. Add meat and seasonings and simmer for 40 minutes. Add parsley and shallots about 5 minutes before serving.

Yield: 6-8 servings

ALLIGATOR SAUCE PIQUANTE

2 cups chopped onion
1/3 cup cooking oil
1/4 cup chopped bell pepper
1/2 cup chopped celery
2 (8-ounce) cans tomato sauce
1 (10-ounce) can Rotel
    tomatoes
2 tablespoons Worcestershire
    sauce
1/4 teaspoon dried basil

1 bay leaf
1/4 teaspoon dried oregano
Salt and pepper to taste
1 (6-ounce) can sliced
    mushrooms
1/4 cup chopped shallots
1/4 cup chopped parsley
2 pounds alligator meat, cubed
    (see note)

Sauté onions in oil until a dark golden brown, stirring often. Add bell pepper and celery and sauté until tender. Add tomatoes, tomato sauce and seasonings; simmer for 10 minutes; then add mushrooms and drained alligator. Cover and cook for 40 minutes. Add shallots and parsley and cook uncovered for 10 more minutes. Serve with rice.

Yield: 8-10 servings

Note: Alligator may be marinated in wine 1 hour before adding to sauce.

DOVE ÉTOUFFÉE AND RICE

8 to 12 doves, seasoned well
    with salt and red pepper
2 tablespoons oil, add more as
    needed
2 cups chopped onion
1 bell pepper, chopped
2 cloves garlic, minced
2 tablespoons chopped celery

2 cups chicken broth
2 tablespoons Worcestershire
    sauce
1 tablespoon chopped parsley
1 tablespoon chopped green
    onion tops
1 (12-ounce) can button
    mushrooms, drained

Brown doves in oil. Remove doves and add onion, bell pepper, garlic and celery to oil and wilt. Return doves to pot and add chicken broth and Worcestershire sauce. Bring to a boil, lower to simmer. Cover and cook until doves are tender. (Check and remove the birds that are cooked first and allow the tougher ones to continue cooking). Add onion tops and parsley and mushrooms. Cook 5 minutes and serve over hot rice.

Yield: 4-6 servings

Mac Beyt

SMOTHERED DOVES

40 doves
Salt, red and black pepper
½ cup oil, more as needed
Water
¾ cup flour
8 cloves chopped garlic

3 cups chopped onion
1 cup chopped celery
2 cups chopped mushrooms,
   fresh or canned
3 quarts water
1 cup chopped parsley

Rub doves with salt, red and black pepper. Put enough oil to cover the bottom of a large thick pot. Brown birds well; add enough water to almost cover the birds. Place in a 350° oven, covered; in about 2 hours most of the birds should be tender. Remove these and add more water, if necessary, to continue cooking the tough birds. When all birds are tender, remove from the pot. Place pot on top of stove and let simmer until all water is evaporated and only oil remains. Add the flour and stir constantly until flour is a chocolate color (roux). Add the garlic, onion, celery and mushrooms. Stir and cook for 20 to 30 minutes. Add 3 quarts water and let simmer for 1½ hours. (DO NOT COVER.) Add more water if necessary. Season to taste. Add parsley. When ready to serve, place birds in gravy to reheat only. Serve over hot cooked rice. This may be reduced to suit needs.

Yield: 20 servings

Juanita Durand

CANARD PRESSÉ
(Pressed Duck)

In the first place ducks must be strangled. This leaves them with rosy breasts. After picking, roast them about 10 minutes.

In the meantime, mash the livers to a paste with 1 part of cognac and 2 parts of Madeira. Slice the duck breasts, keeping the legs, boiling them and serving with lettuce salad. Then the carcass is put into a press and squeezed to get the juice. The juice is then poured over the slices of breast with the liver sauce and a dash of lemon juice.

The whole is placed in a chafing dish and cooked until the sauce thickens, the meat being continually basted with the sauce.

This is an exact copy of a Weeks family recipe!

From the Weeks Family Cookbook

DOVES FROM TOBY

24 doves
Salt and red pepper
1/2 cup oil (not olive oil), add
    more as needed
2 cloves garlic, minced
2 onions, chopped fine
2 stalks celery, chopped fine

2 bell peppers, chopped fine
2 tablespoons Worcestershire
    sauce
1 (10 1/2-ounce) can cream of
    mushroom soup
1/2 cup chopped onion tops
1/2 cup chopped parsley

Clean, dry and season doves with salt and red pepper. Brown in oil in a large, heavy pot (big enough to hold all of the doves). Remove doves as they brown. Add more oil as needed. Add garlic, onion, celery and bell pepper to pot and cook until wilted. Return doves to pot, add soup and Worcestershire sauce. Mix, stir and scrape the bottom of the pot until the doves are well coated. Add 1/2 cup of hot water, lower heat, cover pot and cook until birds are tender. (Check and remove the birds that are cooked first and allow the tougher ones to cook longer.) Add a little water at a time if needed. Add parsley and onion tops before serving. Serve over cooked rice.

This recipe was Toby Veltin's of "Toby's Oak Grove."

WILD DUCK IN SHERRY WINE

1 wild duck
1 teaspoon salt and black
    pepper
Tabasco pepper sauce to taste
1 tablespoon Worcestershire
    sauce

1 whole onion
1 apple, cut in 4 pieces
2 tablespoons butter
1 cup sherry wine
1 cup fresh mushrooms, sliced
Chopped parsley

Dress duck, season with salt, pepper and Tabasco pepper sauce, put whole onion and quartered apple in duck cavity. Heat butter in heavy pot to brown duck on all sides. Cover pot and cook slowly, turning as needed, basting with the wine until golden brown and tender. Add sliced fresh mushrooms and chopped parsley to liquid to make brown gravy. Serve on hot platter with mounds of wild rice.

Yield: 2 servings

Junius A. Winkle

BAKED WILD DUCK

6 ducks
Salt
Pepper, cayenne, white and
  black
1 onion, chopped
1 bell pepper, chopped
1 apple, chopped
1 lemon peel, chopped fine
2 tablespoons olive oil

5 tablespoons flour
6 strips bacon
3 tablespoons of olive oil
2 onions, chopped
2 bell peppers, chopped
1 rib celery, chopped
2 cups water
Garnish: oranges, crabapple
  and parsley

Wash ducks well, season with salt and pepper. Make a stuffing with the onion, bell pepper and apple. Add lemon peel and 2 tablespoons oil and stuff cavities of each duck. Sprinkle ducks with flour; wrap each duck with a strip of bacon. Brown ducks in hot oil in a heavy pan. Pour off excess oil. Add chopped onion, bell pepper, celery and water to ducks. Cover and bake in 350° oven until ducks begin to break at the breastbone (about 2 to 3 hours). Add additional water if needed. Place on a serving platter and garnish with orange slices, crabapple and parsley. Serve gravy with rice.

Yield: 6 servings   *Gigi and Alex Patout*

FRIED FROG LEGS

12 frog legs
1 egg
2 tablespoons water
Salt and pepper

Bread crumbs
Deep fat
Lemon slices, garnish

Dry the frog legs well with paper towels.

Make a wash of 1 egg and 2 tablespoons water. Lightly season the wash with salt and pepper. Do not salt too much because the frog legs will weep.

Dip frog legs into the wash and then into bread crumbs. Place them on wax paper to dry a minimum of 1 hour—can be dried up to ½ day. Fry in deep fat until they float to the top. Turn them over and cook until golden. Do not overcook. Salt and pepper and serve with lemon slices.

Yield: 6 servings   *Mac Beyt*

QUAIL STUFFED WITH SAUSAGE

12 dressed quail
12 teaspoons pure pork
   sausage
12 thin slices bacon
2 cups flour with salt and
   pepper added

2 sticks margarine
3 tablespoons grape or currant
   jelly
2 cups dry red wine

Stuff quail with uncooked sausage. Wrap quail in bacon strip. Roll quail in seasoned flour. Melt margarine in frying pan, add quail and brown. Remove from pan and place in baking dish or deep pan. Add enough of the remaining flour to the drippings in pan to make a brown roux. Add wine and jelly to roux, making enough gravy to cover the birds. Cover pan and bake at 250° until tender, about 1½ to 2 hours.

Yield: 6 servings

Jackie Ferrell

RABBIT OR SQUIRREL SAUCE PIQUANTE

1 rabbit or squirrel cut into
   bite size pieces
1 tablespoon oil
1 tablespoon flour
2 large onions, minced
2 bell peppers, minced
2 cloves garlic, minced
4 stalks celery, minced

1 (16-ounce) can whole
   tomatoes
1 (4-ounce) can mushrooms,
   drained
1 (4-ounce) can sweet peas,
   drained
Salt and pepper to taste
Pinch of sugar

Brown rabbit or squirrel pieces in 1 tablespoon oil until brown. Remove from pot. To make roux, add 1 tablespoon flour to fat and brown (chocolate color), stirring occasionally. Cook onions, bell peppers, garlic, and celery in roux on slow fire with pot covered until soft. Add tomatoes and cook until very tender, about 45 minutes. Put meat in gravy and simmer until meat is tender. Add mushrooms and sweet peas. Season with salt, red pepper and pinch of sugar. Serve over rice.

Yield: 4 servings

Margaret Roane

VENISON CHILI AND BEANS

1 pound pinto beans
2 pounds ground venison
1 large onion, chopped
4 large pods garlic, minced
¼ cup butter
1 tablespoon sugar
1 (16-ounce) can stewed
   tomatoes
1 (16-ounce) can tomato sauce
1 tablespoon salt
Water to cover

1 bay leaf
2 whole cloves garlic
1 teaspoon coriander
   (crushed)
2 teaspoons comino (cumin)
   seed
1 teaspoon oregano
¼ cup pure chili powder (if not
   available, substitute ½ cup
   chili seasoning)
½ teaspoon black pepper

Soak beans overnight. Brown meat, onion and garlic in butter. Add all other ingredients. Cook slowly about 3 hours, or until beans are tender. Add water during cooking if necessary. To thicken slightly, remove about 2 cups mixture, purée in blender, then return to pot.

Yield: 6-8 servings   *Jessamine Musson*

VENISON ROAST

3 to 4 pounds venison roast
3 teaspoons salt
1 teaspoon red pepper

1 onion, chopped fine
1 bell pepper, chopped fine
2 cloves garlic, minced

MARINADE
1 teaspoon Bruce's French
   dressing
¼ cup cider vinegar
¼ cup water
½ cup corn or peanut oil

2 teaspoons salt
½ cup Windsor
   Worcestershire sauce
1 teaspoon Bruce's (red)
   Pepper Sauce

Stir or shake marinade well. Wipe roast with damp cloth. Remove membranes. Rub well with salt and pepper. Make small slits in the roast and stuff with onion, bell pepper and garlic. Put in a deep bowl and cover with marinade. Leave about 3 hours or overnight. Put roast and all marinade in a covered roasting pan with its vent open. Bake about 3 hours in 300° oven. The marinade forms a gravy. Serve with cooked rice.

Yield: 6-8 servings   *Mary Brown*

CHICKEN ALMOND CASSEROLE

6 chicken breasts, cooked and cubed
1 (10½-ounce) can chicken broth
2 (10½-ounce) cans cream of chicken soup
1 cup mayonnaise
2 cups diced celery
1 cup roasted, slivered almonds
2 teaspoons minced onions
½ teaspoon salt
2 tablespoons lemon juice
4 ounces dry Pepperidge Farm bread dressing
1 (10-ounce) package potato chips, crushed

Mix all ingredients and pour over chicken in buttered casserole. Top with Pepperidge Farm dressing and potato chips. Bake for 45 minutes at 350 degrees.

Yield: 6-8 servings   *Vi Bowlin*

CHICKEN—ARTICHOKE CASSEROLE

3 pounds cut-up fryer
6 tablespoons butter
1½ teaspoons salt
½ teaspoon paprika
¼ teaspoon pepper
¼ pound whole mushrooms
2 (14-ounce) cans artichoke hearts (reserve liquid)
2 tablespoons flour
⅔ cup chicken broth
3 tablespoons sherry

Salt, pepper, and paprika the chicken pieces. Brown in 4 tablespoons butter and put in big casserole. Add 2 tablespoons butter to drippings in frying pan and sauté mushrooms 5 minutes. Sprinkle flour over them and brown slightly. Stir in chicken broth and sherry. Cook 5 minutes. While it cooks, arrange artichokes between chicken pieces. Add artichoke liquid to the sauce while cooking. Pour sauce over the chicken, cover, and bake at 375° for 40 minutes.

Yield: 4-6 servings   *Terry Salassi*

KEN'S BIRTHDAY CHICKEN

8 cups chicken, cooked,
  deboned, and cubed
  1 (3-pound) chicken equals
  2 cups
6 (14-ounce) cans artichoke
  hearts, drained and
  quartered
1 pound fresh mushrooms,
  sliced
Chicken broth reserved from
  boiling
1 bunch green onions,
  chopped
2 cloves garlic, pressed

Salt, red and black pepper
  to taste
6 to 8 cups thick white sauce
  (substituting chicken broth
  for milk)
1½ teaspoons white pepper
1½ teaspoons Tabasco
  pepper sauce
8 ounces American cheese,
  grated
8 ounces Gruyere cheese,
  grated
1½ cups dry white wine, room
  temperature

Combine chicken, artichokes and mushrooms. Add green onions and garlic; season lightly with salt, red and black pepper. Make thick white sauce according to basic recipe found on page 91; substitute chicken broth for milk. Add white pepper, Tabasco pepper sauce, both cheeses and wine to white sauce, blend. Adjust seasonings remembering chicken mixture has been seasoned. Mix white sauce with chicken-artichoke mixture. (Using all 8 cups of the white sauce will make a larger amount and make the consistency thinner than using only 6 cups. This is a matter of taste. The thinner consistency could be served over noodles for a variation.) Place in two ovenproof dishes and bake at 350° for 30 to 45 minutes or until heated through.

Yield: 18-20 servings   *Friends of Ken*

CRAB-STUFFED CHICKEN BREASTS

6 chicken breasts, skinned
and boned
Salt and pepper to taste
1/2 cup chopped onion
1/2 cup chopped celery
3 tablespoons butter
1/2 cup dry white wine
1 pound fresh crabmeat

1/2 cup herb seasoned stuffing
mix
2 tablespoons all-purpose flour
1/2 teaspoon paprika
2 tablespoons melted butter
1 recipe Hollandaise Sauce
(see below)
2 ounces shredded Swiss
cheese

Pound chicken to flatten. Sprinkle with a little salt and pepper. Cook onion and celery in 3 tablespoons butter until tender. Remove from heat; add 3 tablespoons wine, crab and stuffing mix; toss. Divide mixture among breasts. Roll up and secure. Combine flour and paprika; coat chicken. Place in 11¾ x 7¼ x 1¾-inch baking dish; drizzle with 2 tablespoons melted butter. Bake at 375° uncovered for 1 hour. Add wine, cheese and Hollandaise Sauce. Heat until cheese melts.

Yield: 6 servings

MICROWAVE HOLLANDAISE SAUCE

1/4 cup butter
2 tablespoons light cream
1/2 teaspoon dry mustard

1/4 teaspoon salt
1 tablespoon lemon juice
2 egg yolks beaten

Place butter in 2 cup glass measure. Microwave on high 1 minute. Stir in rest of ingredients. Microwave on high 1 minute, stirring every 15 seconds. Beat with wire whip until smooth. Sauce can be reheated on high, 1 minute.

Yolanda Trahan

BAKED CHICKEN BREASTS SUPREME

6 (12-ounce size) chicken fryer
  breasts
2 cups sour cream
1/4 cup lemon juice
4 teaspoons Worcestershire
  sauce
4 teaspoons celery salt
2 teaspoons paprika
4-6 cloves garlic, crushed

2 teaspoons salt
1/2 teaspoon white pepper
3/4 cup Italian bread crumbs
  mixed with 3/4 cup plain
  bread crumbs
3/4 cup margarine melted with
  1/4 cup vegetable
  shortening

Bone chicken, remove skin and dry. Mix all ingredients except bread crumbs and margarine mixture. Add chicken to mixture, coating each piece well. Refrigerate overnight.

Next day: Remove chicken and roll in bread crumbs. Place in single layer in shallow pan. Spoon 1/2 of butter mixture over chicken. Bake uncovered 1 hour at 350°, then spoon rest of butter mixture over chicken. Bake an additional 25 minutes or until tender and nicely browned.

Yield: 8 servings   *Yolanda Trahan*

CHINESE LEMON BAKED CHICKEN

1 (3-pound) fryer
1 teaspoon paprika
Dash pepper
1 1/2 teaspoons salt
3/4 cup flour

Juice of 1 lemon
3 tablespoons honey
1/3 cup peanut oil
3 tablespoons melted butter

Cut chicken and mix with paprika, pepper, and salt. Let stand 1/2 hour. Put flour in paper bag, add chicken and shake. Mix lemon juice, honey and oil. In flat baking pan place butter and chicken, skin side down. Bake 30 minutes at 400°. Turn chicken over and pour lemon mixture over chicken. Bake 20-30 minutes until cooked. Baste chicken as it cooks.

Yield: 4-6 servings   *Virginia LaSalle*

CHICKEN CADIEN

1 hen cooked, reserve ½ cup
stock
1 cup very thick white sauce
(recipe for sauce on
page 91)
2 small onions, chopped
1 stalk celery, chopped
1 cup minced green pepper
2 tablespoons margarine

1 cup of mushrooms
6 medium size tomatoes, or
1 large (15½-ounce)
can tomatoes
1 dozen eggs, boiled hard
Tabasco pepper sauce
Worcestershire sauce
Red and black pepper to taste
Cracker crumbs

Steam hen in seasoned water until tender. Cut meat off the bone and dice. When preparing white sauce, use half milk called for and the reserved chicken stock. Brown onions, peppers and celery in margarine. Mix this together with chicken and remaining ingredients, including white sauce. Remove and discard egg whites from boiled eggs and save for another recipe. Add whole egg yolks and stir very lightly so as not to break them up. Season to taste with Tabasco, Worcestershire sauce and pepper. Put into casserole and place casserole in a larger pan which has boiling water in the bottom of it. Cracker crumbs may be sprinkled on top of casserole. Bake at 300° for 30 minutes.

Yield: 6-8 servings   *Weeks Family recipe*

CHINESE CHICKEN I

½ cup sliced onion
2 tablespoons butter
1 (1-pound) can bean sprouts
1 (8-ounce) can water chestnuts, drained and sliced
2 cups chopped celery
½ cup chicken broth
1 (3-ounce) can sliced
mushrooms, reserve liquid

1 cup diced, cooked chicken
3 tablespoons corn starch
¼ cup water
2 tablespoons soy sauce
4 cups hot, cooked rice
½ cup blanched toasted
almonds

Cook onions in butter until tender but not brown. Add bean sprouts and liquid, water chestnuts, celery, chicken broth, mushrooms and liquid and chicken. Heat to boiling. Mix corn starch, water, soy sauce and add to chicken mixture. Return to boil. Serve over rice. Sprinkle with blanched toasted almonds.

Yield: 4-6 servings   *Ellen Minvielle*

CHINESE CHICKEN II

1 (2½ to 3-pound) chicken
skinned, deboned and cut
into bite size pieces
1 large red onion, cut in chunks
1 large bell pepper, cut
in chunks
1 (8½-ounce) can sliced water
chestnuts, drained
1 (8½-ounce) can sliced
bamboo shoots, drained
2 large stalks celery, cut in
chunks
½ cup unsalted peanuts
½ cup green olives
½ cup black olives
1 (15-ounce) can whole
tomatoes, cut into chunks
3 tablespoons soy sauce
Red pepper to taste
Salt to taste

Brown chicken pieces and cover and cook until tender. Add onion, green pepper, water chestnuts, bamboo shoots, celery. Cover and cook until tender. Add remaining ingredients and salt and red pepper to taste. Simmer 15 minutes. Serve hot over chow mein noodles or rice.

Yield: 6 servings

A Friend of The Shadows

DELUXE CHICKEN

1 (3 to 4-pound) chicken cut
up for frying
2 teaspoons salt
1 teaspoon red pepper
2 tablespoons flour
¼ cup salad oil
1 cup chopped onions
⅓ cup chopped bell pepper
⅔ cup chopped celery
1 carrot chopped
1 teaspoon Worcestershire
sauce
1 teaspoon lemon juice
1 recipe cream of mushroom
soup, page 57
1 (5¾-ounce) can Dawn Fresh
mushroom steak sauce
1 tablespoon each chopped
green onion tops and
parsley
¼ cup cooking sherry
(optional)

Sprinkle chicken with salt, pepper and flour. Brown in oil in a 5-quart pot. Chicken must be browned on all sides so that it will have a rich color. Pour off excess fat. Add onions, bell pepper, celery and carrots to browned chicken and let simmer for 10 minutes. Then add Worcestershire sauce, lemon juice, mushroom soup, mushroom steak sauce and sherry. Cook, covered, over low heat about an hour or until chicken is tender. Just before serving add onion tops and parsley. Serve over rice or noodles.

Yield: 4-6 servings

Susie Pharr

DRAMBUIE CHICKEN

2 (3-pound) chickens
1 cup Drambuie
Rind of one lemon
2¼ pounds melted butter

2 tablespoons soy sauce
¼ teaspoon salt
Pepper to taste

Wash chicken and pat dry. Place in roasting pan. Combine rest of ingredients and pour over chicken. Roast chicken covered for 1 hour. Baste every 15 minutes. Uncover and brown for 1 hour.

Yield: 8 servings

Adele Forrest

CHICKEN AND DUMPLINGS

3 pounds chicken
Salt and black pepper
1 stalk celery (optional)
1 (5¾-ounce) can evaporated
  milk

3 chicken bouillon cubes
1 egg
2 cups flour
½ teaspoon salt

Put chicken in Dutch oven; cover with water, season with salt and pepper (heavy on the black pepper) and celery. Cover and cook until done. When done, remove and allow to cool so that chicken can be deboned. (If I am in a hurry, I sometimes boil chicken parts.) Put can of evaporated milk into broth with three chicken bouillon cubes. More water may be added if needed.

Dumplings: Beat 1 egg and add 1 cup chicken broth mixture to mix with flour and ½ teaspoon salt so that flour is consistency to roll out. (Cut juice and egg mixture into flour with fork.) On floured surface roll dough ⅛-inch thick and cut into strips. Drop strips into boiling broth. These will cook in about five minutes. Return chicken to broth and cook on low for a few minutes for gravy to season chicken. Season to taste.

Yield: 6 servings

Suzanne O'Neal

SOUR CREAM ENCHILADAS

4 large onions, chopped
1 clove garlic, chopped
1 (4-ounce) can jalapeño
   peppers, chopped
Salt and pepper to taste
1 large chicken, boiled,
   deboned and cut in small
   pieces
1 tablespoon Worcestershire
   sauce
2 teaspoons chili powder
Tabasco pepper sauce

1 (16-ounce) can tomatoes
1 pound grated American or
   Cheddar cheese
1 dozen corn tortillas
Fat or shortening
1 (10-ounce) can enchilada
   sauce
1 (16-ounce) carton sour
   cream
1 bunch green onion tops,
   chopped

Sauté 3 onions, garlic and jalapeños until tender. Add salt, pepper, chicken, Worcestershire sauce, chili powder, Tabasco pepper sauce and tomatoes. Simmer for 15-20 minutes or until some of the liquid has cooked down. Keep hot. Set aside 1 chopped onion and grated cheese. Dip tortillas in hot fat until done (they become soft). Drain on paper towels and set aside. Fill each tortilla with a heaping spoon of meat mixture, a little grated cheese and roll and seal with toothpicks. Place very close together in baking dish. Sprinkle remaining onion on top of enchiladas. Cover with enchilada sauce. Sprinkle remaining cheese on top. May be frozen at this point. To bake, cover top of enchiladas with green onion tops and sour cream. Bake about 30 minutes at 350.°

Yield: 6 servings

A Friend of The Shadows

ALICE'S FRIED CHICKEN

1 (4-pound) fryer (cut up)
Salt and red pepper
1 egg

½ cup milk or cream
1 cup flour

Season chicken highly with red pepper and salt. Mix 1 egg with milk or cream. Pour over chicken and let stand about 15 minutes. Put 1 cup flour in a paper bag, add chicken and shake. Fry in deep fat on medium heat. Remove pieces as they are done.

Yield: 4 servings

Alice Coleman

CHICKEN WITH HOISIN SAUCE

4 chicken breasts, halved,
  boned, skinned and cut
  into ¾-inch cubes
1 tablespoon cornstarch
1 tablespoon dry sherry
1 tablespoon soy sauce
1 bell pepper, cut into
  ½-inch squares

1 tablespoon vegetable oil
½ pound fresh mushrooms,
  cut into ½-inch cubes
2½ tablespoons Hoisin sauce
  (available oriental grocery)
¼ cup cashews

Sprinkle the cubed chicken with cornstarch, dry sherry and soy sauce. Toss to coat well and set aside. Stir-fry the green pepper in the oil for 1 minute. Put aside, add mushrooms, stir-fry 1 to 2 minutes. Put aside. Stir-fry chicken 2 to 3 minutes until done. Add Hoisin sauce and cashews. Reheat and stir briefly.

Yield: 6 servings

Charlotte Dann

GREEN CHILI CHICKEN KIEV

4 whole chicken breasts,
  halved, boned and skinned
3 tablespoons butter
3 tablespoons old English-
  style sharp cheese spread
2 teaspoons minced onion
1 teaspoon salt

2 tablespoons chopped green
  chilies
¼ cup melted butter
1 cup crushed Cheddar
  cheese crackers
1½ teaspoons taco seasoning
  mix

Flatten each piece of chicken. Beat together butter and cheese spread until well blended (can be done in food processor). Mix in onion, salt and green chilies. Divide mixture equally among the 8 chicken pieces. Roll up each piece, tucking in ends to completely enclose filling. Fasten rolls with toothpicks. Mix together crushed crackers and taco seasoning mix. Dip each chicken roll into melted butter to coat, then coat with crackers and taco mix. At this point, recipe may be frozen. This is a great recipe to make in large quantities and freeze.

To bake: for best results cook in microwave (covered with wax paper) for 10-12 minutes or bake in 350° oven for 30 minutes.

Yield: 8 servings

Trish Fletcher

CHICKEN AND LIMAS A LA VITA

1 2½-pound chicken, cut up
Salt, pepper and red pepper
  to taste
4 tablespoons olive oil
2 tablespoons flour
1 medium onion, chopped fine
1 large tomato, chopped
3 cloves garlic, chopped fine

2 (10-ounce) packages
  Fordhook Lima Beans
½ red bell pepper, sliced thin
½ teaspoon fennel seed
½ teaspoon garni
2 tablespoons fresh parsley
2 cups chicken broth

Season chicken very well and brown in oil; remove and set aside. Add flour to drippings and brown lightly. Add onions and sauté until clear. Add tomatoes and garlic, cover and cook 15 minutes over low heat, stirring occasionally. Add limas, pepper, fennel seed, garni, parsley and chicken broth. Cook 15 minutes more. Place chicken in baking dish. Add lima bean mixture. Bake at 300° until chicken is very tender, basting occasionally. May be served with cooked rice, green salad and white wine.

Yield: 6 servings   *Lillian Vita*

POULET AUX GROS OIGNONS
(Chicken and Large Onions)

1½ tablespoons oil
1 tablespon sugar
1 large fryer, cut up

1 large onion, chopped
½ bell pepper, chopped
Garlic, salt, pepper to taste

Pour oil into a heavy skillet. Sprinkle sugar over the oil. When it is very hot, add chicken and brown well. Add a little water, onion and bell pepper, garlic, salt and pepper to taste. Cook until well done. Delicious to eat with cooked rice.

Yield: 4-6 servings   *Mrs. Collins Dautreuil*

CHICKEN AND OYSTER PIE

½ cup flour
½ cup oil
1 large onion, chopped
1 celery stalk, chopped
½ bell pepper, chopped
2½ to 3 quarts chicken or
    turkey stock
1 quart oysters, reserve liquid
    (amount varies) (optional
    item)

5 to 6 cups cooked cubed
    chicken or turkey
1 bunch green onion tops,
    chopped
½ cup parsley, chopped
Salt, red and black pepper to
    taste
Tabasco pepper sauce to taste
Pie shell or patty shells
1 egg yolk, beaten
2 tablespoons water

Make a dark roux with flour and oil (see basic roux recipe on page 48). Add onions, celery, bell pepper. Cook until wilted. Add hot chicken stock and oyster liquid. Reduce until consistency of thick whipping cream. This may take 3 to 4 hours. Add cubed chicken, green onion tops, parsley, and seasoning. Stir carefully to avoid breaking up chicken pieces. Add oysters and cook until edges curl; about 5 to 7 minutes. If the mixtures becomes thin after adding oysters, add small amounts of roux and cook to thicken. Pour into pie shell and cover with strips of pastry (lattice); glaze with egg yolk and water that have been mixed together. At this point the pie may be frozen. Bake at 350° until mixture bubbles and pastry is golden brown. Serve hot.

Yield: 6-8 servings   *Sherry Landry*

Variation: Serve chicken mixture over rice or serve in patty shells.

SESAME CHICKEN

3 whole, deboned, skinned
    chicken breasts cut in
    1 x 1½-inch pieces

1 (8-ounce) carton sour cream
¾ teaspoon fresh dill

BATTER
1 egg
½ cup water
¾ teaspoon salt

½ cup flour
2 teaspoons sesame seeds

Dip chicken in batter and deep fry. Eat hot, dipped in small carton sour cream mixed with ¾ teaspoon dill seed or fresh dill.

Yield: 6 servings   *Jo Ann Riley*

GOLDEN CHICKEN IN SPAGHETTI

2 large fryers or 1 hen
Pepper and salt, to taste
1 large onion
2 stalks celery
2 green bell peppers, chopped
2 large onions, chopped
1½ sticks margarine

1 (16-ounce) package thin
spaghetti
1 (10-ounce) can Rotel
tomatoes
1½ pounds Velveeta cheese,
cut in chunks
2 cans (17-ounce) tiny English
peas, plus juice

Cut fryers in quarters, wash, barely cover with water; add salt, pepper, onion and celery and cook in a covered saucepan until done. Let cool in broth. Remove and debone, reserving broth. Sauté bell pepper and onion in margarine about 45 minutes. Do not brown. Cook spaghetti in broth, add water if necessary. Do not drain. Add onion, peppers, and chicken to spaghetti; mix together. Add Rotel and cheese. Mix lightly until cheese melts. Mix in peas plus juice. Easier if made a day ahead and refrigerated in casserole dishes. Bake for 45 minutes at 350° before serving. Freezes well. A nice company casserole.

Yield: 18 servings

Grace Shaw

CHICKEN TETRAZZINI

1 (4-pound) chicken
4 tablespoons oil
2 cups water
2 onions, chopped
½ cup celery, chopped
1 bell pepper, chopped

2 cloves garlic, chopped
1 (6-ounce) can tomato paste
2 (8-ounce) cans tomato sauce
Grated cheese
1 (8-ounce) package spaghetti

Cut chicken in pieces and season with salt and pepper. Brown in 3 tablespoons of oil. Add 2 cups water and cook until tender. Remove meat from bone and cut in 1-inch pieces. Set aside. Reserve chicken broth. In 1 tablespoon oil, cook onions, celery, bell pepper and garlic until tender. Add tomato paste, sauce, chicken broth and chicken pieces. Boil spaghetti, drain and rinse, and pour sauce over spaghetti mix. Top with grated cheese and bake ½ hour in 350° oven.

Yield: 4 servings

Margaret Roane

CHICKEN TORTILLA

1 bell pepper
1 onion
1 (10-ounce) can Rotel
  tomatoes
4 tablespoons margarine
1 recipe for mushroom soup,
  page 57

¼ cup jalapeño cheese
1 fryer, boiled, deboned and
  cut up
Tortilla chips
Grated cheese, personal
  preference

Mix first 3 ingredients in blender or processor. Sauté vegetables with margarine. Add cream of mushroom soup, ¼ cup jalapeño cheese and chicken. Layer tortilla chips, chicken mixture, grated cheese, omitting cheese on top. Bake for 30 minutes at 350,° then add grated cheese. Bake until melted or place under broiler.

Yield: 5-6 servings   *Shara Viator*

Note: 1 (10½-ounce) can cream of mushroom soup may be used.

CORNISH HENS
BASTED IN SECRET SAUCE

4 Cornish hens
Salt and pepper to taste
1 stick butter

½ cup honey
½ teaspoon curry powder
1 teaspoon dry mustard

Wash and drain hens, sprinkle with salt and pepper. Melt butter in saucepan, add honey, curry powder and mustard and simmer briefly. Place hens in shallow roasting pan, brush with some sauce. Bake at 375° for 45 minutes. Continue basting with remaining sauce. Also good on chicken.

Yield: 4 servings   *Charlotte Guinn*

GOODBYE TURKEY

5 teaspoons sifted flour
1 teaspoon salt
1/4 teaspoon onion salt
1/4 cup melted butter or
    margarine
2 1/4 cups milk or light cream
1 1/3 cups Minute Rice,
    uncooked

1 1/2 cups turkey broth (or
    chicken bouillon cubes)
1/2 pound grated American
    cheese
1 1/2 cups cooked asparagus
2 cups or 6 slices turkey
2 teaspoons toasted, slivered
    almonds

Combine flour, 1/2 teaspoon salt and onion salt into butter in double boiler. Stir in milk. Cook until thick. Pour Minute Rice from box into 2 quart shallow baking dish. Combine broth, remaining salt and pour over rice. Sprinkle 1/2 of cheese over rice. Add asparagus, then turkey. Pour sauce over all. Sprinkle with remaining cheese. Bake 20 minutes at 375.° Top with almonds.

Yield: 6 servings   *Carolyn Carlon*

TURKEY SAUCE PIQUANTE

2 (8-pound) turkeys, remove
    fat and set aside, about
    8 ounces needed
Fat for frying
1/2 pound chopped onion
1 cup chopped celery
1/2 cup chopped bell pepper
1 quart tomato sauce

1 tablespoon salt
1 teaspoon cayenne pepper
1 quart turkey stock
1/2 cup green onions, chopped
    fine
1/2 cup parsley, chopped fine
2 tablespoons piccalilli sauce

Wash turkeys, disjoint and cut into parts: 4 wings, 4 legs, 4 thighs, and 8 pieces of breast. Simmer turkey necks and backbone pieces for turkey stock. Brown turkey parts until golden brown and set aside. Render turkey fat on low heat and sauté chopped onions, celery, and green pepper in this fat for about 10 minutes. Add tomato sauce, salt, and cayenne pepper and simmer for 30 minutes. Combine turkey stock and fried turkey parts into sauce, cover and simmer on medium heat until tender. Remove from heat and add chopped green onions and parsley, also add the piccalilli. Serve over cooked rice.

Yield: 20 servings   *Junius Winkle*

TURKEY AND TORTILLA

1 (3 to 4-pound) turkey breast
1 stick butter or margarine
1 cup flour
2 cups milk
½ pound fresh mushrooms,
  chopped
4 cups turkey broth
1 onion, chopped

4 (4-ounce) cans of chopped
  green chilies
Salt, pepper, garlic to taste
1 dozen corn tortillas cut into
  1-inch strips
1 pound grated Cheddar
  cheese

Boil turkey breast until tender. Remove skin and cut into bite sized pieces. Reserve broth. Make white sauce using butter, flour and milk. Add mushrooms. Add broth, onion, green chilies and seasonings. In large baking dish, layer tortillas, turkey, sauce mixture, and cheese. Make 2 layers and top with cheese. Bake at 350° for 45 minutes or until bubbly.

Yield: 20 servings

Julaine Porter

SEAFOOD

Circa 1940

This photograph shows the rear of the house as it appeared during Weeks Hall's occupancy. The upper and lower porches are enclosed. Originally, both were open and when the National Trust restored the house to its original plan they were reopened, as shown on the back cover. The back porches are believed to have been enclosed some time between 1834 and 1861, as the two paintings of the house by Adrien Persac in 1861 show both enclosed. During Weeks Hall's years, the enclosed second floor porch served as his sitting room, with a beautiful view of the bayou behind the house.

Weeks Hall and his Aunt Harriet were both collectors of Louisiana furniture. When she died, Weeks Hall inherited many of her good pieces, several of which are in the Shadows today. When the National Trust restored the house, some furnishings were added. Today, the house is furnished in the Empire style (1820-40) in keeping with the antebellum period to which it is restored.

Seafood

CRAB
Coquille.........................203
Croquettes.....................203
Deviled, Virginia...............203
Marinated, and Shrimp..........204
Ravigote.......................204
Stew...........................205
Stew with Shrimp..............205
Stuffed I......................206
Stuffed II.....................206
Stuffed, Neen's...............207
Stuffed Potatoes..............207
Stuffing for Fish..............208

CRAWFISH
Balls..........................210
Boiled.........................208
Cardinale I....................209
Cardinale II...................209
Casserole......................210
Étouffée I.....................211
Étouffée II....................211
Fried I........................212
Fried II.......................212
Quiche.........................213
Shrimp Casserole.............214
Spiced.........................215
Stew I.........................213
Stew II........................214

FISH
Facts About South Louisiana
    Fish........................215
Catfish, Fried.................216
Garfish Balls..................216
Pompano en Papillotte.........217
Redfish Yvonne................218
Sautéed Fish Filets...........220
Skewered Swordfish...........219
Snapper Filets, Captain Bill's....220
Speckled Trout................219
Stuffed........................222
Stuffed, in White Wine.........221
Tuna, Barbecued..............217

OYSTERS
Alexander.....................223
Artichoke Pie.................224

Bienville......................224
Casserole......................226
Creamed Patties I.............225
Creamed Patties II............225
Deviled........................226
Gigi...........................227
Manhattan Style..............227
Pie............................227
Rockefeller...................228
Sherry.........................229
Spaghetti.....................231
Stuffed I......................230
Stuffed II.....................230

SHRIMP
Artichoke Casserole...........232
Avery Island Deviled..........233
Bake I.........................234
Bake II........................234
Barbecued.....................231
Boats..........................232
Boiled.........................233
Broiled........................235
Casserole......................235
Cheese Sauce.................237
Crab, Étouffée................235
Creole I.......................236
Creole II......................236
Creole III (Microwave)........237
Eggplant.......................238
Fettuccine.....................238
Marguerite.....................240
Mosca I........................239
Mosca II.......................239
Ms. Ann.......................240
Mushrooms with Port Wine......241
Newburg.......................241
Pickled........................242
Portuguese....................242
Potted.........................243
Remoulade....................243
Sauce..........................244
Scampi.........................244
Seafood Casserole............246
Stuffed........................245
To Dry.........................246

Refer to additional recipes in "How Men Cook" section.

202

CRAB EN COQUILLE

1 pound crab meat
2 tablespoons butter
1½ tablespoons flour

1 cup milk
1 cup sherry
Salt and pepper to taste

Melt butter, add flour stirring constantly. Add milk slowly and then sherry. Simmer until smooth and creamy. Add crab meat to sauce and mix gently. Put in greased baking shells or pyrex dish. Top with buttered bread crumbs. Bake at 350° for 20 to 25 minutes.

Yield: 4 servings   *A Friend of the Shadows*

CRAB CROQUETTES

4 tablespoons butter
4 tablespoons flour
¾ cup chopped green onions
   with tops

1 cup milk
½ pound crab meat
1 cup bread crumbs
1 egg

Melt butter, add flour, then green onions; blend. Add milk slowly and cook until thick. Mix with crab meat and bread crumbs. Shape and place in refrigerator for about 1 hour to firm up. Dip in bread crumbs, then in beaten egg and in bread crumbs again, and fry in deep fat until golden brown.

Yield: 4 servings   *Sylvia Conrad*

VIRGINIA DEVILED CRABS

1 cup milk
1 egg

2 tablespoons flour
1 tablespoon butter

Place on low fire and cook until thick. When cool, add to the seasoned crab meat recipe shown below:

1 quart crab meat
1 tablespoon olive oil
Pepper and salt

1 tablespoon Worcestershire
   sauce
1 teaspoon dry mustard
½ cup cracker crumbs

Place in crab shells and dust with cracker crumbs. Bake at 350° until brown on top.

Yield: 8-12 servings   *The Weeks Family*

MARINATED CRABS AND SHRIMP

3 dozen boiled crabs with
   3 pounds headless boiled
   shrimp, or 5 dozen crabs
   only

1 large onion, cut into thin
   rings
Bunch of celery, cut in 2-inch
   pieces
1 bell pepper, sliced in rings

Open boiled crabs and clean. Allow the meat to remain in the crab shell. Crack each crab claw so that sauce can penetrate to the claw meat. Do not peel the headless boiled shrimp. Combine ingredients below for sauce:

3 cups imported olive oil
2 cups tarragon vinegar
1 teaspoon Italian seasonings
1/2 teaspoon oregano
1/2 teaspoon sweet basil

2 tablespoons Tabasco pepper
   sauce
5 teaspoons salt
2 tablespoons lemon juice

Using a large plastic container, preferably one that is flat bottomed, arrange a layer of cleaned crabs, claws, boiled shrimp and half of the celery, onion, and bell pepper. Pour 1/2 of the sauce over this. Repeat layers and pour remainder of sauce. Cover and refrigerate. Marinate at least 24 hours, but 48 hours is even better. Toss and stir mixture several times during this period so that sauce completely coats all the seafood. Serve as "finger food" with hot French bread and cold beer.

Yield: 6 servings

Mrs. Donald (Yvonne) Pavy

SEA 1—Top p204

LUMP CRABMEAT RAVIGOTE

5 tablespoons butter
3 tablespoons flour
1 1/2 cups light cream (half
   and half)
1 tablespoon chopped parsley

3 tablespoons chopped green
   onions
Pepper sauce and salt to taste
1 pound lump crab meat (or
   boiled shrimp or peeled
   crawfish)

Make rich sauce in pot with melted butter, flour and cream. Stir well over medium heat. When smooth and thick, add parsley, green onions and seasoning. Very gently, fold in crab meat. Put into individual ramekins and bake for 20 minutes at 350° until bubbly. Also very good as a hot dip.

Yield: 6 servings

Scotty Broussard

CRAB STEW

6 large crabs
1 tablespoon butter
2 tablespoons flour
3 shallots, cut fine

2 cloves minced garlic
3 tablespoons parsley
1 bell pepper, chopped
Salt and pepper

Boil crabs, reserving water. Cut crabs in half. Put butter in iron skillet. Add flour, and make a nice roux. Add seasonings, crabs, and cook 5 minutes; then add 2 cups of water in which they were boiled and cook slowly 10 minutes. Season again, add 2 more cups water, cook 10 more minutes and serve with boiled rice.

Yield: 4 servings   *The Weeks Family*

CRAB AND SHRIMP STEW

1½ to 2 pounds shrimp
1 dozen hardshell crabs
1 cup cooking oil
1 cup flour
1 large onion, chopped
3 to 4 stalks celery, chopped
½ to ¾ cup bell pepper,
  chopped

1 (10-ounce) can Rotel
  tomatoes
Few dashes Worcestershire
  sauce
½ teaspoon monosodium
  glutamate
Salt and pepper to taste
3 tablespoons green onion
3 tablespoons parsley

Peel and devein shrimp and set aside. Reserve shells. Scald crabs in boiling water for 4 to 5 minutes. Break off legs, remove outer shell, and clean well down to the inner shell. Boil cracked crab legs and shrimp shells in about 10 cups water for 30 to 45 minutes to make stock. Strain. Make a brown roux with flour and oil. Add next 3 items and sauté until limp. Add Rotel tomatoes and sauté about 5 minutes. Add strained stock and seasonings and cook until smooth and thick. Add crabs and simmer slowly about 1 hour. Add shrimp and simmer about 7 minutes more. Correct seasoning, add green onion and parsley and serve over cooked rice.

Yield: 8-10 servings   *Keith E. Courrege*

STUFFED CRABS I

½ cup cooking oil
2 pounds onions, chopped fine
1 bunch celery, chopped fine
6 bell peppers, chopped fine
2 tablespoons minced garlic
16 slices toasted bread

4 tablespoons Worcestershire
  sauce
2 sticks butter
4 pounds fresh crab meat
½ cup minced parsley
½ cup chopped onion tops
2 cups bread crumbs

In ½ cup of oil, sauté onions, celery, bell pepper and garlic. Cook until oil rises. Soak toasted bread in water; squeeze as much water out of bread as possible and add to pot. Cook until brown and well blended. Add Worcestershire sauce and butter. Cook until butter comes to top. Add crab meat and mix gently. Add parsley and onion tops. Stir gently. Put filling in crab shells or individual dishes. Top with bread crumbs. Bake at 350.° When ready to serve, garnish with a slice of lemon.

Yield: 48 servings

Mrs. Sam Broussard

STUFFED CRABS II

3 large white onions, chopped
3 bell peppers, chopped
3 ribs celery, chopped
½ cup cooking oil
½ loaf French bread

3 pounds crab meat
2 sticks butter
Cayenne pepper, salt and
  black pepper to taste

Sauté onions, bell pepper and celery in oil. Soak French bread in water and put in colander to drain. When drained of the excess moisture, add bread to onion mixture. Mix well. Add crab meat and butter. Add the rest of the seasonings. Mix carefully. Soak crab shells overnight in soda water. Stuff crab shells or ramekins with mixture. Sprinkle with bread crumbs and put a pat of butter on top. Bake for 30 minutes at 350.° Serve with lemon slices.

Yield: 12 servings

Lillian V. Barrow

NEEN'S STUFFED CRAB

2 medium onions, chopped
fine
3 cloves garlic, minced
2 stalks celery, chopped fine
1 medium bell pepper,
chopped fine
1/2 pound margarine

3 stale or day old hamburger
buns
1 cup evaporated milk
2 eggs, beaten
2 pounds crab meat
1 teaspoon Accent
Salt and pepper to taste

Sauté onions, garlic, celery, bell pepper in 1/2 pound margarine until very, very soft. Crumble hamburger buns and add milk; let soak about 1 minute. Add eggs to hamburger buns and milk. Add crabmeat to sautéed seasonings and mix gently. Add hamburger bun mixture and Accent to this and heat thoroughly. Season to taste. This filling may be put into crab shells or into casserole with bread crumbs on top.

Yield: 8 servings

Susie Pharr

CRAB STUFFED POTATOES

4 Idaho potatoes
1/2 cup butter
1/2 cup light cream
1 teaspoon salt
Pepper to taste

4 teaspoons grated onions
1 cup sharp cheese, grated
1 (6 1/2-ounce) can of lump
crab meat
1/2 teaspoon paprika

Bake potatoes until tender. Cut lengthwise and scoop out potatoes; whip with butter, cream, salt and pepper, onions, and cheese. Using a fork, mix in crab meat and refill potato shell. Sprinkle with paprika, and reheat in a very hot oven for 15 minutes.

Yield: 8 servings

Helen Bernard

CRAB MEAT STUFFING FOR FISH

¼ cup butter or margarine
4 strips bacon, finely cubed
1½ cups celery leaves,
  chopped
¼ cup onion, grated
2 cups soft bread crumbs

4 eggs, well beaten
1½ teaspoons salt
½ teaspoon pepper
Dash of cayenne pepper
Dash of nutmeg
½ pound fresh crab meat

Melt butter in skillet on medium heat. Add bacon and cook until light brown, stirring constantly. Add celery leaves and onions. Cook for 5 or 6 minutes. Stir in bread crumbs, beaten eggs, salt, pepper, cayenne, and nutmeg. Mix well. Remove from heat and add crab meat. This will stuff a 4 to 5 pound fish.

Yield: 6 servings

Sylvia Conrad

BOILED CRAWFISH

SEASONINGS
2 (3¾-ounce) bottles cayenne
  pepper

3 (1 pound, 10 ounce) boxes
  salt

Mix together well and pour in two 1 quart jars.

CRAWFISH
50 pounds live crawfish
1 box salt
5 gallons water

20 gallon pot
1 quart seasoning

Purge live crawfish by dumping crawfish in wash tub; fill with cold water and add 1 box salt. Allow to stand 5 to 10 minutes. Remove crawfish from tub. Meanwhile boil the 5 gallons of water in the 20 gallon pot. Add crawfish and let water return to a boil; cook for 4 minutes covered. Remove crawfish and place in a large container. Sprinkle with 1 quart seasoning as they are added. Cover with newspaper and keep warm. (An ice chest may be used instead of container and newspaper.) Allow to stand a few minutes to let seasonings penetrate. Serve hot.

Yield: 10-12 servings

Sam Broussard

CRAWFISH CARDINALE I

1 stick butter, softened
1 container crawfish fat
2 stalks celery, chopped
1 1/2 cups onion, chopped
1/2 cup bell pepper, chopped
2 cloves garlic, minced
1 teaspoon tomato paste
1 pound crawfish tails, peeled

1/4 cup each, chopped parsley
  and green onions
Salt and pepper
1 teaspoon cornstarch mixed
  with a little cold water
1 1/2 to 2 cups sour cream
French bread

Put butter and crawfish fat in cold skillet and cook over medium heat about 5 minutes. Add next 5 ingredients and cook over medium-high heat until vegetables are wilted—about 5 minutes. Stir frequently. Add crawfish tails and simmer about 10 minutes. Add green onions and parsley and cook until slightly wilted. Season to taste with salt and pepper. Add cornstarch and stir until it "sets." Let simmer a few minutes. Add 1 1/2 cups of sour cream and stir. If more "gravy" is desired, add more sour cream. Serve over toasted slices of French bread.

Yield: 4-6 servings   *Keith E. Courrege*

CRAWFISH CARDINALE II

1 pound crawfish tails
2 medium onions, chopped
1 1/2 sticks butter
3 tablespoons flour
2 cups milk

Salt and pepper
1/2 teaspoon garlic salt
1/2 cup white wine
1 tablespoon tomato paste

Sauté onions in 1/2 stick butter. Add crawfish. Make a cream sauce of 1 stick of butter, flour and add milk gradually to make sauce. Combine white sauce with onions and crawfish. Season with salt, pepper and garlic salt. Add wine and 1 tablespoon tomato paste for color. Good with green salad and French bread.

Yield: 6 servings   *Carol Haik*

CRAWFISH BALLS

4 pounds peeled crawfish tails, cooked
1 bell pepper
1 stalk celery
½ cup chopped green onions
1 to 1½ sticks butter, softened (not margarine)
Salt to taste
1 cayenne pepper or ½ teaspoon ground red pepper
Garlic powder
Bread crumbs

Boil tails in seasoned water 20 minutes, drain, chop. Chop or grind bell pepper, celery, and pepper. Mix all ingredients except bread-crumbs together; season with salt, and red pepper; form balls; roll lightly in bread crumbs. Bake at 400° for 20 minutes. Also good with cooked crab meat.

Yield: 16-18 servings

Earline Rose

CRAWFISH CASSEROLE

¼ stick butter
½ large onion, chopped
½ cup chopped bell pepper
1 pound crawfish tails
1 (10½-ounce) can cream of mushroom soup
2 (7-ounce) cans mushroom steak sauce
1 (10½-ounce) can cream of onion soup
1 beef bouillon cube in 1 cup water
1½ cups raw rice
⅓ cup green onion tops
2 teaspoons dried parsley
Pepper (no salt)

Melt ¼ stick butter. Add onions and bell pepper and sauté—add crawfish, mushroom soup and ⅓ cup water. Add steak sauce and ¼ cup water, onion soup and bouillon. Let boil a few minutes. Add rice, onion tops, parsley and pepper. Mix well. Put in 3-quart cov-ered casserole and bake at 350° for 1 hour. Stir about 10 minutes before done.

Yield: 6-8 servings

Rose Mary Brooks

Note: Shrimp may be substituted for crawfish.

CRAWFISH ÉTOUFFÉE I

1 stick margarine or butter
1 clove garlic, chopped fine
1 large onion, sliced thin
1 container crawfish fat

1 pound crawfish tails (peeled)
Salt, red and black pepper
Green onions and parsley

Melt margarine or butter in iron pot. Add garlic and thinly sliced onion, cook slowly until transparent (do not brown). Add crawfish fat and tails, salt, black and red pepper. Stir well, cover pot and simmer for 20 minutes only. Stir once or twice. When ready to serve, add chopped green onions and parsley. Serve over rice with green salad and hot French bread.

Yield: 3 servings   *Sylvia Conrad*

Variation: 2 onions, chopped; no garlic. Add 2 tablespoons Joyce's Special Seasoning found in sauce section of this book.

CRAWFISH ÉTOUFFÉE II
(with No Crawfish Fat)

1 cup flour
½ cup oil
3 sticks butter
4 large onions
1 stalk celery

4 pounds peeled crawfish tails
Salt, black and red pepper
  to taste
½ cup chopped parsley
½ cup chopped green onions

Make roux with flour and oil, stirring frequently until golden brown. Melt butter and sauté onions and celery until clear and soft. Add crawfish tails, salt and pepper. Cook 5 minutes. Gradually add roux by tablespoons. Add water for desired consistency. Cook 20 minutes. Sprinkle onion tops and parsley over all when done. Serve over cooked rice.

Yield: 16 servings   *Flo Landry*

FRIED CRAWFISH TAILS I

1 cup flour
¾ cup lukewarm water
3 tablespoons vegetable oil

½ teaspoon salt
1 egg white
1 quart crawfish tails, peeled

Mix together flour, water, oil and salt. This may be prepared ahead of time. When ready to cook (or within 2 hours of cooking) fold in 1 egg white stiffly beaten. Season crawfish with salt and pepper; dip in batter and fry only until slightly brown. (Batter will do for about 1 quart of tails.)

Yield: 6-8 servings   Sam Broussard

Note: Serve above with Zippy Sauce found in sauce section.

FRIED CRAWFISH TAILS II
OR FRIED SHRIMP

3 eggs
1 tablespoon mayonnaise
1 tablespoon lemon juice

1 pound cleaned crawfish tails
or 1 pound cleaned shrimp

Beat eggs until fluffy. Add lemon juice and mayonnaise and blend. Then, add the shrimp or crawfish to this mixture and marinate at least 30 minutes before ready to fry.

2 cups yellow corn meal
Salt and pepper to taste

2 teaspoons baking powder
1 cup flour

Mix these dry ingredients in a paper bag. Add a portion of the craw-fish or shrimp at a time and shake. Remove from bag and shake off excess mixture. Drop in deep fat (375°). Fry until brown, turning if necessary as they float. This should not take longer than 3 to 4 minutes. Overcooking will toughen them. Remove and drain on absorbent paper.

Yield: 2-3 servings   Mrs. Donald (Yvonne) Pavy

Note: Serve with Zippy Sauce found in sauce section.

CRAWFISH QUICHE

1 large frozen pie crust,
  defrosted
1 pound peeled crawfish tails
1/4 cup chopped green onions
1/4 cup chopped parsley
1/2 stick butter
1 (4-ounce) can mushrooms,
  drained and sliced
1/4 cup dry sherry or white wine
3 eggs, slightly beaten

1 cup Half and Half
1/2 cup heavy cream
Salt and pepper to taste
1/2 cup grated Gruyère or
  Monterey Jack cheese
1/2 cup grated Parmesan
  cheese
1 fresh tomato, peeled and
  thinly sliced

Partially bake pie shell (3 to 4 minutes) and set aside. Sauté crawfish, green onions, and parsley in butter about 2 minutes. Add mushrooms and sauté another minute or two. Add wine and bring to full boil. Cut off heat and allow to cool. When cool, beat eggs with Half and Half and cream, salt and pepper and add to crawfish mixture. Pour into prepared pie shell, sprinkle with cheeses, and top with sliced tomatoes. Bake for 30 to 45 minutes at 350° or until toothpick inserted in center comes out clean.

Yield: 6 servings main dish
        12 servings appetizer

Keith E. Courrege

CRAWFISH STEW I

2 cups oil
2 cups flour
2 chopped onions
10 ounces crawfish fat

10 pounds crawfish tails
1/2 cup chopped parsley
Salt and pepper to taste

Make a roux with the oil and flour and cook until the color of peanut butter (no darker). Add onions and stir until well cooked. Add crawfish fat and cook slowly (fat will rise when cooked enough). Add water until you get the consistency that you want for the gravy. (Not too much—crawfish will give off some liquid when added.) When ready to eat, heat to boiling—then lower fire; add crawfish tails, salt and pepper, then chopped parsley. Simmer about 15 to 20 minutes—tails will curl when done. Serve with rice.

Yield: 15 servings

Sam Broussard

CRAWFISH STEW II

1 heaping kitchen spoon flour
  (about 1/4 cup)
1/4 cup cooking oil
1 large onion, chopped
1 bell pepper, chopped

1 stalk celery, chopped
1 (1-ounce) package of fat
1 cup water
1 pound crawfish tails
Parsley and green onions

Make a roux of flour and oil. Cook until golden brown. Add onion, bell pepper, and celery to roux; cook until wilted. Add crawfish fat and cook slowly until fat separates from seasonings. Add water; cook for about 1 hour. Crawfish tails are to be added 20 to 30 minutes before serving. Garnish with parsley and green onions.

Yield: 4 servings

CRAWFISH AND SHRIMP CASSEROLE

1 cup chopped onion
1 cup chopped bell pepper
1 cup chopped celery
2 cloves garlic, minced
1 stick butter
1 (10 1/2-ounce) can cream of
  mushroom soup
1 (10 1/2-ounce) can Cheddar
  cheese soup

1 (4-ounce) can pimentos
1 1/2 cups shrimp
1 1/2 cups crawfish tails
2 cups cooked rice
1/4 cup bread crumbs
1/3 cup chopped parsley
1 cup chopped green onions
Salt and pepper to taste

Cook onions, bell pepper, garlic and celery in butter until tender. Add soups, parsley, green onions, shrimp, crawfish, pimentos, salt and pepper. Heat on top of stove—stir in rice and bread crumbs. Put in 3-quart covered casserole dish. Bake for 30 minutes at 350°

Yield: 10-12 servings   *JoAnn Riley*

SPICED CRAWFISH

2 quarts red wine (a good
   California wine)
1 quart water
3 bay leaves
4 cloves garlic
¼ cup Tabasco pepper sauce

2 tablespoons salt
3 sprigs parsley
6 to 8 whole allspice
1 teaspoon tarragon
3 pounds live crawfish

Bring the wine, water, bay leaves, garlic, Tabasco, salt, parsley, all-spice and tarragon to a boil in a deep pot. Lower heat and simmer 10 minutes. Add crawfish and cook 8 to 10 minutes or until done. Drain. Save the bouillon. It can be used for bisque. Chill cooked crawfish well and serve with homemade mayonnaise if desired.

Yield: 4-6 servings *Sylvia Conrad*

LES POISSONS
(Fish)

Facts about South Louisiana fish:

Gaspergou—Firm flesh, slow cooking. Good for courtbouillons and bouillabaisses. Bakes well, can be fried.
Buffalo—Bony, needs tenderloining, firm, slow cooking. When boned can be used in courtbouillons, baked or fried.
Catfish—Can be fried, broiled or baked.
Trout—Soft to medium firm flesh. Best broiled or fried.
Redfish—Medium firm flesh. Good for baking. Also, can be used for courtbouillons or bouillabaisses.
Red Snapper—Use as you would redfish. Also good broiled.
Flounder—Medium firm. Best broiled or fried.
Garfish—Soft, good for fish stews. Good for fishballs.
Lemon Fish—Tough. Good for stews and dishes with long cooking times.
Spade Fish—Similar to gaspergou. Good baked, good for court-bouillons and bouillabaisses.
Perch—Fry or broil.

SEAFOOD

FRIED CATFISH

1½ to 2 pounds catfish filets
Salt and pepper to taste
Garlic powder
Tabasco pepper sauce
Prepared yellow mustard

1 cup yellow cornmeal, lightly
  seasoned with salt and
  pepper
3 tablespoons flour
Cooking oil for deep frying

Season filets with salt, pepper, garlic powder, and Tabasco. Coat filets generously with mustard but don't overdo it. Cut filets into bite-size pieces. Dredge pieces in seasoned cornmeal mixed with flour. Deep fry in about 2 inches of cooking oil in a heavy skillet or Dutch oven until golden brown and crisp. Serve at once with tartar sauce.

Yield: 6 servings

Keith E. Courrege

GARFISH BALLS

2 pounds garfish meat, finely
  ground
3 tablespoons flour
½ bunch fresh parsley,
  chopped fine

Dash nutmeg
2 eggs
4 to 6 green onions, chopped
  fine
Salt, red and black pepper

Mix all ingredients well. Shape into 2-inch balls and drop into simmering seasoned roux.

SEASONED ROUX
½ cup oil
¾ cup flour
1 large onion, chopped fine
½ bell pepper, chopped fine
2 garlic pods, minced

2 stalks celery, chopped fine
1 bay leaf
Salt, black and red pepper
1 quart water

Heat oil in heavy pot. Add flour and stir constantly on medium heat until brown. Add vegetables and sauté for a few minutes. Add 1 quart water and rest of ingredients. Simmer approximately 30 to 45 minutes. Then add garfish balls and continue cooking for 30 to 40 minutes or until fish balls are firm. Serve over fluffy rice.

Yield: 6 servings

Sylvia Conrad

POMPANO EN PAPILLOTTE

6 paper bags or 6 pieces of
  parchment paper
3 cups boiling salted water
1 lemon, cut in slices
1 bay leaf
1/4 teaspoon thyme
6 pompano filets
2 tablespoons butter
3 tablespoons flour

1 onion, minced
1 1/2 cups fish stock
2 tablespoons dry vermouth
1/2 cup boiled shrimp, cut
  into pieces
6 fresh mushrooms, sliced
1/4 teaspoon salt
3 drops Tabasco pepper sauce
2 egg yolks

To boiling salt water add lemon slices, bay leaf, and thyme. Add fish filets and simmer for 15 minutes. Remove the fish. Strain 1 1/2 cups of the water that was used to cook the fish; this is the fish stock. Place fish filets flat in a well oiled paper bag or on individual sheets of parchment paper. Make a thick sauce by melting the butter in a saucepan on simmer flame. To this stir in flour, and add onion, browning the mixture slightly. Add fish stock and vermouth, stirring to make a smooth sauce. Add shrimp, mushrooms, salt and Tabasco pepper sauce. Remove saucepan from heat, cool and beat in egg yolks. Divide the sauce among the filets by placing spoonfuls on each filet. Fold filets and then close the paper bags or fold over the parchment paper so that each fish filet is encased in a separate bag. Bake 10 minutes at 400.° Serve in paper bag.

Yield: 6 servings   *Susie Pharr*

BARBECUED TUNA

2 to 3 pounds fresh tuna filets,
  cut into 2-inch cubes
Red pepper
Black pepper
Salt
Juice of 1 lemon

1/2 teaspoon Worcestershire
  sauce
1 teaspoon prepared mustard
2 tablespoons minced onion
1 (8-ounce) bottle French
  salad dressing

Season fish with the salt and pepper. Mix all other ingredients in a large bowl and marinate cubes of tuna for at least an hour, stirring occasionally so that all of the pieces absorb the flavor. Remove from sauce and grill over hot coals, turning each piece once carefully to avoid breaking up the fish. Depending on the thickness of the pieces, grilling may take 10 or 15 minutes. Use extra sauce to keep fish moist as it cooks. Fish is done when layers will separate. This is delicious and has a very different taste.

Yield: 4-6 servings   *Ed Minvielle*

BAKED REDFISH YVONNE

½ cup cooking oil
¾ cup flour
2 medium onions, chopped fine
½ cup chopped celery
1 bell pepper, chopped fine
2 cloves garlic, chopped fine
2 quarts stewed whole tomatoes (preferably homegrown)
1½ quarts fish stock

3 bay leaves
3 tablespoons chopped green onion tops
3 tablespoons chopped parsley
2 tablespoons sugar or substitute sweetener
Salt and red pepper to taste
1 (8-ounce) can whole mushrooms
6 to 10 redfish filets

Stock preparation: Boil fish heads, bones and seasoning in 2 quarts of water. Reduce to 1½ quarts.

Gravy preparation: Allow at least 2 hours or longer for cooking. Begin by making a roux of the flour and oil, add chopped onions, celery, bell peppers, garlic, and sauté until tender. Add tomatoes, fish stock and bay leaves and simmer for at least 2 hours (gravy needs to be thick, as the gravy will thin out when baking over the fish filets). Add all the remaining ingredients and the gravy is ready for the fish filets. This is best prepared ahead of time and refrigerated. It also freezes very well.

Filet preparation and baking: Cut redfish filets into serving size pieces and place in a large baking pan that is deep enough to hold gravy also. This recipe is for 6 servings, therefore depending on the thickness of your filets, you will need at least 6 pieces or perhaps as many as 10. Leave at least an inch or so of space between filets, to spoon the gravy over each filet, as well as between. Bake for 40 minutes or so at 350°, depending on thickness of filets. Garnish each filet with a thin slice of lemon on top about 5 minutes before taking out of the oven. Serve over hot fluffy rice.

Yield: 6 servings   *Mrs. Donald (Yvonne) Pavy*

SPECKLED TROUT OR REDFISH

2 tablespoons butter, softened
2 tablespoons butter, cut into
 1/2 inch bits
1/4 pound fresh mushrooms,
 cut lengthwise into 1/4 inch
 thick slices
1/4 cup thinly sliced scallions
 including 3 inches of
 green tops

4 (8-ounce) speckled trout
 filets
1 1/2 teaspoons salt
1/2 cup dry white wine
12 medium size uncooked
 shrimp
Hollandaise sauce
Red pepper

Brush baking dish with softened butter and scatter scallions and mushrooms. Place fish over vegetables. Sprinkle with salt and pour in wine. Cover fish with wax paper previously buttered. Butter side on fish. Place in oven and bake at 350° until filets are firm.

In a skillet melt remaining butter until it foams, then add shrimp and stir for 2 or 3 minutes until pink. Set aside. Use recipe on page 87 to prepare Hollandaise sauce. When filets are cooked, strain off liquid and boil until it is reduced to a few tablespoons. Beat that liquid into the Hollandaise sauce. Add red pepper and season to taste. Place shrimp on each filet and spoon the sauce over the top, masking the fish completely. Put under broiler for 30 seconds or until sauce is lightly browned.

Yield: 4 servings   *Helen Bernard*

SKEWERED SWORDFISH

2 pounds swordfish or
 lemonfish
1/2 cup olive oil
3/4 cup lemon juice
1/4 cup grated onion
2 teaspoons salt

1/2 teaspoon fresh ground
 pepper
1 teaspoon paprika
12 to 16 bay leaves
2 teaspoons chopped parsley

Rinse fish and pat dry. Cut fish into 1 1/2 inch cubes. In a glass bowl mix 1/4 cup olive oil, 1/4 cup lemon juice, the grated onion, 1 1/2 teaspoons salt, pepper, paprika, and bay leaves. Toss fish in the mixture. Then cover and marinate in the refrigerator 6 to 8 hours. Turn and baste frequently. Drain and divide fish among 6 to 8 skewers, putting a couple of bay leaves on each skewer. Broil 15 minutes or until brown and tender, turning skewers so as to be sure to brown all sides. Mix together the remaining oil, lemon juice, salt and parsley. Serve with fish.

Yield: 4-6 servings   *Sylvia Conrad*

SAUTÉED FISH FILETS

4 to 6 speckled trout filets
   (or other firm fish)
Milk

Flour
Salt and pepper
Butter

Soak filets in milk, dredge in seasoned flour, then dip in milk, then flour again. Chill for ½ hour, then sauté in butter until nicely browned on both sides.

SEAFOOD SAUCE
1 stick butter
2 tablespoons flour
½ cup chopped green onion
2 teaspoons minced parsley
½ pint oysters, drain and
   reserve liquid
1 (6-ounce) can crabmeat,
   drained
1 (6-ounce) can shrimp, rinsed

1 (4-ounce) can sliced
   mushrooms, drained
1 (14-ounce) can artichoke
   hearts, drained and
   quartered
¼ cup dry vermouth, white
   wine or sherry
Juice of 1 lemon
Parmesan cheese
Salt and pepper to taste

Make roux with butter and flour. Do not brown. Add onions and parsley and cook slowly until soft. Combine oyster liquid, vermouth, and enough water to equal 2 cups liquid. Add to flour mixture and cook until thickened. Add remaining ingredients, except Parmesan cheese. Then salt and pepper to taste. Spoon over cooked fish filets, sprinkle with cheese, and broil until slightly brown on top.

Yield: 4-6 servings   *Barbara Gordy*

CAPTAIN BILL'S BABY SNAPPER FILETS

2 tomatoes
3 tablespoons fresh bread
   crumbs
Salt and pepper
1½ pounds small red snapper
   filets

½ stick butter
½ cup white port wine
1 teaspoon lemon or lime juice
2 tablespoons Parmesan
   cheese
Paprika

Peel and slice tomatoes thinly; arrange slices in 4 buttered ramekins and sprinkle each dish with fresh bread crumbs. Season with salt and pepper. Divide snapper filets among dishes. In a saucepan combine butter, port wine, and lemon or lime juice. Cook over low heat until butter is melted. Increase heat to moderate and boil 3 minutes. Pour mixture over filets and sprinkle with cheese and paprika. Bake for 10 minutes at 500.°

Yield: 4 servings   *Ann Morrow*

BAKED STUFFED FISH IN WHITE WINE

1 (5-pound) fish: redfish, red
  snapper or sea bass
1 tablespoon lemon juice
4 tablespoons butter or
  margarine
4 tablespoons flour
1 large onion, chopped

1 to 2 cloves garlic, minced
1/8 teaspoon cayenne pepper
4 cups water or fish stock
1/2 pound sliced fresh
  mushrooms
2 cups white wine

Rub fish with lemon juice, salt and pepper. Heat butter until melted, add flour, stir until brown. Add onion, garlic and cayenne pepper. Now add water and mushrooms. Pour over fish, add wine. Bake 45 to 55 minutes at 350° or until meat flakes with fork. Baste fish frequently.

Note: Fish may be stuffed before baking with the following recipe.

STUFFING FOR FISH

1/3 cup chopped green onions
  with tops (about six)
1/3 cup chopped bell pepper
1/3 cup finely chopped celery
1 teaspoon garlic powder or
  2 cloves crushed fresh
  garlic (to desired taste)

2 dozen oysters or 1 pound
  shrimp
2 cups Progresso seasoned
  bread crumbs
Salt, black and red pepper

Cook onions, bell pepper, celery, garlic and oysters. Add to bread crumbs. Add small amount oyster liquid until moist. Add salt and pepper. Stuff fish, and bake.

Yield: 4-6 servings

Elaine Conrad

STUFFED FISH

CRAB DRESSING

½ pound butter
3 large onions, chopped
2 bell peppers, chopped
2 stalks celery, chopped
2 pounds crabmeat, cleaned
½ loaf French bread
2 cups seafood stock or water

2 tablespoons salt
1 teaspoon red pepper
1 teaspoon white pepper
1 teaspoon black pepper
1 cup green onion tops, chopped
1 cup chopped parsley

Sauté in butter the onions, bell pepper and celery until very tender, about 45 minutes. Add salt and peppers and cook for 4 minutes. Add crabmeat and mix well; cook for 5 minutes. While the dressing is cooking, dry out the French bread in the oven at 250°; when it becomes hard, remove from oven and cool. In a large bowl, add bread and stock and make a stiff mush. Lower the fire and add bread mush, onion tops and parsley. Mix well and cook until same consistency throughout the dressing. Remove from stove and cool. Dressing should be refrigerated overnight or at least 2 hours. This dressing may be used for stuffed fish, stuffed crabs, shrimp, mushrooms or bell peppers.

Fish: Speckled trout, red fish, red snapper, pompano, lemon fish or any salt water fish; bass or striped bass for fresh water fish. The most important aspect concerning the fish is that it must be FRESH.

The size depends upon how many servings are necessary. A large fish may be stuffed and served whole; smaller fish may be served individually. The most important aspect in cooking the fish is the size pan used. The pan should have about ½ to 1 inch space around the fish and deep enough to hold the sauce, but not deeper than 1½ inches. This aids in removing fish from pan with a spatula.

SAUCE

½ pound butter
1 cup lemon juice
¼ cup Worcestershire sauce
⅛ cup dry vermouth

½ cup chopped green onion tops
½ cup chopped parsley

Mix all ingredients and let cook for about 4 minutes.

Stuff crabmeat dressing inside fish or between 2 filets and place in appropriate size pan. Pour enough sauce over the fish to cover and have enough to go around the ends of fish. If while cooking, it begins to dry, add more sauce. Sprinkle paprika on top for color. Bake at 375° for about 35 to 40 minutes for individual servings or up to 1½ hours for a very large fish.

Yield: 6 servings

Gigi and Alex Patout

OYSTERS ALEXANDER

½ pound butter
2 onions, chopped
1 bell pepper, chopped
1 rib celery, chopped
1 pod garlic, minced
2 pounds shrimp, chopped
4 dozen oysters, drained,
   2 dozen chopped and
   2 dozen whole, keep shells
1 pint oyster water

½ cup parsley, chopped
½ cup green onions, chopped
1 tablespoon lemon juice
1 teaspoon thyme
6 drops Tabasco pepper sauce
Salt and pepper to taste
24 oyster shells cleaned or
   24 ramekins
¼ cup paprika
1 cup Parmesan cheese
1 loaf French bread, ½ soaked
   in oyster water and ½ made
   into dried bread crumbs

Melt butter, add onions, bell pepper, celery and garlic. Sauté until soft. Have ready the chopped shrimp and oysters. Most importantly, cut oysters just back of eye muscles. Add shrimp, oyster water, cook 7 minutes. Add the chopped oysters and cook only 4 minutes. Add soaked ½ loaf of French bread, parsley, green onions, lemon juice, thyme and other seasonings. Cook 10 minutes. Remove from heat, let cool. This is the dressing that will be used to cover oysters. Dressing should be stiff; when baking the oysters, they will give off juice.

Have ready 2 dozen cleaned oyster shells. Place an oyster on each shell. To this sprinkle a little salt and pepper. When dressing has cooled, spoon 2 tablespoons over each oyster or enough to cover completely. Cover oysters thinly, but completely. Repeat this until all oysters are covered with dressing.

Place shells on baking sheet. Mix together ¼ cup of bread crumbs, paprika and Parmesan cheese. Sprinkle lightly over all oyster shells. Place in broiler and/or 450° oven until bread crumbs are brown. This will take about 18 minutes.

Yield: 24 servings
Alex and Gigi Patout

OYSTER-ARTICHOKE PIE

2 dozen fresh oysters, drained, reserve liquid
1 (8-ounce) can artichoke hearts, quartered
½ pound ground sirloin
1 tablespoon olive oil
6 to 8 green onions, sliced
1 cup freshly crushed cracker crumbs
1 (9-inch) deep dish pie crust

Drain oysters well. Keep liquid for later. Rinse artichoke hearts in cold water and drain well. Brown ground sirloin in a tiny amount of olive oil (just enough to keep meat from sticking to skillet), and when brown, add sliced green onions, including tops. Add quartered artichoke hearts and chopped oysters. Toss together lightly. If too dry, add a little of oyster liquid. Simmer slowly until oysters begin to curl on edges. Sprinkle a few cracker crumbs into mixture if it is too moist. Place in pre-baked pie shell. Cover with cracker crumbs. Bake at 350° for 20 minutes. Remove from oven and let cool a little. Slice into 6 or 8 pieces. This can be made ahead and frozen. Just increase to 375° for 1 hour.

Yield: 6-8 servings   *Carol Ann Dumond*

OYSTERS BIENVILLE

1 bunch shallots, chopped fine
3 tablespoons butter
3 tablespoons flour
1½ cups chicken broth
⅔ cup white wine
1 cup minced raw mushrooms
1 cup chopped cooked shrimp
2 egg yolks
2 teaspoons cream
3 dozen oysters in their half shell
Rock salt
Parmesan cheese
Bread crumbs

Sauté shallots in butter, add flour, stirring until light brown. Gradually add chicken broth, wine, mushrooms, and shrimp. Cook slowly for 10 minutes; thicken the sauce with egg yolks beaten with cream and heat without allowing it to come to a boil. Set aside.

On 6 pie pans, put a layer of rock salt. Place 6 oysters in their half shell on each pan. Bake the oysters in their own juice, at 350° for about 6 minutes. Take out of oven and cover each oyster with some sauce. Sprinkle lightly with bread crumbs and grated Parmesan cheese. Return the oysters to the oven for about 10 minutes, or until browned.

Yield: 3 dozen   *Scotty Broussard*

CREAMED OYSTER PATTIES I

4 dozen oysters
1 tablespoon butter
1 tablespoon flour
1 small onion, grated
1 (4-ounce) can chopped
   mushrooms and liquid

Salt, black and red pepper
   to taste
2 tablespoons chopped
   parsley and green onions
1/4 teaspoon lemon juice
1 dozen patty shells

Cook oysters in their own liquid. Bring to a boil then simmer over a low flame for 10 minutes. Melt butter in saucepan. Add flour and blend until smooth. Add onion, mushrooms and liquid, and seasonings. Add parsley and green onions. Add oysters and lemon juice. Cook 5 minutes and then pour into patty shells. Bake for 15 minutes at 425.°

Yield: 12 servings

L. J. Freyou

CREAMED OYSTER PATTIES II

3 teaspoons butter, melted
3 teaspoons flour
1/2 cup liquid from oysters
1 1/2 cups heavy cream
Salt and pepper to taste

2 egg yolks
1 pint oysters
2 tablespoons dry sherry
4 to 6 patty shells
Parsley, chopped

Melt butter and blend in flour. Cook for a few minutes. Stir in oyster liquid and 1 cup cream and continue stirring until sauce is thick and smooth. Season with salt and pepper. Then gradually stir in remaining cream mixed with the egg yolks. Continue stirring until thoroughly heated (don't boil). Heat oysters in their remaining liquid, then drain. Add sherry to sauce, then the heated oysters. Serve in patty shells and sprinkle with parsley.

Yield: 4-6 servings

Sylvia Conrad

OYSTER CASSEROLE

½ cup chopped onions
1 cup chopped celery
½ cup chopped celery leaves
2 cloves garlic, minced
½ cup finely chopped parsley
1 stick butter
1 cup bread crumbs
4 dozen oysters and oyster
   liquid

1 cup milk
2 beaten eggs
½ pound fresh button
   mushrooms (or canned)
2 hard boiled eggs, chopped
Salt, black and red pepper
   to taste
½ cup dry Sauterne wine

Steam onions, garlic, celery and celery tops and parsley in butter, but do not brown. Moisten bread crumbs in oyster liquid for approximately 4 to 5 minutes. Stir in milk to which 2 beaten eggs have been added. Add mushrooms, oysters and chopped eggs. Season with salt, black and red pepper. Stir in Sauterne wine and bake 45 minutes or until solid, in 325° oven. This is delicious used as stuffing for duck or turkey.

Yield: 6-8 servings

Alicia Conrad Stewert

DEVILED OYSTERS

3 dozen oysters, drained
2 cups celery, chopped fine
2 onions, chopped fine
1 pod garlic, minced
½ cup butter or margarine

3 eggs, hard-boiled
6 slices toasted bread,
   crumbled
4 sprigs parsley, chopped fine

Sauté onions, celery and garlic for 20 minutes in butter. Cut oysters in 2 or 3 pieces. Add to seasonings and cook 5 minutes longer. Remove from fire. Mash eggs with fork, then add eggs and parsley with crumbled bread. Will fill about 12 oyster shells or a shallow casserole. Bake at 350° about 20 minutes.

Yield: 12 servings

Mrs. L. O. Broussard, Sr.

OYSTERS GIGI

24 pieces of bacon
48 oysters, drained
2 cups flour, seasoned with salt and pepper

3 eggs
1 beer
2 cups Italian bread crumbs

Fry bacon for 2 minutes. Cut bacon strips in half. Take ½ strip of bacon and wrap around each oyster and secure with a toothpick. Take bacon-wrapped oyster and roll in seasoned flour. Beat eggs and beer well for beer batter. Dip floured oysters in beer batter then roll in bread crumbs. Do all 48 oysters at one time. Deep fat fry oysters until the bread crumbs turn dark brown.

Yield: 6 servings   *Gigi Patout*

OYSTERS MANHATTAN STYLE

2 dozen oysters
½ cup butter
½ teaspoon paprika
½ teaspoon salt

1 tablespoon finely chopped parsley
3 strips of bacon cut into 4 pieces each

Use 3 to 6 freshly opened oysters for each person. Place them individually on cleaned half shell. Cream butter, paprika, salt, and chopped parsley. Put a piece of mixture on each oyster, then cover the oyster with a thin piece of bacon. Set on a baking sheet and bake at 450° for 10 minutes or until bacon is crisp. Serve with a quarter of lemon.

Yield: 6-8 servings   *The Weeks Family*

OYSTER PIE

Use the recipe for Creamed Oyster Patties II and fill a casserole or pie dish with the mixture. Top with a rich pastry which has been rolled and chilled for 30 minutes. Bake in 450° oven for approximately 15 minutes. Reduce heat to 350° and bake another 5 minutes or until crust is browned.

Yield: 4-6 servings   *Sylvia Conrad*

OYSTERS ROCKEFELLER

1 (15-ounce) can top quality
  spinach
1 cup chopped shallots
  (tops only)
1 cup shredded lettuce
1 cup chopped parsley
1 cup chopped celery leaves
2 sticks melted margarine
  or butter

1 cup Parmesan cheese
2/3 cup bread crumbs
1 1/2 ounces absinthe
3/4 teaspoon salt
3/4 teaspoon Tabasco pepper
  sauce
3 dozen oysters
Rock salt

Heat spinach, put in blender, and blend thoroughly. Add shallots, lettuce, parsley and celery leaves and 2 sticks butter (or margarine) and blend thoroughly. Pour into saucepan and add salt, Tabasco pepper sauce, 1/4 cup cheese and bread crumbs. Cook slowly about 15 minutes. Add absinthe.

Drain oysters for 1/2 hour or longer in colander. Place oyster shells on coarse salt in shallow pan and put oyster in each shell. Place in 375° oven until some of the juice comes out of the oysters and the edges curl. Remove from oven and pour juice out of shells into salt in pan (use tongs or pliers to handle). Cover each oyster with sauce and sprinkle well with remaining Parmesan cheese. Cook under broiler or in hot oven until sauce browns slightly on top. This is enough sauce for approximately 36 oyster shells.

Yield: 3 dozen

Barbara Patout

OYSTERS SHERRY

MUSHROOM SAUCE
3 tablespoons butter
3 tablespoons flour
1½ cups Half and Half

1 cup minced mushrooms,
use processor
1 teaspoon salt
½ teaspoon pepper

Melt butter, add flour and cook for 3 minutes. Remove from heat and beat the Half and Half into the mixture with a wire whisk. Add mushrooms, salt and pepper. Return to heat; bring to a boil, then lower heat and cook until thick.

OYSTER MIXTURE
3 dozen oysters, drained and
reserve 1 cup liquid
1 (14-ounce) can artichoke
hearts, drained
1 cup finely chopped celery
¼ cup finely chopped bell
pepper
½ cup finely chopped green
onions
1 stick butter
1 cup sliced fresh mushrooms

½ cup white wine, preferably
vermouth
2 tablespoons minced parsley
Salt, red and black pepper
to taste
Tabasco pepper sauce and
lemon juice to taste
2 cups rough bread crumbs,
freshly made from French
bread
Butter bits for top

Cook oysters in their own liquid until edges begin to curl; reserve liquid after draining. Chop into small pieces when cool enough to handle. Chop artichoke hearts.

Sauté celery, bell pepper, onions, garlic in the butter until softened. Add sliced mushrooms and cook until mushroom liquid evaporates. Add mushroom sauce, artichoke hearts, oyster liquid, and wine to pot. Cook until well blended and thickens again. Add oysters and let come to a boil again. Remove from heat and add parsley, salt, pepper, lemon juice and Tabasco pepper sauce to taste. Gradually add the bread crumbs until mixture gets thick. Adjust seasonings if necessary. Place in individual ramekins and dot with butter bits. May sprinkle with more bread crumbs if desired. Can also be placed in large fireproof casserole dish. Bake at 350° until hot.

Yield: 8-10 servings

Sherry Landry

STUFFED OYSTERS I

½ cup butter
1 onion, chopped fine
½ bell pepper, chopped fine
4 dozen oysters
1 (4-ounce) sleeve Saltine
  crackers made into crumbs
1 cup evaporated milk

Salt, very little if any
¼ teaspoon pepper
1 tablespoon parsley, chopped
  fine
1 tablespoon green onion tops,
  chopped
Bread crumbs

Sauté onion and bell pepper in butter until soft, stirring constantly. Drain oysters well. Cut oysters in half if they are large and add to onion and bell pepper. Cook until oysters curl. Add cracker crumbs that have been soaked in milk. Add pepper, salt to taste, parsley and onion tops. Serve with bread crumbs on top. Bake at 350° for 30 minutes.

Yield: 8-10 servings

Susie Pharr

STUFFED OYSTERS II

1 whole loaf stale French
  bread
1 pint oyster juice
½ pound butter or margarine
2 onions, chopped
1 bell pepper, chopped
1 cup celery, chopped
1 pod garlic, chopped
2 pounds cooked peeled
  shrimp

4 dozen fresh raw oysters
½ cup parsley, chopped
½ cup minced green onion
  tops
1 tablespoon lemon juice
Dashes of hot sauce to taste
1 cup grated Parmesan
  cheese
¼ cup paprika

Soak ½ of the French bread in oyster liquid and squeeze out. Toast remaining ½ of loaf in slow oven until crisp enough to crumb or process to crumbs. Melt butter, add onions, bell pepper, celery and garlic. Cook until wilted. Add shrimp that have been chopped, 2 dozen oysters, cut into small bite-size pieces, and oyster liquid. Cook 10 minutes. Add soaked French bread, parsley, green onion tops, lemon juice, and hot sauce. Cook 10 minutes. Remove from heat and cool. Place remaining 2 dozen oysters in individual rame-kins (ovenproof dishes) or 1 large ovenproof casserole dish. Cover with above dressing completely. Sprinkle with remaining ½ French bread, crumbling bread on top. Sprinkle Parmesan cheese and paprika on top. Bake for 20 minutes at 400.°

Yield: 8-10 servings

Carol Ann Dumond

OYSTER SPAGHETTI

4 to 6 dozen oysters with juice
¼ cup oil
¼ cup olive oil
¾ cup flour
2 onions
3 large pods garlic, minced
1 bell pepper, finely chopped
2 stalks celery, finely chopped
1 (6-ounce) can tomato paste
1 (10-ounce) can Rotel
  tomatoes
1 (8-ounce) can tomato sauce
2 teaspoons oregano
½ teaspoon thyme
½ teaspoon sweet basil
3 bay leaves
Salt, red and black pepper to
  desired taste
½ lemon, sliced thin

Drain oysters keeping juice for sauce. Make a roux with oil, olive oil and flour. When this is golden brown add onions, garlic, bell pepper and celery and cook for a few minutes. Add tomato paste, Rotel tomatoes and tomato sauce. Stir well. Add approximately 1 quart water and water from oysters. Then add oregano, thyme, basil, bay leaves, salt, black and red pepper and lemon slices. Simmer for 1 hour in covered pot. Add oysters 20 minutes before serving. Serve over hot buttered spaghetti with lots of fresh Parmesan cheese, grated. Shrimp may be added if desired.

Yield: 6-8 servings   *Sylvia Conrad*

BARBECUED SHRIMP

24 large shrimp, shelled,
  deveined, tails left on
24 slices bacon
1 to 2 large onions, sliced
2 cloves garlic
2 tablespoons brown sugar
2 tablespoons soy sauce
3 tablespoons dry sherry
½ tablespoon ground ginger
½ tablespoon chili powder

Cut shrimp down back and open out like a butterfly. Place a slice of onion on the shrimp, fold up and wrap in a slice of bacon; hold together with a toothpick. Mix rest of ingredients together for the marinade and pour over the shrimp. Leave in marinade for 1 hour. Turn shrimp 2 or 3 times. Barbecue over medium fire until the shrimp are cooked and bacon is crispy.

Yield: 4-6 servings   *Penny Fenton*

SHRIMP AND ARTICHOKE CASSEROLE

1 stick butter or margarine
3 tablespoons flour
¾ cup milk
¾ cup heavy cream or
    Half and Half
Worcestershire sauce to taste
Salt and freshly ground pepper
Tabasco pepper sauce to taste
¼ cup parsley
½ cup grated Parmesan
    cheese
2 tablespoons sherry or
    Madeira wine (optional)

1 (14-ounce) can artichoke
    hearts, drained and sliced
2 pounds shrimp, cooked,
    peeled, and deveined
¾ cup chopped onion
½ cup chopped bell pepper
½ cup chopped celery
8 ounces fresh mushrooms,
    sliced
1 teaspoon paprika
Parmesan cheese, grated
    for top

Melt 3 tablespoons butter or margarine; stir in flour. When blended, gradually add milk and cream or Half and Half, stirring constantly until thickened and smooth. Add Worcestershire sauce, salt, pepper, and Tabasco pepper sauce to taste, parsley, and Parmesan cheese. Sherry or Madeira wine is optional. Arrange artichoke hearts in buttered 3-quart baking dish. Scatter shrimp evenly over artichokes. In separate skillet melt remaining 5 tablespoons butter or margarine and sauté onion, bell pepper and celery until soft. Add mushrooms and cook until mushroom liquid evaporates (approximately 6 minutes). Spoon sautéed mixture over shrimp. Pour cream sauce over shrimp; sprinkle with more Parmesan cheese and paprika. Bake at 300° degrees for 30 minutes or until hot and bubbly.

Yield: 6 servings   *Nancy Lewis*

Note: More Half and Half may be added to the sauce if necessary.

SHRIMP BOATS

12 large baking potatoes
2 (10-ounce) packages frozen
    shrimp
1 cup margarine
2 cups grated sharp cheese

1 tablespoon salt
¼ cup grated onion
1½ cups light cream
½ teaspoon red pepper

Bake potatoes at 350° for 45 minutes. Boil shrimp, chop. Cut potatoes in half lengthwise, scoop out, reserve shells. Whip potatoes with margarine, cheese, salt, onion, cream, pepper; mix in shrimp. Refill shells. Sprinkle with paprika. Reheat 15 minutes.

Yield: 12 servings   *Jackie Turnage*

AVERY ISLAND DEVILED SHRIMP

1 egg, slightly beaten
1/4 teaspoon salt
1/8 teaspoon Tabasco pepper
  sauce
1 pound cleaned raw shrimp
1 cup bread crumbs
1/4 cup butter
1 onion, finely chopped
1 clove garlic, minced
1 (10 1/2-ounce) can consommé

1/2 cup white wine
2 tablespoons bottled steak
  sauce
1 1/2 teaspoons dry mustard
1/2 teaspoon salt
1/2 teaspoon Tabasco pepper
  sauce
Juice of 1 lemon
4 cups hot cooked rice

Mix egg, 1/4 teaspoon salt, 1/8 teaspoon Tabasco pepper sauce. Coat shrimp with egg, then crumbs. Brown in butter and remove shrimp. Keep hot while sauce cooks.

Deviled Sauce: In butter used to fry shrimp (add more if needed to make 2 tablespoons), cook onion and garlic until tender. Add remaining ingredients except lemon juice and rice; reduce in volume to 1/2. Add lemon juice just before serving. Arrange shrimp on rice and pour the Deviled Sauce over all.

Yield: 6 servings   *A Friend of the Shadows*

BOILED SHRIMP

5 pounds frozen shrimp
5 tablespoons salt
1 tablespoon red pepper
1 tablespoon black pepper

1 tablespoon Worcestershire
  sauce
Juice and parts of 2 lemons
1 green pepper, cut up

In large pot, cover shrimp with cold water and add all ingredients. When water comes to a full boil, let boil for 1 minute. Remove from fire and let set in water for 8 minutes. Drain and serve. Serve with potato salad and garlic bread.

Yield: 4 servings   *Sue Dauterive*

SHRIMP BAKE I

1 (4-ounce) can mushrooms,
  drained
¼ stick margarine
2 cups cooked shrimp
2 cups cooked rice
1 cup chopped bell pepper
1 cup chopped onion
½ cup chopped celery

¼ cup chopped pimento
1 (12-ounce) can whole
  tomatoes, drained
¾ teaspoon salt
½ teaspoon chili powder
Garlic powder to taste
1 stick margarine, melted

Sauté mushrooms in margarine. Combine with other ingredients. Place in greased casserole. Pour melted margarine over all. Bake for 30 minutes at 300°

Yield: 4-6 servings

Jackie Turnage

SHRIMP BAKE II

5 pounds shrimp with heads
  or 3 pounds of headless
  shrimp
1½ pounds of butter
4 tablespoons salt
2 tablespoons black pepper
2 tablespoons red pepper
2 large onions, thinly sliced
1 pod garlic, minced
2 medium oranges with
  peeling, sliced or 1 can
  mandarin slices

1 cup chopped green onion
  tops
2 bell peppers, chopped
4 hot peppers, chopped
2 lemons with peel, sliced
  thinly
2 tablespoons Worcestershire
  sauce
French bread

Use pan about 2 inches deep. Place shrimp in pan and place all the ingredients on top. Stir slowly. Put in 350° oven for 30 minutes. Stir gently every 5 or 10 minutes. (When body separates from shell remove from oven.) Serve hot. Dip French bread in the gravy and have lots of paper towels.

Yield: 4 servings

Mac Beyt

BROILED SHRIMP

Take 2 POUNDS OF LARGE SHRIMP. Wash well and season with salt, pepper and melted butter. Put the shrimp in the oven and broil until done. Put on hot plates and serve with the following sauce.

3 tablespoons butter (melted)
1 clove minced garlic
2 tablespoons Worcestershire
  sauce

6 drops of Tabasco pepper
  sauce
2 teaspoons lemon juice
1 tablespoon minced celery
Salt to taste

Put the sauce in individual ramekins, peel the shrimp at the table and dip them in the sauce.

Yield: 2-4 servings   *Old Weeks Family recipe*

SHRIMP CASSEROLE

1 stick butter
½ cup chopped onion
½ cup chopped bell pepper
Salt and pepper to taste
1 (10-ounce) can Rotel
  tomatoes
1 (10¾-ounce) can cream of
  onion soup

1 (10¾-ounce) can cream of
  chicken soup
1 (10¾-ounce) can cream of
  mushroom soup
2 pounds raw shrimp (peeled
  and seasoned with salt
  and pepper)
2 cups uncooked rice

Melt butter. Sauté onions and bell pepper. Add tomatoes and soup, mix well. Add rice and raw shrimp and mix well. Add salt and pepper, bake covered for 1 hour at 350°.

Yield: 10-12 servings   *Adele Wormser*

SHRIMP AND CRAB ÉTOUFFÉE

3 sticks margarine
4 medium onions, chopped
2 bell peppers, chopped
6 ribs celery, chopped

2 pounds cleaned shrimp
1 dozen cleaned crab bodies
6 sprigs parsley, chopped
6 green onion tops, chopped

Melt margarine, sauté onions, bell peppers and celery until wilted, then add shrimp. Cook covered until shrimp are almost done. Add crabs for about 5 minutes or until hot. Add parsley and onion tops. I always do this with leftover crabs.

Yield: 6-8 servings   *Mrs. Herbin P. Breaux*

SHRIMP CREOLE I

2 pounds of lake shrimp
2 tablespoons butter
2 tablespoons flour
1 large onion, chopped
1 bell pepper, chopped
2 sprigs parsley, chopped
2 stalks celery, chopped

3 cloves garlic
2 bay leaves
1 (12-ounce) can tomatoes
Salt to taste
½ pod red pepper or pepper
  to taste

Wash shrimp well, peel, and devein. Put butter in a deep pot and when melted, add flour and make a roux. Put in next 7 ingredients, and cook for 10 minutes. Season with salt and pepper. Cook sauce for 10 minutes. Add shrimp and cook for 20 minutes. Serve hot.

Yield: 4 servings   *Old Weeks Family recipe*

SHRIMP CREOLE II

2 pounds fresh shrimp
1 large onion, chopped
1 to 2 cloves garlic, chopped
½ green pepper, chopped
2 stalks celery, chopped
3 tablespoons cooking oil
1 (6-ounce) can tomato paste

½ lemon, sliced
½ cup water
Salt, black pepper and red
  pepper
Green onion tops and parsley,
  chopped

Shell and devein shrimp; set aside. Sauté onion, garlic, bell pepper, and celery in oil until wilted in a 2-quart iron pot. Add tomato paste and stir well. Add shrimp, lemon slices, and ½ cup water, salt, black and red pepper. Cover and simmer for 20 to 25 minutes. Add chopped green onion tops and parsley. Serve over rice with tossed green salad and hot garlic bread.

Yield: 4-6 servings   *Sylvia Conrad*

SHRIMP CREOLE III (MICROWAVE)

2 pounds shrimp
½ cup flour
½ cup oil
1 cup chopped onion
½ cup chopped celery
¼ cup chopped green onions
6 cloves garlic, chopped

¼ cup chopped parsley
1 (15-ounce) can tomato sauce
15 ounces water
1 teaspoon salt
½ teaspoon pepper
¼ teaspoon cayenne pepper

Peel shrimp, set aside. In 2½ or 3-quart casserole dish, combine flour and oil, blend well. Cook on high for about 10 minutes or until roux is a deep caramel color. Stir frequently. Add onions and celery. Sauté 3 minutes. Stir and add green onions, parsley and garlic. Sauté 2 more minutes. Stir tomato sauce, water and seasonings into roux. Cook on high for 10 minutes. Add shrimp, stir and simmer for 10 more minutes or until shrimp are cooked. Serve over hot rice.

Yield: 4-6 servings

Penny Fenton

SHRIMP IN CHEESE SAUCE

6 tablespoons butter
8 tablespoons flour
1 teaspoon salt
¼ teaspoon white pepper
2 cups milk

1 cup grated cheese
1 pound raw, cleaned,
   deveined shrimp
Bread crumbs

Melt butter over low heat. Add flour and seasonings. Stir until blended. Remove from heat. Gradually add milk and return to heat. Cook, stirring constantly until thick. Add grated cheese. Add raw shrimp and cook until done (about 10 minutes). Serve over toast or in ramekins with bread crumbs on top.

Yield: 4 servings

Flo Landry

SHRIMP AND EGGPLANT

3 medium eggplants
½ block margarine
2 stalks celery, chopped fine
2 onions, chopped fine
3 cloves garlic, minced

½ bell pepper, chopped fine
2 pounds peeled shrimp
1 (10-ounce) can Rotel
  tomatoes
Salt and pepper to taste

Parboil eggplant. Drain and sauté chopped onion, bell pepper, celery, and garlic in margarine. Add boiled, peeled and chopped eggplant and shrimp. Add Rotel tomatoes. Season to taste. Cook for about 30 minutes. Pour mixture in greased casserole. Cover with seasoned bread crumbs. Bake for about 30 minutes at 350.°

Yield: 6-8 servings

Clara Landry

SHRIMP FETTUCCINE

3 pounds peeled, deveined
  shrimp
1 stick butter
3 ounces dry vermouth
6 tablespoons sour cream
¼ cup chopped fresh parsley

1 tablespoon corn starch
3 (8-ounce) packages thin
  noodles, cooked and
  buttered
½ cup grated Parmesan and
  Romano cheese

Combine shrimp and butter in large skillet and cook about 10 minutes or until pink. Add vermouth and bring to boil; then add sour cream, parsley, and corn starch mixed with 2 tablespoons cold water. Cook until thick. Serve over cooked noodles which have been tossed with butter and grated cheese.

Yield: 8 servings

French House Restaurant

SHRIMP MOSCA I

1 pound washed, peeled and
  deveined shrimp
2 teaspoons rosemary
2 bay leaves
1 teaspoon thyme
1 teaspoon oregano
½ cup lemon juice

1 teaspoon each of basil,
  pepper, Worcestershire
  sauce
Tabasco pepper sauce to taste
2 pods garlic, crushed
½ cup olive oil
¼ cup vegetable oil
½ cup wine vinegar

Mix ingredients and marinate shrimp overnight. Use very hot electric fry pan. Cook shrimp with marinade. Cook about 5 minutes.

Yield: 4 servings   *Penny Fenton*

SHRIMP MOSCA II

1 pound peeled, deveined
  shrimp
1 stick butter
⅓ cup Worcestershire sauce
1 teaspoon salt
1 teaspoon black pepper
1 teaspoon red pepper

2 teaspoons garlic juice
1 teaspoon thyme
2 teaspoons rosemary (put in
  cheesecloth bag)
½ teaspoon celery salt
½ cup Progresso bread
  crumbs

Peel and devein shrimp; set aside. Put all ingredients except shrimp and bread crumbs in saucepan and cook slowly on low fire for 5 minutes. Do not boil! Put raw shrimp in 1½-quart pyrex dish. Pour sauce and bread crumbs over shrimp and bake at 400° for 15 minutes. Serve in ramekins.

Yield: 4 servings   *Elenore Mestayer*

SHRIMP MARGUERITE

1¼ cups chopped onion
1 chopped bell pepper
2 small pods garlic, minced
1 stick margarine
1 to 1½ pounds raw, peeled
  shrimp
1 (10-ounce) can Rotel
  tomatoes
1 (10¾-ounce) can cream of
  mushroom soup
½ cup water
¼ cup chopped pimentos
1½ teaspoons salt
½ teaspoon red pepper
4 slices bread
3 cups cooked rice (1½ cups
  raw rice, cooked)
¼ cup chopped parsley
Bread crumbs

Sauté vegetables in margarine. Add shrimp and tomatoes. Cook 5 minutes. Add soup, water, and pimentos and cook 5 minutes. Add salt and red pepper. Soak bread in a bowl of water, squeeze out excess water and add bread to mixture. Add the cooked rice and parsley. Pour into 3-quart greased casserole, cover with bread crumbs and dot with butter. Bake 30 minutes at 400.°

Yield: 4-5 servings

Sue Dauterive

SHRIMP MS. ANN

30 large shrimp, peeled
Salt and pepper
2 sticks butter
½ cup lemon juice
¼ cup dry vermouth
¼ cup Worcestershire sauce
½ cup onion tops, chopped
  fine
½ cup parsley, chopped fine

Butterfly shrimp, with tail on. Season with salt and pepper and arrange on a baking sheet in rows. Simmer butter, lemon juice, dry vermouth and Worcestershire sauce over low heat for 10 minutes. Add chopped onion tops and parsley to sauce. Pour over shrimp. Broil for about 10 minutes until shrimp are cooked. Serve as an appetizer or main dish with vegetables.

Yield: 4 servings

Alex and Gigi Patout

SHRIMP AND MUSHROOMS WITH PORT WINE

(Grand Prize Winner, MORNING ADVOCATE Cookbook Contest, 1976)

½ cup green onions, chopped
½ cup parsley, chopped
3 cloves garlic, minced or pressed
1½ sticks butter
¾ pound fresh mushrooms, sliced

1 pound raw, peeled shrimp
½ cup seasoned bread crumbs
½ cup Port wine (do not substitute)

Sauté green onions, parsley, and garlic in butter. Add mushrooms and sauté a few minutes. Add shrimp and sauté on medium heat 5 to 6 minutes. Add bread crumbs and mix thoroughly. Add wine and heat until well heated throughout. Serve as appetizer or first course.

Yield: 6-8 servings   *Keith E. Courrege*

SHRIMP NEWBURG

¼ cup butter
¼ cup flour
½ teaspoon salt
¼ teaspoon pepper
2 cups milk
2 egg yolks, beaten

2 cups cooked and deveined shrimp
1 tablespoon sherry
Pinch marjoram
Tabasco pepper sauce, to taste
1 dozen patty shells

Melt butter in heavy saucepan, blend in (stirring to keep smooth) flour and seasonings. Cook over low heat, stirring until mixture is smooth and bubbly. Remove from heat. Stir in milk gradually until smooth. Bring to boil; stirring constantly, boil 1 minute. Add beaten egg yolks to hot mixture a little at a time, blend thoroughly. Just before serving, stir in shrimp, sherry, marjoram, and Tabasco pepper sauce. Serve in patty shells.

Yield: 1 dozen   *Adele Wormser*

PICKLED SHRIMP

1 quart water	2 stalks celery, chopped
6 sliced garlic cloves	2 large bay leaves
1 large onion, sliced	2 pinches thyme
8 sprigs parsley	2½ pounds raw peeled shrimp
½ lemon rind and juice	

Simmer the first 8 ingredients for 20 minutes. Add shrimp and bring to boil again, then simmer for 10 minutes. Drain and cool shrimp. In shallow pan arrange shrimp in layers with:

2 medium sliced onions	1 box bay leaves

Pour over each layer some of this mixture:

1 cup salad oil	2½ tablespoons capers and
¾ cup warmed vinegar	juice
1½ teaspoons salt	¼ cup Worcestershire sauce
2½ teaspoons celery seed	1 tablespoon yellow mustard
	Tabasco pepper sauce to taste

After pouring sauce over shrimp, onions, and bay leaves, cover pan and store in refrigerator not less than 24 hours. Will keep a week or more. When serving arrange entire mixture on large platter with toothpicks and crackers.

Yield: 6 servings   *Juanita Winkle*

PORTUGUESE SHRIMP

1 stick butter or margarine, melted	1 teaspoon red pepper
	1 tablespoon Worcestershire
⅔ cup olive oil	sauce
1 teaspoon garlic, crushed	2 teaspoons black pepper
½ cup lemon juice	2 quarts of shrimp, unpeeled,
2½ teaspoons salt	with heads on

Mix first 7 ingredients. Arrange shrimp on shallow pan in rows very close together and spoon sauce evenly over shrimp. Sprinkle black pepper over shrimp and marinate 1 hour or longer. Bake 10 to 15 minutes at 350°

Yield: 2 quarts   *Mrs. Barbara Patout*

POTTED SHRIMP

1 pound raw shrimp
¼ pound butter
½ teaspoon nutmeg

½ teaspoon mace
1 lemon sliced thin

Peel and devein shrimp. Melt butter, add rest of ingredients except lemon. Cook and stir until shrimp turn pink. Place shrimp in ramekins or casserole dish closely packed but don't mash. Pour butter sauce over top of shrimp and refrigerate until thoroughly chilled and firm. Serve on lettuce leaves and garnish with lemon slices.

Yield: 4 servings   *Alicia Conrad Stewart*

SHRIMP REMOULADE

2 pounds peeled cooked
   shrimp
¼ cup olive oil
¼ cup cooking oil
¼ cup vinegar
1 cup finely chopped celery
⅓ cup chopped parsley
2 tablespoons grated onion
½ cup creole mustard

3 tablespoons paprika
½ teaspoon black pepper
½ teaspoon salt
2 scant tablespoons
   horseradish
½ teaspoon Tabasco pepper
   sauce
1 tablespoon mayonnaise

Mix all ingredients, except shrimp, together in large bowl. This may be put in a blender, if you wish. Then add shrimp and marinate in refrigerator for 3 days. Serve with melba rounds.

Yield: 4-6 servings   *Scotty Broussard*

SHRIMP SAUCE

½ cup oil
¾ cup flour
2 onions, chopped fine
2 stalks celery, chopped fine
3 cloves garlic, minced
1 bell pepper, chopped fine

1 (6-ounce) can tomato paste
2 quarts hot water
Salt and red pepper to taste
2 pounds cleaned shrimp
    (more if desired)

Make a roux using flour and oil. When this is golden brown, add chopped onions, celery, garlic, and bell pepper. Sauté for a minute or so. Then add tomato paste. Then sauté a little more. Add water, salt and pepper and let this cook for about 3 hours. Add shrimp and cook for 20 minutes before serving. Serve over spaghetti or rice.

Yield: 2 quarts   *Clara Landry*

SHRIMP SCAMPI

2 cloves garlic, minced
1 teaspoon salt
¼ teaspoon black pepper
¼ cup olive oil

2 pounds shrimp, shelled and
    cleaned
2 tablespoons chopped
    parsley
Juice of 1 lemon

Combine garlic, salt, pepper, and oil. Arrange shrimp in single layer in broiler pan. Brush oil mixture over shrimp. Let stand about 1 hour to blend flavors. Broil shrimp slowly, turning once every 5-7 minutes until cooked. Sprinkle with parsley and lemon juice.

Yield: 4-6 servings   *Sylvia Conrad*

STUFFED SHRIMP

2 sticks butter
2 large onions, chopped fine
2 stalks celery, chopped fine
½ cup bell pepper, chopped
  fine
2 cups crab meat
2 cups shrimp, boiled,
  peeled and ground
4 tablespoons green onions
4 tablespoons parsley
1 teaspoon salt
¼ teaspoon red pepper
¼ teaspoon black pepper
4 eggs, well beaten
8 tablespoons bread crumbs
4 dozen large shrimp, peeled
  and seasoned
1 cup evaporated milk
½ cup water
Salt
1⅓ cups fish fry
Oil for deep fat frying

For dressing melt butter. Sauté onions, celery, bell pepper on low fire until clear. Add crab meat, shrimp, green onions, parsley, and salt and pepper. Cook on low fire about 3 minutes. Add eggs and bread crumbs. Stir well.

Split raw shrimp. Place about 1 tablespoon stuffing on each shrimp. Shape into oblong ball. Beat eggs with milk. Roll ball in fish fry, then egg mixture; then again in fish fry. Fry in deep fat for 5 minutes or until brown.

Yield: 8 servings   *Mrs. Roy (Flo) Landry*

SEAFOOD

SEAFOOD CASSEROLE

1 cup onion, chopped
1 cup bell pepper, chopped
1 cup celery, chopped
2 cloves garlic, chopped
1 stick margarine
1 (10¾-ounce) can mushroom
   soup
1 (10¾-ounce) can Cheddar
   cheese soup

1 (4-ounce) jar pimentos
3 cups seafood (any kind)
1 teaspoon salt
Parsley
Onion tops
2 cups cooked rice
¼ cup bread crumbs

Cook onion, bell pepper, garlic, and celery in margarine until tender. Add soups, parsley, onion tops, seafood, pimento and salt. Simmer, stir in rice and bread crumbs. Pour into large casserole dish and top with bread crumbs. Bake 30 to 40 minutes at 325°.

This recipe is good with any variation of seafood. I usually use crab and shrimp; crawfish is also tasty.

Yield: 10-12 servings

Rachel Inzerella

TO DRY SHRIMP

Take fresh raw shrimp and wash well. Put into fast boiling water (using 1 ounce pure rock salt to 3 gallons water). Boil 5 minutes. Remove and spread shrimp out on drying platform. This should be made of clean, unpainted lumber and be built 3 feet from the ground and placed in full hot sun. If the weather is dry and hot (in the 90s) the drying takes only 1 day, but if humid or cooler, much longer. After shrimp are dry, place in clean crocker (burlap) sack and beat sack against a drum to break the loosened hulls free. Remove the hard dry bodies of shrimp to save for cooking and gumbo, or good as a snack with beer.

Juanita Winkle

BREADS, DRESSINGS, JELLIES, JAMS AND RELISHES

Circa 1940

The little Summer House (often referred to as the "Gazebo") overlooking the Bayou Teche, is located at the back of the Shadows' garden. The original structure installed by Weeks Hall was destroyed in 1963 by a hurricane and rebuilt in 1971 from the plans of 1928. The second Summer House was a gift of Richard Koch, Shadows restoration architect from New Orleans, to the memory of his friend Weeks Hall. A plaque in the floor commemorates the gift.

The bayou seen from the Summer House is still a navigable waterway and is busy with barge and pleasure boat traffic. The Summer House today provides an escape from routine with a blend of graceful, moss-hung oaks in the garden and a medley of bayou sounds.

Breads, Dressings, Jellies, Jams and Relishes

BREADS
  Biscuits
    Angel......................249
    Cheese.....................249
    Easy Beaten................250
    Helen's....................250
    Yam........................251
  Breads
    Banana.....................251
    Brioche....................252
    Brown......................252
    Cajun......................253
    Celebration................253
    Cinnamon...................254
    Coffee Cake, Surprise......254
    Cranberry Nut..............255
    Cream Cheese Braid.........256
    Irish Soda.................257
    Italian Herb...............257
    Louisiana Grits............255
    Poppy Cheese Loaf..........258
    Pumpkin....................258
    Pumpkin Nut................258
    Riverboat Sweet............259
    Strawberry.................259
    Sweet Potato I.............260
    Sweet Potato II............260
  Cornbreads
    Jalapeño, Hot..............261
    Jalapeño, Miss Edith's.....261
    Momma's....................264
    Spoon Bread, Fluffy........262
    Yam........................262

Muffins
    Bran, Refrigerator.........265
    Sausage....................266
    Yam-Pecan..................266
  Rolls
    Croissant Refrigerator.....267
    Doughnuts-Beignets.........263
    Light......................267
    Griddlecakes...............265
DRESSINGS
    Cornbread..................263
    French Bread...............264
CHUTNEY
    Apple......................273
    Fruit......................274
    Peach......................274
JAMS AND PRESERVES
    Fig I......................268
    Fig II.....................268
    Fig-Strawberry.............268
JELLIES
    Blackberry.................269
    Pepper.....................269
    Port Wine..................269
PICKLES
    Beets and Eggs, Pickled....270
    Bread and Butter...........270
    Freezer....................271
    Mirliton...................271
    Squash.....................271
    Watermelon.................272
RELISHES
    Chow Chow, Aunt Marie's....272
    Corn and Cabbage...........273
    Green Tomato-Green Pepper...273

Refer to additonal recipes in "How Men Cook" section.

ANGEL BISCUITS

1 package dry yeast
2 tablespoons very warm water
5 cups all-purpose flour
1 teaspoon baking soda
3 teaspoons baking powder

2 tablespoons sugar
1½ teaspoons salt
¾ to 1 cup shortening
2 cups buttermilk

Dissolve yeast in warm water. Sift dry ingredients into a large bowl; cut in shortening with a pastry blender. Add buttermilk and yeast mixture. Stir until thoroughly moistened.

Turn dough out onto floured board—roll to ½-inch thickness and cut biscuits. Place on ungreased baking sheet. Bake at 400° for 12 to 15 minutes until lightly browned.

Yield: 2½ dozen 2-inch biscuits   *Carolyn Sutton*

Note: Dough may be refrigerated in plastic bag or covered bowl until ready to use—keeps well several days. Remove from refrigerator, roll and cut—let sit about 15 minutes until the biscuits reach room temperature before baking.

CHEESE BISCUITS

1 pound grated sharp cheese
1 pound butter (no substitute)

4 cups regular flour
Red pepper

Mix cheese and butter, add flour and red pepper and mix well. Roll into small balls and bake on ungreased cookie sheet at 400° for 10 minutes. Do not brown.

Yield: 180 biscuits   *Mrs. Bernard (Bootsie) Trappey*

Note: These will freeze baked or unbaked.

EASY BEATEN BISCUITS

2½ cups all-purpose flour
½ teaspoon salt
½ teaspoon baking powder

½ cup lard or vegetable
  shortening
7 to 8 tablespoons ice water

Insert steel chopping blade in food processor. Place flour, salt, baking powder and lard in food processor container. Process at medium until mixture is coarse, using start/stop technique. With machine running at high speed, add water in steady stream through feed tube until dough forms a ball; let machine run 2 minutes.

Roll dough on floured surface to ¼-inch thickness. Cut into rounds. Place biscuits on ungreased cookie sheet; prick tops of biscuits with tines of fork. Bake at 400° for 25 minutes, or until golden brown. Serve hot.

Yield: 1 dozen

Beverly Shea

HELEN'S BISCUITS

4 cups all-purpose flour
2 tablespoons baking powder
1 tablespoon plus 1 teaspoon
  sugar
1 teaspoon baking soda

1 teaspoon salt
⅔ cup chilled unsalted sweet
  butter
1½ cups buttermilk
¼ cup melted butter

Mix flour, baking powder, sugar, baking soda, and salt in a medium size bowl. Cut in chilled butter until mixture resembles coarse crumbs. Stir in buttermilk. Turn dough onto floured board. Knead lightly, about 10 strokes. Roll dough 1¼-inch thick. Cut into 3-inch circles. Arrange biscuits with sides touching in buttered 9-inch square pan. Brush tops with melted butter. Bake at 450° until golden, about 25 minutes. Serve warm.

Yield: 8 large biscuits

Helen Johnson
Helen's Cafeteria

YAM BISCUITS

1¾ pounds (scant) fresh yams
½ cup solid white shortening
1½ cups all-purpose flour
2 teaspoons baking powder
1 teaspoon salt
¼ cup sugar

Scrub the yams in cold water, do not pare; cover them with boiling water and boil in a covered saucepan just until tender when pierced with a fork. Drain. Remove skins and mash. Measure enough to make 2 cups; reserve any remaining for some other use. With a spoon, beat the shortening into the 2 cups mashed hot yams until blended; cool.

In a medium-size bowl stir together the flour, baking powder, salt and sugar. Add the yam mixture and work together until blended. If dough is very sticky, add flour sparingly.

On a pastry cloth with a stockinet-covered rolling pin, roll out dough ½-inch thick. With a floured round 2-inch cutter, cut out biscuits. Place slightly apart on an ungreased cookie sheet. Bake in a preheated 450° oven until browned—15 to 18 minutes. (Bottoms of biscuits will be very dark, but they will not taste scorched.) Rush to the table while they are still puffy and hot; they will sink slightly as they cool. Serve with plenty of butter.

Yield: 2 dozen   *Barbara Schwing*

Note: Mashed yams are available in cans. You do not need to cook your own.

BANANA BREAD

3 bananas mashed fine
½ cup shortening
1 cup sugar
1 teaspoon baking soda
1 cup flour
2 eggs
½ cup nuts

Cream bananas, shortening and sugar. Sift soda and flour together and add alternately with eggs to banana mixture. Add nuts. Bake in a greased loaf pan at 350° approximately 40 minutes, until toothpick in center comes out clean.

Yield: 1 loaf   *Dorothy Griffin*

Variation: 2 cups flour and no nuts. Bake in two loaf pans.

Mrs. Tom Uncapher

BRIOCHE

½ cup milk
1 package yeast
¼ cup lukewarm water
1 stick margarine
1 teaspoon salt

⅓ cup sugar
3 whole eggs
1 separated egg
3¼ cups flour

Scald milk. Dissolve yeast in water. Cream margarine with salt and sugar. Add milk and yeast mixture to margarine and sugar. Beat 3 whole eggs and 1 egg yolk. (Reserve white of egg for brushing tops of rolls.) Add beaten eggs to yeast mixture. Stir in flour until just mixed well. Leave wooden spoon in dough (to help dough rise up spoon) and cover with a dish towel. Set in warm place to rise to double its size, about 2 hours. Stir down dough; then leaving spoon in, cover bowl with foil and towel, and refrigerate overnight. When ready to bake, stir down and lightly knead dough on floured surface. Do not overknead. Make into rolls, placing a little top knot on each roll, and place in generously buttered muffin or fluted edged tins. Let rolls rise in tins. Brush tops of rolls with beaten egg white (do this very gently). Bake at 425° for 10 minutes until tops are browned.

Yield: 2 dozen rolls

BROWN BREAD

5 cups graham flour
1½ cups sugar
3½ cups buttermilk or sour
    milk
1 cup nuts

1 cup raisins
4 teaspoons baking soda
1 teaspoon salt
¼ cup shortening

Mix together and bake 1 hour at 325° in two greased and floured loaf pans.

Yield: 2 loaves

*A Weeks Family recipe
Mrs. William G. Weeks*

CAJUN BREAD

1 loaf French bread
1 cup mayonnaise
2 cloves garlic (minced)
3 cups cheddar cheese
  (grated)

¼ cup chopped parsley
½ cup chopped green onion
  tops
Tabasco pepper sauce to taste

Slice bread in half lengthwise. Mix all other ingredients and spread on bread. Bake at 350° until hot and cheese melts.

Yield: 10 servings

Friends of the Shadows

CELEBRATION BREAD

4 cups sifted flour
2 teaspoons baking powder
1 teaspoon baking soda
1 teaspoon salt
1¼ cups granulated sugar
⅔ cup shortening
3 eggs

2 cups applesauce
1 cup chopped nuts
1 (16-ounce) can red sour
  pitted cherries (well
  drained) and reserve liquid
2 teaspoons almond extract

Sift flour, baking powder, soda and salt; set aside. Blend sugar and shortening until creamy. Add eggs and beat well. Add flour mixture alternately with applesauce. Stir in nuts, drained cherries and extract. Pour into 2 greased 9 x 5 x 3-inch loaf pans. Bake at 350° 45 to 55 minutes or until tests done. Remove from pans while warm and when cool spread with cherry glaze.

CHERRY GLAZE
1 teaspoon almond extract
2 tablespoon reserved cherry
  juice

1 tablespoon margarine
  (melted)
1 cup powdered sugar

Blend all ingredients until smooth and spread on cold loaves.

Yield: 2 loaves

Yolanda Trahan

CINNAMON BREAD

2 egg whites well beaten
½ cup milk
½ cup butter or shortening
1 cup sugar

2 egg yolks beaten
1½ cup flour
2½ teaspoons baking powder
1 teaspoon cinnamon

Mix together egg whites and milk. Cream together the butter, sugar and egg yolks and add to the milk mixture. Sift together flour, baking powder and cinnamon and add to the creamed mixture. Bake in oiled loaf pan at 300° for 30 minutes. When done pour 1 tablespoon melted butter over top and sprinkle with mixture of sugar and cinnamon.

Mrs. W.S. Torian

SURPRISE COFFEE CAKE

Combine and set aside:

1½ cups brown sugar plus
    1 tablespoon

1 cup chopped pecans

Mix in large bowl for 2 minutes:

2 cups flour
1 cup sugar
2 teaspoons baking powder
1 teaspoon salt
1 (3-ounce) package instant
    vanilla pudding

1 (3-ounce) package instant
    butterscotch pudding
1 teaspoon vanilla
4 eggs
1 cup water
¾ cup oil

Pour ½ batter in 13 x 9 x 2-inch greased pan; sprinkle ½ sugar mixture, pour rest of batter and top with remaining sugar mixture. Bake at 350° for 40 minutes. Serve warm. This is served at the Shadows Jazz Brunch.

Yield: 1 coffee cake

Yolanda Trahan

CRANBERRY NUT BREAD

2 cups flour
1 cup sugar
1 1/2 teaspoons baking powder
1/2 teaspoon baking soda
1 teaspoon salt
1/4 cup shortening
3/4 cup orange juice

1 tablespoon grated orange
   rind
1 egg
1/2 cup chopped nuts
2 cups fresh cranberries,
   chopped coarsely

Sift flour, sugar, baking powder, baking soda and salt. Cut in shortening until it resembles coarse cornmeal. Combine orange juice and rind with egg. Pour all at once into dry ingredients, mixing just enough to dampen. Carefully fold in nuts and cranberries. Spoon into greased loaf pan (9 x 5 x 3). Spread corners and sides slightly higher than center. Bake at 350° about one hour—until crust is golden brown or toothpick inserted comes out clean. Remove from pan. Cool. Store overnight for easy slicing.

Yield: 1 loaf

Beverly Shea

LOUISIANA GRITS BREAD

2 cups well cooked grits
1 large heaping tablespoon
   butter
1 cup sifted flour
Pinch salt

1 teaspoon Royal baking
   powder
2 cups milk
3 eggs separated, beaten

Put the hot grits in a bowl—add the butter and salt and beaten yolks of eggs, then add the milk. Put baking powder with flour into the mixture and fold in the whites of the eggs. Pour this into a baking dish and bake in a hot oven until brown (about 15 minutes).

Old Weeks Family recipe

CREAM CHEESE BRAID

1 cup sour cream
½ cup sugar
1 teaspoon salt
½ cup melted margarine

2 packs dry yeast
½ cup warm water
2 beaten eggs
4 cups flour

Heat the sour cream over low heat, stir in sugar, salt and margarine. Cool to lukewarm. Sprinkle yeast over warm water in a bowl; stir until yeast is dissolved and add sour cream mixture, eggs, and flour. Combine these, forming a dough. Cover dough in bowl and place in refrigerator overnight.

The next day; divide in four pieces. Roll each piece on well-floured board to 12 x 18-inch rectangle. Spread cream cheese filling on each and roll like a jelly roll. Pinch edges and fold ends under, placing seam down on greased baking sheet. Slit each roll at 2-inch intervals about ⅔ of the way through to resemble a braid. Cover them and let them rise in a warm place until double in bulk (about an hour). Bake at 375° for 12 to 15 minutes. Spread with glaze while warm.

CHEESE FILLING

2 (8-ounce) packages cream
    cheese (soft)
¾ cup sugar

1 egg
⅛ teaspoon salt
2 teaspoons vanilla

Mix all ingredients and beat well.

GLAZE

2 cups confectioner's sugar
4 tablespoons milk

2 teaspoons vanilla

Combine and glaze bread.

Yield: 4 breads

A Friend of the Shadows

IRISH SODA BREAD

1 tablespooon butter or
  margarine
4 cups flour

1 teaspoon baking soda
1 teaspoon salt
1 to 1½ cups buttermilk

Cut butter into flour. Stir in baking soda and salt. Beating constantly with mixer or large spoon, add buttermilk to form firm ball. Knead dough several minutes, then form a ball. With floured hands flatten dough to a circle about 2 inches high on a greased, lightly floured cookie sheet. Cut cross ½-inch deep in center. Bake at 425° for 35 to 45 minutes. Cool slightly on rack. Place on board in center of table and let each break off a portion.

Yield: 1 loaf

Arthur C. Tomlinson

ITALIAN HERB BREAD

1 pound frozen bread dough
½ stick melted butter
1 pound Italian or pork sausage
¼ to ½ cup salad olives or
  black olives
¼ cup green onion tops
  (optional)

¼ cup Romano or Parmesan
  cheese
½ cup each Mozzarella and
  Cheddar cheese
½ teaspoon Italian seasonings
Black pepper and salt

Let dough rise, roll out to 9 x 6 inches, brush with some melted butter, cover and let rise. Cook sausage, cool thoroughly and grind. Sprinkle sausage over risen dough. Add onion tops, all cheeses, olives and seasonings. Roll like a jelly roll and pinch edges to seal. Lay on seam, let rise another ½ hour. Bake at 350° for 35 to 45 minutes. Fix a salad and you have a meal.

Yield: 6-8 servings

Shara Viator & Yolanda Trahan

POPPY CHEESE LOAF

3¾ cups biscuit mix
1 cup shredded sharp cheese
 (4-ounce package)
1 tablespoon poppy seed
1 tablespoon minced instant
 onions

1½ teaspoons garlic salt
1½ cups milk
1 egg
1 teaspoon poppy seed

Stir together biscuit mix, cheese, poppy seed, onion, garlic salt, milk and egg until all of the mixture is dampened. Beat vigorously by hand 1 minute or 150 strokes. Pour into well-greased 9 x 5 x 3 loaf pan. Spread evenly. Sprinkle 1 teaspoon poppy seeds over top. Bake in 350° oven for 55 to 60 minutes.

Yield: 1 loaf

Beverly Shea

PUMPKIN BREAD

3 cups sugar
1 cup salad oil
4 eggs
1¼ teaspoons salt
1 teaspoon cinnamon
1 teaspoon nutmeg

⅔ cup water
2 cups pumpkin
3½ cups flour
3 teaspoons soda
1 cup chopped nuts

Combine all ingredients and mix with an electric mixer. Divide batter into 3 greased loaf pans and bake at 350° for 1 hour or until toothpick comes out clean.

Yield: 3 loaves

Mrs. Tom Uncapher

PUMPKIN NUT BREAD

1 cup sugar (white or brown or
 equal parts of each)
¼ cup soft shortening
2 eggs
1 cup pumpkin pie mix

2 cups biscuit mix
1 or 2 teaspoons pumpkin pie
 spice
1 cup chopped nuts

Cream shortening with sugar. Add eggs and pumpkin. Stir until well blended. Add biscuit mix and spice, blending well. Stir in nuts last. Pour into greased loaf pan (9 x 5 x 3) and bake 50 to 55 minutes in a 350° oven. Will also make 12 medium size muffins, if desired.

Yield: 8 servings

Barbara Schwing

RIVERBOAT SWEET BREAD

1 cup butter
1 cup sugar
4 eggs
2 cups flour
½ teaspoon cinnamon
½ teaspoon nutmeg
½ teaspoon baking powder
½ teaspoon salt

¼ cup fruit brandy
¼ cup cream or evaporated
milk
1 package (9-ounce)
mincemeat
2 tablespoons flour
1 tablespoon cocoa

Cream butter and sugar—add eggs one at a time beating well after each addition. Sift dry ingredients together. Add alternately to butter mixture with combined brandy and cream. In separate bowl, crumble mincemeat and coat well with the flour and cocoa. Fold into batter, pour into greased and floured 9-inch loaf pan. Bake at 325° for 1 hour and 15 minutes—or until nicely browned. Slice and serve with hot tea or coffee—may also be toasted.

Yield: 1 loaf

Celene Boudreaux LeBlanc
& Juanita Winkle

STRAWBERRY BREAD

3 cups flour
1 teaspoon baking soda
1 teaspoon salt
1 teaspoon cinnamon
2 cups sugar

4 eggs, beaten
1¼ cups chopped pecans
1½ cups vegetable oil
1 pint whole, frozen and
undrained strawberries

Stir dry ingredients together. Make a deep well in center. Mix remaining ingredients; pour into well. Stir just enough to mix all ingredients. Pour into 2 oiled loaf pans. Bake at 350° for 1 hour. Cool in pans 10 minutes, then turn out to cool.

Yield: 2 loaves

SWEET POTATO BREAD I

3 cups sugar
1 cup cooking oil
5 eggs
3½ cups sifted flour
2 teaspoons baking soda
½ teaspoon salt

1 teaspoon cinnamon
1 teaspoon nutmeg
⅔ cup water
1 (15-ounce) can sweet
   potatoes, mashed
1 cup nuts (optional)

Combine sugar and oil; beat well. Add eggs and beat. Combine dry ingredients and add to egg mixture alternately with water. Stir in sweet potatoes and chopped nuts. Pour batter into 3 greased loaf pans. Bake at 350° for one hour. Makes 3 small loaves. This makes a good gift and freezes well.

Yield: 3 small loaves   *Judy McIlhenny*

SWEET POTATO BREAD II

½ cup butter
½ cup shortening
2⅔ cups sugar
4 eggs
2 cups cold, mashed sweet
   potatoes
3½ cups flour, sifted

1 teaspoon salt
1 teaspoon cinnamon
1½ teaspoons nutmeg
2 teaspoons baking soda
1 cup chopped walnuts
⅔ cup cold, strong coffee

Cream butter, shortening and sugar; add eggs, one at a time, mixing well after each addition. Blend in sweet potatoes. Sift together dry ingredients; add nuts. Stir into creamed mixture alternately with cold coffee. Pour batter into 2 greased 9 x 5 x 3-inch loaf pans and 8 greased muffin pan cups. Bake at 375° for 1 hour for loaves and 25 minutes for muffins. Cool 10 minutes.

Yield: 2 loaves and 8 muffins   *Beverly Shea*

HOT JALAPEÑO CORNBREAD

1 cup chopped onion
4 pods garlic, minced
1 cup whole kernel corn
3 eggs
2½ cups milk
½ cup chopped pimentos
½ cup chopped hot jalapeño
    peppers

3 cups cornbread mix
2 tablespoons sugar
½ teaspoon salt
½ pound bacon, cooked crisp
    and crumbled
1½ cups grated sharp cheese

Combine ingredients and bake in a 9 x 13-inch oiled pan at 300°
for 3 hours.

Yield: 12 servings

Jo Ann Riley

"MISS EDITH'S" JALAPEÑO PEPPER CORNBREAD

1½ cups yellow corn meal
1 teaspoon salt
3 teaspoons baking powder
2 eggs, slightly beaten
⅔ cup salad oil

1 cup sour cream
1 (16-ounce) can cream corn
3 jalapeño peppers, seeded
    and chopped
1 cup grated Cheddar cheese

Combine dry ingredients. Add eggs, oil, and sour cream and stir
until blended. Stir in corn and peppers. Put ½ batter in well greased
8 x 8 x 2-inch pan. Sprinkle ½ cheese over batter. Pour remaining batter over cheese and top batter with remaining cheese. Bake
at 350° for 40 minutes.

Yield: 8 servings

Mrs. Edith Duncan

YAM CORN BREAD

2 cups sifted all-purpose flour
2 cups yellow cornmeal
2½ tablespoons baking
   powder
2 teaspoons salt
½ cup sugar

4 eggs
¾ cup milk
⅓ cup salad oil
2⅔ cups Bruce's cut or whole
   yams, drained and mashed

Sift flour with cornmeal, baking powder, salt and sugar; set aside. Beat eggs, milk and oil together in large bowl until smooth. Add yams and beat until blended. Add flour mixture, stirring only until flour mixture is moistened. Spoon batter into two greased 9-inch pans. Bake in 425° oven 35 to 40 minutes or until bread tests done. Cut into squares. Serve warm with butter. Extra yam corn bread may be frozen in foil for future use. Thaw, then reheat (wrapped) in 425° oven until warmed throughout.

Yield: 2 loaves

Bruce's Foods

FLUFFY SPOON BREAD

1½ cups boiling water
1 cup yellow cornmeal
1 tablespoon butter or
   margarine (softened)
3 eggs separated

1 cup buttermilk
1 teaspoon salt
1 teaspoon sugar
1 teaspoon baking powder
¼ teaspoon baking soda

In large bowl stir boiling water into cornmeal; to prevent lumping stir until mixture is cool. Blend in butter and egg yolks. Stir in buttermilk, salt, sugar, baking powder and baking soda. Beat egg whites just until soft peaks form; fold into batter. Pour into greased 2-quart casserole and bake 45 to 50 minutes at 375° Serve hot with butter. This is a light soufflé type bread that is spooned onto the plate and eaten with a fork. Delicious with oven fried chicken.

Yield: 8-10 servings

Phyllis Peterson

ORIGINAL FRENCH MARKET DOUGHNUTS—BEIGNETS

1 package yeast
1/2 cup lukewarm water
1 cup boiling water
1/4 cup vegetable shortening
1/2 cup sugar
1 tablespoon salt

1 cup evaporated milk
2 eggs, well beaten
4 cups flour
3 1/2 cups flour, approximately
Oil for deep frying
Powdered sugar

Dissolve yeast in warm water and set aside. Pour 1 cup boiling water over shortening, sugar, and salt. Add milk, yeast mixture and eggs. Stir in 4 cups flour and beat vigorously. Add remainder of flour to make a soft dough (may not take all the flour). Oil bowl and place dough inside and cover. Refrigerate and store until needed. Roll out dough to 1/4-inch and cut into preferred shape. The traditional shape is a rectangle approximately 2 x 3 inches. Deep fry at 350.° Sprinkle with powdered sugar and serve.

Yield: 4 dozen

A Friend of the Shadows

CORNBREAD DRESSING

1 pound giblets and/or 1/2
   pound of sausage
2/3 cup of butter
1/2 cup chopped onions
1/2 cup chopped bell pepper

1/2 cup chopped celery
Salt and pepper to taste
2 quarts of crumbled
   cornbread, cooked
Chicken or turkey stock

Chop giblets. Sauté in butter until cooked. If using sausage omit the butter and cook the sausage with the giblets. Add the onion, bell pepper and celery; cook until wilted. Add the cornbread. Season with salt and pepper to taste, moisten with stock to the consistency that you prefer. Toss lightly. Use to stuff turkey or chicken or turn into a shallow, buttered casserole dish and bake at 350° until brown on top.

Yield: 2 quarts

A Friend of the Shadows

FRENCH BREAD DRESSING

2 loaves French bread
1 pound margarine
1 pound ground beef
½ pound sausage mix (pork)
1 bunch celery
2 large onions
1 bunch green onions
8 cloves garlic, minced
2 large bell peppers

6 to 8 cups water
Salt to taste
½ to 1 teaspoon Tabasco
  pepper sauce
2 tablespoons parsley,
  chopped
2 eggs
1 pint oysters (optional)

The night before the dressing is to be made, slice French bread into thin slices and place on cookie sheets to dry overnight. When ready to make dressing, if bread is not completely dry, put in slow oven until thoroughly dry. It must be dry enough to crush with a rolling pin.

Melt margarine in large (8-quart size, at least) pot. Add meats and cook over medium fire.

Chop or grind celery, onions, garlic and bell peppers, add to meat mixture and cook until vegetables are clear. Crush bread into fine crumbs with rolling pin. Put into large mixing bowl. Add water until mixture is very moist but not runny.

Add seasonings: salt, Tabasco and parsley. Add bread and mix well. Cook for 10 more minutes. Taste and add more seasoning if necessary. Remove from fire and add eggs and mix fast and well. Put into casserole and bake in 350° oven for 45 minutes to 1 hour, or until the top is crusted and browned and bubbly.

Yield: 12-14 servings

Juanita Winkle

MOMMA'S CORNBREAD

1 cup yellow cornmeal
1 teaspoon salt
1 tablespoon baking powder
1 tablespoon sugar (optional)

2 eggs, beaten
½ cup milk
¼ to ⅓ cup bacon drippings

Mix dry ingredients; set aside. Heat the skillet, corn pone pans or 8 x 8-inch baking pan in a 450° oven. Add the bacon drippings to skillet to warm. Add eggs and milk and heated bacon drippings to dry ingredients; stir. Pour back into skillet and bake for 10 minutes in pone pans or 15 to 20 minutes in skillet or pan.

Yield: 6 servings

GRIDDLECAKES

⅔ cup oatmeal ground in food
   processor or blender
1⅓ cups whole wheat flour
⅔ cup yellow corn meal
⅔ cup white flour
4 teaspoons baking powder

2 teaspoons baking soda
2 teaspoons salt
1½ sticks cold butter
4 eggs
4 cups buttermilk
¼ cup table syrup

Mix dry ingredients well (can be done day before and refrigerated). Cut cold butter in tiny bits and blend into dry ingredients with pastry blender. Beat eggs, add to buttermilk, add syrup then blend into dry mixture. Cook on griddle like pancakes. Serve with syrup or sour cream and cinnamon sugar.

I promise that you will never be able to eat "pancake mix" again after you have tasted these delicious and nutritious griddlecakes. I usually mix up a double or triple batch of the dry ingredients and keep it as a "mix" in the refrigerator. I have found that 1 cup of "mix," 3 tablespoons of butter, 1 egg and 1¼ cup buttermilk will serve 2 adults and 2 children.

Yield: 6-8 servings   *Adele Guillot*

REFRIGERATOR BRAN MUFFINS

4 cups All-Bran
2 cups Nabisco 100% bran
2 cups boiling water
1 quart buttermilk
1 cup shortening
3 cups sugar

4 eggs
5 cups flour
½ teaspoon salt
5 teaspoons baking soda
2 teaspoons baking powder

Pour boiling water over the bran mixture. Add buttermilk and let stand. Cream shortening, sugar, and eggs. Add creamed mixture to bran mixture. Mix flour, salt, soda, and baking powder and add to other mixture. Spoon out (don't stir) into greased muffin cups. Will keep in the refrigerator for six weeks. Bake in 375° oven for about 20 minutes or until golden brown.

Yield: 1 gallon mix   *Beverly Shea*

SAUSAGE MUFFINS

½ pound bulk pork sausage,
  browned, crumbled
  —reserve drippings
Melted butter
2 cups regular flour

¼ cup sugar
1 tablespoon baking powder
½ teaspoon salt
1 egg
1 cup milk

Brown sausage. Add butter to drippings to make ¼ cup. Sift dry ingredients together in large bowl. In a small bowl beat together egg and milk, stir in drippings. Add this to dry ingredients. Stir 20 strokes and then add sausage. Stir 5 times more. Fill buttered muffin cups ¾ full. Bake at 400° for 20 minutes. Great for brunch.

Yield: 12-15 muffins   *Barbara Schwing*

YAM-PECAN MUFFINS

2 cups sifted flour
2 teaspoons baking powder
½ teaspoon salt
1 teaspoon cinnamon
1 teaspoon nutmeg
⅓ cup sugar
1 egg

1 cup milk
1 cup mashed yams
¼ cup melted butter
1 cup chopped pecans
2 teaspoons grated orange rind
1 tablespoon sugar
1 teaspoon cinnamon

Sift flour, baking powder, spices, and sugar together. In small bowl beat egg, add milk, yams, and butter. Blend. Add to flour mixture with pecans and orange rind. Stir until dry ingredients are moistened and batter is lumpy. Spoon into buttered muffin pan. Sprinkle with sugar mixed with cinnamon. Bake at 425° for 25 minutes until tester comes out clean.

Yield: 12 muffins   *Barbara Schwing*

CROISSANT REFRIGERATOR ROLLS

4 sticks margarine
2 cups milk
2 packages dry yeast
3 teaspoons sugar
¼ cup water

4 eggs, beaten
8 cups flour, sifted
½ teaspoon salt
½ cup sugar

Melt margarine and add milk gradually. Dissolve yeast and 3 teaspoons sugar in ¼ cup water. Add beaten eggs. Add yeast mixture to butter. Add flour, salt and ½ cup sugar. Place in tightly covered bowl and refrigerate overnight or at least 8 hours. The next day, divide dough into 6 wedges while still in bowl. Each wedge makes one dozen rolls. Roll each piece out in a 10-inch circle. Cut each circle into 12 pie shaped pieces. Roll each piece individually, starting at the large end. Place on a greased cookie sheet and let rise 2½ to 3 hours. Bake at 425° about 8 minutes.

Yield: 4 dozen

Nancy Lewis

LIGHT ROLLS

1 envelope of dry yeast
1 cup milk
1 stick butter
½ cup sugar

4½ cups of sifted flour
½ teaspoon salt
2 eggs, beaten

Dissolve yeast in ¼ cup warm water. Set aside. Heat milk to boiling; pour over butter and sugar. Add yeast when cool. Add 2 cups flour. Add eggs. Beat well in electric mixer or by hand if you have enough energy. Add balance of flour, (about 2½ cups) with ½ teaspoon salt. Mix in this last with a wooden spoon. Turn out on a floured board. Knead until smooth. Let rise until double. Punch down. Shape into pocket rolls. Let rise. Bake in an oiled pan at 400° about 15 to 20 minutes.

Yield: 2-3 dozen

Cathi Gibbens

FIG PRESERVES I

4 quarts figs, rinsed   **2 quarts sugar (8 cups)**
1 lemon, sliced thinly

Place all ingredients in a large pot, covered. Simmer until figs are transparent, 2 to 3 hours. Stir frequently to prevent scorching. Place in sterilized jars. Seal.

Yield: 4 pints

Sylvia G. Conrad

FIG PRESERVES II

12 cups sugar   **Red food coloring**
12 cups water   **24 cups figs**
1 lemon, seeded and minced   **1 box (8-ounce) baking soda**

Combine sugar, water and lemon and a few drops of food coloring in a large container; bring to a boil. Let syrup boil while preparing figs. Place figs in sink. Sprinkle baking soda over figs; pour large kettle of boiling water over all. Let figs stand in water 1 or 2 minutes. Remove from boiling water; plunge into cold water. Let stand 1 or 2 minutes. Scoop figs up in colander; hold under running water to wash clean. Prick each fig with a fork and transfer to syrup. (Pricking with fork will allow them to "plump"). Cook approximately 20 minutes or until figs begin to absorb some of the syrup. Do not overcook. Turn off heat. Cover. The next day reheat figs; seal in sterilized jars. Cool. Never tighten rings once jars have been cooled, it will break the seal. (If thicker syrup is desired, remove figs from syrup and put figs in sterilized jars. Boil syrup until desired consistency is obtained and then pour over figs. Seal jars.)

Yield: 12-14 pints

Nancy Lewis

FIG—STRAWBERRY JAM

4 cups peeled, mashed figs   **1 (6-ounce) package**
3 cups sugar   **strawberry Jello**

Mix all. Cook 30 minutes. Put in sterilized jelly jars. Seal.

Yield: 5 to 6 8-ounce jars

Yvonne Pavy

BLACKBERRY JELLY

With the delicious bread Mrs. Broussard brings along a little jar of homemade blackberry jelly. "The blackberries were such a delight this year—so beautiful," she exclaims. She said there is nothing to making the jelly...First, she and her husband pick the blackberries fresh off the bush. Then she presses them through a cloth to gather the juice; for each cup of juice she adds two cups of sugar, and this she boils in a large container for 20 minutes. This yields two pints.

Yield: 2 pints   *Juanita Winkle*

PEPPER JELLY

6 bell peppers
18 small hot peppers
19½ cups sugar

4½ cups cider vinegar
12 drops red food color
3 (6-ounce) bottles Certo

Grind peppers and combine with sugar and vinegar. Bring to foaming boil. Skim. Remove from heat, add food coloring and let stand 5 minutes. Add Certo and pour into jars immediately.

Yield: 24 (8-ounce) jars   *Shadows Service League*

PORT WINE JELLY

4 cups ruby port wine
6 cups sugar
2 tablespoons lemon juice

1 (6-ounce) bottle Certo fruit
pectin

Mix wine, sugar and lemon juice in a large saucepan. Bring to a low boil, stirring constantly. When boiling, turn off heat and at once stir in Certo. Pour into sterilized jelly glasses. Cover with ⅛ inch hot paraffin.

Yield: 10 half-pint glasses   *Bootsie Minvielle*

PICKLED BEETS AND EGGS

2 (16-ounce) cans small whole beets
1 cup cider vinegar
¼ cup sugar

1 teaspoon salt
⅛ teaspoon ground cloves
1 medium onion, sliced
12 small eggs, hard boiled

Drain beets, reserve 1 cup juice. In medium saucepan, combine vinegar, sugar, salt, cloves, onion, and reserved beet juice; bring to a boil, stirring occasionally. Add beets; simmer, uncovered for 10 minutes.

Peel eggs, and place in half gallon jar. Slowly pour in beets and liquid; stir gently to distribute eggs evenly.

Let cool, cover, then refrigerate. Wait at least 24 hours before serving.

Yield: ½ gallon jar   *A Friend of the Shadows*

BREAD AND BUTTER PICKLES

1 cup salt
1 cup sliced onions

12 sliced cucumbers

Cover with water and soak overnight.

SYRUP
3 cups white vinegar
1 teaspoon celery seed
2 cups sugar

1 cup water
1 teaspoon mustard seed

Add drained cucumbers to syrup. Bring to boil. Add ½ teaspoon turmeric. Bottle and seal in sterilized quart jars.

Yield: 3-4 quarts   *Cathi Gibbens*

FREEZER PICKLES

2 quarts cucumbers, peeled
   and sliced thin
1 medium onion, sliced thin

1 tablespoon salt
1½ cups sugar
½ cup white vinegar

Mix cucumbers, onion and salt, let stand 2 hours, drain well. Then mix sugar and vinegar well and pour over cucumbers. Pack into freezer containers and freeze. Pickles are ready to eat in 3 to 4 days.

Yield: 2 quarts
A Friend of the Shadows

Note: If cucumbers are large, they may be halved or quartered.

MIRLITON PICKLES

5 mirlitons, peeled and sliced
4 to 5 onions, chopped
2 to 3 bell peppers, chopped
½ cup salt
5 cups cider vinegar

5 cups sugar
2 teaspoons mustard seed
1 teaspoon turmeric
½ teaspoon whole cloves

Mix first 4 ingredients and let stand for 2 to 3 hours.

Mix next 5 ingredients and boil for 5 minutes. Drain mirliton mixture and add to hot vinegar mixture and bring to full boil. Pack in hot, sterilized jars and seal.

Yield: 3-4 quarts
Keith Courrege

SQUASH PICKLES

4 quarts small yellow squash
6 medium white onions
⅓ cup plain salt
5 cups sugar

3 cups cider vinegar
2 tablespoons mustard seed
1½ teaspoons celery seed
1½ teaspoons turmeric

Slice squash, onion and add salt. Cover with ice, mix, let stand 3 hours. Drain and heat with other ingredients. Put in sterilized jars and seal.

Yield: 10 pints
Harriet Shea

WATERMELON PICKLES

Take one tablespoon of powdered lime. (The kind used to make lime water for babies). Put it in one quart of water, pour over 6 cups peeled cut up pieces of watermelon rind and let set for 2½ hours. Drain, cover with fresh water, cook until almost tender. Let stand overnight. Make a syrup of 7 cups sugar, one pint vinegar, ½ teaspoon oil of cloves, ½ teaspoon oil of cinnamon. Cook to syrup consistency (10 minutes). Drain watermelon pieces and put in syrup, bringing to a good boil. Let stand overnight. Bring to boil again, let stand overnight. If syrup is still thin, drain, boil down. Place pieces in hot jars, pour boiling syrup over, seal.

Yield: 6 cups
Cathi Gibbens

AUNT MARIE'S CHOW CHOW

½ gallon chopped cucumbers (do not peel)
½ gallon chopped white onions
½ gallon chopped green tomatoes (do not peel)
1 gallon shredded cabbage (about 2 medium heads)
9 pints of white vinegar
3 pints water

¾ box of salt
Red pepper to taste
2 teaspoons celery seed
2 teaspoons whole allspice
1½ cups sugar
3 ounces dry mustard
1 pint salad oil
1 cup flour
1 ounce turmeric

Prepare vegetables, soak overnight in a crock with 3 pints vinegar and 3 pints of water to which salt has been added.

In a large pot boil 4 pints vinegar with red pepper to taste, celery seed and allspice. Thoroughly mix the remaining 2 pints of vinegar, sugar, mustard, salad oil, flour and turmeric. Add to the boiling vinegar, cook until thick. Add the thoroughly drained vegetables and cook 10 minutes. Cool, put in sterilized jars and seal.

Yield: 14 pints
Jeanne Conrad

CORN AND CABBAGE RELISH

12 ears uncooked corn
2 large onions
1 large red bell pepper
1 small cabbage
2 large green bell peppers
1½ cups sugar

¼ cup salt
2 tablespoons dry mustard
½ teaspoon turmeric
4 cups vinegar
¼ cup flour

Cut corn from cob. Chop other vegetables. Mix thoroughly. Heat 2 cups vinegar to boiling point. Add sugar, salt, mustard, and flour and turmeric which have been combined with 2 cups cold vinegar. Let boil till thick. Add vegetables. Cook ½ hour. Seal in hot sterilized jars.

Yield: 6-7 half-pints   *Cathi Gibbens*

GREEN TOMATO—GREEN PEPPER RELISH

4 cups green tomatoes
4 cups green bell peppers
   (may be mixed with red
   bell peppers for color)
4 cups onion
4 cups cabbage

1 small red, hot pepper
   (optional)
2 cups white vinegar
4 cups sugar
1 or 2 teaspoons celery seed
   (optional)
3 tablespoons salt

All vegetable measurements are after being chopped or coarsely ground. Mix all ingredients and boil 10 minutes, then seal in sterilized jars.

Yield: 7 quarts

APPLE CHUTNEY

18 medium-sized sour apples
3 red bell peppers
3 large white onions
9 green tomatoes
3 cups cider vinegar
3 cups sugar

1 teaspoon mace
2 tablespoons salt
2 teaspoons cinnamon
1 teaspoon ginger
1½ teaspoons allspice
2 cups seedless raisins

Peel and core apples, seed the peppers, peel onions, core green tomatoes and put all through coarse food chopper. Heat vinegar, sugar, spices and raisins and bring to boil. Stir in the chopped apples, onions, tomatoes and peppers. Cook at rolling boil, stirring constantly, until thick (about 30 minutes). Fill into sterilized jars and seal hot.

Yield: 6 pints   *Juanita Winkle*

PEACH CHUTNEY

4 pounds ripe peaches
2 white onions
½ pound raisins
1 clove garlic, peeled
½ cup preserved or
   crystalized ginger
1 small chili pepper

4 cups brown sugar, firmly
   packed
2 cups cider vinegar
2 teaspoons ginger
1 tablespoon salt
2 tablespoons mustard seed

Scald, peel and cut up peaches. Put onions, raisins and garlic, pepper and ginger through food grinder. Mix all ingredients together in a kettle and bring to a quick boil. Simmer slowly for about an hour, stirring frequently to prevent scorching, until chutney is thick and brown in color. Pour into hot sterilized jars and seal.

Yield: 3 pints   *Juanita Winkle*

FRUIT CHUTNEY

4 pounds ripe apples or
   peaches (as preferred)
3 large white onions
1 clove garlic, peeled and
   sliced
2 cups seedless raisins
½ cup diced crystalized ginger
2 to 4 teaspoons ground
   ginger, according to taste
1 tablespoon red pepper

2 tablespoons mustard seed
2 teaspoons cinnamon
1 teaspoon nutmeg
1 teaspoon grated lemon rind
2 tablespoons lemon juice
2 cups white corn syrup
2 cups brown sugar, packed
2 cups cider vinegar
1 tablespoon salt
1 small chili pepper

Wash and cut up apples (peel and dice) or peaches (do not peel), onions and garlic. Mix all ingredients together in a kettle and bring to a quick boil. Simmer slowly for about ¾ to 1 hour, stirring frequently to prevent scorching, until chutney is thick and brown in color. Pour into hot sterilized jars and seal.

Yield: 6 pints   *Juanita Winkle*

Note: Any other fruit (fresh, dried or candied) may be added or substituted as desired. Also, other spices may be added if desired. I have also added chopped celery and shredded or sliced raw carrots and sweet potatoes, which add to the bulk of ingredients and do not take away from the taste.

SWEETS

Circa 1940

This statue is one of a group depicting the four seasons. They were bought and placed in the four corners of the formal garden by Weeks Hall. This statue, "Winter," huddles against the cold in a tropical garden. Weeks Hall's influence can best be seen in the gardens, for it was there that he lavished much of his attention, arranging the flowers and plants with the eye of an artist. His efforts created a lush atmosphere around the house.

During the antebellum period, however, the grounds were very different indeed. Although Mary Clara Weeks, mistress of the Shadows, was an avid gardener, whose books on horticulture are still on display at the house, it was necessary to maintain a working garden to meet the family's needs. Therefore, in addition to Mary Clara's flower beds, vegetable gardens and poultry shared the grounds.

It is Mary Clara, too, that we can thank for the lovely moss-hung live oaks that surround the house. She planted them in the 1830's, and they have grown to provide cool shade to a once sunny garden spot. One oak still bears the original hitching ring.

Sweets

CAKES
Angel Food, Heavenly 277
Apple 278
Better than Anything 277
Blitz Torte 278
Chocolate, Aunt Maud's 279
Chocolate Cream Cheese 280
Chocolate Éclair 279
Coke 281
Cream, Italian 281
Fruit 282
Fudge 283
Pecan 282
Pound, Chocolate 284
Pound, Cream Cheese 283
Pumpkin-Walnut 284
Pumpkin-Walnut Roll 285
Red Velvet, Waldorf Astoria 286
Spiced Amaretto-Toffee Roll 287
Strawberry Shortcake,
    Old-Fashioned 285

CANDIES
Almond Roca 316
Buttermilk Pralines 320
Chocolate Candy, Easy 317
Chocolate Truffles 316
Divinity 317
"Elmer's Gold Brick" 317
Mints, Butter 318
Peanut Brittle 318
Peanut Butter Fudge 318
Pecan Brittle 319
Pecan Pralines I 319
Pecan Pralines II 319
Pecan Turtles 320
Sugared Pecans 320

COOKIES
Almond Cakes 308
Brownies, Neen's Very Easy 308
Butterscotch-Oatmeal 309
Chinese 309
Chocolate-Caramel Squares 309
Christmas Wreaths 310
Congo Squares 310
Cream Cheese Squares 310
Gingerbread Men 311
Great and Easy Bars 311
Lemon Mardi-Gras Squares 312
Lemon Squares 312
Les Oreilles De Cochon 313
Mandelbrodt (Jewish Cookies) 314
Peanut Blossoms 313
Pecan Cocoons 314
Pecan Crisp 314
Praline 315

Refrigerator 315
Russian Rocks 315

DESSERTS
Ambrosia, Eugenie's 296
Apple Strudel 296
Birds' Nests 297
Bread Pudding, Walnut Fudge 299
Bread Pudding with Whiskey
    Sauce 298
Charlotte Russe 297
Chocolate Charlotte, Frozen 300
Chocolate-Cream Cheese
    Delight 299
Chocolate Velvet Cream 301
Cobbler, Easy Apple 300
Cobbler, Old-Fashioned Sweet 301
Cobbler, Yam, Trappey's
    Minute-Made 302
Eggnog Dessert, Frozen 302
Floating Island 303
Fruit Trifle 302
Ice Cream, Best Vanilla 303
Ice Cream Crunch, Coffee 304
Ice Cream Squares, Caramel 304
Lemon Sherbet 305
Mocha Brandy Parfait, Frozen 305
Pots De Crème 305
Soufflé Froid au Chocolat 306
Soufflé, Strawberries 21 306
Strawberries and Cream Dessert . . 307
Strawberry Crème, Brandied 307
Wine Jelly Dessert 308

FROSTINGS, FILLINGS AND SAUCES
Fillings for Crêpes, Jelly Rolls, Layer
    Cakes or Petit Fours 288
Hard Sauce 289
Pecan Filling 288
Velvet Rum Sauce 288
Whipped Cream Frosting 287

PIES
Crust, Basic 289
Crust, Food Processor 289
Banana Cream 290
Banana Split 290
Chocolate 291
Chocolate Amaretto Mousse 291
Fudge, Superb 292
Lemon Meringue 292
Peach Parfait 293
Peanut Butter, Chocolate Crust . . . 293
Pecan, Black Bottom 294
Pecan, Deluxe 294
Pecan, Grandmother's 294
Pumpkin Chiffon with Chocolate-
    Walnut Crust 295
Summer 295

Refer to additional recipes in "How Men Cook" section.

HEAVENLY ANGEL FOOD CAKE

1 cup plus 2 tablespoons cake
 flour
¾ cup granulated sugar
1½ cups egg whites (11 to 13,
 depending on size of eggs
 used) at room temperature

½ teaspoon salt
1½ teaspoons cream of tartar
1 cup sifted granulated sugar
1 teaspoon vanilla extract
1 teaspoon almond extract

Sift flour and ¾ cup sugar together 5 times. Beat egg whites and salt until foamy. Add cream of tartar and continue beating until stiff, 2½ to 3 minutes. Sprinkle in the 1 cup sifted sugar and beat only until blended. Add extracts. Sprinkle in flour/sugar mixture evenly and mix quickly to blend. Pour into ungreased tube pan and bake at 375° for 30 to 35 minutes.

Yield: 16 servings   *Alva L. Lamperez*

BETTER THAN ANYTHING CAKE

1 (18-ounce) package yellow
 cake mix
1 (3-ounce) package vanilla
 instant pudding
4 eggs
6 ounces German sweet
 chocolate, divided
 (4 ounces grated, and
 2 ounces melted)
½ cup oil
½ cup water

1 (8-ounce) carton sour cream
1 (6-ounce) package chocolate
 chips
½ cup chopped pecans
½ stick butter
Few grains salt
1 teaspoon vanilla
1 (16-ounce) box powdered
 sugar
2 tablespoons milk to thin,
 approximately

Mix cake mix, pudding, eggs, 4 ounces grated chocolate, oil, water and sour cream on medium speed for 10 minutes. Stir in chips and nuts. Bake in greased and floured tube pan 55 minutes at 350.° Cool 10 minutes. Icing: melt 2 ounces chocolate with butter; add salt, vanilla and powdered sugar. Add milk sparingly to a spreadable consistency. Ice cake while warm.

Barbara Schwing

APPLE CAKE

1½ cups vegetable oil
1½ cups white sugar
½ cup brown sugar
2 eggs, beaten
2 teaspoons vanilla
3 cups flour

1 teaspoon cinnamon
1½ teaspoons soda
1 teaspoon salt
3 cups of apples, chopped
½ cup of pecans

Mix oil, sugars, eggs, vanilla and beat well. Add all remaining ingredients which have been mixed together. Knead dough. Bake at 350° in greased tube pan about 1½ hours.

Yield: 16 servings   *Ollie Vidrine*

BLITZ TORTE

CAKE
½ cup shortening
½ cup sugar
3 eggs, separated
½ teaspoon vanilla

5 tablespoons milk
1 cup cake flour
1½ teaspoons baking powder
1 teaspoon salt

MERINGUE
3 egg whites
½ cup sugar

½ cup nut meats

FILLING
½ pint whipping cream or 1 (8-ounce) carton of Cool Whip
Sliced, sugared strawberries or drained, canned pineapple or
   sliced, sugared peaches

Cream shortening and sugar. Add well beaten egg yolks, vanilla and milk. Fold in sifted flour, baking powder and salt. Use 9-inch cake pans. Place in cake tins which have been lined with oiled paper. (Batter will not seem very thick.)

Beat whites of eggs until stiff; gradually add ½ cup sugar. Spread equally over cake batter. Sprinkle with nuts. Bake at 350° for 25 to 30 minutes. Test with toothpick for doneness. Turn out carefully on cake rack. When cool, place nut side of one layer up. Fill with whipped cream and sugared fruit. Place other layer meringue side up.

Yield: 12 servings   *Cathi Gibbens*

AUNT MAUD'S CHOCOLATE CAKE

CAKE

2 cups sugar
2 cups flour
1 stick butter or margarine
½ cup shortening
4 tablespoons cocoa
1 cup water

½ cup buttermilk
1 teaspoon baking soda
1 teaspoon cinnamon
1 teaspoon vanilla
2 eggs, slightly beaten

ICING

1 stick butter or margarine
2 tablespoons cocoa
4 tablespoons milk

¾ pound of powdered sugar
1 teaspoon vanilla
1 cup chopped nuts

Sift sugar and flour into large bowl. Bring butter, shortening, cocoa, and water to a boil. Remove from heat and pour over sugar-flour mixture. Stir well. Add remainder of cake ingredients. Mix well. Pour into an 11 x 16-inch greased pan. Bake 20 minutes at 400° or until toothpick inserted in center comes out clean. Cool a little before icing.

For icing, bring butter, cocoa and milk to a boil. Remove from heat and add sugar, vanilla and nuts. Beat well (about 1 minute) and spread over warm cake.

Yield: 24 squares   *Maureen Doerle*

CHOCOLATE ÉCLAIR CAKE

2 (3-ounce) vanilla instant
  pudding
2 cups whipped topping
3 cups milk
Honey graham crackers
2 tablespoons butter
2 tablespoons white corn syrup

2 squares semi-sweet
  chocolate or 1 cup plus
  1 tablespoon chocolate
  chips
2 tablespoons milk
½ cup powdered sugar

Beat pudding and milk on slow speed until thick. Stir in whipped topping and mix well. In bottom of 9 x 13 x 2-inch pan, layer whole graham crackers and then put half of pudding mixture on top. Repeat layers ending with graham crackers on top. For topping melt chocolate and butter over low heat. Stir in rest of ingredients and spread over top layer of graham crackers. Refrigerate. Cut into squares to serve.

Yield: 8-10 servings   *Shara Viator*

CHOCOLATE CREAM CHEESE CAKE

The frosting comes from part of the batter.

2 (3-ounce) packages cream
  cheese, softened
½ cup margarine, softened
1 teaspoon vanilla
1½ pounds sifted powdered
  sugar
¼ cup milk, at room
  temperature
4 squares (1 ounce each)
  unsweetened chocolate,
  melted and cooled

4 tablespoons margarine,
  softened
3 eggs
2¼ cups all purpose flour
1 teaspoon baking powder
1 teaspoon baking soda
1 teaspoon salt
1¼ cups milk

Cream together cream cheese, the ½ cup margarine, and the vanilla. Alternately beat in sugar and the ¼ cup milk. Blend in chocolate. Remove 2 cups for frosting; cover and refrigerate. Cream together remaining chocolate mixture and 4 tablespoons margarine. Add eggs; beat well. Mix together dry ingredients, and beat into creamed mixture alternately with the remaining milk. Turn into two greased and floured 9 x 1½-inch round cake pans. Bake in 350° oven for 30 minutes. Cool in pans for 10 minutes. Remove; cool on racks. Remove frosting from refrigerator 15 minutes before frosting cake.

Yield: 12 servings

Ann Hayes

COKE CAKE

2 cups flour
2 cups sugar
1 cup Coke
2 sticks margarine
2 tablespoons cocoa

½ cup buttermilk
2 eggs
1 teaspoon soda
1 teaspoon vanilla
1½ cups small marshmallows

Sift together flour and sugar and set aside. Bring Coke, margarine and cocoa to boil. Pour this over sifted flour and sugar. To this add buttermilk, beaten eggs, soda, vanilla and marshmallows. Mix well and pour into greased and floured sheet cake pan. Bake for 45 minutes at 350°.

ICING

1 stick margarine
2 tablespoons cocoa
6 tablespoons Coke

1 box confectioner's sugar
1 cup pecans

Bring margarine, cocoa and Coke to a boil. Pour over sugar and add pecans. Ice cake while still warm. Cut into serving pieces from pan.

Yield: 20 servings   *Mrs. Gordie White*

ITALIAN CREAM CAKE

1 stick margarine, softened
½ cup vegetable shortening
2 cups sugar
5 eggs, separated
2 cups flour

1 teaspoon soda
1 cup buttermilk
1 teaspoon vanilla
1 small can coconut
1 cup chopped pecans

Cream margarine and shortening. Add sugar and beat until smooth. Add egg yolks. Combine flour and soda and add to creamed mixture, alternately with buttermilk. Add coconut and nuts. Fold in beaten egg whites. Bake in two 8-inch pans at 350° for 30 minutes. Ice with frosting below.

FROSTING

½ stick margarine, softened
1 (1-pound) box confectioner's
   sugar

1 (8-ounce) package cream
   cheese, softened
½ teaspoon vanilla

Beat all ingredients until smooth. Frost cake.

Yield: 12 servings   *JoAnn Riley*

FRUIT CAKE

1 pound butter
1 pound brown sugar
8 eggs, separated
Juice of 2 oranges and 1 lemon
3½ cups flour
2 teaspoons nutmeg
1 teaspoon mace
1 teaspoon ground cloves
1 teaspoon salt
2 teaspoons ground cinnamon
1 teaspoon baking soda

1 pound raisins
1 cup candied cherries,
   chopped
1 cup candied pineapple,
   chopped
1 pound pitted dates
   (not sugared)
1 cup currant jelly
1 cup molasses
1 cup strong black coffee
1 pound chopped pecans

Cream butter and brown sugar, add beaten egg yolks and juices and mix until smooth. Sift flour and add dry spices, soda and salt. In a bowl put all chopped fruit, add 1 cup flour and spice mixture and mix together. In another bowl, mix jelly, molasses and coffee. Add fruit and nuts to creamed butter and sugar mixture. Then add remaining flour alternately with jelly mixture. Stir in stiffly beaten egg whites and mix well. Pour into a greased and floured tube pan and bake at 250° for 2 to 3 hours or until nicely browned and firm; test by pressing top. Cool.

Yield: 20 servings   *Ione S. Woods*

PECAN CAKE

2 cups sugar
1 stick margarine
4 eggs

2 squares melted
   unsweetened chocolate
2 cups flour
6 cups shelled pecans

Cream together sugar and margarine. Add eggs one at a time, beating well after each addition. Add melted chocolate and mix well. Sift flour and mix with pecans. Pour chocolate mixture into flour and pecans, mix well. Grease tube pan and line with oiled heavy brown paper. Cover top of batter with oiled paper also. Bake for 2 hours at 250°

Yield: 16 servings

Note: May be baked in 2 small loaf pans, prepared as above.

FUDGE CAKE

2 sticks butter
2 cups sugar
4 eggs
1½ cups flour

6 tablespoons cocoa
2 teaspoons vanilla
2 cups chopped nuts

Blend butter and sugar. Add eggs one at a time and beat. Sift flour and cocoa together and add to above mixture. Add vanilla and pecans. Pour into greased pan (9 x 13) and bake at 350° for 30 minutes. Frost with Fudge Icing below.

FUDGE ICING
4 cups sugar
1 can Carnation milk
1 stick butter
1 (12-ounce) package semi-
   sweet chocolate chips

1 pint jar marshmallow creme
3 cups pecans
1 teaspoon vanilla

Combine sugar, milk and butter. Cook, stirring constantly to 236° on candy thermometer. Remove from fire, add chocolate chips, marshmallow creme, and blend until chocolate is melted. Add pecans and vanilla and pour over cake. Whatever is left may be poured into a buttered pan and used as fudge.

Yield: 24 servings   *Susie Pharr*

CREAM CHEESE POUND CAKE

3 sticks butter
1 (8-ounce) package cream
   cheese
3 cups sugar

1 teaspoon vanilla
6 eggs
3 cups cake flour

Cream butter, cream cheese, sugar and vanilla together until smooth. Add eggs, one at a time, beating well after each addition. Then add flour until well blended. Bake 1½ hours in greased and floured tube pan at 325.° Cake may be topped with ½ cup chopped pecans before baking. Sprinkle with sifted powdered sugar after baking.

Yield: 12-16 servings   *Penny Fenton*

CHOCOLATE POUND CAKE

½ pound butter (2 sticks)
½ cup shortening
3 cups sugar
5 eggs
3 cups flour

½ teaspoon baking powder
½ teaspoon salt
4 tablespoons cocoa
1 cup milk
1 tablespoon vanilla

Cream butter, shortening, sugar, and eggs. Mix dry ingredients together, sift, and add alternately with milk. Add vanilla. Bake in greased and floured tube pan for 1 hour and 20 minutes at 325° (Use a large tube pan as it makes a big cake.) Ice with Chocolate Frosting below.

CHOCOLATE FROSTING
1 box powdered sugar
1 stick margarine
6 tablespoons milk

3 tablespoons cocoa
1 teaspoon vanilla
½ cup nuts

Mix all ingredients except nuts. Bring to boil. Remove from heat and add nuts. Allow to cool somewhat, then pour over warm cake.

Yield: 12 servings   *Shereen Minvielle*

PUMPKIN-WALNUT CAKE

3 cups flour
2 teaspoons baking powder
2 teaspoons baking soda
1 teaspoon salt
3½ teaspoons cinnamon

4 large eggs
2 cups sugar
1½ cups corn oil
2 cups pumpkin, canned
1½ cups chopped walnuts

Sift together first 5 ingredients, set aside. Beat eggs well, and gradually add sugar until thick and lemon colored. While still beating constantly, add oil slowly. With mixer at low speed, add dry ingredients alternately with pumpkin, beginning and ending with dry ingredients. Beat until smooth and add walnuts. Pour into ungreased tube pan. Bake at 350° until toothpick comes out clean, about 1 hour and 10 minutes. Drizzle warm cake with Praline Glaze below.

PRALINE GLAZE
⅔ cup brown sugar
½ stick margarine
½ cup chopped walnuts

1 tablespoon cream or
   evaporated milk

Cook together until it starts to thicken. Pour over warm cake.

Yield: 20 slices   *A Friend of the Shadows*

PUMPKIN-WALNUT ROLL

3 eggs
1 cup sugar
2/3 cup canned pumpkin
1 teaspoon lemon juice
3/4 cup flour
1 teaspoon baking powder

2 teaspoons cinnamon
1 teaspoon ginger
1/2 teaspoon nutmeg
1/2 teaspoon salt
1 cup chopped walnuts

Beat eggs on high speed of mixer for 5 minutes. Gradually beat in 1 cup sugar. Stir in pumpkin and lemon juice. Fold dry ingredients into pumpkin. Spread in greased and floured jelly roll pan. Sprinkle chopped walnuts over top of batter. Bake for 15 minutes at 375.º Lay a dish towel flat and sprinkle it with powdered sugar. Turn warm cake out onto towel, nut side down, and roll towel and cake up in jelly roll fashion. Let cool. Fill with cream cheese filling below.

FILLING

1 (8-ounce) package cream
   cheese, softened
1 cup powdered sugar

4 tablespoons softened
   margarine
1/2 teaspoon vanilla

Combine all ingredients together and beat until smooth. Gently unroll cake in towel. Carefully spread filling on side of cake without nuts. Spread all the way to outer edges. Carefully roll cake back up jelly roll style. This is a great Thanksgiving or Christmas dessert.

Yield: 8 servings   *Barbara Schwing*

OLD-FASHIONED STRAWBERRY SHORTCAKE

2 cups sifted flour
1/3 cup sugar
4 teaspoons baking powder
1/2 teaspoon salt

1/8 teaspoon nutmeg
1/2 cup soft butter
1 egg
1/3 cup milk

Mix first 5 ingredients together in a bowl. Cut in butter until mixture is like coarse meal. Beat together egg and milk and add to flour mixture. Bake in greased 10 x 12-inch pan for 25 minutes at 350.º Cut into squares and serve with fresh sweetened strawberries and sweetened whipped cream.

Juanita Winkle

WALDORF ASTORIA RED VELVET CAKE

½ cup vegetable shortening
1 cup sugar
2 eggs
¼ cup red food coloring
2 tablespoons cocoa
1 cup buttermilk

2¼ cups cake flour
1 teaspoon salt
1 teaspoon vanilla
1 teaspoon baking soda
1 tablespoon vinegar

Cream shortening, sugar, eggs. Make a paste of food coloring and cocoa and add to creamed mixture. Add buttermilk alternately with sifted flour and salt; add vanilla. Add baking soda to vinegar (this will bubble up). Then add this to batter, blending instead of beating. Bake in two 8-inch greased and floured cake pans for 24 to 30 minutes at 350.° Cool, split layers to make 4 layers and ice as below.

FROSTING
3 tablespoons flour
1 cup milk
1 cup sugar

1 teaspoon vanilla
1 cup butter, softened

Cook flour and milk until very thick, stirring constantly. Cool. Cream sugar, butter and vanilla until very fluffy. Add cooled mixture to this. Mix until well blended. Should be the consistency of whipped cream. Frosts four 8-inch layers.

Yield: 8-10 servings   *Barbara Schwing*

SPICED AMARETTO-TOFFEE ROLL

3 eggs
1 egg yolk
1/2 cup sugar
1/2 teaspoon vanilla
1/2 cup flour
1 teaspoon cinnamon
1/4 teaspoon cardamom
1/4 teaspoon nutmeg
2 tablespoons butter, melted
Powdered sugar

1 (8-ounce) carton frozen
   whipped topping
4 (1 1/8-ounce) English toffee
   candy bars, crushed
1 1/2 tablespoons amaretto or
   other almond flavored
   liqueur
Maraschino cherries, for
   garnish

Line a 15 x 10-inch jelly roll pan with waxed paper, then grease and flour paper. Combine eggs, egg yolk, sugar, and vanilla and beat at high speed 5 to 6 minutes until thick and tripled in volume. Combine flour and spices, mixing well; fold into egg mixture. Fold in butter, blend well. Spread batter evenly in prepared pan and bake at 350° for 11 to 13 minutes. Sift powdered sugar onto a rectangular kitchen towel, and turn out warm cake immediately onto towel. Peel off waxed paper and, starting at narrow end, roll up cake and towel together. Let cool in towel. Combine whipped topping, crushed candy and amaretto. Unroll cake; remove towel. Spread cake with 2/3 of whipped topping mixture, and reroll. Place on serving plate, seam side down. Spoon remaining whipped topping mixture down center of cake. Garnish with maraschino cherries, if desired.

Yield: 8-10 servings   *A Friend of the Shadows*

WHIPPED CREAM FROSTING

2 tablespoons flour
1/2 cup milk
1/4 cup butter
1/4 cup vegetable shortening

1/2 cup sugar
1 teaspoon vanilla
3 tablespoons marshmallow
   creme (optional)

Mix flour and milk in saucepan, cook until thick. Cool. Cream butter and shortening 4 minutes, gradually adding sugar and beat for 4 more minutes. Add flour paste and beat another 4 minutes. Add vanilla and blend in marshmallow creme.

Yield: 1 cup

FILLINGS FOR CRÊPES, JELLY ROLLS, LAYER CAKES OR PETIT FOURS

RASPBERRY-KIRSCH FILLING

¾ cup raspberry preserves   3 tablespoons kirsch

Melt preserves in small pan over low heat. Strain through sieve to remove seeds. Cool and stir in kirsch. Brush onto layers.

Yield: ¾ cup

COFFEE FILLING

¼ cup coffee liqueur   1 tablespoon water
1 tablespoon granulated sugar   2 teaspoons instant coffee

Stir all ingredients together and brush over cake layer or for a thicker filling, add 1½ cups sweetened whipped cream to fill crêpes or jelly rolls.

CHOCOLATE FILLING

1 (12-ounce) package   16 tablespoons butter cut into
   semisweet chocolate chips   pats (2 sticks)
                             2 cups confectioner's sugar

Melt chocolate chips and butter over low heat, stirring constantly. Remove from heat, cool and add confectioner's sugar.

A Friend of the Shadows

PECAN FILLING FOR A CAKE

1 cup ground pecans   1 teaspoon vanilla
¾ cup sugar   ½ cup water

Bring all ingredients to a boil and cook about 10 minutes or until thick enough to spread. Cool and spread between layers.

Yield: 1 cup   *A Weeks Family recipe*

VELVET RUM SAUCE

½ cup butter or margarine   ½ cup light cream, or 1
1 cup sugar   (6-ounce) can evaporated
2 tablespoons rum, or   milk
   1 teaspoon rum extract   1 teaspoon nutmeg

Combine all ingredients and heat to boiling over low heat. Serve warm over fruit cobblers, custards, bread pudding, etc.

Yield: 1 cup   *Debbie Schwing*

HARD SAUCE

¼ cup butter or margarine
1½ cups confectioner's sugar

1 teaspoon rum extract
2 tablespoons milk

Cream butter or margarine until fluffy. Beat in sugar a little at a time; then beat in rum extract and milk until smooth. Chill. Spoon onto baked fruit or fruit pies or warm bread pudding, etc.

Yield: 2/3 cup   *Barbara Schwing*

Note: 1 tablespoon milk and 1 tablespoon rum may be used in place of the rum extract and 2 tablespoons milk.

FOOD PROCESSOR PIE CRUST, NEVER FAIL

1½ cups unbleached flour or
**   regular flour**
¼ teaspoon salt

1 stick of butter
¼ cup cold water

Place flour and salt in processor bowl with butter cut into 8 parts. Process with blade until finely ground, about 15 to 30 seconds. Slowly add the ice water with motor running until dough lumps, 30 seconds or less. Remove, separate into 2 portions and roll out on floured surface. It takes less time to make this recipe than to read it!

Yield: 1 top and bottom crust   *Sonja Klein Viator*

BASIC PIE CRUST

1¼ cups flour
¼ teaspoon salt
Pinch of sugar

1 stick butter (chilled)
¼ cup vegetable shortening
3 to 4 tablespoons ice water

Sift flour, salt, and sugar into large mixing bowl. Cut butter and shortening into small pieces and cut into flour mixture rapidly. When shortening is the size of tiny peas, add water gradually, mixing lightly until dough holds together. Don't overwork. Shape into a ball and refrigerate for ½ hour. Place on a floured surface and roll out to ⅛-inch thickness, 2 inches larger than pie pan. Transfer to pan by rolling dough onto rolling pin and unroll into pan. Trim edges and flute. Dough can be refrigerated several days before using or it can be frozen. Prick bottom of shell to bake. Cook in 400° oven until golden brown, approximately 10 minutes.

BANANA CREAM PIE

⅓ cup flour
⅔ cup sugar
¼ teaspoon salt
2 cups milk, scalded
3 slightly beaten egg yolks,
   in separate container

2 tablespoons butter
½ teaspoon vanilla
2 large or 3 small bananas
1 (9-inch) baked pastry shell
3 egg whites
3 tablespoons sugar

Mix flour, sugar, and salt in double boiler and whisk in milk gradually. Cook until very thick, stirring constantly. Add scant ¼ cup of this mixture to egg yolks, then stir this into remaining hot mixture. Cook 2 minutes; cool. Add butter and vanilla. Slice bananas into pie shell and pour cooled mixture over bananas. Make meringue with egg whites and sugar. Spread on top of custard. Bake at 350° for 12 to 15 minutes.

Yield: 8 servings

Carla Mouton

BANANA SPLIT PIE

3 cups crushed vanilla wafers
1½ sticks melted margarine
1 stick margarine
2 eggs
3 cups sifted confectioner's
   sugar
1 (3-ounce) box chocolate
   pudding instant mix
1 (6-ounce) jar cherries,
   drained

3 medium bananas, sliced and
   dipped into pineapple juice
   to prevent browning
1 (15¼-ounce) can crushed
   pineapple, very well
   drained
1 (12-ounce) container Cool
   Whip whipped topping
1 cup crushed pecans

Mix vanilla wafers and margarine and press into 9 x 13-inch pan. Mix together margarine, eggs, and confectioner's sugar and beat with mixer for 10 minutes. Spread over crust. Mix instant pudding according to package directions and spread over egg mixture. Layer remaining ingredients in order given. Refrigerate overnight.

Yield: 20 servings

Shara Viator
Carolyn Sorci
Adele Wormser

CHOCOLATE PIE

20 chocolate Oreo cookies,
    crushed
¼ cup melted butter

1 quart coffee ice cream,
    softened

Mix crushed cookies and butter and press into a 9-inch pie pan. Spread ice cream over pie crust.

SAUCE

3 ounces unsweetened
    chocolate, melted
¼ cup butter
⅔ cup sugar

⅔ cup evaporated milk
1 teaspoon vanilla
1 pint whipped cream
½ cup chopped pecans

Bring chocolate, sugar and butter to a boil. Gradually add milk and cook until thick. Cool and add vanilla. Spread over ice cream and return to freezer. Before serving top with whipped cream and cover with chopped pecans. Serve immediately.

Yield: 8 servings   *Bootsie Trappey*

CHOCOLATE AMARETTO MOUSSE PIE

1 (12-ounce) package
    semi-sweet chocolate
    chips (2 cups)
4 tablespoons margarine
1 (14-ounce) can condensed
    milk

¼ cup water
¼ cup Amaretto liqueur
2 cups heavy cream, whipped
Sliced almonds for garnish
¼ teaspoon salt

Melt 1 cup chocolate chips and 2 tablespoons margarine. Pour into foil lined 9-inch pie pan and smooth over bottom and up sides of pan. Freeze until firm about 30 minutes. Combine remaining chips with remaining margarine, milk and salt and melt. Stir in water and cook until blended. Add amaretto and cook and stir over low heat about 5 minutes until thickened. Cool to room temperature. Fold 1½ cups whipped cream into chocolate mixture and refrigerate. When chocolate shell is firm, lift out of pan and peel off foil. Place shell on serving dish and fill with chocolate amaretto filling. Garnish with remaining whipped cream and almonds. Chill about 3 hours to set.

Yield: 8 servings   *Barbara Schwing*

SUPERB FUDGE PIE

½ cup margarine
3 squares unsweetened
  chocolate
4 eggs
3 tablespoons white corn
  syrup
1½ cups sugar

¼ teaspoon salt
1 teaspoon vanilla
1¼ cups vanilla wafers,
  crushed
¼ cup melted margarine
¼ cup sugar

Melt margarine and chocolate over low heat. Place eggs in a bowl and beat, add syrup, sugar, salt and vanilla. Combine slightly cooled chocolate with egg mixture. Set aside. Make crust by blending vanilla wafers, sugar and margarine together and pressing into 9-inch pie pan. Pour in filling and bake for 25 to 30 minutes at 350.° Serve warm with ice cream. Best if eaten the same day it is made.

Yield: 8 servings   *Curtis Thomas*

LEMON MERINGUE PIE

½ cup sugar
4 tablespoons cornstarch
¼ teaspoon salt
1½ cups water
3 egg yolks
½ cup sugar
2 tablespoons margarine

⅓ cup fresh lemon juice
1½ teaspoons grated lemon
  rind
1 (9-inch) baked pastry shell
3 egg whites
6 tablespoons sugar

Combine sugar, cornstarch and salt in top of double boiler. Gradually blend in water. Cook, stirring constantly, over boiling water until thickened. Cover and cook 10 minutes longer, stirring occasionally. Meanwhile beat together egg yolks and sugar. Blend a little of the hot mixture into yolks; then stir yolks into remaining hot mixture. Cook over boiling water 2 minutes, stirring constantly. Add margarine, lemon juice and lemon rind. Cool and pour into baked shell. Beat egg whites until foamy, add sugar gradually and beat until stiff peaks form. Spread meringue over pie. Bake at 350° for 15 to 20 minutes until golden. Cool away from drafts.

Yield: 8 servings   *Juanita Winkle*

PEACH PARFAIT PIE

3½ cups sliced peaches,
peeled and sweetened
with ¾ cup sugar
1 (3-ounce) package lemon
Jello mix

½ cup cold water
1 pint vanilla ice cream
1 (9-inch) baked pie shell
½ cup heavy cream, whipped
and sweetened to taste

Let peaches stand in sugar for 15 minutes; then drain and reserve liquid. Add enough water to peach liquid to make 1 cup. Heat this to boiling and add Jello. Stir to dissolve. Cut ice cream in about 6 pieces and add to hot Jello liquid. Stir to melt, chill ½ hour. Fold in peaches. Pour into pie shell. This will be quite runny but will set. Refrigerate until set. Top with whipped cream and a few sliced peaches which have been sprinkled with lemon juice to prevent from turning brown.

Yield: 8 servings   *Ganelle Goodwin*

CHOCOLATE CRUST PEANUT BUTTER PIE

1 (6-ounce) package
semi-sweet chocolate
pieces, melted
1 9-inch pie shell, baked
1 (8-ounce) package cream
cheese, softened

⅓ cup peanut butter
⅔ cup sugar
1 tablespoon milk
1 cup heavy cream, whipped
Chopped peanuts

Spread melted chocolate chips over bottom and up sides of baked pie crust. Chill to firm chocolate. Combine cream cheese, peanut butter, sugar, and milk until well blended. Fold in whipped cream. Pour into crust. Chill overnight. Garnish with chopped peanuts.

Yield: 8 servings   *Barbara Schwing*

BLACK BOTTOM PECAN PIE

1 unbaked 9-inch pastry shell
1/4 cup corn starch
1/3 cup bourbon
3 eggs
3/4 cup sugar

1/2 cup margarine, melted
1/2 cup light corn syrup
1 cup chopped pecans
1 (6-ounce) package
    semi-sweet chocolate
    chips

Dissolve corn starch in bourbon, set aside. In large bowl beat eggs. Add sugar, margarine, corn syrup and bourbon-corn starch mixture. Stir in pecans and chocolate chips. Pour into pie shell. Bake at 350° for 30 to 35 minutes. (Filling should be slightly less set in center of pie than around edges.) Chocolate chips will settle on bottom of pie while baking, thus giving the pie its name.

Yield: 8 servings   *Barbara Schwing*

DELUXE PECAN PIE

3 eggs
1 cup sugar
1/2 teaspoon salt
2 tablespoons butter, melted
1/2 cup dark corn syrup

1/2 cup whipping cream
1 cup pecan halves
1 teaspoon vanilla
1/4 cup brandy
1 (9-inch) unbaked pie shell

In small bowl, beat eggs, sugar, salt, butter, syrup and cream. Stir in pecans, vanilla, and brandy. Pour into pastry. Bake 40 to 50 minutes at 375° until filling is set, and knife inserted into center of pie comes out clean. If crust browns too quickly, crimp a strip of foil around the edge of crust.

Yield: 8 servings   *A Friend of the Shadows*

GRANDMOTHER'S PECAN PIE

1 cup white corn syrup
1 cup sugar
2 tablespoons flour, stirred
    into sugar

1 tablespoon melted butter
3 eggs, separated
1 3/4 cups pecans
1 (8-inch) pie crust, unbaked

Mix corn syrup, sugar, flour, melted butter, egg yolks, and pecans together. Beat egg whites until stiff, then fold into other mixture. Pour into crust. Bake at 350° for 45 minutes.

Yield: 8 servings   *Carolyn Sorci*

PUMPKIN CHIFFON PIE WITH CHOCOLATE-WALNUT CRUST

1 (6-ounce) package
chocolate chips
2 tablespoons vegetable
shortening
1 cup finely chopped walnuts
1/4 cup sugar
1 envelope unflavored gelatin
1/2 teaspoon salt

1/2 teaspoon cinnamon
1/4 teaspoon nutmeg
3/4 cup milk
2 eggs, separated
1 cup canned pumpkin
1 teaspoon vanilla extract
1/2 cup heavy cream, whipped

For crust, melt chips over hot water with shortening. Stir in walnuts. Press over sides and bottom of 9-inch foil lined pie pan. Chill in refrigerator until firm (1 hour). Lift shell from pan, peel off foil, and replace shell in pan. For filling, combine in large saucepan sugar, gelatin, salt, cinnamon and nutmeg. Stir in milk, egg yolks, and pumpkin. Cook over medium heat until mixture boils and gelatin dissolves. Remove from heat, and add vanilla. Pour mixture into small bowl, which is set in ice. Chill until mixture mounds when dropped from spoon, about 30 minutes. Meanwhile, beat egg whites until soft peaks form, gradually adding sugar until peaks are stiff. Fold into pumpkin mixture along with whipped cream. Pour mixture into chocolate walnut crust. Chill to set at least 1 hour.

Yield: 8 servings   *Barbara Schwing*

SUMMER PIE

1 ready made graham cracker
crust
1 (14-ounce) can condensed
milk

1 (8-ounce) container Cool
Whip whipped topping
1 (6-ounce) can frozen
lemonade
1/4 cup graham cracker crumbs

Bake pie crust and cool. Mix milk, Cool Whip whipped topping and lemonade together with a hand mixer. Pour into pie crust and sprinkle with graham cracker crumbs. Refrigerate.

Yield: 8 servings   *Carolyn Sorci*

EUGENIE'S AMBROSIA

4 oranges
6 bananas
3 apples
1 (10-ounce) can peeled
    grapes, seedless
2 eggs

1 cup sugar
½ pint cream or 1 (10-ounce)
    can evaporated milk
1 tablespoon lemon juice or
    cider vinegar

Peel and section oranges. Slice bananas. Peel and dice apples. In heavy saucepan cream eggs and sugar. Add cream or milk. Stir constantly over low heat. Remove when thickened and add lemon or vinegar. Pour hot mixture over all fruit. Serve chilled.

Yield: 10-12 servings

Pim Mixon

APPLE STRUDEL

¼ to ½ cup seedless dark
    raisins
3 tablespoons cognac or
    brandy
2 cups pared, thinly sliced,
    tart apples
½ cup chopped walnuts
¼ cup granulated sugar
4 tablespoons unsalted butter
    or margarine

1 tablespoon grated lemon
    peel
½ teaspoon ground cinnamon
½ teaspoon vanilla
½ cup fine dry bread crumbs
½ cup apricot preserves
6 frozen phyllo strudel leaves,
    thawed
Melted clarified butter
Powdered sugar

Soak raisins in 2 tablespoons cognac for 2 hours. Combine raisin mixture, apples, walnuts, sugar, 2 tablespoons melted butter, lemon peel, cinnamon and vanilla in large bowl. Cook and stir bread crumbs in remaining 2 tablespoons butter in small skillet until light brown. Heat apricot preserves in small pan over low heat until hot; stir in 1 tablespoon cognac. Heat oven to 350° Layer phyllo leaves on kitchen towel, brushing each leaf with clarified butter. Spread entire surface with hot apricot mixture; sprinkle with bread crumbs. Spoon apple mixture along longest end of leaves in a 3-inch strip, leaving a ½-inch border. Lift towel, using it to roll leaves over filling, jelly roll fashion from longest end closest to filling. Place strudel diagonally, seam side down on lightly buttered 15 x 10-inch jelly roll pan. Brush with butter. Score strudel diagonally, through top few leaves, into equal sections. Bake at 350° until apples are tender and strudel is brown and crisp, 45 to 50 minutes. Cool to lukewarm; sprinkle with powdered sugar. Cut into servings.

Yield: 16 servings

Sue McDonough

BIRDS' NESTS

1 cup finely chopped walnuts
1 tablespoon packed brown
  sugar
Dash cinnamon
6 frozen phyllo strudel leaves,
  thawed

½ cup unsalted butter, melted
½ lemon
1½ cups sugar
1¼ cups water

Make walnut filling by mixing nuts, brown sugar and cinnamon together. Place phyllo leaves between barely dampened kitchen towels to prevent drying. Place 1 phyllo leaf on clean surface; brush top surface with butter. Fold in half lengthwise; brush with butter. Sprinkle 1 tablespoon walnut filling on long end of phyllo leaf. Roll phyllo leaf, starting at long folded edge, to 1 inch from edge. Form into ring, leaving 1 inch in center of ring. Fold overhanging phyllo under ring. Place on buttered jelly roll pan (15 x 10-inch). Repeat with remaining phyllo leaves. Place 1 tablespoon walnut filling in center of each ring. Brush with butter. Bake until golden at 400°, about 40 minutes. Make lemon peel syrup by cutting thin yellow peel from lemon and cut into strips. Squeeze juice from lemon. Heat lemon peel, juice, sugar and 1¼ cups water in 2 quart pan over medium heat, stirring occasionally, to boiling; reduce heat and simmer uncovered, stirring occasionally, 10 minutes. Pour syrup over each hot pastry. Cool completely.

Yield: 6 individual nests   *Sue McDonough*

CHARLOTTE RUSSE

1 quart milk
¼ cup sugar or to taste
4 egg yolks
2 teaspoons vanilla

4 rounded tablespoons corn
  starch
2½ dozen ladyfingers
3½ pints cream, whipped
1 cup pecans, ground fine

Heat milk; do not boil. Add sugar. Break egg yolks into bowl, beat. Add a little warm milk. Beat together. Add rest of milk. Add vanilla. Slowly add corn starch. Cook slowly over low fire to prevent curdling. Cook until thick. Line bowl with ladyfingers. Pour mixture into bowl. Allow to cool, then top with whipped cream. Sprinkle with pecans. Refrigerate.

Yield: 10 servings   *Mildred Swatloski*
Recipe of Mrs. Paul Simon

BREAD PUDDING WITH WHISKEY SAUCE

PUDDING

1 loaf French bread or 8 stale
  hamburger buns
1 quart milk
2 cups sugar
8 egg yolks

1 stick melted butter
2 teaspoons vanilla
1/8 teaspoon salt
1/2 cup raisins (optional)

Soak bread in milk for a couple of hours. Mash well. Beat sugar and egg yolks, add melted butter, vanilla and salt. Pour over bread and milk, fold in raisins. Put in a 10 x 12-inch ovenproof dish. Put dish in a pan of water and bake at 300° for 50 to 60 minutes or until a silver knife inserted comes out clean. Remove from oven and top with meringue; spread to outer edges. Return to 350° oven for 10 minutes.

MERINGUE RECIPE

2 tablespoons corn starch
4 tablespoons cold water
1 cup boiling water
8 egg whites

16 tablespoons sugar
2 teaspoons vanilla
Pinch of salt

Blend corn starch and cold water in pan. Add boiling water, cook until clear and thick. Let stand until completely cool. Beat whites until foamy; gradually add sugar and beat until stiff. Turn to low speed and add salt and vanilla; gradually add corn starch mixture; turn machine to high and beat well.

WHISKEY SAUCE

1 cup sugar
6 tablespoons corn starch
1 cup water

3 tablespoons lemon juice
4 tablespoons butter
1 cup bourbon whiskey

In a small saucepan, mix the sugar and cornstarch; stir in the water and lemon juice until smooth. Add butter and bring to a boil; lower heat and cook until smooth and thickened, about 3 minutes. Remove from heat and stir in whiskey. Cool, stirring occasionally. Serve warm over bread pudding.

Yield: 8-10 servings

Mac Beyt

WALNUT FUDGE BREAD PUDDING

1½ cups milk
¾ cup sugar
1 (6-ounce) package
    semi-sweet chocolate
    pieces
½ teaspoon cinnamon

1½ cups coarse dry bread
    crumbs, torn from bread
    several days old
1 tablespoon margarine
1 egg
⅛ teaspoon salt
½ cup chopped walnuts
Sweetened whipped cream

Grease 6 individual ramekins and place in baking pan with 1 inch water surrounding cups. Mix milk, sugar, chocolate, cinnamon and bread crumbs in top of double boiler. Cook and stir over hot water until chocolate is melted and mixture thick. Stir in margarine. Remove from heat. Gradually add egg beaten with the salt, to the chocolate mixture, stirring constantly. Mix in the nuts. Spoon into ramekins. Bake at 350° for about 50 minutes. Remove dishes to wire rack. Serve warm or chilled topped with whipped sweetened cream and walnut halves.

Yield: 6 servings

Barbara Schwing

CHOCOLATE-CREAM CHEESE DELIGHT

1 stick margarine
1 cup flour
½ cup chopped nuts
1 cup powdered sugar
1 (8-ounce) package cream
    cheese

1 (16-ounce) container Cool
    Whip whipped topping
1 (6-ounce) package
    chocolate instant pudding
2½ cups milk
Chopped pecans or grated
    sweet milk chocolate

Melt margarine; add flour and nuts. Pat into 9 x 13-inch pan and bake 15 minutes at 350.° Cream powdered sugar, cream cheese, and 1 cup whipped topping. Spread over cooled crust. Mix chocolate pudding mix with milk; beat until thick. Pour over cream cheese layer. Spread remaining whipped topping over all and sprinkle pecans or chocolate over top.

Yield: 12-15 servings

Shereen Minvielle
Sue Dauterive

FROZEN CHOCOLATE CHARLOTTE

1 tablespoon butter or
  margarine
2 tablespoons sugar
2 (3-ounce) packages fresh
  ladyfingers
¼ cup white crème de menthe
1 (12-ounce) package
  semi-sweet chocolate
  pieces

3 tablespoons instant coffee
½ cup boiling water
6 eggs, separated
½ cup sugar
1 teaspoon vanilla
2½ cups heavy cream
1 (4-ounce) bar sweet baking
  chocolate

Butter 9-inch springform pan and then sprinkle with 2 tablespoons sugar. Split ladyfingers but do not separate. Brush flat surfaces with crème de menthe. Line pan with ladyfingers, crème de menthe side up. Melt chocolate on top of double boiler, stirring occasionally. Dissolve coffee in ½ cup boiling water. Beat egg yolks in small bowl until foamy. Beat in sugar gradually until thick. At low speed add coffee, chocolate and vanilla. With clean beaters, beat egg whites in large bowl until stiff. Stir 1 cup beaten whites into chocolate mixture. Fold chocolate mixture back into remaining egg whites. Beat 1½ cups heavy cream until stiff and fold into chocolate mixture. Pour into ladyfinger lined pan. Freeze until firm. Whip remaining cream and decorate Charlotte. Before serving allow semi-sweet bar to soften slightly in low oven; make chocolate curls with vegetable peeler. Firm curls in refrigerator and sprinkle over whipped cream. Allow to thaw 1 hour at room temperature before serving. Remove springform ring and cut into wedges.

Yield: 10-12 servings   *Barbara Schwing*

EASY APPLE COBBLER

6 medium size apples, peeled
  and sliced
2 tablespoons sugar
1 teaspoon cinnamon
1 (18-ounce) package yellow
  cake mix

1 cup walnuts, chopped
  (optional)
1 stick margarine, melted
Light cream

Combine apples, sugar and cinnamon, sprinkle with ¼ cup of dry cake mix and toss until apples are evenly coated. Spoon into buttered 8-inch square baking pan. Cover and bake at 350° for 30 minutes. Remove from oven. Mix remaining cake mix and walnuts, drizzle butter over this and toss until large crumbs form. Sprinkle evenly over apple mixture and bake 20 minutes longer or until topping is puffed and golden. Serve warm with cream.

Yield: 8 servings   *Connie Goodwin*

CHOCOLATE VELVET CREAM

CRUST

1 ⅓ cups chocolate wafers, finely crushed

⅓ cup melted butter
½ cup chopped nuts

Combine ingredients and press onto bottom of 9-inch springform pan. Bake at 325° for 10 minutes.

FILLING

1 (8-ounce) package cream cheese, softened
¼ cup sugar
1 teaspoon vanilla
3 eggs, separated

1 cup semi-sweet chocolate pieces
¼ cup sugar
1 cup heavy cream, whipped
¾ cup chopped nuts

Combine cream cheese, sugar and vanilla, beating until well blended. Stir in 3 beaten egg yolks, semi-sweet chocolate which has been melted. Beat 3 egg whites until soft peaks form. Gradually beat in ¼ cup sugar; fold into chocolate mixture. Fold in whipped cream and nuts. Pour over crumb crust, freeze. Before serving, garnish as you wish with whipped cream, etc. This dessert may be frozen for weeks. Allow 1 hour at room temperature before serving.

Yield: 8-10 servings

Susie Pharr
Mrs. Sam Broussard

OLD-FASHIONED SWEET COBBLER

4 cups fresh or frozen sliced fruit: apples, peaches, blackberries, pears or other suitable fruit in its natural juice

1 cup milk
1 cup sugar
1 cup flour
2 teaspoons baking powder
Pinch of salt

Prepare fruit and set aside. Stir until fairly smooth the milk, sugar, flour, baking powder and salt. Place fruit into 9 x 12-inch baking dish; pour batter over fruit and bake in 375° oven for about 45 minutes or until brown.

Yield: 8-10 servings

Sonja Klein Viator

TRAPPEY'S MINUTE-MADE YAM COBBLER

2 (15-ounce) cans Sugary Sam
  mashed yams
1 cup dark brown sugar
8 tablespoons corn starch
1/4 cup water
1 (19-ounce) box white
  cake mix

1 1/4 block butter or margarine
1/2 pound pecan halves
  (chopped nuts or shredded
  coconut may be
  substituted)

Dissolve sugar and corn starch in 1/4 cup water; mix thoroughly with mashed yams. Pour into large pyrex baking dish (1 1/4-inch deep). Over layer of yams, pour çake mix directly from box. Cut margarine or butter to 1/8-inch slices and space evenly over cake mix. Top with pecan halves spaced evenly over cake. Bake for 30 to 45 minutes or until evenly brown at 350°.

Yield: 16 servings   *B. F. Trappey's Sons, Inc.*

FROZEN EGGNOG DESSERT

3 dozen ladyfingers
1 (16-ounce) box
  confectioner's sugar
1/2 pound butter

5 eggs, separated
6 tablespoons bourbon
1 cup chopped pecans

Line springform pan with ladyfingers. Cream sugar and butter. Add egg yolks which have been beaten to sugar-butter mixture. Mix in bourbon. Beat egg whites until stiff and fold into mixture. Then add nuts. Pour into pan. Freeze. May be garnished with whipped cream and nuts when served.

Yield: 8 servings   *Mrs. Provost Minvielle*

FRUIT TRIFLE

1 pound cake, broken into
  pieces and sprinkled with
  apricot brandy
2 1/2 pints whipping cream,
  whipped

Sliced strawberries, bananas,
  cherries, fresh pineapple,
  pears
Peaches, mandarin orange
  sections, (canned, drained)
1 1/2 cups chopped pecans

Layer cake, whipped cream, nuts and all fruits 3 times in large glass bowl, ending with whipped cream and nuts. Let set overnight.

Yield: 12 servings   *Shayne Wormser*

FLOATING ISLAND

½ cup sugar
½ teaspoon salt
1 tablespoon corn starch
2 cups milk

4 eggs, separated
1 teaspoon vanilla
⅓ cup sugar

Mix ½ cup sugar, salt, and corn starch in saucepan. Scald milk, then pour over sugar mixture slowly, stirring well. Add beaten egg yolks, mixing thoroughly, then cook slowly until mixture thickens and coats spoon. Cool, add vanilla. Beat egg whites until stiff, gradually beating in ⅓ cup sugar. Beat until peaks form. Gently fold whites into custard, being careful not to break up too small. The whites will float through the custard like little islands, hence the name. Chill.

Yield: 6 servings   *Bootsey Minvielle*

BEST VANILLA ICE CREAM

6 cups milk
8 large eggs
2 cups sugar

½ teaspoon salt
2 tablespoons vanilla
1 pint Half and Half

Scald 6 cups milk (may use lowfat). In saucepan combine eggs, sugar and salt. Then beat with rotary beater until well blended. Add scalded milk, gradually blending with spoon. Cook until mixture coats spoon—do not boil. Remove from heat. Add vanilla and cool. Strain and add Half and Half. Chill well before freezing in electric ice cream freezer.

Yield: ½ gallon   *Carolyn Sutton*

Variation: For peach ice cream, add 1 quart sugared, chopped peaches after ice cream has been chilled and before freezing process.

COFFEE ICE CREAM CRUNCH

½ cup softened margarine
¾ cup firmly packed brown
  sugar
2½ cups rice crispy cereal

1 cup chopped pecans
½ gallon coffee ice cream
1 jar fudge ice cream topping

Cream margarine; gradually adding brown sugar, beat until light and fluffy. Stir in cereal and nuts. Spread ½ of crumb mixture in buttered 13 x 9-inch pan. Spread ice cream evenly over crumb mixture. Spread fudge sauce over and then rest of crumb mixture. Cover and freeze until firm. Let stand at room temperature a few minutes before slicing.

Yield: 15 servings

Barbara Schwing

CARAMEL ICE CREAM SQUARES

CRUST
2 cups flour
¾ cup oatmeal (uncooked)
1 cup melted margarine

1 cup chopped pecans
½ cup brown sugar

Combine all ingredients and crumble on a cookie sheet. Bake at 400° for 15 to 20 minutes, stirring to brown evenly. Press ½ crumbs in bottom of 11 x 16-inch pan.

FILLING
½ gallon vanilla ice cream
1 (12-ounce) jar caramel ice
  cream topping

1 cup chopped pecans
½ gallon chocolate ice cream

Layer the vanilla ice cream over crust by slicing a rectangular half gallon to fit bottom of pan. Then pour caramel sauce evenly over ice cream. Top with pecans. Then repeat, layering chocolate ice cream. End by topping with the other ½ of the crumb crust mixture. Cover with foil and store in freezer several hours before cutting into squares to serve.

Yield: 20 servings

Carolyn Sutton
Mrs. Tom Uncapher

LEMON SHERBET

¾ cup lemon juice
Grated rind of half lemon
1¾ cups sugar

1 quart milk
White of 1 egg, beaten

Mix together and freeze in refrigerator freezer.

Yield: 1 quart   *A Weeks Family recipe*

FROZEN MOCHA BRANDY PARFAIT
(A sipping dessert)

½ gallon vanilla ice cream
½ gallon chocolate ice cream
½ cup brandy

1 cup strong black coffee
1 cup dark crème de cacao

Whirl all in blender until well mixed. Place in a large gallon container. Make a day ahead of time to allow the mixture to freeze as much as possible. Because of the liqueurs, it will not freeze solid. When ready to serve, place in stemware with a dollop of whipped cream on top and sprinkle with chocolate shavings.

Yield: 20 servings   *Carol Ann Roberts Dumond*

POTS DE CRÈME

1 (6-ounce) package semi-
    sweet chocolate morsels
    (1 cup)
1 cup milk chocolate morsels

½ cup sugar
3 eggs
1 cup hot milk
Whipped cream for garnish

In blender combine chocolate, sugar and eggs. Pour in hot milk and blend on medium speed until mixture is smooth. Pour into pots de crème or demitasse cups and chill several hours. Garnish with whipped cream if desired. Must be kept refrigerated until ready to serve.

Yield: 6 servings   *Juanita Winkle*

SOUFFLÉ FROID AU CHOCOLAT

2 (1-ounce) squares
  unsweetened chocolate
½ cup confectioner's sugar
1 cup milk
1 envelope unflavored gelatin
  (softened in 3 tablespoons
  cold water)

¾ cup sugar
1 teaspoon vanilla
¼ teaspoon salt
2 cups whipping cream,
  whipped

Melt chocolate squares over hot water. When melted, stir in confectioner's sugar and mix well. Heat milk just until a film shows on the surface and stir slowly into melted chocolate. Cook, stirring constantly, until it reaches the boiling point, but do not boil. Remove from heat and mix in softened gelatin, sugar, vanilla, and salt. Place in refrigerator until slightly thickened. Beat mixture until light and airy.

In separate bowl, whip cream until it holds its shape. Combine the 2 mixtures and pour into a 2-quart soufflé dish. Chill 2 to 3 hours in refrigerator or until ready to serve.

Yield: 8 servings   *Nancy Lewis*

STRAWBERRIES 21 SOUFFLÉ

ICE CREAM BASE
2 coconut macaroons,
  crumbled
4 teaspoons Grand Marnier
1 pint vanilla ice cream,
  softened

½ pint heavy cream,
  whipped
2 tablespoons almonds,
  chopped and toasted
2 teaspoons powdered sugar

Add macaroons and Grand Marnier to ice cream; fold in whipped cream. Spoon into ice cream mold. Sprinkle with almonds and powdered sugar. Cover with plastic wrap; freeze until firm.

SAUCE
1 (10-ounce) package frozen
  strawberries or
1 pint fresh strawberries

4 tablespoons sugar
6 tablespoons Grand Marnier

Thaw frozen strawberries; heat in saucepan. Remove from heat; add Grand Marnier. If using fresh berries, cap, wash and mash in saucepan. Add sugar and simmer 2 to 3 minutes. Remove from heat; add Grand Marnier.

Unmold ice cream on serving plate. Serve with warm sauce.

Yield: 4-6 servings   *Nancy Lewis*

STRAWBERRIES AND CREAM DESSERT

1 ⅓ cups condensed milk
⅓ cup lemon juice
1 tablespoon grated lemon
  rind
1 cup whipping cream,
  whipped

1 pint fresh strawberries,
  hulled and halved
1 (8-ounce) package
  ladyfingers
Few whole strawberries for
  garnish

Combine condensed milk, lemon juice and lemon rind. Fold ½ cup whipped cream into condensed mixture. Split ladyfingers and line 9 x 5-inch loaf pan, sides and bottom. Fold strawberries into whipped cream/condensed milk mixture and pour over ladyfingers. Refrigerate 3 hours until firm. To remove, run spatula or knife around inside of pan. Invert on plate. Spread remaining ½ cup whipped cream on top and garnish with whole berries.

Yield: 8 large slices   *A Friend of the Shadows*

BRANDIED STRAWBERRY CRÈME

½ cup sugar
2 envelopes plain gelatin
¼ teaspoon salt
2¼ cups milk
½ cup brandy

1 pint sour cream
1 teaspoon vanilla
2 cups sliced strawberries
¼ cup sugar
¼ cup brandy

Blend sugar, gelatin, salt and milk together in saucepan. Heat, stirring constantly, until gelatin and sugar are dissolved. Remove from heat. Stir in brandy. Cool. Blend in sour cream and vanilla until smooth. Turn into ring mold sprayed with Pam. Unmold after set and serve with brandied strawberries and fresh mint sprigs. To make brandied strawberries, combine strawberries, sugar and brandy and let stand at least ½ hour and chill before serving.

Yield: 6 servings   *A Friend of the Shadows*

WINE JELLY DESSERT

1 envelope unflavored gelatin
½ cup cold water
½ cup sugar

1 lemon (grated rind and juice)
1½ cups port wine
Whipped cream for topping

Soak gelatin in cold water in a 2-cup fireproof measuring cup. Next place cup in a saucepan with a little water and heat the gelatin and water until the gelatin is completely dissolved; add sugar, stir until sugar has dissolved. Add lemon rind and lemon juice and wine. Cool, strain and pour into 4 wine glasses. Place in refrigerator until firm. Top with whipped cream just before serving.

Yield: 4 servings   *Mildred W. Dauterive*

ALMOND CAKES

1 stick butter
2 cups sugar
1 egg yolk, beaten
⅓ teaspoon soda

½ pint sour milk
1 teaspoon almond extract
Sifted flour

Cream butter and sugar together. Add beaten egg yolk, and soda which has been dissolved in sour milk. Add almond extract and enough flour to make a stiff dough. Roll thin and cut into shapes. In the center of each cookie, press a blanched almond. Dust with granulated sugar and bake on floured tins at 300° for 8 to 10 minutes.

Yield: 3 dozen   *Pattie Weeks Torian*

NEEN'S VERY EASY BROWNIES

1 stick margarine
1 cup sugar
2 eggs
¾ cup flour

3 tablespoons cocoa
1 teaspoon vanilla
1 cup chopped pecans

Blend margarine and sugar. Add eggs one at a time and blend. Sift flour and cocoa and add to above mixture. Add vanilla and pecans. Pour into a greased 8 x 8-inch pan and bake for 25 minutes at 350°

Yield: 16 brownies   *Susie Pharr*

BUTTERSCOTCH-OATMEAL COOKIES

1½ cups shortening
1 cup brown sugar
1 cup white sugar
3 eggs
1 (12-ounce) package
    butterscotch chips

2¼ cups flour
1½ teaspoons soda
3 cups oatmeal
2 teaspoons vanilla
1½ tablespoons hot water

Mix all together and drop by spoonfuls on cookie sheet. Bake 8 to 10 minutes at 375.°

Yield: 5 dozen

Linda Matthews

CHINESE COOKIES

2 egg whites
2 cups chopped pecans

1½ cups brown sugar
1 teaspoon vanilla

Beat egg whites until stiff. Add remaining ingredients. Mix and drop by spoonfuls on a greased cookie sheet. Bake for 10 minutes at 350.°

Yield: 4 dozen

Mrs. Collins Dautreuil

CHOCOLATE-CARAMEL SQUARES

1 (14-ounce) bag light colored
    caramels
⅔ cup evaporated milk
1 (18½-ounce) package
    German chocolate
    cake mix

¾ cup margarine or butter,
    softened
1 cup chopped nuts
1 (6-ounce) package
    semi-sweet chocolate
    chips

Combine caramels and ⅓ cup evaporated milk in top of a double boiler; heat, stirring constantly, until caramels are completely melted. Remove from heat. Combine cake mix, remaining ⅓ cup milk, butter, until dough holds together; stir in nuts. Press half of cake mixture into greased 13 x 9 x 2-inch baking pan. Bake at 350° for 6 minutes. Sprinkle chocolate morsels over crust. Pour caramel mixture over chocolate chips, spreading evenly. Crumble remaining cake mixture over caramel mixture. Return pan to oven, bake 15 to 18 minutes. Cool. Chill 30 minutes; cut into small bars.

Yield: 24 squares

Vivian Duhe

CHRISTMAS WREATHS

½ cup slightly salted butter
  or margarine
30 large marshmallows
2½ to 3 teaspoons green food
  coloring

1½ teaspoons vanilla extract
4 cups corn flakes
Red cinnamon candies

In a 2-quart saucepan, melt butter and marshmallows over moderate heat, stirring constantly. When melted, remove from heat and stir in food coloring and vanilla. Stir in corn flakes. Drop mixture onto wax paper, 1 tablespoon at a time. Decorate with candies. Let stand at least 30 minutes and cool. Be sure to butter hands very well before shaping into a wreath.

Yield: 3 dozen   *Yolanda Trahan*

CONGO SQUARES

2 sticks margarine, softened
1 (16-ounce) box brown sugar
3 eggs
1 teaspoon vanilla
2¾ cups flour

2 teaspoons baking powder
½ teaspoon salt
1 (12-ounce) package
  chocolate chips
1 cup chopped nuts

Cream margarine and brown sugar together well. Add eggs and beat until fluffy. Add vanilla. Sift flour, baking powder and salt together and add to creamed mixture. Stir in chips and nuts. Bake in two 7 x 9-inch greased pans at 325° for 25 minutes. Do not overbake but test for doneness.

Yield: 48 squares   *Barbara Schwing*

CREAM CHEESE SQUARES

1 (18-ounce) yellow cake mix
  (any flavor cake mix may
  be used)
1 tablespoon water
1 stick soft margarine
1 egg

1 cup chopped pecans
1 (8-ounce) package cream
  cheese
3 eggs
1 (16-ounce) box powdered
  sugar

Mix the cake mix, water, margarine and egg, and press into 9 x 13-inch pan. Spread with pecans. Mix cream cheese, eggs and powdered sugar well and pour over first layer. Bake at 350° for 35 to 45 minutes. Cut while slightly warm and remove when cool.

Yield: 24 squares   *Mac Beyt*

GINGERBREAD MEN

1 cup brown sugar, packed
1/3 cup shortening
1 (12-ounce) bottle dark
  molasses
2/3 cup water

1 teaspoon each ginger,
  allspice, cinnamon and
  cloves, all ground
6 1/2 cups self-rising flour
Decorator's icing
Trims (gumdrops, raisins,
  peanuts, etc.)

In a large mixer bowl mix sugar, shortening and molasses. Blend in water gradually. On low speed blend dry ingredients gradually into molasses mixture. Cover bowl; chill 24 hours. Roll dough 1/4-inch thick on floured cloth-covered board. Cut out cookies. With spatula carefully transfer cookies to lightly greased baking sheet. Bake 10 to 12 minutes at 350° Cool slightly, remove from sheet. Spread with decorator's icing and decorate with trims.

DECORATOR'S ICING
4 cups confectioner's sugar
1 teaspoon vanilla

4 tablespoons light cream

Mix all together until smooth and of spreading consistency. Tint portions as desired. Frost cookies.

Yield: 3 dozen   *Juanita Winkle*

GREAT AND EASY BARS

1/2 cup margarine
1 1/2 cups graham cracker
  crumbs
1 (17-ounce) can condensed
  milk

1 (6-ounce) package semi-
  sweet chocolate chips
1 (3 1/2-ounce) can flaked
  coconut
1 cup pecans, chopped
1 cup walnuts, chopped

In 13 x 9-inch baking pan melt margarine. Sprinkle crumbs over margarine. Pour condensed milk over crumbs evenly. Evenly layer chocolate chips, coconut, pecans and walnuts. Press down gently. Bake at 325° 25 to 30 minutes or until lightly browned. Cool completely before cutting.

Yield: 24-30 bars   *Renee T. Richard*

LEMON MARDI GRAS SQUARES

1 ½ cups sifted flour
½ teaspoon salt
¼ teaspoon baking powder
3 eggs, separated
1 cup powdered sugar

½ cup butter
1 cup sugar
⅓ cup lemon juice
2 tablespoons grated lemon
rind

Sift dry ingredients. Beat egg whites until soft mounds form; add powdered sugar gradually, beating after each addition. Beat until stiff peaks form. Cream butter and sugar well. Add egg yolks, one at a time. Beat for 1 minute. Add lemon juice alternately with dry ingredients to creamed mixture and mix well. Add rind; fold in egg whites. Pour in greased and floured 9 x 13-inch pan. Bake for 25 to 30 minutes at 350.° Frost with topping below.

TOPPING
1 cup powdered sugar
1 tablespoon cream

2 tablespoons butter
Chopped nuts

Mix sugar, cream and butter together and spread over warm squares. Sprinkle with nuts.

Yield: 24 squares   *Susie Pharr*

LEMON SQUARES

1 stick butter, melted
¼ cup powdered sugar
1 cup flour
2 eggs

1 cup sugar
2 tablespoons flour
¾ teaspoon baking powder
2 tablespoons lemon juice

Mix first 3 ingredients together and press in 9 x 9-inch pan. Bake at 350° for 30 minutes. Beat eggs until light, add sugar, flour, baking powder and lemon juice. Spread over crust and bake for 30 minutes.

Yield: 40 squares   *JoAnn Riley*

LES OREILLES DE COCHON

2 cups flour
½ teaspoon baking powder
½ teaspoon salt

½ stick margarine
2 eggs
1 teaspoon vinegar

Mix all together in food processor until it forms a ball and leaves side of container. (Or mix by hand as for pastry.) Pinch a small piece and shape into a ball. Roll paper thin between 2 pieces of saran wrap. Deep fat fry one at a time. Drop in hot fat and place a fork or old-time clothespin in center and give a twist until pastry seems slightly twisted. Remove fork or clothespin and fry until lightly brown. Drain on paper towel. Fill with chopped pecans and syrup made as follows.

SYRUP

1½ cups cane syrup
Pinch of salt

1 cup chopped pecans

Cook syrup and salt to soft ball stage. Add chopped nuts and pour over each l'oreille de cochon.

Yield: 2 dozen

Mrs. Sam Broussard

PEANUT BLOSSOMS

1¾ cups flour
1 teaspoon soda
½ teaspoon salt
½ cup sugar
½ cup brown sugar, packed
½ cup shortening
½ cup peanut butter

1 egg
2 tablespoons milk
1 teaspoon vanilla
1 (12-ounce) bag chocolate
   kisses
Granulated sugar

Combine first 10 ingredients and mix on low speed until dough forms. Shape into balls, roll in granulated sugar, place on ungreased cookie sheet and bake for 10 to 12 minutes at 375.° While still hot on cookie sheet, press kisses in center of each cookie. Remove from sheet and cool.

Yield: 3-4 dozen

Susie Pharr

MANDELBRODT
(Jewish Cookies)

2 eggs
½ cup oil
1 tablespoon butter
1 teaspoon almond extract
¾ cup sugar

1 teaspoon baking powder
Pinch of salt
½ cup almonds or walnuts
2 cups sifted flour

Mix all ingredients, adding flour last. Grease cookie sheet. Form 3 loaves from dough on cookie sheet. Bake 28 to 30 minutes at 350°. Take out of oven and slice while hot. Put back in oven for 5 minutes on one side and 5 minutes on other side to brown.

Yield: 3 dozen   *Brenda LaBiche*

PECAN COCOONS

⅞ cup margarine
4 tablespoons confectioner's
   sugar
2 cups flour

1 tablespoon water
2 teaspoons vanilla
1 cup pecans, chopped
Powdered sugar

Cream margarine and sugar. Add 1 cup flour and mix well. Add water and remainder of flour. Knead and add vanilla and pecans. Pinch off small ball of dough. Roll in shape of a small finger. Bake about 15 minutes at 350° and roll in powdered sugar. Store in a tightly covered container.

Yield: 4 dozen   *Mrs. Sam Broussard*

PECAN CRISP COOKIES

½ cup shortening
½ cup butter
1 (16-ounce) box light brown
   sugar
2 eggs
2½ cups flour

¼ teaspoon salt
½ teaspoon baking soda
1 teaspoon vanilla
1 cup pecans, finely chopped
Pecan halves

Cream shortening and butter thoroughly; gradually add brown sugar and cream well. Add well beaten eggs. On slow speed of mixer, add the flour that has been sifted together with salt and soda. Add vanilla. Stir in finely chopped pecans. Drop from spoon onto a greased cookie sheet, 2 inches apart. Top with pecan halves. Bake for about 10 minutes at 350°.

Yield: 5-6 dozen   *Julie Harris*

314

PRALINE COOKIES

1 egg white
1 cup brown sugar

1½ to 2 cups chopped pecans
1 teaspoon vanilla

Beat egg white until stiff and add sugar and mix well. Add pecans and vanilla. Drop by teaspoons on greased cookie sheet. Bake for 30 minutes at 275.° Remove immediately!

Yield: 3 dozen   *Eva Schexnayder*

REFRIGERATOR COOKIES

1 cup vegetable shortening
1 teaspoon salt
1 cup brown sugar
1 cup white sugar

2 eggs
3 cups sifted flour
½ teaspoon baking soda
1 cup nuts, chopped

Blend shortening with salt and sugar. Add eggs one at a time, mixing well. Add flour and stir soda and nuts into first mixture. Shape into roll about 2½ inches in diameter. Roll in a paper and chill 2 hours. With sharp knife, cut thin slices of chilled dough and place on greased cookie sheet and bake at 375° until delicately brown.

Yield: 5-6 dozen   *Pat Wells*

RUSSIAN ROCKS

2 cups brown sugar
1 cup margarine
1 teaspoon baking soda
¼ cup hot water
3 eggs, well beaten
3½ cups flour

1 teaspoon cinnamon
1 teaspoon nutmeg
1 tablespoon cocoa
1 teaspoon ginger
1 pound dark raisins
4 cups pecans

Mix brown sugar and margarine. Add soda and water. Beat eggs well in small mixer bowl. Add to sugar/margarine mixture. Sift flour and spices together and add to mixture. Coat nuts and raisins in a little flour and stir into batter. Refrigerate overnight. Grease baking sheet lightly and drop by spoonfuls. Bake for 15 minutes at 350.°

Yield: 16 dozen   *Juanita Winkle*

ALMOND ROCA

1 cup butter (not margarine)
1 cup sugar
1 cup coarsely chopped
   almonds

1 (8-ounce) bar German
   chocolate
Finely chopped almonds

Melt butter and sugar together in heavy saucepan over medium heat. Stir constantly and watch closely to avoid burning. Cook to 240.° Add nuts, cook to 300.° Pour onto cookie sheet. Depth of candy should be approximately ¼ inch. Cool, then cover with melted German sweet chocolate. Sprinkle finely chopped almonds on top.

Yield: ¾ pound

Jessamine Musson

Note: Chocolate covering can be eliminated and served as almond brittle.

CHOCOLATE TRUFFLES

7 ounces bittersweet
   chocolate, cut into 1-inch
   pieces
½ cup whipping cream
2 tablespoons butter
¾ cup powdered sugar,
   measured, then sifted

2 egg yolks
1 to 2 tablespoons dark rum
   (to taste)
Unsweetened cocoa and/or
   coarsely chopped toasted
   walnuts

Combine chocolate, cream and butter in top of double boiler over simmering water. Add sugar and yolks and whisk until smooth. Remove from heat, add rum. Place pan in flat glass dish and chill until malleable, about 2 hours in refrigerator or 1 hour in freezer. Shape into small balls about the size of large olives, and roll in cocoa and/or nuts. Place in paper candy cups and refrigerate until hardened.

Yield: 2½-3 dozen

Barbara Schwing

EASY CHOCOLATE CANDY

1 (12-ounce) package
  chocolate chips
1 (14-ounce) can condensed
  milk

1 cup nuts, chopped
1 cup miniature marshmallows

Heat and melt chocolate and condensed milk. Then fold in nuts and marshmallows. Pour into 9 x 13-inch buttered pan.

Yield: 1½ pounds   *Carolyn Sorci*

DIVINITY

2 cups sugar
½ cup corn syrup
½ cup water

2 egg whites
½ teaspoon vanilla
1 cup pecans, chopped

Boil sugar, syrup, and water to 265.° Beat egg whites until stiff. Pour syrup over egg whites, beating constantly. Add vanilla and nuts. Drop by rounded teaspoonfuls onto foil. Let stand until dry. Store in container or tin that is airtight.

Yield: 1 pound   *JoAnn Riley*

"ELMER'S GOLD BRICK" CANDY

4½ cups sugar
1 (13-ounce) can evaporated
  milk
1 stick margarine
1 (6-ounce) package
  chocolate chips

3 cups pecans or walnuts
1 (12-ounce) package
  Hershey's kisses
1 (7-ounce) jar marshmallow
  creme

Bring sugar, milk and margarine to soft boil stage on a candy thermometer. Remove from fire and beat by hand for a few minutes. Add remaining ingredients, mix and pour into two 8-inch square buttered pans. Cool and cut into squares.

Yield: 5 pounds   *Ella Shepherd*

OLD-FASHIONED BUTTER MINTS

1 stick butter
2 tablespoons condensed
   milk
1 tablespoon water
½ teaspoon oil of peppermint
   (may be obtained from
   druggist)

1½ (16-ounce) boxes
   confectioner's sugar
Food color of your choice to
   tint mints

Put all ingredients together and knead well. Add food coloring. Shape into long rolls about ½ inch thick and cut each roll into bite size pieces with kitchen scissors.

Yield: 4 dozen   *Sis Lamperez*

PEANUT BUTTER FUDGE

½ cup butter or margarine
1 (16-ounce) box light brown
   sugar
½ cup milk

¾ cup smooth or crunchy
   peanut butter, as preferred
1 teaspoon vanilla extract
1 (16-ounce) box
   confectioner's sugar

In medium saucepan, melt butter, stir in brown sugar and milk. Bring to a boil, boil and stir 2 minutes. Remove from heat; stir in peanut butter and vanilla. Mix in confectioner's sugar; beat until smooth. Spread into buttered 9-inch square pan. Chill until firm. Cut into squares.

Yield: 3½ pounds   *Barbara Schwing*

PEANUT BRITTLE

2 cups sugar
1 cup light corn syrup
1 cup water
¼ teaspoon salt

1½ cups raw peanuts
1 tablespoon butter
¼ teaspoon baking soda

Combine sugar, corn syrup and water in saucepan. Cook to 236° on candy thermometer, stirring constantly. Add salt and peanuts and continue cooking to hard crack stage (300°). Stir constantly. Remove from heat, add butter and soda, stir lightly. Pour evenly onto well greased wax paper, cool partially, lifting around edges with a knife. Cool until firm, then turn. Cool completely and break into pieces.

Yield: 3 dozen pieces   *Juanita Winkle*

PECAN BRITTLE

2 cups pecan pieces
1 cup sugar

1 cup white corn syrup
1 tablespoon baking soda

Butter a baking sheet before you start. Mix pecans, sugar, and syrup together in heavy saucepan. Bring to a boil, stirring constantly. Wipe down sides with damp pastry brush and cook without stirring to a hard crack stage (300°). Remove from heat immediately and quickly stir in soda. It's supposed to foam, so don't worry. Pour mixture immediately onto buttered sheet. When cool enough to touch, stretch to make as thin as possible. When thoroughly cool, break into pieces. Store in an airtight container.

Yield: 1 pound   *Bootsey Minvielle*

PECAN PRALINES I

3 cups white sugar
1 cup brown sugar
1 (17-ounce) can condensed
    milk
1 cup sweet milk
1/2 cup light corn syrup

2 quarts pecans
1/2 cup honey
1 stick butter or margarine
Dash salt
1 teaspoon vanilla

Mix all ingredients except nuts and vanilla; cook to soft ball stage on candy thermometer. Add pecans and cook 10 minutes. Add vanilla. Cool, beat until candy loses its gloss. Pour by teaspoonfuls onto waxed paper.

Yield: 4 dozen   *Mrs. Sam Broussard*

PECAN PRALINES II

1 1/2 cups white sugar
3/4 cup brown sugar
Dash salt
1/2 cup evaporated milk

1/2 stick margarine
2 cups pecans
1 teaspoon vanilla

Cook sugar, salt and milk until it boils; cook to soft ball stage, add butter and let it remain on fire until completely melted. Remove from fire and beat until thick. Add nuts and vanilla. Drop by teaspoonfuls onto waxed paper. If too thick to handle, reheat to consistency desired.

Yield: 2 1/2 dozen   *Rachel Inzerella*

BUTTERMILK PRALINES

2 cups sugar
1 cup buttermilk
1 teaspoon baking soda

Pinch of salt
4 tablespoons butter
2 cups pecans

Mix sugar, buttermilk, baking soda and salt. Cook over medium heat, stirring carefully to prevent sticking. Cook to soft ball stage (236-238°). Remove from heat and add pecans and butter, stir; cool slightly. Beat until begins to harden; pour rapidly on foil by spoonfuls.

Yield: 12 large pralines

Betty Fleming

PECAN TURTLES

CRUST
2 cups flour
1 cup brown sugar

½ cup soft margarine

FILLING
⅔ cup butter
½ cup brown sugar
1 cup pecan halves

1 (6-ounce) package
    chocolate chips

Mix crust ingredients and press into ungreased 13 x 9-inch pan. Melt butter and mix with brown sugar and pour over pecans which have been layered onto crust. Bake 18 to 22 minutes until bubbly in preheated 350° oven. Sprinkle chocolate chips over all, allowing them to melt and then spread to cover. Cool and cut into squares.

Yield: 48 squares

Betty LeBlanc

SUGARED PECANS

2 cups sugar
1 cup cream
2 tablespoons light corn syrup

2 tablespoons butter
½ teaspoon vanilla
4 to 5 cups pecan halves

Combine sugar, cream, corn syrup and butter. Cook to 234.° Remove from heat and add vanilla. Add as many nuts as syrup will cover. Fold over and over gently with wooden spoon (to keep from breaking up nuts) until coating loses its gloss and begins to sugar. Pour onto waxed paper and break apart or drop in clusters.

Yield: 2½ pounds

Rachel Inzerella

HOW MEN COOK

Circa 1923

Weeks Hall and Hollywood's D. W. Griffith are shown on the lawn of the Shadows during the filming of "The White Rose," a pre-talkie film. During the 1920's and 30's, Weeks Hall revived the gaiety and sparkle of antebellum hospitality. He was a friend of many celebrities who were visitors to the Shadows. Among them were H. L. Mencken, Max Ernst, Sherwood Anderson, Tex Ritter, Walt Disney, Cecil B. DeMille, and Henry Miller. To keep a record of his famous guests, Weeks Hall had them sign the door to his studio, in place of a guestbook. The prized door can be seen at the Shadows today and looks almost like a "Who's Who" of the 20's through the 40's.

Weeks Hall had a great sense of pride in the Shadows, and this feeling caused him to do all in his power to preserve the house for posterity. He often expressed the fear that if he did not do something to protect the house in his lifetime, after his death it might be demolished and "replaced by a hamburger stand." He wanted to be sure that the house would survive, and his dream came true.

Before his death, the National Trust for Historic Preservation agreed to accept the property. Weeks Hall was an early preservationist, and through his foresight, the Shadows now stands as a house museum, interpreting the history and culture of the bayou country.

How Men Cook

BEVERAGES
Bayless Special................323
Old Fashioned................323
Old Fashioned (in Bulk)........323
Planter's Punch, Jacob's........324
APPETIZERS
Boudin Balls.................324
Mushroom Pâté................324
Oyster Rockefeller Dip..........325
SALADS
Fire and Ice.................325
Pineapple Jewel...............326
SOUPS
Courtbouillon, Red Fish........327
Cream of Carrot with Thyme......328
Cream of Chicken with Sausage...329
Cream of Leek and Lettuce......328
Cream of Squash.............329
Gumbo, Crab.................330
Onion, Easy Homemade........330
VEGETABLES
Beans, Hot and Spicy...........331
Cream Corn..................331
Easy Maque Choux.............332
Rice, Fried...................332
Spinach Pies.................333
Spinach Timbales..............333
Vegetable Casserole, Classic.....334
SAUCE
Chateaubriand................334
CHICKEN
Breasts, Company..............335
Breasts, with Pecan Stuffing......335
Chinese Brown................336
Creole and Oyster Pie..........336
Creole Étouffée...............337
Garlic, Forty.................337
Lemon, Baked................338
MEATS
Cassoulet....................339
Chili, Old Fashioned...........342
Elias La' Ha' Mishwie...........340
Grillades and Grits............338
Jambalaya, Keith's............340

Leighton's Enchiladas..........34
Steak with Oysters.............34:
Tamales, Sydney Louviere's......34:
WILD GAME
Venison Roast, Charlie's........34:
(Woodcock) Bécasse Acadian.....34
Duck
Mallards, Tony's..............34!
Teal, Stuffed.................34
Wild, Magnalite...............34!
SEAFOOD
Barbecued Fish...............34(
Crab Chops..................34(
Crawfish Étouffée, Hallman's.....34!
Crawfish Yvonne..............34
Crêpe Batter, Basic............34!
Crêpes, Woody's Seafood.......34!
Lobster, Cajun................35(
Lobster, Yucatan..............35(
Oyster Stew..................35(
Shrimp a la Mr. B.............35
Shrimp and Crab Stew.........35
Shrimp Fettuccini, Wayne's......35:
Snapper Filet Robert...........35:
BREAD
Cajun Cowboy Cornbread......35<
Chicken and Cornbread Dressing..35:
Onion Bread.................35<
DESSERT
Banana Pudding..............35!
Carrot Cake..................35!
Coconut Layer Cake...........35(
Custard for Homemade Ice
   Cream...................35:
Jim's Dessert................35
Rum or Brandy Balls..........35!
Strawberry Dessert............35!
SUNDAY BRUNCH
Eggs Benedict................35!
Hollandaise Sauce.............35!
Ramos Gin Fizz...............35!
**LE FROMAGE DE LA TÊTE
DU COCHON**
(Hogshead Cheese)...........36(

BAYLESS SPECIAL

3 parts gin
1 part bourbon
½ part GOOD red grenadine

1 part fresh orange juice
1 part fresh lemon juice

Shake over ice, strain and serve.

Be sure the grenadine is of a good variety. Add or subtract the grenadine to adjust the sweetness.

Jack Bayless

OLD FASHIONED

Pour 2 ounces of water into a large old-fashioned glass; add 1 heaping teaspoonful of sugar; stir well and dissolve that sugar. Add 3 or 4 dashes of Angostura bitters with the sugar and water. Add 3 ounces of straight bourbon whiskey (preferably 8 year old whiskey or better and *not more* than 86 proof); add one half ounce of cherry juice; fill up the glass with ice and stir well to chill this drink. Garnish with slice of orange and a cherry. Sit back quietly and drink freely.

Yield: 1 serving

Jacob S. Landry

MEN 1—Middle p323

OLD FASHIONED
(in Bulk)

Pour 1 pint of water into a large vessel; add 2 heaping tablespoonsful of sugar; stir well to dissolve the sugar. Add 8 to 10 dashes of Angostura bitters and stir well to blend in the bitters with the sugar and water; add 1 fifth of straight bourbon whiskey (preferably 8 years old or better and not more than 86 proof). Add 4 or 5 ounces of cherry juice; stir well and keep in the refrigerator, and when being served, pour over ice into an old-fashioned glass and garnish with a slice of orange and a cherry.

Yield: 1½ quarts

Jacob S. Landry

MEN 1—Bottom p323

JACOB'S PLANTER'S PUNCH

Start drink just like you would a lemonade—add sugar to about a quart of water, then add about a quart of lemon juice, having the end product with the sweetness or tartness you would like if you were making a lemonade; then add a fifth of Bacardi rum (dark preferred); mix well, then add about a quart of good, fresh orange juice. If you wish you may add about a half cup of grenadine syrup, but this is optional and doesn't improve the taste but does give the drink a richer color. The quality of the lemons and oranges you use will have a direct bearing on the quality of your punch.

Yield: 1 gallon   *Jacob S. Landry*

BOUDIN BALLS

1 pound cooked boudin   **Seasoned bread crumbs**
1 or 2 eggs, beaten slightly   **Cooking oil**

Remove the boudin from the casing. Form dressing into balls about the size of walnuts. Dip balls in beaten egg and then into seasoned bread crumbs. Deep-fry balls in cooking oil at about 325° until lightly browned. Drain on paper towels. Serve hot with toothpicks.

(This is a simple and excellent party appetizer or hors d'oeuvre and is excellent to serve to boudin lovers who might be reticent about eating boudin at social gatherings in the usual messy fashion.)

Yield: 20—25 servings   *Keith E. Courrege*

Note: Boudin recipe on page 169.

MUSHROOM PÂTÉ

½ pound fresh mushrooms,   **1 (8-ounce) package cream**
  chopped   **cheese**
2 tablespoons butter   **¾ teaspoon garlic salt**

Sauté mushrooms in butter until tender and liquid has evaporated. Processor all ingredients until smooth. Refrigerate, covered, for 3 hours before serving. Serve with melba or toast points.

Yield: 1½ cups   *Wayne Peltier*
                                            Peltier's Catering

OYSTER ROCKEFELLER DIP

1 stick butter
1 cup celery, chopped
2 bunches green onions, chopped
1 bunch parsley, chopped
1 (10-ounce) package frozen chopped spinach, defrosted
3 cloves garlic, minced
1 teaspoon salt or to taste
Red pepper to taste
Pinch of thyme

2 teaspoons lemon juice
1 1/2 tablespoons Worcestershire sauce
1/2 teaspoon monosodium glutamate
1 teaspoon sugar
6 anchovy filets, mashed, or 2 tablespoons anchovy paste
1 ounce Pernod or Herbsaint
6 dozen oysters, drained and juice reserved
Seasoned bread crumbs

Sauté celery in butter until limp. Add onions, parsley, spinach and garlic for 15 minutes. Remove from heat. Add next 9 ingredients and mix well. Blend mixture, part at a time, until smooth. Add oyster liquid and blend. In large skillet, sauté oysters just until edges start to curl. Remove from heat. Chop oysters and stir into blended sauce mixture. Heat 4 to 5 minutes. Add seasoned bread crumbs until it is of proper dipping consistency. Transfer to chafing dish and keep warm. Use as dip with cocktail crackers or potato chips.

Yield: 20-25 servings   *Keith E. Courrege*

FIRE AND ICE SALAD

SAUCE
3/4 cup vinegar
1/4 cup water
1 1/2 teaspoons celery seed
1 1/4 teaspoons mustard seed

1/2 teaspoon salt
4 teaspoons sugar
1/8 teaspoon cayenne pepper
1/8 teaspoon black pepper

SALAD
6 large ripe tomatoes
2 green peppers
1 red onion sliced thin

2 cucumbers, peeled, seeded and sliced
2 avocados, peeled and sliced

Combine all sauce ingredients and bring to a boil (one minute) then remove from heat. Peel tomatoes and cut them in chunks; slice green peppers in strips. Place in bowl with onions and pour sauce over. Refrigerate 4 hours or longer. Just before serving, add cucumber and avocados.

Yield: 6-8 servings   *Curtis R. Thomas*

PINEAPPLE JEWEL

2 envelopes unflavored gelatin
1¼ cups cold water
1 cup sugar
⅔ cup vinegar
½ cup pineapple juice
1 tablespoon chopped green
 onion
1 tablespoon soy sauce
1 teaspoon salt
2 or 3 dashes garlic powder

1 (8-ounce) can pineapple
 chunks, drained
1 cup coarsely chopped green
 pepper
1 cup seeded, bite-size,
 drained tomatoes
Lettuce
Mayonnaise
Chopped candied ginger

Sprinkle gelatin over ¼ cup cold water and let stand 5 minutes to soften. Combine sugar, remaining water, vinegar, pineapple juice, green onion, soy sauce, salt and garlic powder. Cook over moderate heat, stirring constantly until sugar is dissolved. Add softened gelatin and heat, stirring until gelatin is dissolved. Cool until slightly thickened. Stir in pineapple, green pepper and tomato. Pour into oiled 5¼ to 6 cup mold, or individual serving molds. Chill until firm, 4 to 5 hours. Unmold on serving plate and garnish with lettuce. Serve topped with mayonnaise and sprinkled with chopped candied ginger.

Yield: 8-10 servings   *Keith Courrege*

RED FISH COURTBOUILLON

2 (10-pound) red fish
3 large carrots
3 stalks celery
2 cups oil
3½ to 4 cups flour
2 (15-ounce) cans tomato
  sauce
3 onions, chopped
3 bell peppers, chopped

1 stalk celery, chopped
2 gallons fish stock
Salt, red and black pepper to
  taste
Tabasco pepper sauce to taste
1 cup green onion tops
½ cup chopped parsley
½ cup cooked chopped eggs
Lemon slice per serving

Filet red fish and cut into bite size pieces; set aside. Place the bones, carrots and celery in a large gumbo pot. Simmer for 45 minutes to 1 hour. Remove and discard the bones and vegetables. Strain the stock through a cheesecloth twice. Make a roux with oil and flour; cook slowly until light golden brown. Cool; add tomatoes and cook slowly. Now you are about to embark on one of the Cajuns' most notable sayings: "Cook until oil separates on the edges." This may take up to 3 hours. (Please don't throw the recipe up in the air and say, "He must be out of his mind." Give it a chance, it is well worth the experience. Anyway, you need to do something while you are making the stock.) After separation, add onions, bell peppers and celery and cook until soft. Set aside and cool. Place stock pot on medium heat and bring to slow boil. Add roux slowly, a little at a time. Cook for about 45 minutes to an hour, stirring frequently. Add seasonings; cook for 15 minutes. Add fish; cook 15 minutes. Add onion tops and parsley 5 minutes before serving. Serve over rice in gumbo bowls. Garnish with chopped eggs and lemon slices. Serve with hot French bread.

Yield: 10-12 servings   *Alex Patout*

CREAMED LEEK AND LETTUCE SOUP

1½ cup minced, well washed
   leek
1 cup minced onion
1 clove garlic, minced
Salt and pepper to taste
½ stick butter
2 potatoes, peeled and thinly
   sliced

½ head Boston lettuce
   coarsely chopped
3 cups chicken stock or broth
1 cup milk
1 cup cream
Tabasco pepper sauce to taste
Chives or onion tops

In a large sauce pan, sweat leek, onion, garlic, salt and pepper in butter. Cover for 20 minutes and cook until vegetables are very soft. Add potatoes, lettuce, chicken stock and simmer for 25 minutes. Pureé mixture in blender and return to pan. Add milk, cream and Tabasco pepper sauce, and simmer for 5 minutes. Correct for salt and pepper. Divide among 6 heated bowls. Garnish with chives or onion tops. (Watercress may be used instead of lettuce.)

Yield: 6 servings   *Gordon M. Millet*

Definition: Sweat means to remove all liquid.

CREAM OF CARROT SOUP WITH THYME

1 pound carrots, scraped
   and sliced
4 cups Chicken Broth
1 onion, chopped

4 tablespoons butter
Salt and pepper to taste
1 cup heavy cream
½ teaspoon powdered thyme

Simmer carrots in chicken broth until tender, about 15 minutes. In another pan, sauté onions in butter until limp but not browned. Purée all in blender or food processor. Add salt and pepper, cream and thyme and bring back to boil, stirring constantly. Serve hot or chilled with a sprinkling of chopped parsley for garnish.

Yield: 6 servings   *Dan Regard*

CREAM OF CHICKEN WITH SAUSAGE SOUP

1/2 pound butter (2 sticks)
1 cup of flour
2 medium onions, chopped
4 stalks celery, chopped
2 quarts homemade or canned
   chicken stock
1 1/2 to 2 pounds fully cooked
   smoked sausage, cut in
   bite-size slices

3/4 cup Half and Half
Meat from boiled chicken,
   removed from bones and
   in bite size
Salt to taste
Pepper to taste
1 tablespoon thyme
   (powdered or rubbed)

Melt butter in soup pot. Add flour and cook 3 to 5 minutes over medium heat stirring constantly. Add vegetables and sauté until slightly tender. Add chicken stock and simmer 20 minutes or until vegetables are fully tender. Add sausage and simmer another 10 to 15 minutes. Add chicken and Half and Half; simmer and add salt, pepper and thyme as desired. Serve plain or over hot rice.

Yield: 8-10 servings   *L. Hallman Woods*

CREAM OF SQUASH SOUP

1/2 stick of butter
1 onion, chopped
1 to 1 1/2 pounds yellow squash,
   sliced

4 cups chicken broth
Salt and pepper to taste
1 cup heavy cream
1/4 teaspoon powdered thyme

Sauté onions in butter until soft. Set aside. Simmer squash in chicken broth until just tender, about 10 to 15 minutes. Mix squash, broth and onion and purée in blender of food processor. Return mixture to saucepan on stove. Add cream and thyme and heat until very hot but not boiling. Serve.

Yield: 5-6 servings   *Keith Courrege*

CRAB GUMBO

1 dozen large crabs
1 kitchen spoon lard
2 pounds okra
4 medium onions
5 tomatoes
4 cloves garlic, minced

3 ears tender corn, cut from
  cob
1 tablespoon sifted flour
1 red pepper
Salt to taste
1 tablespoon vinegar

Wash the crabs thoroughly, then boil them in just enough water to cover and cook until done, (about 20 minutes after the water begins to boil) saving the water the crabs were boiled in. Remove the shells, saving all the fat from the upper shells, and picking out all the meat of the crab. Put the lard in a large pot. Have the okra cut up in round slices and add it to the hot lard; fry until dry. Add the onions, chopped up tomatoes, and minced garlic. Fry all together, then add 4 quarts of the water in which the crabs were boiled. Add salt to taste, and set it all to boil about 2 hours. Meanwhile, add the flour to the corn, and about half an hour before serving, add the crab meat and the corn with the flour. The gumbo must be thick and highly seasoned. Just before serving, add one tablespoon of vinegar to prevent the gumbo from being ropy. Serve with rice.

Yield: 6-8 servings *A Weeks Family recipe*

EASY HOMEMADE ONION SOUP

4 medium yellow onions
¼ cup butter
1 tablespoon flour
2 (10-ounce) cans beef
  consommé

Toasted rounds of French
  bread
½ pound Swiss cheese,
  shredded
Salt and pepper to taste

Peel and slice onions into rings. Heat butter in a saucepan. As soon as it is melted, add sliced onions. Stir lightly, to avoid breaking rings. A wooden spoon is ideal. When rings are wilted and beginning to turn golden, sprinkle flour around and mix lightly. Gradually pour in 2 soup cans of consommé. Stir constantly to avoid sticking. When soup begins to boil, lower flame, cover pan and simmer for 15-20 minutes. When ready to serve, ladle soup into individual bowls. Place a toasted French bread round on top and sprinkle with shredded Swiss cheese.

Yield: 4 servings *Captain Albert Waterson*

HOT AND SPICY BEANS

1 pound lean ground chuck
1 large onion, chopped
1 bell pepper, chopped
1 package Chili-O-mix
3 tablespoons catsup

1 (42-ounce) can pork and
  beans
2 cloves garlic
2 large jalapeño or chile
  peppers, chopped

In large saucepan lightly brown ground chuck, drain, then add onion and bell pepper and cook until tender. Add all remaining ingredients and can of beans and cook on low fire for about 1½ hours, stirring occasionally. If mixture becomes too thick before fully cooked a little water may be added. Season to taste; this recipe is best hot and spicy.

Yield: 8-10 servings

Harold Tauzin

Note: Could be used as dip.

CREAM CORN

1 large onion, finely chopped
½ bell pepper, finely chopped

1½ sticks butter
3 (12-ounce) cans niblet corn

Sauté onion and bell pepper in 4 tablespoons butter until tender. Add drained corn. Add more butter as desired; use your own judgement.

TOPPING
1 carton whipping cream

Whip as usual with sugar. Put about 2 tablespoons on top of each serving of hot corn.

Yield: 6-8 servings

Joe Davis

EASY MAQUE CHOUX

4 slices bacon, chopped
1 large onion, chopped
1 bell pepper, chopped
2 cloves garlic, minced
1 (10-ounce) can Rotel
tomatoes, drained and
chopped (optional)

4 (16-ounce) cans yellow
whole kernel corn or same
amount frozen
4 tablespoons butter
½ teaspoon salt or to taste

Cook bacon on medium heat in heavy saucepan until not quite brown. Add next 3 ingredients and sauté until limp. Add Rotel tomatoes and sauté 2 to 3 minutes. Blend 1 can corn, undrained, in blender until smooth and add to above. Add other 3 cans of corn (drained), butter, and salt. Cook slowly over medium-low heat, stirring frequently, until mixture is thick.

Yield: 10-12 servings

Keith Courrege

FRIED RICE

8 slices bacon, cooked crisp
and crumbled
Bacon drippings reserved
from above
1 large onion, chopped
1 cup chopped celery
½ cup chopped bell pepper
½ pound boiled ham, chopped
½ pound bulk pork sausage,
cooked and crumbled

1 pound smoked sausage,
cooked and cut into ⅓-
inch slices
3 egg omelet, slivered finely
6 cups cold, cooked long grain
rice
½ teaspoon salt
¼ teaspoon sugar
½ teaspoon monosodium
glutamate
5 tablespoons soy sauce
⅓ cup chopped green onion

Fry bacon and remove from drippings. Cook onion, celery, and bell pepper in bacon drippings until limp. Add ham, bacon, pork sausage, smoked sausage, and egg and heat through thoroughly. Add salt, sugar, monosodium glutamate, and rice and mix thoroughly with a fork. Sprinkle rice mixture with soy sauce, while stirring, until rice takes on a golden brown color and until mixture is piping hot. Add green onions, mix well, and serve.

Yield: 10-12 servings

Keith E. Courrege

SPINACH PIES

2 unbaked 9-inch pie shells
2 tablespoons butter or
   margarine
2 cups minced, peeled onion
2 (10-ounce) packages frozen,
   chopped spinach, thawed
6 eggs

2 (15-ounce) containers
   cottage cheese (small curd)
1½ teaspoon salt
¼ teaspoon pepper
¼ teaspoon ground nutmeg
½ cup Parmesan cheese,
   grated

Heat oven to 400° Prick pie shells all over with a fork and bake 15 minutes until lightly browned. In a large skillet melt butter over moderate heat; add onion and cook until soft, stirring occasionally. Squeeze spinach to remove as much moisture as possible. Add spinach to onion and toss over heat until all liquid has evaporated; remove skillet from heat. Mix remaining ingredients in a large bowl. Add spinach-onion mixture and mix until it looks like green and white marble. Pour half the filling into each pie shell. Turn oven down to 350° and bake pies 45 minutes until tops are golden and filling is set. Remove pies from oven and cool to room temperature. Cut each pie in six wedges to serve.

Yield: 12 servings   *Robert Benoit*

SPINACH TIMBALES

2 (10-ounce) packages frozen
   chopped spinach, cooked
2 eggs, beaten
¼ cup seasoned bread crumbs
¼ cup grated Parmesan
   cheese

¼ cup chopped green onion
¼ cup melted butter
2 cloves garlic, minced pinch
   of thyme
Salt and pepper to taste

Mix all ingredients thoroughly. Make individual molds in demitasse coffee cup and place on thick seasoned tomato slices in shallow baking dish. Bake at 350° in preheated oven about 20 minutes. May be served as is or with a little hollandaise sauce drizzled over the top.

Yield: 6-8 servings   *Keith E. Courrege*

CLASSIC VEGETABLE CASSEROLE

Fresh vegetables
2 pounds ground beef
3 onions, chopped
3 cloves garlic, chopped
1 loaf French bread
2 sticks butter

¼ cup oyster sauce
Salt
Pepper
2 tablespoons thyme
1 can chicken broth

Cook vegetables of your choice that are fresh and in season (squash, mirlitons, eggplant, tomato, etc.), by steaming or boiling so that 1½ or 2 quarts of cooked vegetables remain.

In the meantime, cook ground beef in a large pot until brown, add onions and sauté until slightly tender. Add chopped garlic, 1 loaf of French bread (chopped into bread crumbs in the food processor) and butter.

When the vegetables are tender, add them to the above. Add oyster sauce (available at Oriental supermarkets), salt and pepper to taste and thyme. Add chicken broth and stir vigorously until fully blended. The mixture should be fairly loose. If more liquid is needed, add more chicken broth.

Pour into greased casserole dish and bake 1 hour at 375.°

Yield: 6-8 servings   *Hallman Woods*

CHÂTEAUBRIAND SAUCE

½ pound butter
½ lemon (juice and grated peel)
1 (10-ounce) can mushroom steak sauce
1 (4-ounce) can mushroom pieces, drained

½ cup green onion tops
Dash soy sauce
Dash Worcestershire sauce
Dash Tabasco pepper sauce
2 ounces Burgundy wine

Melt butter; add all other ingredients and simmer until hot. Serve on steaks and other beef.

Yield: 2 cups   *E. A. LaSalle, Sr.*

CHICKEN BREASTS WITH PECAN STUFFING

10 (6-ounce) deboned
   chicken breasts
2 small onions
1 bell pepper
2 celery stalks
1 pound ground pork
1 egg

2 teaspoons sweet basil
½ teaspoon allspice
Black and red pepper
Salt to taste
½ pint whipping cream
1 cup finely chopped pecans

Process 2 of the 10 chicken breasts in a food mill or grinder and set aside. Finely chop onions, bell pepper, and celery and mix well with pork. Add egg, basil, and allspice and season with salt and pepper. Season 8 chicken breasts and pound to thickness of a crêpe, but not to the extent that meat breaks apart. In the center of each breast, thinly layer the pork mixture, the whipping cream and pecans and then the ground chicken. Begin rolling the breast, making sure that all stuffing is well secured. Place on a baking tin (fold side down) and refrigerate for at least 12 hours. One hour before serving, preheat oven and bake at 350° for 45 minutes or until golden brown.

Yield: 6-8 servings

Wayne Peltier
Peltier's Catering

COMPANY CHICKEN BREASTS

8 chicken breasts halved
   and deboned
Onion flakes
Dried beef (one foil package)

8 slices bacon
1 pint sour cream
2 cans cream of mushroom
   soup

Sprinkle the chicken with onion flakes and wrap a slice of dried beef around each one. Place them in a pan and lay bacon slices on top of each piece. Mix sour cream and mushroom soup together (you may wish to add a little milk also). Pour this over the meat and bake uncovered in a 325° oven for 1 hour.

Yield: 6 to 8 servings

Curtis Thomas

CHINESE BROWN CHICKEN

1 clove garlic, chopped
1 tablespoon coarsely
   chopped ginger root
1 tablespoon chopped green
   onion
1 cup peanut oil
1 fryer, deboned, cut into
   1½-inch pieces

Salt and red pepper to taste
¼ cup cornstarch
3 tablespoons soy sauce
1 teaspoon sugar
2 tablespoons white wine
Chicken stock

Fry first 3 ingredients in peanut oil about 30 seconds over moderately high heat. Remove and discard. Season chicken with salt and pepper and sprinkle lightly with corn starch. Cook chicken in oil until lightly browned. Add soy sauce, sugar, and wine. Add chicken stock to just barely cover chicken. Cover pot and cook over medium heat until stock is almost gone and a thick, brown gravy remains. Serve with rice and Chinese vegetables.

Yield: 6-8 servings
Keith E. Courrege

CREOLE CHICKEN AND OYSTER PIE

3 heaping tablespoons flour
1 stick butter
1 cup chopped green onion
½ cup chopped celery
¼ cup chopped parsley
2½ dozen oysters, drained
   (reserve juice)

2 whole chicken breasts,
   deboned, skinned, cooked,
   and cut into bite size pieces
Few dashes of Tabasco pepper
   sauce
Pinch of thyme
Bay leaf, crumbled
1 (10-biscuits) can biscuits

On medium heat cook flour in butter, stirring constantly, until flour turns a rich chocolate brown. Add green onions, celery, and parsley and sauté until vegetables are limp. Add oysters and cook until edges curl. Add reserved oyster juice until sauce is thick and makes a heavy gravy. If too thick, add a little chicken broth to get the proper consistency. Add chicken and gently simmer until bubbly hot. Pour into 2 quart casserole. Top with biscuits. Bake in preheated 400° oven until biscuits are puffed and nicely browned.

Yield: 6-8 servings
Keith E. Courrege

CREOLE CHICKEN ÉTOUFFÉE

1 broiler-fryer chicken, cut into
   serving pieces
Salt and pepper
Flour
3 tablespoons cooking oil
1 large onion, chopped
½ bell pepper, chopped
2 stalks celery, chopped

2 cloves garlic, crushed
½ to ¾ pound cooked,
   smoked sausage, cut into
   bite size pieces
1 tablespoon chopped green
   onion
1 tablespoon chopped parsley

Season chicken pieces, coat with flour, and brown in oil over medium high heat. Remove chicken from pot and lower heat. Add onion, bell pepper, celery and garlic to pot and sauté until limp but not brown. Return chicken to pot, add sausage, cover pot, and simmer gently over medium-low heat for 1 to 1½ hours. If there is too much fat, skim off the grease. If the gravy is too thick, add a little water or chicken broth. Correct seasoning, add green onion and parsley, and serve over cooked rice or noodles.

Yield: 6-8 servings   *Keith E. Courrege*

FORTY GARLIC CHICKEN

1 broiler-fryer chicken, cut into
   serving pieces
1½ teaspoons salt
Pepper to taste
Dash of nutmeg
40 cloves of garlic (Yes, 40!!)
3 tablespoons olive oil

3 tablespoons butter, melted
2 stalks of celery, thinly sliced
4 tablespoons minced parsley
½ cup heavy cream or
   evaporated milk
½ cup sherry

Season chicken with 1 teaspoon salt, pepper and nutmeg. Set aside. Parboil garlic in boiling water for 30 seconds. Drain and remove skins. Mix olive oil and butter and dip chicken pieces to coat. Pour remaining oil mix to coat bottom of 1½ to 2 quart casserole that has a cover. Layer ½ the garlic, celery, and parsley in the casserole and top with ½ the chicken pieces. Layer other ½ of garlic, celery, and parsley and ½ teaspoon salt. Top with remaining ½ of the chicken pieces. Pour cream and wine over all. Bake, covered, in a preheated 350° oven for 1 hour and 15 minutes to 1 hour and 30 minutes; stir sauce and baste occasionally. Serve with hot, crusty French bread. The garlic becomes mild and soft and is delicious spread on the bread!

Yield: 6 servings   *Keith E. Courrege*

BAKED LEMON CHICKEN

1 chicken, cut up
1 cup flour
Salt to taste
Red pepper to taste
1 to 2 teaspoons paprika
1/2 cup melted butter

1 clove garlic, minced
2 tablespoons salad oil
1/4 teaspoon salt
1/4 cup lemon juice
1 tablespoon minced onion
1/2 teaspoon thyme

Roll chicken in mixture of flour, salt, pepper and paprika. Arrange skin side down in buttered, shallow baking dish. Brush with butter. Bake at 350° to 400° for 30 minutes. Mix remaining ingredients and brush over chicken. Bake 30 minutes longer.

Yield: 4-6 servings   *Carroll DeBlanc*

GRILLADES AND GRITS

4 to 5 pounds round steak, cut
   1/4 to 3/8-inch thick, trimmed
   and cut into pieces approximately 1/3 pound each
Seasoned flour (with salt
   and pepper)
1/4 cup cooking oil
2 medium onions, chopped
5 stalks celery, chopped
2 bell peppers, chopped
3 cloves garlic, chopped

2 (16-ounce) cans whole
   tomatoes
3 bay leaves
1 tablespoon thyme (rubbed)
1/4 cup sugar
Salt
Black pepper
Red pepper
2 (10-ounce) cans beef broth
1/2 cup green onions, chopped

Dredge meat in seasoned flour and brown in the cooking oil in a heavy pot that has a cover. After meat is browned on both sides, set aside and pour out all but 2 or 3 tablespoons of oil. Sauté onions, celery, bell pepper, and garlic until slightly tender. Add 2 cans tomatoes with juice after having blended them in a food processor 30 seconds. Add bay leaves, thyme, sugar, and salt and pepper to taste. Add 1 can beef broth and simmer gently 20 minutes, partially covered. Then add meat to the pot and cover with the gravy. Continue to cook gently and partially covered until the meat is tender. Check for seasoning again. If the gravy becomes too thick, add more beef broth. If it is too thin, corn starch may be used to thicken it to the desired consistency.

Serve over hot grits prepared according to package directions topped with green onions.

Yield: 8-10 servings   *L. Hallman Woods*

CASSOULET

This casserole dish of white beans and meat is very popular throughout the provinces of France and has almost as many different versions as there are provinces. It is prepared with many different combinations of meats such as pork, lamb, duck, goose, wild game, etc. It is time-consuming to prepare and this recipe is condensed for sake of brevity. It is intended primarily for the cook who has a reasonable amount of culinary know-how.

Prepare in advance of final assembly:

1 pound or 2 cups dried Great Northern white beans cooked with onion, garlic, and salt pork and seasoned with green onion and parsley and cooked until done but not too thick.
1 small domestic duck baked to a golden brown and cut into small serving pieces
½ pound each lean pork and lamb cut into 1 to 1½-inch chunks, sautéed in tomato and white wine gravy seasoned with onion, garlic, celery, bay leaf and thyme
½ pound pork sausage (plain, smoked, or garlic-flavored) cooked and cut into ½-inch slices
¾ cup seasoned bread crumbs
4 tablespoons duck fat or butter

Preheat oven to 400.° Rub inside of fairly deep 4 to 5 quart ovenproof casserole with cut clove of garlic. Put layer of beans in bottom, add layer of mixed meats, layer of beans, layer of meat, and end up with layer of beans on top. If there doesn't appear to be enough liquid, add liquid from beans or chicken broth. When adding meat to dish, be sure to include some of the gravy. Spread top with bread crumbs and drizzle with fat or butter. Heat casserole on top of stove until bubbling then put into upper third of oven and bake uncovered until crust forms on top, about 15-20 minutes. Push crust down gently into dish, reduce heat to 350.° and continue to bake until crust forms. Push crust down into dish. This can be repeated 2 or 3 times and baked for a total of about an hour. More liquid can be added if needed. Leave final crust intact for serving. Serve with French bread and dry white wine.

Yield: 10-12 servings   *Keith E. Courrege*

ELIAS LÁ HÁ MISHWIE

(Lebanese Shish Kabob)

4 pounds choice heavy beef
   sirloin steak, 2 inches thick
Salt and red pepper

4 large onions
1 French bread cut lengthwise

Cut steak into cubes about 2 inches by 1 inch. Cut peeled onions into fourths. Break onions apart and place into bowl with meat cubes. Season to taste and mix well. Place on skewers starting with meat and alternating with onion, ending with meat. Cook over charcoal pit with briquets being completely gray. Place skewers over coals turing each rod constantly to seal in flavor. During cooking process, dunk skewers between French bread three times; this allows bread to absorb onion and steak juices. Cooks rapidly.

Yield: 8 servings   *Darryl Elias*

KEITH'S JAMBALAYA

¾ pound fresh pork
¾ pound slice of ham
1 pound smoked sausage
⅓ cup bacon drippings
1 large onion, chopped
½ bell pepper, chopped
1 cup celery, chopped
2 cloves garlic, pressed
4 chicken bouillon cubes
4 cups hot water
¼ cup chopped green onion

2 cups long grain rice
1 (10-ounce) can Rotel
   tomatoes, drained and
   chopped
¼ cup chopped parsley
2 tablespoons Worcestershire
   sauce
1 teaspoon Accent
Salt and red pepper to taste
¼ teaspoon powdered thyme
1 or 2 bay leaves

Cook pork, ham, and sausage. Cut into bite-size chunks and set aside.

Cook onion, bell pepper, celery, and garlic in bacon drippings until wilted (do not brown) and set aside.

Dissolve bouillon cubes in hot water and set aside.

Wash rice several times in cold water, rubbing between the hands, until water is clear. Drain well and put into heavy Dutch oven or large casserole with tight-fitting cover. Add other ingredients, stir well, cover, and bake in 350° oven for about 1 hour. Uncover and stir gently with a fork. If too moist, leave uncovered, reduce heat to 225° and cook for 15 to 30 minutes longer. Serve with tossed green salad and hot French bread.

Yield: 10-12 servings   *Keith E. Courrege*

LEIGHTON'S ENCHILADAS

1 small onion, chopped
1 small bell pepper, chopped
3 cloves garlic, chopped
2 tablespoons oil
1 pound lean ground beef or
 ½ beef and ½ pork
Salt, red and black pepper
 to taste
1 large onion, grated

2½ cups Velveeta cheese,
 grated
1 package (12 count) frozen
 corn tortillas, defrosted
 according to package
 directions
1 (14-ounce) can Hormel hot
 chili, without beans

Brown the chopped small onion, peppers and garlic slightly in oil. Add the ground meat. Cook, season with salt, red and black pepper. Meanwhile, grate large onion to fine pieces like pulp. Place defrosted tortillas one at a time in greased baking pan. Place small amount of meat in center of tortilla; spread a little of pulpy onion and grated Velveeta cheese over meat. Fold tortillas and secure with toothpicks. Now spread remaining pulpy onion and grated cheese over this. Once all 12 enchiladas are made, heat chili; add ¼ can of water to this and heat to boiling. Pour over enchiladas and bake at 350° for about 20 to 25 minutes or until cheese is melted.

HOT SAUCE FOR ENCHILADA

In ground meat drippings, heat thinly sliced onion rings and bell pepper rings. Add a dash of chili powder. Add 8 ounces stewed tomatoes and all the hot pepper desired. Mash well and serve over enchiladas for extra hotness. Ground jalapeño peppers are good for this, also.

Yield: 12 servings   *Leighton Devillier*

OLD FASHIONED CHILI

1 large bell pepper, chopped
2 large onions, chopped
2 pounds ground beef
2 tablespoons oil
1 (16-ounce) can whole
 tomatoes
1 (10-ounce) can Rotel
 tomatoes
1 (14-ounce) can Austex chili
 without beans

Salt and pepper to taste
1 (6-ounce) can tomato paste
1 (6-ounce) can water
2 to 3 (15-ounce) cans
 Trappey's red kidney beans
 in chili gravy
½ cup chili powder

Brown bell pepper, onion and meat in oil until onions are clear and meat is gray. Add all the remaining ingredients to pot and simmer 2 to 2½ hours.

Yield: 8 servings   *Calise T. Trahan*

SIDNEY LOUVIERE'S TAMALES

5 pounds lean beef, ground
2 pounds lean pork, ground
1 bunch celery
4 large onions
2 large bell peppers
8 cloves garlic
12 ounces yellow corn meal

1 (22-ounce) box corn flakes,
 crushed
Salt and red pepper to taste
Chili powder to taste
4 (12-ounce) cans tomato
 sauce
Corn husks or papers

Process celery, onions, bell peppers and garlic until fine. Mix all the ingredients except chili powder and tomato sauce. Sprinkle chili powder on top of mixture until it turns red and is thickly coated. Mix well. Remove one large tablespoon of mixture and place on husks or papers and roll. Put in a large shallow pot and layer until all the mixture is used. Pour the sauce over the tamales and add water to cover. Bring to a boil, reduce to simmer, cover pot and cook for several hours. Taste to determine if cooked.

Yield: 4-6 dozen   *Talbot Giroir*

STEAK WITH OYSTERS

Rib-eye steaks (1 per person)

For each steak, use:

1 cup fresh mushrooms, sliced
2 tablespoons butter or
margarine
3 tablespoons chopped green
onion
2 tablespoons chopped
parsley
6 to 12 oysters, drained
depending on size

1 tablespoon Worcestershire
sauce
2 to 3 dashes lemon juice
2 to 3 dashes Tabasco pepper
sauce
¼ teaspoon seasoned salt
Dash or 2 of dry sherry

Place steaks in sizzling platter, and let sit for a few minutes while oven broiler is pre-heating. Put steak under broiler and cook to desired degree.

While steak is cooking, sauté mushrooms about 3 minutes in the butter. Add green onions and parsley and cook, stirring well, until wilted (about 2 to 3 minutes). Add oysters, then rest of ingredients, and cook on medium heat until edges of oysters curl. Steaks should be just about done by this time. Season steaks with salt and top with oyster-mushroom mixture and serve.

Yield: Rib-eye steaks (1 per person)   *Keith E. Courrege*

CHARLIE'S VENISON ROAST

Deer roast, 8 to 10 pounds
Salt and pepper to taste
3 onions, chopped
2 cloves garlic, chopped

1 bell pepper, chopped
1 package dry Lipton onion
soup
½ pound bacon

Wash deer roast several times in cold water. Pat dry with paper towels, season with salt and pepper, and set aside.

Mix 2 tablespoons of onions, 1 clove of garlic and 1 tablespoon of bell pepper with dry soup mix. Pepper may be added but no salt. Make punctures in roast and stuff with this mixture.

Place roast in roasting pan and cover entire roast with strips of bacon. Place remaining onions, bell pepper, and garlic in roasting pan. Cover and cook in oven at 275° for 3½ to 4 hours. If too much gravy has been made, remove roast and cook gravy down to desired amount. Serve over rice.

Charlie Toups

BÉCASSE ACADIAN
(Woodcock)

12 woodcock	Butter
Black pepper to taste	Paprika
Red pepper	1 tablespoon cooking oil
Salt	½ cup beef bouillon

Prepare 12 fat woodcock for roasting with black pepper, red pepper and salt. Refrigerate for 3 to 6 days. Preheat oven to 400.° Paint woodcock with butter and sprinkle with paprika before cooking breast up in black iron pot (cover later) with 1 tablespoon oil to grease pan. Baste with ½ cup beef bouillon and juices for 1 hour. Finish cooking on hot surface burner approximately ½ hour and use cover as needed.

SAUCE

6 to 8 oysters	½ cup beef bouillon
1 pound fresh cooked mushrooms	¼ cup pepper jelly
	⅓ cup Madeira wine
⅓ cup green onion	Calvados or Grand Marnier
¼ cup chopped parsley	

Remove birds and place in shallow serving dish in warm oven. Chop 6 to 8 large oysters and mix with juices and drippings in iron pot with cooked mushrooms, green onion tops, chopped parsley, beef bouillon, and Madeira wine. Reduce by boiling. Add large cooking spoon of pepper jelly; stir. When smooth, pour over birds and flambé with Calvados or Grand Marnier.

Serve with creamed cabbage and rice dressing.

Yield: 6-8 servings

Daniel L. Regard

STUFFED TEAL DUCK

Stuff ducks with sausage mixture of ½ beef and ½ pork seasoned with salt and red pepper. Salt and pepper ducks and wrap in bacon. Cook over low heat in a deep barbecue pit until tender.

Robert Chastant

TONY'S MALLARDS SUPREME

4 mallards, dressed
Salt and pepper to taste
4 onions, chopped
4 sticks celery, chopped
1 bell pepper, chopped
1 cup bacon fat

2 (10-ounce) cans chicken
  broth
1 cup Burgundy wine
½ cup onion tops, chopped
½ cup parsley, chopped
1 (8-ounce) can sliced
  mushrooms, reserve liquid

Season ducks with salt and pepper. Mix chopped onions, celery and bell pepper and add to cavity of each duck. Secure each cavity with a toothpick or two. In black iron pot heat bacon fat and brown ducks to a golden brown. Add chicken broth, wine, and enough water to cover ducks. Bring to a boil and reduce fire to simmer. Cook until tender, about 3 to 4 hours. Remove ducks from pot and add onion tops, parsley, mushrooms and mushroom juice. Thicken with a little flour and cook for a few minutes. If more gravy is needed, water may be added.

Yield: 8 servings

Tony Schwing

MAGNALITE WILD DUCKS

2 wild ducks
Salt, red and black pepper
garlic powder
2 tablespoons cooking oil
1 teaspoon sugar

2 onions, chopped
1 bell pepper, chopped
4 ground artichokes
  (Jerusalem artichokes)

Wash ducks several times in cold water. Pat dry with paper towels. Season ducks with salt, pepper and garlic powder. In Magnalite roasting pan (a thick heavy roasting pan may be substituted) put oil and sprinkle sugar on bottom of pan. Over medium to high heat, let sugar cook to a golden color. Immediately place ducks in roaster and brown. Reduce heat to low and add remaining ingredients to roaster. Cover and cook for 4 hours. DO NOT REMOVE LID. If too much gravy has been made in the cooking process, remove ducks and reduce to desired amount. Serve over rice.

Yield: 2-4 servings

Ira C. Toups

BARBECUED FISH

Redfish or drum
Salt and ground pepper
Lemon juice

Dry Italian salad dressing mix
Butter

Remove head and clean redfish or drum. Do not scale. Using electric knife, cut in half lengthwise along backbone (as in fileting). Eight hours before cooking, season well with salt and pepper and dry Italian salad dressing mix.

Cook (scales down) over a medium charcoal fire, basting with mixture of butter and lemon juice, being careful not to overcook. Do not turn. Serve scales down, scooping fish away from scales to eat.

Rene Broussard

CRAB CHOPS

2 tablespoons onion, chopped
**   fine**
3 tablespoons margarine or
**   butter**
2 tablespoons flour
1 cup milk
1 pound crab meat

20 crackers, rolled into crumbs
Salt and red pepper to taste
1 egg, beaten
6 small crab claws, shelled
Cracker meal for dredging
Oil for frying

Sauté onion in margarine, add flour and then milk to make medium thick white sauce. Cool slightly before using. Mix crab meat, cracker crumbs, seasoning, egg and parsley. Add only enough white sauce to keep the ingredients together, and shape into 6 balls. Press a crab claw into each. Pack firmly between hands, forming an oblong or round patty. Roll in cracker meal.

Put about ½ inch of oil in pan and fry on one side until brown and turn over to brown the other side. Do not crowd pan.

Yield: 6 servings

Peter W. Patout

CRAWFISH YVONNE

3 tablespoons butter
3 tablespoons flour
1 pound butter
1 quart chopped bell peppers
2 quarts chopped onions
1 quart chopped celery
3 ounces crawfish fat
¼ cup each salt and white
pepper, or to taste

Red pepper to taste
5 to 6 drops Tabasco pepper
sauce, or more to taste
3 pounds crawfish tails
½ gallon water
1 cup chopped green onion
tops
1 cup chopped fresh parsley

To make roux, melt 3 tablespoons butter and stir in 3 tablespoons flour. Cook slowly over low heat, stirring often, until the color of peanut butter. The color is vital; make sure it is a golden brown and not too dark. Set aside.

Melt 1 pound butter in a large skillet and add the gallon of mixed peppers, onions and celery. Sauté slowly over low heat, stirring often for 30 to 45 minutes. Do not let it stick or burn. Add 3 table-spoons of roux. Thoroughly stir into vegetables, making certain all is well mixed, evenly colored and no oil floating on top or at sides of dish. If oil begins to separate, simply keep stirring until blended in. Add crawfish fat to pot and continue stirring. Season with salt and pepper and Tabasco pepper sauce. Let simmer 5 minutes, stirring occasionally to keep from sticking or separating.

Meanwhile, pour tails into large bowl and wash in about ½ gallon water. When thoroughly rinsed, pour water into sauce. Stir and cook 10 to 15 minutes. Add crawfish tails and simmer another 5 to 10 minutes until flavors blend and sauce is slightly thickened.

Top with green onion tops and parsley and serve in bowls over hot rice.

Yield: 8 servings   *Alex Patout*

HALLMAN'S CRAWFISH ÉTOUFFÉE

1 pound of crawfish tails
1 onion
1 stalk celery
¼ bell pepper
1 stick butter

½ teaspoon tomato paste
2 ounces crawfish fat
½ teaspoon flour
½ cup green onion tops
Parsley to garnish

Chop onion, celery and bell pepper. Sauté in butter until tender. Add ½ teaspoon tomato paste and crawfish fat and mix tails. Add ½ teaspoon flour to thicken. Cook 10 minutes, then add ½ cup green onion tops and parsley. Cook 3 minutes.

Yield: 2-4 servings

Hallman Woods

BASIC CRÊPE BATTER

1 cup cold milk
4 eggs
2 cups sifted flour

1 cup cold water
1 teaspoon salt
4 tablespoons melted butter

Whirl all ingredients in the blender. Store in the refrigerator several hours. Heat a 6 to 7-inch crêpe pan or iron skillet until a drop of water dances. Grease thoroughly with a piece of salt pork or bacon rind. Pour scant ½ cup of batter into the pan and swirl rapidly until batter covers the bottom. Immediately pour off batter that does not adhere. Cook until browned, lift edge and with fingers turn. Cook a few seconds on the other side. It won't be prettily browned but it doesn't matter. Regrease and reheat pan to the smoking point before each crêpe. You may store well-wrapped crêpes in the refrigerator with a piece of wax paper between each crêpe. These freeze well so they are worth the little time involved. This recipe is for meat or vegetable crêpes, not desserts.

Yield: 25-30 6 or 7-inch crêpes
     or 20 8-inch crêpes

Gulf Coast Catering Co.

WOODY'S SEAFOOD CRÊPES

Prepare 8 to 10 (8-inch) crêpes. See Basic Crêpe Recipe.

FILLING

½ stick butter
1 clove garlic, pressed
½ cup green onions, minced
½ cup water chestnuts, minced
4 cups prepared seafood: crab, lobster, shrimp or a combination

¼ cup Madeira
⅛ teaspoon cayenne
¼ teaspoon nutmeg
1 teaspoon salt
½ teaspoon dry mustard
½ cup parsley, minced

Melt butter, sauté garlic and onions until soft, but not browned. Add water chestnuts and 3 cups seafood. Cook for 2 minutes. Add wine and seasonings; toss over moderate heat until liquid almost evaporates. Stir in parsley and set aside.

SAUCE

4 tablespoons butter
4 tablespoons flour
2 cups fish stock or clam juice
½ cup milk
1 cup grated Gruyère or mild Swiss, (4-ounce)
1 cup heavy cream
½ teaspoon salt
½ teaspoon Lawry's Seasoned Salt

Cayenne to taste
Pinch of garlic powder
¼ teaspoon saffron
1 tablespoon vermouth
1 tablespoon lemon juice
1 tablespoon Madeira
1 cup remaining seafood
1 tablespoon minced chives

Melt butter for sauce, stir in flour until smooth and gradually add stock. Stir over low heat until thick and smooth. Add milk, cheese, cream, salts, cayenne and garlic powder. Dissolve saffron in vermouth and add with lemon juice and Madeira. Carefully stir in 1 cup remaining seafood and chives. Check for seasoning.

PIE

Stir ½ cup of sauce into the filling. In a buttered 9-inch pie plate, layer crêpes and filling, beginning and ending with the crêpes. Wrap and store overnight or freeze. Store remaining sauce. If frozen let thaw 1 hour before baking. Pour 1 cup of sauce over pie and bake 30 minutes in a 350° oven or 1 hour if pie has been frozen. Cut in pie shaped wedges "au table" and pass remaining sauce.

Robert Woodburn

CAJUN STYLE LOBSTER

Lobster tails
Salt, red and black pepper
Egg and milk batter

Fish fry coating mixture
Oil for deep frying

Cut lobster tails in half leaving shell intact. Season liberally. Roll tails in egg batter and then roll in fish fry. Fry in deep fat. Tails are done when they float to surface.

Ira C. Toups

YUCATAN LOBSTER — GARLIC STYLE

2 lobster tails
2 cloves garlic
Juice of ½ lime

Salt and pepper to taste
1 tablespoon margarine

Cut lobster tails in half, leaving shell on. Place remaining ingredients in a mortar and make a paste. Spread this paste on meat of each lobster tail. Place in a covered skillet and cook on low to medium heat until done, approximately 10 to 15 minutes depending on size of lobster.

Yield: 2 servings

Ira C. Toups

OYSTER STEW

2 medium onions, chopped
½ bell pepper, chopped
3 cloves garlic, chopped
1 stalk celery, chopped
½ cup chopped parsley
4 tablespoons oil

1 quart hot water
1 tablespoon flour
1 quart unwashed oysters
Salt and red pepper to taste
½ cup chopped green onion
tops

Sauté onions, bell pepper, garlic, celery and parsley in 3 tablespoons oil. Add hot water and boil for 10 minutes. Heat 1 tablespoon oil and add flour; brown until golden to make a roux. Add roux to boiling water. When this is all dissolved, add oysters and juice and bring to a boil. Reduce heat to simmer, cover pot and cook for 50 minutes. Add salt and pepper to taste and serve over rice. (May be topped with chopped green onion tops.)

Yield: 6 servings

Rusty Brown

SHRIMP A LA MR. B

Shrimp
1 pound jar yellow mustard
1 package Zatarain's crab
  boil spices

2 ounces Trappey's Mexi-Pep
  hot sauce

Remove crab boil from bag and add to yellow mustard. Add 2 ounces Mexi-Pep hot sauce. Roll shrimp in mixture. Place in baking dish and bake in oven at 350° for 20 minutes. Remainder of mustard sauce can be refrigerated and used later.

Bernard Trappey

SHRIMP AND CRAB STEW

7 pounds shrimp with heads on
2 dozen crabs
3 cups oil
5 to 6 cups flour
3 (10-ounce) cans Rotel
  tomatoes
5 onions, chopped
3 bell peppers, chopped

3 stalks celery, chopped
2 gallons stock
Salt, red and black pepper
  to taste
Tabasco pepper sauce to taste
1 cup chopped green
  onion tops
½ cup chopped parsley

Remove heads; peel shrimp; set shrimp aside. Peel crabs; take off legs and claws. Break crab in half, slice each half between the shells to expose the crabmeat; set sliced crabs aside. Place shrimp heads, peelings, crab claws and legs into large gumbo pot. Cover with 3 gallons water and boil for 45 to 60 minutes reducing to 2 gallons. Strain stock and discard shrimp and crab remains. Make a roux with oil and flour; cook to a shade of gold, then add tomatoes and continue to cook until it is brown. Add onions, bell pepper and celery and cook until soft. Place stock on medium heat and when boiling, add roux gradually, a little at a time, to make a thick sauce. Be sure to stir frequently. When a thick sauce is obtained, let it simmer for at least 45 minutes, stirring frequently. Add seasoning and cook for another 15 minutes; add crabs and cook another 20 minutes; add shrimp and cook 10 minutes. Add onion tops and parsley 5 minutes before serving. Serve over rice in gumbo bowl with hot French bread!

Yield: 15-20 servings

Alex Patout

WAYNE'S SHRIMP FETTUCCINE

2 pounds peeled and deveined
   shrimp
Salt, red, black pepper to taste
1 1/2 sticks of unsalted butter
6 to 10 cloves of garlic

1 package of fettuccine
   noodles, boiled and
   drained
1/2 cup chopped parsley

Season shrimp with salt, red pepper and black pepper. Sauté 1 1/2 pounds of the shrimp in 1 stick of the butter until pink. In food processor, chop garlic and remaining 1/2 pound of shrimp. Add garlic-shrimp mixture to cooked shrimp and continue to cook for 10 minutes. Add remaining 1/2 stick butter, melt and pour mixture over noodles. Add parsley, toss and serve.

Yield: 4-5 servings   *S. Wayne Peltier*

SNAPPER FILET ROBERT

4 filets snapper seasoned with
   Tony Chachere's seasoning
   (green can)
1 medium onion, chopped
3 cloves garlic
1/4 pound clarified butter
1 1/2 cups crab meat
2 tablespoons chopped parsley
1 pint seasoned chicken broth
1/8 teaspoon paprika
1/4 teaspoon black pepper

Dash each thyme, tarragon,
   dill weed (optional)
1 pound shrimp, peeled and
   deveined
1/3 cup white dry wine
1 tablespoon lemon juice
2 tablespoons cornstarch
   dissolved in 1/4 cup cold
   water
Garnish-lemon slices and
   parsley

Pat dry filet of snapper, sprinkle with Tony Chachere's seasonings. Set aside. Grease large baking dish with oil and place 2 seasoned filets in dish.

In shallow pan, add onion and garlic to clarified butter and sauté until onion is clear. Spoon 1 tablespoon of onion, garlic and butter mixture over each filet. Pack crabmeat on top of both filets and sprinkle with parsley. Cover with other two seasoned filets and sprinkle with remainder of butter.

Simmer 1 pint chicken broth, paprika and all other seasonings for 30 minutes (low heat), add shrimp and continue to simmer for 10 minutes. Add wine and lemon juice and thicken with cornstarch mixture and pour over filets. Bake in moderate hot oven (375-400°) for 15 minutes. Garnish with lemon slices and chopped parsley before serving.

Robert Benoit

CHICKEN AND CORNBREAD DRESSING

1 large hen
Tabasco pepper sauce to taste
Salt to taste
1 cup yellow corn meal
1 cup all-purpose flour
4 teaspoons baking powder
¼ teaspoon sugar (if desired)
½ teaspoon salt
1 cup milk
1 egg
½ cup corn oil
1 large onion, chopped
1 large bell pepper, chopped
5 cloves garlic
1 cup celery, sliced
2 hard boiled eggs, chopped
1 (2-ounce) jar pimentos
6 stuffed green olives, chopped
1 (3-ounce) can pitted black olives, chopped
½ sleeve crackers, broken up
1 egg, beaten well (separate for soufflé dressing)
Green onions, chopped
Parsley, chopped
3 chicken bouillon cubes, in one cup water

Cut hen into pieces and boil in water with salt and Tabasco pepper sauce to taste until meat falls off the bone. Cool and debone. Retain broth. Refrigerate chicken, then cut into pieces with kitchen scissors. Mix corn meal, flour, baking powder, sugar, salt, milk, egg and ¼ cup oil and put into greased 8-inch pan and bake 20 to 25 minutes at 475° in preheated oven. After cornbread is cool, break it up and put it into a large pan. Cook onion, bell pepper, celery and garlic in remaining ¼ cup of oil, covered, over low fire until tender. Cool. Add cooked vegetables and chicken pieces to cornbread. Add the hard boiled eggs, pimentos, green olives and black olives, crackers, and beaten egg. Add chopped green onions and parsley to taste. Mix very well with large spoon, adding enough chicken broth to make a very moist dressing so it will not dry out while cooking. If extra broth is needed to make dressing moist, add three chicken bouillon cubes in one cup of water. Put in baking dish and bake at 375° for about 30 to 40 minutes.* (If you want a soufflé dressing, retain the egg white of the raw egg and beat until firm, adding about 1 teaspoon sugar while beating. Fold into cornbread mixture. Fill baking dish about half full as it will rise.) *Up to this point freezes very well.

Yield: 8 servings   *L. J. Freyou*

CAJUN COWBOY CORNBREAD

4 strips bacon
1½ cups cornbread mix
   (prepared mix without
   sugar)
½ cup milk
2 eggs
1 (8-ounce) can yellow whole
   kernel corn, well drained

1 large onion, chopped fine
2 jalapeño peppers, chopped
   fine
1 cup sharp cheese, grated
2 tablespoons cooking oil
1 tablespoon plain cornmeal

Fry bacon crisp, then cool and crumble (save drippings). In bowl, mix lightly prepared cornbread mix, milk and eggs. Add saved bacon drippings and mix in remaining ingredients (except cooking oil). Preheat iron skillet with the cooking oil in 425° oven and just before pouring in batter, sprinkle plain cornmeal over bottom of skillet to prevent sticking. Pour in batter. Bake at 425° for about 45 minutes, until browned.

Yield: 4-6 servings

Junius A. Winkle

ONION BREAD

1 loaf of French bread
1 stick unsalted butter, melted
1 onion, thinly sliced
Sweet basil

White cheese (Swiss,
   Mozzarella, jalapeño),
   grated

Slice bread lengthwise for two open-faced breads. Spread butter on each half and layer the onion slices. Lightly season with basil, and top with cheese. Bake at 350° until golden around edges and center of bread.

Wayne Peltier

BANANA PUDDING

1 (12-ounce) box vanilla
  wafers
4 bananas
1 (12-ounce) container Cool
  Whip

1 (8-ounce) can Eagle Brand
  condensed milk
1 (3-ounce) package instant
  vanilla pudding mix
2 cups milk

In 13 x 9-inch pan layer vanilla wafers alternately with bananas. Mix remaining ingredients, beat well. Pour over wafers and bananas. Refrigerate until set.

Armond Goodwin

CARROT CAKE

2 cups flour
1½ teaspoons baking soda
2 teaspoons baking powder
1 teaspoon salt
2 teaspoons cinnamon
2 cups sugar

1½ cups oil
4 eggs
2 cups grated carrots
½ cup chopped nuts
1 (8-ounce) can crushed
  pineapple, drained

Sift together flour, baking soda, baking powder, salt and cinnamon. Add sugar, oil and eggs and beat well. Add carrots, nuts, and drained pineapple. Bake in 350° oven for 40 to 45 minutes for sheet cake and 30 to 35 minutes for 2-layer cake.

ICING

1 (8-ounce) package cream
  cheese
½ cup margarine (soft)

1 teaspoon vanilla
1 pound box confectioner's
  sugar

Mix the first three ingredients, then beat in one pound confectioner's sugar.

Yield: 12 servings

Hallman Woods

COCONUT LAYER CAKE

1 (18.5-ounce) box, Duncan   1 teaspoon almond extract
   Hines white cake mix

Prepare three 8 or 9-inch cake layers from white cake mix according to package directions and add almond extract to batter before baking. Bake according to package directions. Cool before adding filling.

FILLING

1 cup fresh grated coconut   ¾ cup sugar
   (frozen may be used)   1 (5¾-ounce) can evaporated
2 tablespoons butter   milk

Cook filling ingredients in heavy saucepan, stirring for about 10 minutes on medium heat until thick and of spreading consistency. Assemble cake layers and spread filling between layers, but not on top.

ICING

1⅓ cups sugar   2 to 3 tablespoons
2½ tablespoons water   confectioner's sugar
2 tablespoons white corn   ½ teaspoon pure vanilla
   syrup   extract
2 egg whites, beaten stiff   1 teaspoon almond extract
           1 cup grated coconut

Mix first 3 ingredients and cook in saucepan until it reaches 238° on candy thermometer. Add slowly to beaten egg whites, beating vigorously until smooth and creamy. Add confectioner's sugar and beat until smooth. Add flavoring extracts. Ice top and sides of cake and sprinkle with grated coconut.

Yield: 12-16 servings   *Keith Courrege*

CUSTARD FOR HOMEMADE ICE CREAM

12 eggs
4 cups sugar
8 tablespoons flour
1 teaspoon salt

1 gallon milk
2 (15-ounce) cans Carnation
milk
3 tablespoons vanilla

Separate eggs and set egg whites aside for later use. In large mixing bowl thoroughly mix egg yolks with sugar, flour and salt. Gradually add a portion of the milk until dry ingredients are dissolved. Put all in large saucepan including remaining ingredients (except egg whites). Bring to a boil and immediately lower heat to simmer. Cook for about 15 minutes stirring constantly. Remove from heat. Beat egg whites until fluffy and fold into mixture. After cooling for 2 to 3 hours it is ready for freezing in home freezer.

Yield: 24 servings   *Harold Tauzin*

JIM'S DESSERT

1 (18-ounce) package Duncan
Hines yellow cake mix
1 (3-ounce) package instant
vanilla pudding
1 (8-ounce) package cream
cheese, softened

1 (8-ounce) can crushed
pineapple, drained
1 (8-ounce) container Cool
Whip whipped topping
Chopped nuts

Mix and bake mix according to directions in 9 x 13-inch pan. Cool. Mix instant pudding according to direction in a blender or mixer. Add cream cheese to pudding mix. Spread pudding mixture on cake. Spread well-drained pineapple on top of mixture. Spread whipped topping on top and sprinkle with nuts. Refrigerate for several hours.

Gulf Coast Catering Co.

RUM OR BRANDY BALLS

1 (10-12-ounce) box crushed
  vanilla wafers
2 tablespoons cocoa
1 cup confectioners sugar

1 cup very finely chopped
  walnuts or pecans
2 tablespoons light corn syrup
1/2 cup rum or brandy

Mix all together. Form into 1-inch balls and roll in confectioners sugar. Store in airtight container in refrigerator.

Yield: 3 dozen   *Armond Goodwin*

STRAWBERRY DESSERT

2 envelopes unflavored gelatin
1/2 cup cold water
1/2 cup hot water
1 cup sugar
1/2 teaspoon salt
Juice of 1 lemon
1 (16-ounce) frozen
  strawberries, sliced

1 (16-ounce) container Cool
  Whip whipped topping
1 (4-ounce) container Cool
  Whip whipped topping
1 prepared angel food cake
Red food coloring
Shredded coconut

Dissolve 2 envelopes unflavored gelatin in cold water. Add hot water to this after dissolved. Add sugar, salt and lemon juice. Add frozen strawberries including juice and refrigerate until slightly thick. Remove from refrigerator and fold in large container of whipped topping. Break angel food cake into small pieces and combine with the strawberry mixture. Pour into a 9 x 13-inch pan and refrigerate over night. Before serving, frost with small container of whipped topping which has been tinted with red food coloring. Sprinkle with coconut.

Curtis Thomas

SUNDAY BRUNCH

A late Sunday morning breakfast—for leisurely and relaxed dining, to be followed by absolutely nothing, except a nap!

Ed Haile

HOLLANDAISE SAUCE

¾ cup water
1 tablespoon fresh lemon juice
2 tablespoons butter
2 egg yolks*
⅛ teaspoon salt

⅛ teaspoon Tabasco pepper sauce
⅛ teaspoon paprika
1 tablespoon corn starch

In top of double boiler, heat the water, lemon juice, salt, Tabasco pepper sauce, and paprika. Dissolve cornstarch in a little cold water and add to above mixture, stirring constantly until thickened. Remove from heat and stir in beaten egg yolks and 1 tablespoon butter. Stir well until butter is melted. Return to heat, add the other tablespoon butter, and continue stirring until it reaches the consistency of very thick cream. Will be enough to use for 4 eggs in Eggs Benedict (see recipe).

*Instead of throwing the egg whites away, use them in making a Ramos Gin Fizz (see recipe). This is a delightful and refreshing drink to sip while making the Hollandaise Sauce.

EGGS BENEDICT

4 large eggs
4 English muffin halves
4 slices Canadian bacon
Hollandaise sauce

Water, sufficient for poaching
1 tablespoon white vinegar
2 tablespoons butter
½ teaspoon paprika

Heat water and vinegar in a 2-quart pot until bubbles begin to form. Gently add eggs to water, folding the white over the yellow, and poach for about 2 minutes. Remove eggs with a slotted spoon and place in a bowl of warm water. Cook the bacon until it's almost crisp. Keep warm.

Butter the muffins and place under broiler until brown. Place on a plate the muffin half, then the bacon, then an egg (drain well) and overlay with Hollandaise Sauce. Sprinkle a pinch of paprika over the sauce and serve immediately. Serves 4 (or 2 if really hungry). Serve with chilled bottle of Amourosé.

RAMOS GIN FIZZ

White of one egg
1 teaspoon powdered sugar
1 tablespoon sweet cream
Juice of ½ lemon

2 ounces gin
⅛ teaspoon orange flower water

Combine the egg white, powdered sugar and cream in a shaker and beat until frothy. Add the remaining ingredients and shake well with ice. Strain into an 8 ounce tumbler and fill with chilled soda water.

Yield: 1 serving

LE FROMAGE DE LA TÊTE DU COCHON
(Hogshead Cheese)
TRADITIONAL CAJUN DELICACY

This is an adaptation of an old Cajun recipe which used the actual head of a butchered hog. Due to the difficulty of obtaining this particular ingredient, the recipe has been changed to use ingredients that are more readily available. The end result, however, is just as tasty. It is best to take a couple days to make this, although that is not mandatory.

FIRST DAY
3 to 4 pounds pork shoulder roast
4 pig's feet or pork shanks
Salted water to cover

1 onion, coarsely chopped
2 cloves garlic, sliced
1 teaspoon vinegar
1 teaspoon lemon juice

Simmer above ingredients 3 to 4 hours until meat falls off bones. Let cool enough to handle. Strain broth and set aside. Pick meat off bones, discarding fat and gristle. Chop meat finely and put in covered container. Refrigerate meat and broth overnight.

NEXT DAY
Broth should be firmly congealed with layer of fat on top. If not *firmly* congealed, add gelatin during this next cooking. Skim fat off and discard, and set broth aside.

1 onion, minced
1 stalk celery, minced

2 cloves garlic, crushed
2 tablespoons butter

Sauté above in the butter until limp. Add chopped meat, broth and the following seasonings:

½ teaspoon each powdered bay leaf, thyme, basil, sage and paprika

1½ tablespoons Worcestershire sauce
Salt and pepper to taste

Simmer for 20 to 30 minutes, and if gelatin is needed, soften 1 or 2 envelopes unflavored gelatin in a little cold water and add to hot mixture. Add ½ cup chopped parsley, 1 cup chopped green onion and salt and pepper to taste (mixture should be highly seasoned). Cook until liquid is reduced and mixture is thick and gooey. Pour into pans or molds and chill until congealed. Serve as spread with crackers.

Yield: serves 20 to 30 people, as an appetizer   *Keith Courrege*

Note: Pig's feet and shanks may be omitted if necessary and gelatin alone can be used to congeal mixture.

Notes

Shadows-On-The-Teche...Come See Us!

PAN AND BAKING DISH SIZES

COMMON KITCHEN PANS TO USE AS CASSEROLE WHEN THE RECIPE CALLS FOR

4-cup baking dish:
9-inch pie plate
8-inch layer cake pan
7⅜ x 3⅝-inch loaf pan

8-cup baking dish:
8 x 8-inch square pan
11 x 7-inch baking pan
9 x 5-inch loaf pan

6-cup baking dish:
8 or 9-inch layer cake pan
10-inch pie plate
8½ x 3⅝-inch loaf pan

10-cup baking dish:
9 x 9-inch square pan
11¾ x 7½-inch baking pan
15 x 10-inch jelly-roll pan

12-cup baking dish and over:

13½ x 8½-inch glass baking pan	12 cups
13 x 9-inch metal baking pan	15 cups
14 x 10½-inch roasting pan	19 cups

TOTAL VOLUME OF SPECIAL BAKING PANS

Tube pans:

7½ x 3-inch bundt pan	6 cups
9 x 3½-inch kugelhupf tube or bundt pan	9 cups
9 x 3½-inch angel cake pan	12 cups
10 x 3¾-inch bundt pan	12 cups
10 x 4-inch kugelhupf tube pan	16 cups
10 x 4-inch angel cake pan	18 cups

Melon mold:

7 x 5½ x 4-inch mold	6 cups

Springform pans:

8 x 3-inch pan	12 cups
9 x 3-inch pan	16 cups

Ring molds:

8½ x 2¼-inch mold	4½ cups
9¼ x 2¾-inch mold	8 cups

Charlotte mold:

6 x 4¼-inch mold	7½ cups

Brioche pan:

9½ x 3¼-inch pan	8 cups

HANDY SUBSTITUTIONS

Ingredient Called For	Substitution
1 cup self-rising flour	1 cup all-purpose flour plus 1 teaspoon baking powder and ½ teaspoon salt
1 cup cake flour	1 cup sifted all-purpose flour minus 2 tablespoons
1 cup all-purpose flour	1 cup cake flour plus 2 tablespoons
1 teaspoon baking powder	½ teaspoon cream of tartar plus ¼ teaspoon soda
1 tablespoon cornstarch or arrowroot	2 tablespoons all-purpose flour
1 tablespoon tapioca	1½ tablespoons all-purpose flour
2 large eggs	3 small eggs
1 egg	2 egg yolks (for custard)
1 egg	2 egg yolks plus 1 tablespoon water (for cookies)
1 cup commercial sour cream	1 tablespoon lemon juice plus evaporated milk to equal 1 cup; or 3 tablespoons butter plus ⅞ cup cup sour milk
1 cup yogurt	1 cup buttermilk or sour milk
1 cup sour milk or buttermilk	1 tablespoon vinegar or lemon juice plus sweet milk to equal 1 cup
1 cup fresh milk	½ cup evaporated milk plus ½ cup water
1 cup fresh milk	3 to 5 tablespoons nonfat dry milk solids in 1 cup water
1 cup honey	1¼ cups sugar plus ¼ cup liquid
1 (1-ounce) square unsweetened chocolate	3 tablespoons cocoa plus 1 tablespoon butter or margarine
1 tablespoon fresh herbs	1 teaspoon dried herbs or ¼ teaspoon powdered herbs
¼ cup chopped fresh parsley	1 tablespoon dehydrated parsley
1 teaspoon dry mustard	1 tablespoon prepared mustard
1 pound fresh mushrooms	6 ounces canned mushrooms

INDEX

A

ex's Eggplant Dressing.............107
ice's Fried Chicken................193
ligator
Balls.............................179
Fried.............................179
Sauce Piquante................91, 180
Smothered........................179
mond(s)
Bacon Cheese Spread.............28
Cakes.............................308
Chicken Casserole...............186
Roca..............................316
maretto Stone Sour...............17
nchovy Wine Cheese Spread.........28
ngel Biscuits.....................249
ppetizer(s)
Almond Bacon Cheese Spread.......28
Anchovy Wine Cheese Spread........28
Artichoke Balls...................28
Bacon and Oysters.................29
Boudin Balls......................324
Braunschweiger Spread.............29
Cheddar Cheese Puffs..............29
Cheese Ball.......................30
Cheese Straws.....................30
Chicken Glacé.....................31
Crab Ball.........................30
Crabmeat Spread...................31
Crab Triangles....................32
Crawfish, Scandinavian............32
Eggplant Antipasto................33
Eggplant Caviar...................107
Ham Balls, Festive................33
Hidden Treasures..................34
Hogshead Cheese...................360
Jezebel Sauce.....................34
Maureen's Cheese..................34
Mushroom Caps, Stuffed............36
Oyster Log, Smoked................38
Pastellitoes......................35
Pecans, Peppered..................35
Ripe Olive Curry..................36
Shrimp and Mushrooms with
    Port Wine.....................241
Shrimp Canapes....................37
Shrimp de Jonghe..................37
Shrimp Ms. Ann....................240
Shrimp Remoulade..................243
Spinach Balls.....................38
Toast Cups........................36
Vegetables, Marinated.............37
Appetizer(s), Dips
Artichoke.........................39
Chicken, Hot......................39

Crabmeat..........................40
Crawfish or Shrimp................40
Curry, Basic......................41
Mushroom, Hot.....................41
Oyster Rockefeller................325
Shrimp, Lemony....................42
Spinach...........................42
Taco..............................43
Appetizer(s), Pâté
Chicken Liver I...................43
Chicken Liver II..................43
Curry.............................44
Mushroom..........................324
Pork..............................44
Apple
Cake..............................278
Chutney...........................273
Cobbler, Easy.....................300
Strudel...........................296
Artichoke
Asparagus.........................95
Balls.............................28
Casserole, Chicken................186
Casserole, Dressing...............95
Casserole, Noodle.................132
Casserole, Shrimp and.............232
Casserole, Spinach Cheese.........96
Dip...............................39
Florentine........................96
Pie, Oyster-......................224
Salad I...........................69
Salad II..........................69
Salad, Hearts of..................69
Soup, Cream of....................55
Soup, Cream of Mushroom and.......57
Stuffed...........................97
Asheville Salad...................82
Asparagus
Artichoke.........................95
Mushrooms and.....................108
Aunt Marie's Chow Chow............272
Aunt Maud's Chocolate Cake........279
Avery Island Deviled Shrimp.......233
Avocado
Guacamole Salad...................70
Molded Salad......................70
Soup, Cream of....................55

B

Bacon and Oysters.................29
Baked Acorn or Butternut Squash...113
Baked Chicken Breasts Supreme.....189
Baked Eggs........................125
Baked Kibbe.......................163
Baked Lemon Chicken...............338

Baked Redfish Yvonne................218
Baked Stuffed Fish in White Wine.......221
Baked Swiss Cauliflower..............103
Baked Wild Duck...................183
Banana(s)
  Bread.........................251
  Pudding.......................355
  Split Pie......................290
Barbecue(d)
  Fish.......................... 346
  Sauce, Brown's Texas.............. 86
  Shrimp........................ 231
  Tuna.......................... 217
Basic Crêpe Batter..................348
Basic Pie Crust....................289
Basic White Sauce—Thin, Medium
  and Thick..................... 91
Bayless Special....................323
Bean(s)
  Casserole, Green................. 97
  Charlotte's Mexican Medley.......... 71
  Green, Medley................... 98
  Hot and Spicy...................331
  Lima, Bake, Super................ 98
  Limas a la Vita, Chicken and........ 195
  Red, Creamy.................... 99
  Salad, Spanish.................. 71
  Soup, Pinto.................... 64
Bécasse Acadian (Woodcock)..........344
Beef
  Brisket........................149
  Brisket with Mop Sauce..............150
  Daube and Potatoes...............150
  Daube Glacé....................151
  Dry Fried Beef...................151
  East Indian Beef Curry.............153
  Elias La Ha Mishwie...............340
  Grillades and Grits................338
  Party Beef with Herb Biscuits.........152
  Pastellitoes..................... 35
  Peppered......................153
  Short Ribs, Sweet and Sour..........154
  Smothering—Cajun Style............149
  Stew Bake.....................154
  Stew, Daddy's...................155
  Stroganoff.....................155
Beef, Ground
  Cabbage Rolls...................100
  Chili for Hot Dogs................160
  Chili, Missouri..................160
  Chili, Old Fashioned..............342
  Chili, Sante Fe..................161
  Eggplant Baskets.................159
  Enchiladas, Leighton's.............341
  Green Enchilada Casserole..........161
  Holiday Spaghetti................165
  Kibbe, Baked...................163

Lasagne.........................134
Meatballs and Spaghetti, French
  Style.........................165
Meat Balls, Mama Vita's Red Gravy.....164
Meat Loaf, Sauce Piquante.......... 91
Swiss Loaf......................171
Tamales........................162
Tamales, Sidney Louviere's..........342
Beef, Steak(s)
  Flank, Grilled, and Mushrooms........157
  Pepper........................156
  Round, Sauerbraten...............157
  Round, Smothered, with Onions......158
  San Marco......................158
  Sugar.........................159
  Tenderloin Filet, Stuffed............156
  with Oysters....................343
Beets
  Chinese....................... 99
  Pickled, and Eggs................270
Best Vanilla Ice Cream...............303
Better Than Anything Cake............277
Beverage(s)
  Amaretto Stone Sour.............. 17
  Bayless Special..................323
  Bloody Marys, Frozen.............. 17
  Bourbon Slush................... 17
  Cherry Bounce.................. 18
  Daiquiri, Frozen................. 18
  Eggnog....................... 18
  Egg Nog, Old Virginia Recipe........ 19
  Gin Buck...................... 19
  Margarita, Frozen................ 19
  Mint Julep..................... 20
  Mint Julep, Southern.............. 20
  Old Fashioned..................323
  Old Fashioned (in Bulk)............323
  Old Fashioneds.................. 20
  Pink Squirrel................... 21
  Ramos Gin Fizz..................359
  Sazerac....................... 21
  Spiced Tea..................... 25
  Whiskey Sour................... 21
  Wines........................ 26
(See also Wines, Suggestions for Serving)
Birds' Nests.......................297
Biscuits (See Breads)
Bisque(s)
  Corn and Crab Bisque.............. 51
  Crawfish and Shrimp Bisque......... 54
  Crawfish Bisque I................ 52
  Crawfish Bisque II................ 53
Blackberry Jelly....................269
Black Bottom Pecan Pie..............294
Black-eyed Pea Jambalaya............142
Blitz Torte.......................278
Bloody Mary Soup.................. 59

366

Boiled Crawfish. 208
Boiled Shrimp. 233
Boudin. 169
Boudin Balls. 324
Bourbon Slush. 17
Brandied Strawberry Crème. 307
Braunschweiger Spread. 29
Bread(s)
  Banana. 251
  Brioche. 252
  Brown. 252
  Cajun. 253
  Celebration. 253
  Cinnamon. 254
  Coffee Cake, Surprise. 254
  Cranberry Nut. 255
  Cream Cheese Braid. 256
  Irish Soda. 257
  Italian Herb. 257
  Louisiana Grits. 255
  Onion. 354
  Orange French Toast. 130
  Poppy Cheese Loaf. 258
  Pumpkin. 258
  Pumpkin Nut. 258
  Riverboat Sweet. 259
  Strawberry. 259
  Sweet Potato I. 260
  Sweet Potato II. 260
Bread(s), Biscuit(s)
  Angel. 249
  Cheese. 249
  Easy Beaten. 250
  Helen's. 250
  Herb, Party Beef with. 152
  Yam. 251
Bread(s), Cornbread(s)
  Cajun Cowboy. 354
  Fluffy Spoon. 262
  Hot Jalapeño. 261
  Jalapeño Pepper, "Miss Edith's". 261
  Momma's. 264
  Yam. 262
Bread(s), Dressing(s)
  Chicken and Cornbread. 353
  Cornbread. 263
  French Bread. 264
Bread(s), Muffin(s)
  Bran Muffins, Refrigerator. 265
  Sausage. 266
  Yam-Pecan. 266
Bread(s), Roll(s)
  Croissant Refrigerator. 267
  Doughnuts—Beignets, Original
    French Market. 263
  Light. 267
Bread and Butter Pickles. 270

Bread Pudding with Whiskey Sauce. 298
Breakfast Casserole. 125
Brioche. 252
Brisket. 149
Brisket with Mop Sauce. 150
Broccoli
  Casserole. 98
  Casserole, Cauliflower and, Mary's. 102
  Cauli-, Bake. 102
  Marinated, Tangy. 99
Broiled Shrimp. 235
Brown Bread. 252
Brownies, Neen's Very Easy. 308
Brown's Texas Barbeque Sauce. 86
Brussels Sprouts-Ham Kabobs. 168
Buttermilk Pralines. 320
Butterscotch-Oatmeal Cookies. 309

C

Cabbage
  Casserole. 100
  Casserole-Meatless. 101
  Relish, Corn and. 273
  Rolls. 100
Caesar Salad. 74
Cajun Bread. 253
Cajun Cowboy Cornbread. 354
Cajun Mustard Sauce. 87
Cajun Rice Dressing I. 144
Cajun Rice Dressing II. 145
Cajun Sausage, Fresh. 170
Cajun Style Lobster. 350
Cake(s)
  Amaretto-Toffee Roll, Spiced. 287
  Angel Food. 277
  Apple. 278
  Better than Anything. 277
  Blitz Torte. 278
  Carrot. 355
  Chocolate, Aunt Maud's. 279
  Chocolate Cream Cheese. 280
  Chocolate Éclair. 279
  Coconut Layer. 356
  Cream, Italian. 281
  Fruit. 282
  Fudge. 283
  Pecan. 282
  Pound, Chocolate. 284
  Pound, Cream Cheese. 283
  Pumpkin-Walnut. 284
  Pumpkin-Walnut Roll. 285
  Red Velvet, Waldorf Astoria. 286
  Strawberry Shortcake, Old-Fashioned. . 285
Cakes (See also Fillings and Frostings)
California Blue Cheese Dressing. 83
Canard Pressé (Pressed Duck). 181

Candy(ies)
  Almond Roca 316
  Butter Mints, Old Fashioned 318
  Chocolate, Easy 317
  Chocolate Truffles 316
  Divinity 317
  "Elmer's Gold Brick" 317
  Fudge, Peanut Butter 318
  Peanut Brittle 318
  Pecan Brittle 319
  Pecans, Sugared 320
  Pralines, Buttermilk 320
  Pralines, Pecan I 319
  Pralines, Pecan II 319
  Turtles, Pecan 320
Candy Cane Surprise Punch 23
Captain Bill's Baby Snapper Filets 220
Captain's Salad 81
Caramel Ice Cream Squares 304
Carrot(s)
  a L'Orange 101
  Cake 355
  Casserole, Squash and 116
  Ring Mold, Fourteen Karat 72
  Salad, Piquant 71
  Soup, Cream of 56
  Soup, Cream of, with Thyme 328
Casserole(s)
  Artichoke Asparagus 95
  Artichoke Dressing 95
  Artichoke Spinach Cheese 96
  Breakfast 125
  Broccoli 98
  Cabbage 100
  Cabbage, Meatless 101
  Cassoulet 339
  Cauli-Broccoli Bake 102
  Cauliflower and Broccoli, Mary's 102
  Cauliflower, Baked Swiss 103
  Cauliflower, Holiday 103
  Cauliflower-Wild Rice 104
  Cheese and Potato 112
  Chicken Almond 186
  Chicken and Limas a la Vita 195
  Chicken-Artichoke 186
  Chicken-Spinach Noodle 133
  Chicken Tetrazzini 197
  Chicken Tortilla 198
  Crawfish 210
  Crawfish and Shrimp 214
  Eggplant I 105
  Eggplant II 106
  Eggplant III 106
  Eggs, Cheese and Bread 125
  English Pea 111
  Green Bean 97
  Green Enchilada 161

Green Rice 141
Lima Bean Bake 98
Mirliton (Vegetable Pear) 108
Mushrooms and Asparagus 108
Noodle Artichoke 132
Okra-Bacon 109
Oyster 226
Pork Chop 168
Potato 111
Potato, Cheddar Cheezy Hash Brown . . . 112
Rice and Mushroom 138
Seafood 246
Seafood Rice 139
Shrimp 235
Shrimp and Artichoke 232
Shrimp and Eggplant 238
Shrimp Bake I 234
Shrimp Bake II 234
Shrimp Marguerite 240
Squash I 116
Squash II 117
Squash III 117
Squash, Acorn or Butternut, Baked . . . 113
Squash and Carrot 116
Squash and Tomatoes 119
Squash, Summer 118
Tomato I 119
Tomato II 120
Turkey and Tortilla 200
Turkey, Goodbye 199
Vegetable, Classic 334
Wild Rice 139
Wild Rice and Oyster 140
Yam/Bourbon 121
Yams with Pineapple 122
Cassoulet 339
Cauliflower
  Baked Swiss 103
  -Broccoli Bake 102
  Casserole, and Broccoli, Mary's 102
  Holiday 103
  Pickled Garden Salad 75
  Soup, Cream of 56
  -Wild Rice 104
Celebration Bread 253
Champagne Punch 22
Champagne Salad 72
Charlie's Venison Roast 343
Charlotte Russe 297
Charlotte's Mexican Medley 71
Chateaubriand Sauce 334
Cheddar Cheese Puffs 29
Cheese
  Ball 30
  Biscuits 249
  Casserole, and Potato 112
  Casserole, Eggs, and Bread 125

Cheddar, Hash Brown Potatoes 112
Cream Cheese Braid 256
Fondue 131
Grits, Garlic 131
Maureen's 34
Pie, Mexican 130
Sauce, Welsh Style 87
Straws 30
Tiropites (Cheese Triangles) 39
Cherry Bounce 18
Chicken
    Almond Casserole 186
    Artichoke Casserole 186
    Baked Lemon 338
    Breasts, Baked, Supreme 189
    Breasts, Company 335
    Breasts, Crab Stuffed 188
    Breasts, with Pecan Stuffing 335
    Cadien 190
    Chinese I 190
    Chinese II 191
    Chinese Brown 336
    Chinese Lemon Baked 189
    Deluxe 191
    Dip, Hot 39
    Drambuie 192
    Dressing, and Cornbread 353
    Dumplings 192
    Enchiladas, Sour Cream 193
    Étouffée, Creole 337
    Forty Garlic 337
    Fried, Alice's 193
    Glacé 31
    Golden, in Spaghetti 197
    Gumbo Filé with Oysters 49
    Jambalaya 142
    Ken's Birthday 187
    Kiev, Green Chili 194
    Lasagne 135
    Limas a la Vita 195
    Okra Gumbo 48
    Pâté, Liver I 43
    Pâté, Liver II 43
    Pie, and Oyster 196
    Pie, and Oyster, Creole 336
    Poulet aux Gros Oignons 195
    Salad, Cobb 77
    Salad, Country Fair 78
    Salad, Curried 78
    Sauce Piquante 90
    Sausage Jambalaya 143
    Sesame 196
    Soup, Cream of, with Sausage 329
    -Spinach Noodle Casserole 133
    Tetrazzini 197
    Tortilla 198
    with Hoisin Sauce 194

Chili
    for Hot Dogs 160
    Missouri 160
    Old Fashioned 342
    Sante Fe 161
    Venison and Beans 185
Chinese Beets 99
Chinese Brown Chicken 336
Chinese Chicken I 190
Chinese Chicken II 191
Chinese Cookies 309
Chinese Lemon Baked Chicken 189
Chocolate
    Cake, Aunt Maud's 279
    Candy, Easy 317
    Candy, "Elmer's Gold Brick" 317
    Caramel Squares 309
    Charlotte, Frozen 300
    Cream Cheese Cake 280
    Cream Cheese Delight 299
    Éclair Cake 279
    Pie 291
    Pie, Amaretto Mousse 291
    Pie, Crust, Peanut Butter 293
    Pound Cake 284
    Soufflé Froid au 306
    Truffles 316
    Velvet Cream 301
Chow Chow, Aunt Marie's 272
Christmas Wreaths 310
Chutney
    Apple 273
    Fruit 274
    Peach 274
Cinnamon Bread 254
Citrus Dressing 83
Classic Vegetable Casserole 334
Cobb Salad 77
Coconut Layer Cake 356
Coffee Ice Cream Crunch 304
Coffee Punch 22
Coke Cake 281
Company Chicken Breasts 335
Condiments (See Jams, Jellies, Preserves,
Pickles, Chutney)
Congo Squares 310
Cookie(s)
    Almond Cakes 308
    Bars, Great and Easy 311
    Brownies, Neen's Very Easy 308
    Butterscotch-Oatmeal 309
    Chinese 309
    Christmas Wreaths 310
    Cocoons, Pecan 314
    Gingerbread Men 311
    Les Oreilles de Cochon 313
    Mandelbrodt 314

Peanut Blossoms.................313
Pecan Crisp....................314
Praline.......................315
Refrigerator..................315
Russian Rocks.................315
Squares, Chocolate-Caramel........309
Squares, Congo.................310
Squares, Cream Cheese............310
Squares, Lemon.................312
Squares, Lemon Mardi Gras.........312
Corn
  Bisque, and Crab................ 51
  Couche Couche, Mère's...........132
  Cream........................331
  Fritters......................104
  Indian.......................104
  Maque Choux..................105
  Maque Choux, Easy.............332
  Pudding......................105
  Relish, and Cabbage............273
  Soup, Mama's.................. 61
Cornbread(s) (See Breads)
Cornbread Dressing.................263
Cornbread Dressing, and Chicken.......353
Cornish Hens Basted in Secret Sauce....198
Country Fair Chicken Salad........... 78
Crab(s)
  Ball............................ 30
  Bisque, Corn and................ 51
  Chops........................346
  Croquettes....................203
  Deviled Virginia...............203
  Dip........................... 40
  Eggs and, in Brandy Cream Sauce.....126
  en Coquille....................203
  Étouffée, Shrimp and............235
  Gumbo.......................330
  Marinated, and Shrimp...........204
  Potatoes, Stuffed...............207
  Ravigote, Lump Crabmeat.........204
  Spread, Crabmeat............... 31
  Stew........................205
  Stew, and Shrimp...............205
  Stew, Shrimp and...............351
  Stuffed I......................206
  Stuffed II.....................206
  Stuffed Chicken Breasts..........188
  Stuffed, Neen's................207
  Stuffing, for Fish...............208
  Triangles...................... 32
Cranberry Nut Bread................255
Crawfish
  Balls.........................210
  Bisque I...................... 52
  Bisque II..................... 53
  Bisque, and Shrimp............. 54
  Boiled........................208

Cardinale I.....................209
Cardinale II....................209
Casserole.....................210
Casserole, and Shrimp...........214
Dip, or Shrimp................. 40
Étouffée I......................211
Étouffée II.....................211
Étouffée, Hallman's.............348
Fried, Tails I...................212
Fried, Tails II..................212
Pasta........................133
Quiche.......................213
Scandinavian.................. 32
Spiced.......................215
Stew I.......................213
Stew II......................214
Yvonne......................347
Cream Cheese Braid..............256
Cream Cheese Pound Cake.........283
Cream Cheese Squares............310
Cream Corn...................331
Creamed Oyster Patties I.........225
Creamed Oyster Patties II.........225
Creamed Soup(s) (See Soups)
Creamy Red Beans............... 99
Creole Chicken and Oyster Pie........336
Creole Chicken Étouffée............337
Creole Okra....................110
Crêpe(s)
  Basic Batter...................348
  Fillings for...................288
  Seafood, Woody's..............349
Croissant Refrigerator Rolls.........267
Crown Roast of Lamb..............166
Crustless Quiche.................127
Cucumber(s)
  Salad Ring................... 74
  Salad, Tomato and............. 82
  Soup, Cold................... 58
Curried Chicken Salad............. 78
Curried Rice....................140
Curried Zucchini Soup............ 61
Curry Dip (Basic)................ 41
Curry Pâté..................... 44
Custard for Homemade Ice Cream......357

D

Daddy's Courtbouillon............. 63
Daddy's Stew...................155
Daube and Potatoes..............150
Daube Glacé...................151
Daube Glacé, Veal...............171
Delicious Potato Salad............ 77
Deluxe Chicken.................191
Deluxe Pecan Pie................294
Dessert(s)
  Ambrosia, Eugenie's............296

370

Apple Strudel. 296
Banana Pudding. 355
Birds' Nests. .297
Bread Pudding, Walnut Fudge. 299
Bread Pudding, with Whiskey Sauce. . . .298
Charlotte, Frozen Chocolate. 300
Charlotte Russe. 297
Chocolate-Cream Cheese Delight. 299
Chocolate Velvet Cream. 301
Cobbler, Easy Apple. 300
Cobbler, Old-Fashioned Sweet. 301
Cobber, Yam, Trappey's Minute-Made. .302
Eggnog, Frozen. 302
Floating Island. 303
Fruit Trifle. 302
Ice Cream, Best Vanilla. 303
Ice Cream Crunch, Coffee. 304
Ice Cream, Custard for Homemade. 357
Ice Cream Squares, Caramel. 304
Jim's. 357
Lemon Sherbet. 305
Parfait, Frozen Mocha Brandy. 305
Pots de Crème. 305
Rum or Brandy Balls. 358
Soufflé Froid au Chocolat. 306
Soufflé, Strawberries 21. 306
Strawberries and Cream. 307
Strawberry Crème, Brandied. 307
Strawberry Dessert. 358
Wine Jelly Dessert. 308
Deviled Oysters. 226
Dilled Hot Potato Salad. 77
Dip(s)
  Artichoke. 39
  Chicken, Hot. 39
  Crabmeat. 40
  Crawfish or Shrimp. 40
  Curry (Basic). 41
  Mushroom, Hot. 41
  Oyster Rockefeller. 325
  Shrimp, Lemony. 42
  Spinach. 42
  Taco. 43
Divinity. 317
Doughnuts-Beignets, Original French
  Market. 263
Dove Étouffée and Rice. 180
Doves (see Game)
Doves from Toby. 182
Drambuie Chicken. 192
Dressing(s) (See also Bread Dressings
  and Stuffings)
  Artichoke Casserole. 95
  Eggplant, Alex's. 107
  Rice and Oyster. 145
  Rice, Cajun I. 144
  Rice, Cajun II. 145

Rice, Shrimp and Oyster. 146
Dry Fried Beef. 151
Ducks (See Game)

E

East Indian Beef Curry. 153
Easy Apple Cobbler. 300
Easy Beaten Biscuits. 250
Easy Chocolate Candy. 317
Easy Homemade Onion Soup. 330
Easy Maque Choux. 332
Eggnog. 18
Eggnog Dessert, Frozen. 302
Eggplant
  Antipasto. 33
  Beef in Eggplant Baskets. 159
  Casserole I. .105
  Casserole II. 106
  Casserole III. 106
  Caviar. 107
  Dressing, Alex's. 107
  Shrimp and. 238
  Soup, Cream of. 56
Egg(s)
  Baked. 125
  Benedict. 359
  Breakfast Casserole. 125
  Casserole, Cheese and Bread. 125
  Crab in Brandy Cream Sauce. 126
  Creole. 126
  Pickled Beets and. 270
  Plantation. 128
  Quiche, Crawfish. 213
  Quiche, Crustless. 127
  Quiche, Shadows Service League. 127
  Ranchero. 128
  Shrimp Soufflé with Sauce. 129
  Supper. 127
  Toast, Orange French. 130
Elias La Ha Mishwie. 340
"Elmer's Gold Brick" Candy. 317
Enchilada(s)
  Casserole, Green. 161
  Leighton's. 341
  Sour Cream. 193
English Pea Casserole. 111
Étouffée(s)
  Crawfish I. 211
  Crawfish II. .211
  Crawfish, Hallman's. 348
  Creole Chicken. 337
  Dove. 180
  Shrimp and Crab. 235
Eugenie's Ambrosia. 296

F

Facts about South Louisiana Fish. 215

Fairmont Spinach Salad............... 80
Festive Ham Balls.................... 33
Fig(s)
  Preserves I........................268
  Preserves II.......................268
  -Strawberry Jam....................268
Filling(s)
  Chocolate..........................288
  Chocolate and Cream Cheese........301
  Coffee.............................288
  Cream Cheese.......................256
  Pecan, for a Cake..................288
  Raspberry Kirsch...................288
Fillings for Crêpes, Jelly Rolls, Layer Cakes
  or Petit Fours.....................288
Fire and Ice Salad...................325
Fish
  Barbecued..........................346
  Catfish, Fried.....................216
  Courtbouillon, Daddy's............. 63
  Courtbouillon, Sauce Piquante...... 90
  Crabmeat Stuffing for..............208
  Filets, Sautéed....................220
  Garfish Balls......................216
  Les Poissons (Facts about South
    Louisiana Fish)..................215
  Pompano en Papillotte..............217
  Red Fish Courtbouillon.............327
  Redfish Yvonne, Baked..............218
  Sauce Piquante..................... 90
  Snapper Filet Robert...............352
  Snapper Filets, Captain Bill's.....220
  Speckled Trout or Redfish..........219
  Stuffed............................222
  Stuffed, Baked in White Wine.......221
  Swordfish, Skewered................219
  Tuna, Barbecued....................217
Fisherman's Tartar Sauce............. 92
Floating Island......................303
Fluffy Spoon Bread...................262
Food Processor Pie Crust, Never Fail.....289
Forty Garlic Chicken.................337
Fourteen Karat Ring Mold............. 72
Freezer Pickles......................271
French Bread Dressing................264
French Onion Soup.................... 62
French Style Meatballs and Spaghetti....165
Fried Alligator......................179
Fried Catfish........................216
Fried Crawfish Tails I...............212
Fried Crawfish Tails II or Fried Shrimp....212
Fried Frog Legs......................183
Fried Rice...........................332
Frog Legs (See Game)
Frosting(s)
  Chocolate I........................279
  Chocolate II.......................284

Coke.................................281
Cream Cheese.........................281
Decorator's..........................311
Fudge................................283
Whipped Cream........................287
White................................286
White, Cooked........................356
Frozen Bloody Marys.................. 17
Frozen Chocolate Charlotte...........300
Frozen Daiquiri...................... 18
Frozen Eggnog Dessert................302
Frozen Fruit Salad................... 72
Frozen Margarita..................... 19
Frozen Mocha Brandy Parfait..........305
Fruit (See Individual Types)
Fruit Cake...........................282
Fruit Chutney........................274
Fruit Trifle.........................302
Fudge Cake...........................283
Fudge Pie, Superb....................292

G

Game, Alligator(s)
  Balls..............................179
  Fried..............................179
  Sauce Piquante.....................180
  Smothered..........................179
Game, Dove(s)
  Étouffée and Rice..................180
  From Toby..........................182
  Smothered..........................181
Game, Duck(s)
  Canard Pressé (Pressed Duck).......181
  Mallards, Tony's Supreme...........345
  Teal, Stuffed......................344
  Wild, Baked........................183
  Wild, in Sherry Wine...............182
  Wild, Magnalite....................345
  Wild, Salad........................ 79
Game, Other
  Frog Legs, Fried...................183
  Quail Stuffed with Sausage.........184
  Rabbit or Squirrel Sauce Piquante.....184
Game, Venison
  Chili and Beans....................185
  Roast..............................185
  Roast, Charlie's...................343
Game, Woodcock
  Bécasse Acadian....................344
Garfish Balls........................216
Garlic Cheese Grits..................131
Garlic Mayonnaise.................... 84
Gazpacho............................. 59
Gin Buck............................. 19
Gingerbread Men......................311
Glaze(s)
  Cherry.............................253

Praline..........................284
Sugar..........................256
Golden Chicken in Spaghetti..........197
Goodbye Turkey.....................199
Grandmother's Pecan Pie..............294
Great and Easy Bars..................311
Greek Grape Salad..................73
Green Bean Casserole...............97
Green Bean Medley..................98
Green Chili Chicken Kiev.............194
Green Chili Squash..................116
Green Enchilada Casserole...........161
Green Rice.........................141
Green Tomato-Green Pepper Relish.....273
Griddlecakes.......................265
Grillades and Grits..................338
Grillades, Sauce Piquante............90
Grilled Flank Steak and Mushrooms......157
Grits
    Baked..........................131
    Garlic Cheese....................131
    Grillades and.....................338
    Mère's Couche Couche............132
Guacamole Salad....................70
Gumbo(s)
    Chicken and Okra.................48
    Chicken, Filé with Oysters...........49
    Crab...........................330
    Roux...........................48
    Seafood and Okra................50
    Shrimp.........................49
    Shrimp and Okra.................50
    Z'Herbes........................51

H

Hallman's Crawfish Étouffée..........348
Ham Kabobs-Brussels Sprouts.........168
Hard Sauce.........................289
Hearts of Artichoke Salad.............69
Hearty Cajun Potato Soup.............65
Heavenly Angel Food Cake...........277
Helen's Biscuits....................250
Hidden Treasures....................34
Hogshead Cheese....................360
Holiday Cauliflower..................103
Holiday Spaghetti...................165
Hollandaise Sauce....................87
Hollandaise Sauce for Food Processor...88
Hot and Spicy Beans.................331
Hot Chicken Dip......................39
Hot Jalapeño Cornbread.............261
Hot Mushroom Dip...................41
Hot Tamales........................162

I

Ice Cream(s) (See Desserts)
Icing(s) (See Frostings)

Indian Corn........................104
Indian Spinach......................80
Irish Soda Bread...................257
Italian Cream Cake.................281
Italian Herb Bread.................257

J

Jacob's Planter's Punch..............324
Jalapeño Hot Sauce..................88
Jambalaya
    Black-eyed Pea..................142
    Chicken........................142
    Chicken and Sausage............143
    Jambalaya......................141
    Keith's.........................340
Jam(s) and Preserves
    Fig Preserves I..................268
    Fig Preserves II.................268
    Fig-Strawberry Jam..............268
Jelly(ies)
    Blackberry......................269
    Pepper.........................269
    Port Wine......................269
Jelly Rolls, Fillings for..............288
Jezebel Sauce......................34
Jim's Dessert......................357
Joyce's Special Seasoning...........88

K

Keith's Jambalaya..................340
Ken's Birthday Chicken.............187
Kraut Salad.........................80

L

Lamb
    Crown Roast of.................166
    Leg of, with Mustard-Crumb
        Coating....................166
    Rolled Shoulder of, and Yams.......167
    Shanks in Red Wine.............167
Lasagne...........................134
Leek and Lettuce Soup, Cream of......328
Le Fromage de la Tête du Cochon
    (Hogshead Cheese)............360
Leg of Lamb with Mustard-Crumb
    Coating........................166
Leighton's Enchiladas...............341
Lemon
    Dip, Lemony Shrimp.............42
    Pie, Meringue...................292
    Sherbet........................305
    Squares........................312
    Squares, Mardi Gras............312
Les Oreilles de Cochon.............313
Les Poissons (Facts about South
    Louisiana Fish).................215
Light Rolls........................267

Lobster
  Cajun Style. 350
  Yucatan, -Garlic Style. 350
Louisiana Grits Bread. 255
Lump Crabmeat Ravigote. 204

M

Magnalite Wild Ducks. 345
Make Ahead Oriental Salad. 75
Mama's Corn Soup. 61
Mamma Vita's Red Gravy with Meat
  Balls. 164
Mandelbrodt. 314
Maque Choux. .105
Marinated Crabs and Shrimp. 204
Marinated Vegetable Bowl. 76
Marinated Vegetables. 37
Mary's Cauliflower and Broccoli
  Casserole. 102
Maureen's Cheese. 34
Mayonnaise
  Garlic. 84
  Never Fail Homemade. 84
Meat (See Individual Types)
Mère's Couche Couche. 132
Mert's Creamed Spinach. 114
Mexican Cheese Pie. 130
Microwave Hollandaise Sauce. 188
Milk Punch. 23
Mint Julep. 20
Mirliton Casserole (Vegetable Pear). 108
Mirliton Pickles. 271
"Miss Edith's" Jalapeño Pepper
  Cornbread. 261
Missouri Chili. .160
Molded Avocado Salad. 70
Momma's Cornbread. 264
Muffins (See Breads)
Mushroom(s)
  Asparagus, and. 108
  Caps, Stuffed. 36
  Dip, Hot. 41
  Pâté. 324
  Rice and, Casserole. 138
  Shrimp, with Port Wine. 241
  Soup, Cream of. 57
  Soup, Cream of Artichoke and. 57
  Veal Pies, with. 172
Mustard Greens, Smothered. 109

N

Neen's Stuffed Crab. 207
Neen's Very Easy Brownies. 308
Never Fail Homemade
  Mayonnaise. 84
Newburg Sauce. 89
Noodle Artichoke Casserole. 132

O

Okra
  -Bacon Casserole. 109
  Creole. 110
  Gumbo, Chicken. 48
  Gumbo, Seafood. 50
  Gumbo, Shrimp. 50
  Tomatoes, Smothered. 110
Old Country's Red Sauce. 89
Old Fashioned. .323
Old Fashioned (in bulk). 323
Old-Fashioned Butter Mints. 318
Old Fashioned Chili. 342
Old Fashioneds. 20
Old-Fashioned Strawberry
  Shortcake. 285
Old-Fashioned Sweet Cobbler. 301
Old Virginia Recipe for Egg Nog. 19
Olive Oil Spaghetti. 134
Onion
  Bread. 354
  Soup a L'Oignon. 62
  Soup, Easy Homemade. 330
  Soup, French Onion. 62
Orange French Toast. 130
Original French Market Doughnuts
  -Beignets. 263
Osso Bucco. 176
Oyster(s)
  Alexander. 223
  Bacon and. 29
  Bienville. 224
  Casserole. 226
  Casserole, Wild Rice. 140
  Chicken Gumbo Filé. 49
  Deviled. 226
  Dressing, Rice and. 145
  Dressing, Rice, Shrimp and. 146
  Gigi. 227
  Log, Smoked. 38
  Manhattan Style. 227
  Patties I, Creamed. 225
  Patties II, Creamed. 225
  Pie. 227
  Pie, Artichoke. 224
  Pie, Chicken and. 196
  Pie, Creole Chicken and. 336
  Rockefeller. 228
  Rockefeller Dip. 325
  Sherry. 229
  Soup Lafayette. 64
  Spaghetti. 231
  Steak with. 343
  Stew. 350
  Stuffed I. 230
  Stuffed II. 230

P

Pancakes (See Griddlecakes)
Parmesan Primavera.................137
Party Beef with Herb Biscuits.........152
Pasta(s)
   Fettuccine, Shrimp.................238
   Fettuccine, Shrimp, Wayne's.........352
   Fettuccine, Spinach...............136
   Lasagne..........................134
   Lasagne, Chicken................135
   Noodle, Artichoke Casserole.........132
   Noodle, Spinach Ring...............136
   Parmesan Primavera...............137
   Salad............................135
   Spaghetti, French Style Meatballs and..165
   Spaghetti, Golden Chicken in.........197
   Spaghetti, Holiday..................165
   Spaghetti, Olive Oil................134
   Spaghetti, Oyster.................231
   Spaghetti, Tomato-Salad............. 83
   Spaghetti with Green Sauce.........137
   -Spinach Noodle, Chicken Casserole...133
   Tetrazzini, Chicken................197
   Vermicelli Vinaigrette...............138
Pastellitoes.........................35
Pâté
   Chicken Liver I..................... 43
   Chicken Liver II.................... 43
   Curry............................ 44
   Mushroom........................324
   Pork............................ 44
Peach Chutney......................274
Peach Parfait Pie...................293
Peanut
   Blossoms........................313
   Brittle..........................318
Peanut Butter
   Fudge..........................318
   Pie, Chocolate Crust..............293
Pea(s)
   Black-eyed, Jambalaya..............142
   English, Casserole.................111
Pecan(s)
   Brittle..........................319
   Cake..........................282
   Cocoons.........................314
   Cookies, Crisp...................314
   Muffins, Yam-...................266
   Peppered........................ 35
   Pie, Black Bottom.................294
   Pie, Deluxe.....................294
   Pie, Grandmother's................294
   Pralines I........................319
   Pralines II.......................319
   Stuffing, Chicken Breasts with.......335
   Sugared.........................320
   Turtles..........................320

Pedigreed Sausage and Peppers........170
Peppered Beef.....................153
Peppered Pecans.................... 35
Pepper Jelly.......................269
Pepper Steak......................156
Pickled Beets and Eggs..............270
Pickled Garden Salad................ 75
Pickled Shrimp.....................242
Pickles
   Bread and Butter.................270
   Freezer.........................271
   Mirliton........................271
   Squash.........................271
   Watermelon......................272
Pie(s)—Dessert
   Banana Cream...................290
   Banana Split.....................290
   Chocolate.......................291
   Chocolate Amaretto Mousse........291
   Crust, Basic.....................289
   Crust, Food Processor, Never
     Fail..........................289
   Fudge, Superb...................292
   Lemon Meringue.................292
   Peach Parfait....................293
   Peanut Butter, Chocolate Crust.......293
   Pecan, Black Bottom..............294
   Pecan, Deluxe...................294
   Pecan, Grandmother's.............294
   Pumpkin Chiffon with Chocolate-Walnut
     Crust........................295
   Summer........................295
Pie(s)—Other
   Chicken and Oyster...............196
   Chicken and Oyster, Creole.........336
   Mexican Cheese..................130
   Oyster.........................227
   Oyster-Artichoke.................224
   Spinach....................114, 333
   Veal, with Mushrooms.............172
   Vegetable.......................122
Pineapple Jewel.....................326
Pink Squirrel....................... 21
Pinto Bean Soup.................... 64
Piquant Carrot Salad................. 71
Plantation Club Salad Dressing......... 85
Plantation Eggs....................128
Planters Punch..................... 23
Pompano en Papillotte...............217
Poppy Cheese Loaf.................258
Poppy Seed Dressing................ 84
Pork
   Cassoulet.......................339
   Chop Casserole..................168
   Ham Balls, Festive................ 33
   Ham Kabobs-Brussels Sprouts........168
   Honduras.......................169

Le Fromage de la Tête du Cochon
   (Hogshead Cheese)............360
   Pâté.............................44
Port Wine Jelly.....................269
Portuguese Shrimp..................242
Potato(es) (See also Yams)
   Casserole.........................111
   Casserole, Cheese and.............112
   Cheddar Cheezy Hash Brown.......112
   Crab Stuffed.....................207
   Daube and.......................150
   Puffs.............................113
   Salad, Delicious...................77
   Salad, Dilled Hot..................77
   Shrimp Boats.....................232
   Soufflé..........................113
   Soup, Cream of....................58
   Soup, Hearty Cajun................65
Pots de Crème.....................305
Potted Shrimp.....................243
Poulet aux Gros Oignons............195
Poultry (See Individual Types)
Praline(s)
   Buttermilk........................320
   Pecan I..........................319
   Pecan II.........................319
   Cookies.........................315
Pumpkin
   Bread...........................258
   Chiffon Pie with Chocolate-Walnut
     Crust..........................295
   Nut Bread.......................258
   Walnut Cake.....................284
   Walnut Roll......................285
Punch
   Candy Cane Surprise...............23
   Champagne.......................22
   Coffee............................22
   Fruit, Spirited.....................24
   Milk..............................23
   Planters..........................23
   Planters, Jacob's.................324
   Punch............................22
   Red Rooster Christmas Drink........24
   Sangria...........................24
   Sangria, White.....................25
   Wassail...........................25

Q

Quail (See Game)
Quail Stuffed with Sausage............184
Quiche
   Crawfish.........................213
   Crustless........................127
   Shadows Service League............127

R

Rabbit or Squirrel Sauce Piquante......184

Ramos Gin Fizz....................359
Red Fish Courtbouillon..............327
Red Rooster Christmas Drink..........24
Refrigerator Bran Muffins............265
Refrigerator Cookies................315
Relish(es)
   Chow Chow, Aunt Marie's..........272
   Corn and Cabbage................273
   Green Tomato-Green Pepper........273
Remoulade Sauce...............70, 89
Rice
   Casserole, and Mushroom..........138
   Casserole, Seafood...............139
   Casserole, Wild Rice..............139
   Casserole, Wild Rice and Oyster.....140
   Cauliflower-Wild Rice..............104
   Curried..........................140
   Dressing, and Oyster..............145
   Dressing, Cajun I.................144
   Dressing, Cajun II................145
   Dressing, Shrimp and Oyster.......146
   Fried............................332
   Green...........................141
   Jambalaya.......................141
   Jambalaya, Keith's...............340
   Spinach and......................115
   Vegetable........................143
Ripe Olive Curry....................36
Riverboat Sweet Bread..............259
Rolled Shoulder of Lamb and Yams.....167
Rolls (see Breads)
Round Steak Sauerbraten............157
Roux..............................48
Rum or Brandy Balls................358
Russian Rocks.....................315

S

Salads, Fruit
   Champagne.......................72
   Frozen...........................72
   Greek Grape......................73
   Pineapple Jewel..................326
   Strawberry Delight................73
   Yum-Yum........................73
Salads, Poultry and Game
   Chicken, Country Fair..............78
   Chicken, Curried..................78
   Cobb.............................77
   Duck, Wild.......................79
Salads, Seafood
   Seafood..........................79
Salads, Vegetable
   Artichoke I........................69
   Artichoke II.......................69
   Artichoke, Hearts of...............69
   Asheville.........................82
   Avocado, Molded..................70

Bean, Spanish. 71
Caesar. 74
Captain's. 81
Carrot, Piquant. 71
Cucumber Ring. 74
Fire and Ice. .325
Fourteen Karat Ring Mold. 72
Garden, Pickled. 75
Guacamole. 70
Kraut. 80
Marinated Bowl. 76
Mexican, Charlotte's. 71
Oriental, Make Ahead. 75
Pasta. 135
Potato, Delicious. 77
Potato, Dilled Hot. 77
Seven Layer. 76
Spinach. 81
Spinach, Fairmont. 80
Spinach, Indian. 80
Tomato and Cucumber. 82
Tomato Aspic. 82
Tomato-Spaghetti. 83
Salad Dressing(s)
Blue Cheese, California. 83
Citrus. 83
Mayonnaise, Garlic. 84
Mayonnaise, Never Fail Homemade. . . 84
Pastoral. 85
Plantation Club. 85
Poppy Seed. 84
Salmon, Sauce Piquante. 91
Sangria. 24
Sante Fe Chili. 161
Sauce Piquante. 90
Sauce Piquante Variations. 90
Sauce(s)
Barbeque, Brown's Texas. 86
Basting. 156
Chateaubriand. 334
Cheese, Welsh Style. 87
Chili. 160
Green. 137
Hollandaise. 87, 359
Hollandaise, for Food Processor. 88
Hollandaise, Microwave. 188
Jalapeño Hot Sauce. 88
Mop Sauce. .150
Mushroom. .229
Mustard, Cajun. 87
Newburg. 89
Piquante. 90
Piquante, Variations. 90
Red, Old Country's. 89
Remoulade. 70, 89
Seafood, White Wine. 92
Secret Sauce. 198

Shrimp. 244
Tartar, Fisherman's. 92
White, Thin, Medium and Thick. 91
Wine and Oyster. 344
Zippy. 92
Sauce(s)—Sweet
Hard. 289
Velvet Rum. 288
Whiskey Sauce for Bread Pudding. 298
Sauerkraut
Kraut Salad. 80
Sausage
Boudin. 169
Boudin Balls. 324
Cajun, Fresh. 170
Jambalaya, and Chicken. 143
Muffins. 266
Pedigreed and Peppers. 170
Quail Stuffed with. 184
Soup, Cream of Chicken and. 329
Swiss Loaf. .171
Sautéed Fish Filets. 220
Sazerac. 21
Scaloppine a la Marsala. 175
Scaloppini, Veal. 175
Scandinavian Crawfish. 32
Seafood (see Individual Types)
Seafood and Okra Gumbo. 50
Seafood Casserole. 246
Seafood Rice Casserole. 139
Seafood Salad. 79
Seasoning, Joyce's Special. 88
Sesame Chicken. 196
Seven Layer Salad. 76
Shadows Service League Quiche. 127
Sherbet, Lemon. 305
Shrimp
à la Mr. B. .351
and Eggplant. 238
and Mushrooms with Port Wine. 241
Avery Island Deviled. 233
Bake I. 234
Bake II. 234
Barbecued. 231
Bisque, Crawfish and. 54
Boats. 232
Boiled. 233
Broiled. 235
Canapes. 37
Casserole. .235
Casserole, and Artichoke. 232
Casserole, Crawfish and. 214
Creole I. 236
Creole II. 236
Creole III (Microwave). 237
de Jonghe. 37
Dip, Crawfish or. 40

Dip, Lemony. 42
Dressing, Rice, and Oyster. 146
Étoufée, and Crab. 235
Fettuccine. 238
Fettuccine, Wayne's. 352
Fried. 212
Gumbo. 49
Gumbo, Okra and. 50
in Cheese Sauce. 237
Marguerite. 240
Marinated, Crabs and. 204
Mosca I. 239
Mosca II. 239
Ms. Ann. 240
Newburg. 241
Pickled. 242
Portuguese. 242
Potted. 243
Remoulade. 243
Sauce. 244
Sauce Piquante. 90
Scampi. 244
Soufflé with Sauce. 129
Stew, and Crab. 351
Stew, Crab and. 205
Stuffed. 245
To Dry. 246
Sidney Louviere's Tamales. 342
Skewered Swordfish. 219
Smoked Oyster Log. 38
Smothered Alligator. 179
Smothered Doves. 181
Smothered Okra and Tomatoes. 110
Smothered Round Steak with Onions. . . . 158
Smothering—Cajun Style. 149
Snapper Filet Robert. 352
Soufflé
    Froid au Chocolat. 306
    Potato. 113
    Shrimp, with Sauce. 129
    Strawberries 21. 306
Soup(s)
    a L'Oignon. 62
    Corn, Mama's. 61
    Courtbouillon, Daddy's. 63
    Courbouillon, Red Fish. 327
    Gazpacho. 59
    Onion, Easy Homemade. 330
    Onion, French. 62
    Oyster, Lafayette. 64
    Pinto Bean. 64
    Potato, Hearty Cajun. 65
    Strawberry. 59
    Turtle I. 65
    Turtle II. 66
    Vichyssoise. 60
    Vichyssoise, Spinach. 60

Zucchini, Curried. 61
Soup(s), Cream of
    Artichoke. 55
    Avocado. 55
    Carrot. 56
    Carrot, with Thyme. 328
    Cauliflower. 56
    Chicken with Sausage. 329
    Eggplant. 56
    Leek and Lettuce. 328
    Mushroom. 57
    Mushroom and Artichoke. 57
    Potato. 58
    Squash. 329
Sour Cream Enchiladas. 193
Southern Mint Julep. 20
Spanish Bean Salad. 71
Speckled Trout or Redfish. 219
Spiced Amaretto-Toffee Roll. 287
Spiced Crawfish. 215
Spiced Tea. 25
Spinach
    Artichokes Florentine. 96
    Balls. 38
    Casserole, Artichoke, Cheese. 96
    Creamed, Mert's. 114
    Dip. 42
    Fettuccine. 136
    Noodle Ring. 136
    Pie. 114
    Pies. 333
    Rice, and. 115
    Salad. 81
    Salad, Captain's. 81
    Salad, Fairmont. 80
    Salad, Indian. 80
    Timbales. 333
    Vichyssoise. 60
Spirited Fruit Punch. 24
Squash
    Acorn or Butternut, Baked. 113
    and Tomatoes. 119
    Casserole I. 116
    Casserole II. 117
    Casserole III. 117
    Casserole, Carrot. 116
    Casserole, Summer. 118
    Green Chili. 116
    Pickles. 271
    Soup, Cream of. 329
    Spaghetti, Stuffed. 115
    Stuffed. 118
Squirrel or Rabbit Sauce Piquante. 184
Steak San Marco. 158
Steak with Oysters. 343
Stew
    Beef, Bake. 154

Crab. 205
Crab and Shrimp. 205
Crawfish I. 213
Crawfish II. 214
Daddy's. 155
Oyster. 350
Shrimp and Crab. 351
Veal Ragout with Onions and
  Chestnuts. .174
trawberry(ies)
Bread. 259
Crème, Brandied. 307
Dessert. 358
Dessert, and Cream. 307
Salad, Delight. 73
Shortcake, Old-Fashioned. 285
Soufflé 21. 306
Soup. 59
tuffed
Artichokes. 97
Crabs I. 206
Crabs II. 206
Fish. 222
Mushroom Caps. 36
Oysters I. 230
Oysters II. 230
Shrimp. 245
Squash. 118
Squash, Spaghetti. 115
Teal Duck. 344
Tenderloin Filet. 156
tuffing
Crabmeat, for Fish. 208
Pecan Chicken Breasts with. 335
ugared Pecans. 320
ugar Steak. 159
ummer Pie. 295
ummer Squash Casserole. 118
unday Brunch. .359
uperb Fudge Pie. 292
uper Lima Bean Bake. 98
uper Yams. 122
urprise Coffee Cake. 254
weet and Sour Short Ribs. 154
weet Potato Bread I. 260
weet Potato Bread II. 260
weet Potatoes (See Yams)
weets (see Cakes, Candy, Cookies, Desserts,
ies)
wiss Loaf. 171

T

aco Dip. 43
angy Marinated Broccoli. 99
iropites (Cheese Triangles). 39
oast Cups. 36
o Dry Shrimp. 246

Tomato(es)
Aspic. 82
Casserole I. 119
Casserole II. 120
Okra, Smothered and. 110
Salad, and Cucumber. 82
Salad, Spaghetti. 83
Squash and. 119
Tony's Mallards Supreme. 345
Trappey's Minute-Made Yam Cobbler. 302
Tuna, Barbecued. 217
Turkey
Goodbye. 199
Sauce Piquante. 199
Tortilla, and. 200
Turnip(s)
Puff. 121
You Can't Believe It's. 120
Turtle
Soup I. 65
Soup II. 66

V

Veal
Daube Glacé. .171
Osso Bucco. 176
Pies with Mushrooms. 172
Ragout with Onions and Chestnuts. 174
Risotto. 173
Scalloppine a la Marsala. 175
Scaloppini. 175
Vegetable(s) (See also Individual Names)
Casserole, Classic. 334
Marinated Bowl. 76
Pear (Mirliton). 108
Pie. 122
Rice. 143
Vegetable Sauces (see Sauces)
Velvet Rum Sauce. 288
Venison (See also Game)
Venison Chili and Beans. 185
Venison Roast. 185
Venison Roast, Charlie's. 343
Vermicelli Vinaigrette. 138
Vichyssoise. 60
Vichyssoise, Spinach. 60
Virginia Deviled Crabs. 203

W

Waldorf Astoria Red Velvet Cake. 286
Walnut Fudge Bread Pudding. 299
Wassail. 25
Watermelon Pickles. 272
Wayne's Shrimp Fettuccine. 352
Welsh Style Cheese Sauce. 87
Whipped Cream Frosting. 287
Whiskey Sour. 21

White Sangria. 25
White Wine Seafood Sauce. 92
Wild Duck in Sherry Wine. 182
Wild Duck Salad. 79
Wild Rice and Oyster Casserole. 140
Wild Rice Casserole. 139
Wine Jelly Dessert. 308
Wines, Suggestions for serving with:
  Beef, Italian Dishes, Cheeses. 26
  Lamb, Veal, Pork. 27
  Poultry. 27
  Seafood. 27
Woodcock (Bécasse Acadian). 344
Woody's Seafood Crêpes. 349

Y

Yam(s)
  Biscuits. 251
  Bread, Sweet Potato I. 260
  Bread, Sweet Potato II. 260
  Casserole, -Bourbon. 121
  Cobbler, Trappey's Minute-Made. 302
  Corn Bread. 262
  Lamb, Rolled Shoulder of, and. 167
  Muffins, -Pecan. 266
  Pineapple. 122
  Super. 122
You Can't Believe It's Turnips. 120
Yucatan Lobster-Garlic Style. 350
Yum-Yum Salad. 73

Z

Z'Herbes Gumbo. 51
Zippy Sauce. 92
Zucchini
  Pie, Vegetable. 122
  Soup, Curried. 61